The Small Town Planning Handbook

Second Edition

Second Edition
Copyright 1995 by the American Planning Association
Chicago, Illinois
Paperback copies ISBN 1-884829-02-3
Hardbound copies ISBN 1-884829-03-1
Library of Congress Catalog Card Number 94-71489

The first edition of this book was published in 1988 by the
American Planning Association.

Printed in the United States of America

Contents

Acknowledgments

We wish to thank Katherine Daniels for her many thoughtful comments on the manuscript. Jim Segedy was a great help, especially on matters of small town design. Jerry Knox, Bob Burke, Gary Mattson, and Dennis Gale offered many good suggestions. Frank So of the American Planning Association gave us much encouragement and valuable advice on revising the *Handbook*. Any remaining mistakes remain the sole responsibility of the authors.

About the Authors

Thomas L. Daniels is Director of the Agricultural Preserve Board of Lancaster County, Pennsylvania. John W. Keller is a Professor of Regional and Community Planning at Kansas State University and is Planning Director of Pottawattomie County, Kansas. Mark B. Lapping is Provost and Academic Vice-President at the University of Southern Maine.

I always think of Heaven
as a small town with a bandstand
in the park, and a great many trees. . .
and I would know everyone in it, and none of
them would ever die, or move
away, or age, or alter.

Anne Tyler

Preface

The first edition of *The Small Town Planning Handbook* explained how to create a comprehensive community plan and how to draft zoning and subdivision regulations and a capital improvements program to implement the plan. In this edition, we seek to go further in responding to the needs of small towns in the areas of physical design and local economic development. At the same time, we have updated information and added more illustrations. We have been pleased to hear that the *Handbook* has helped many communities to achieve a greater sense of purpose and direction and to improve their quality of life. Also, we have been gratified that the *Handbook* has been used as a text in college planning classes.

Diversity and change are the two most prominent features of rural and small town America. Socially, small towns and rural counties are among the most and least diverse places. Of the 30 most ethnically diverse counties, 14 are rural. By comparison, all of the 50 least ethnically diverse counties are rural, and half of these are located in just two states, Iowa and Nebraska. Economic diversity is apparent in the differing levels of wealth among communities and in the importance of different industries and jobs. Some rural counties, especially those adjacent to metropolitan counties, are quite well-off. Meanwhile, other more remote counties remain desperately poor. On average, rural counties have a higher percentage of people living below the poverty line and in substandard housing than urban counties.

Change is another important aspect of small towns, particularly in population and jobs. The 1980s showed a pattern of population decline in most of rural America. Although the decline may be only temporary in some places, other communities continued to experience a steady outmigration of young and middle-age residents. The popular image of rural employment is in farming, but in recent decades only a minority of rural dwellers have earned a living just from the traditional rural industries of farming, ranching, forestry, mining, and fishing. Manufacturing, government jobs, and a growing trade and service sector now account for over four-fifths of rural employment. And over the past 20 years, many people from urban areas have moved to small towns or the countryside. But more remote rural areas have not shown prosperity and growth.

This handbook is aimed at helping small towns and rural counties gain a greater sense of purpose and direction. Planning for change—for desirable change—must be aimed at promoting development that will meet local needs. At the same time, planning should discourage development that will reduce the community's financial strength, physical appearance, or environmental quality.

Good community planning results from common sense and an orderly, open approach to finding out local needs, setting goals and priorities, and taking action. Part One of this handbook presents a step-by-step method of developing a town comprehensive plan. Part Two explains the drafting and application of land use regulations which put the town plan into action. Together, the town plan and regulations serve to guide both public officials and private citizens in making decisions that will affect the future growth of their community. Part Three offers several strategies for economic development and small town design, while maintaining a sense of direction in order to create a sustainable community well into the future.

A number of books on small town planning have been written lately, but most have serious flaws. First, they try to apply urban planning practices and techniques to small towns. In most cases, this does not work. Small towns differ from large cities not only in size, but also in attitude, economic base, appearance, and aspirations. Second, many handbooks for planning and economic development in rural communities are written by a regional, state, or federal agency. Although these handbooks are of some use, they lack a truly local perspective.

We are rural and small town planners. We have lived and worked in rural communities. We have taught rural and small town planning in land grant universities. As practicing planners, we share 30 years of day-to-day experience in small towns, counties, rural-service agencies, and planning departments, including hundreds of evenings before rural planning commissions.

This handbook is intended for use in small cities, rural counties, and towns of about 1,000 to 10,000 people. Some communities have been operating with a long outdated community plan, others have modified their zoning and subdivision ordinances without referring to their plan, and still other places have never drafted or implemented a plan.

In Part One of this handbook, we discuss how to put together a community plan and a land use map. In Part Two, we explain how zoning ordinances, subdivision regulations, capital improvements programs, and other land use controls are used to put a community plan into action. Land use regulations and capital spending programs should reflect the community's goals and the land use map included in the plan. Decisions of the planning commission on development proposals and community programs depend on common sense, personal judgment, and the circumstances of each particular proposal. Personal values as well are likely to enter into these decisions. But these development decisions should be consistent with the goals and objectives of the community plan and the zoning and subdivision ordinances, and other regulations.

In Chapters 21 through 23, we present methods of guiding the physical design of small towns, economic development issues and techniques, and how to put together a strategic plan for the community. This strategic plan links the comprehensive plan and land use and design ordinances with the economic development effort.

Since the first edition of *The Small Town Planning Handbook* appeared, we have had the opportunity to test our ideas and advice in communities ranging from 450 to 12,000 people. Many of the planning strategies and techniques contained in the handbook can be successfully transferred to communities and counties of up to 25,000 people.

What we offer is a planning guide and a way of thinking to help make planning an effective way to improve your community. But the success of the planning effort will depend on the dedication, pride, and hard work of the people in your community. We wish you much success.

Thomas L. Daniels
John W. Keller
Mark B. Lapping

A commitment to place is an important feature of rural life.

—CALVIN HOBBS

Planning in Small Towns: An Overview

There are over 13,000 small towns in the United States. These towns of under 10,000 inhabitants are mostly found in rural settings in the Great Plains, Midwest, and Southeast. Small towns share the common trait of being an incorporated political unit with a distinct local government. Yet, small towns are different from one another not only in size and location, but also in economic base and social conditions. These differences make planning in small towns a special challenge.

A BRIEF HISTORY OF SMALL TOWNS IN AMERICA

Throughout America's history, some towns have prospered, others merely survived, and more than a few have faded away. The majority of America's small towns were settled in the 17th, 18th, and 19th centuries. On the East Coast and in the Midwest, towns grew up about five or six miles apart. In the Great Plains, the arrival of the railroads increased the average distance between small towns to almost 30 miles—about the limit of a steam locomotive before water was depleted. The West, with its lack of navigable rivers, imposing mountain ranges, and vast amount of desert, was settled by foot, horse, and rail. But the location of settlements was actually the result of booms, land rushes, opportunity, climate, and even pure folly.

Beginning in the late 18th century and throughout most of the 19th century, the federal government pursued a policy of conquering the continent. To stimulate settlement, transportation, communications, and commerce, the government sold millions of acres into private hands and granted millions more to states, railroads, and homesteaders. But the free market, driven by individual buyers and sellers, largely determined the location of new developments. Where land speculators, town jobbers, and farmers were successful, towns arose. Some towns aspired to be the new Chicago or another New York. But many towns also failed to become more than artists' drawings or lines on a plat map.

These early town plans contained a street layout, building lots, parks, a central business district, and residential neighborhoods. These original town plans, unfortunately, were one-time blueprints. They could not guide future additions to the towns, show how to provide new roads, or account for the many changes that would occur in the community.

In the 19th century, towns generally fulfilled three purposes: to function as retail and service centers to surrounding farmers; to process and ship farm products, timber, and minerals; and to provide protection. Across an enormous and expanding frontier, settlers needed a network of service center towns. Farming reigned as the primary source of livelihood in rural areas. And several towns began as forts on the frontier.

The 1890s and the first decade of the 20th century are often regarded as the heyday of small town America. Small towns prospered as the nation grew in population, thanks in part to a large influx of Europeans. Industries expanded and farm commodity prices rose, bringing about the golden age of American agriculture. Farmers had money to spend in town, and most townspeople enjoyed an orderly middle-class lifestyle. Main Street was the economic and social heart of the community with the general store, barbershop, saloon, bank, and livery stable. Schools, newspapers, and opera houses thrived. Despite the railroad and telegraph, communication and transportation were still slow enough to make small towns isolated from most national and international affairs.

It was not until after World War II with the coming of the interstate highways and telecommunications that rural areas truly entered into the mainstream of everyday national life. Yet, this integration with the national economy and culture also spelled a decline in the importance of rural areas in national affairs.

World War II drew thousands of young men and women away from the rural areas, initiating a 30-year exodus to urban/suburban America. This era of mass society—mass production, marketing, and communications—found small towns competing for a limited market. Farm numbers dwindled as farm size increased, and the countryside carried the stigma of being hick.

Railroads began to falter in the 1920s from a combination of government regulation and competition from cars and trucks. From 1945 to 1970, the competition with planes, cars, and busses drove nearly all privately held railroads out of the passenger service business. Trucking often proved more flexible and as fast in hauling freight. Thousands of routes and spur lines were abandoned and a large number of towns lost rail service. Again in the 1980s with the deregulation of rail, bus, and trucking service, many small, out-of-the-way places were dropped.

In the 1970s, the human scale of small towns, the back-to-the-land ethic, and a philosophy of "Small Is Beautiful" touched off a net migration of population from urban areas to nonmetropolitan counties. America's rural population actually increased faster than its urban population for the first time in 150 years! Yet, many rural places lost population in the 1980s. The decade of inmigration was quickly replaced by outmigration and population loss because of the hard times in the rural economy. It is possible that in many states the rate of rural population loss is actually increasing in the 1990s.

Small towns have been undergoing profound changes in the past few decades. Near metropolitan areas, hundreds of small towns have been swallowed up into suburbia. More Americans now reside in suburbs than in inner cities or rural areas. In remote rural areas, many communities have struggled to survive. Some towns have become recreation and tourist attractions; others have benefited from the growth in federal and state government programs; and still others have enjoyed growth as retirement communities thanks in part to social security payments and Medicare. The planning goals and objectives in these different towns will vary considerably. For example, economic development is not a problem for towns near metropolitan areas, but it is a matter of life or death to remote communities. Conversely, environmental quality is often less of a concern in remote places than in towns experiencing rapid development.

The reasons for towns to exist in the 19th century were quite different from the reasons today. Nineteenth century towns were outposts on the frontier and primarily served surrounding farmers. In the 1990s, the farms are fewer and larger, and retail merchandise and services are increasingly being concentrated in regional centers of more than 25,000 people. Many towns within a 40-mile radius of these regional centers have become bedroom communities. Those small towns beyond commuting distance of a regional center will struggle to retain residents and economic activity. Among the more remotely situated towns, county seats will have an advantage in attracting new businesses because they tend to have greater financial and population resources than do neighboring communities.

Today, small towns are attractive because of their human scale of buildings, affordable housing, lack of traffic congestion, and tight-knit social fabric. Recent polls have shown that most Americans would prefer to live in a small town, rather than a city or suburb. Also, there has been renewed interest in the design of small towns. The mix of residential and commercial uses, the emphasis on walking rather than the automobile, and the human scale of buildings are seen as contributing to both a pleasant environment and a closer, more sociable community.

But two trends will continue to shape small towns for the foreseeable future: the drop in federal grants and greater competition among towns to draw and promote new businesses. In the 1980s, the federal government forced more planning, public services, and economic development efforts down to the state and local levels. At the same time, federal grant programs were cut, with federal revenue sharing to communities completely eliminated in 1987. In fact, federal grants to small communities fell by more than 50 percent between 1985 and 1987. This means that small towns will have to become more self-reliant and will need to plan carefully and strategically to make their communities good places in which to live and work.

Federal programs often require small towns to comply with regulations that were designed for large cities. For example, the Safe Drinking Water Act of 1974 requires community water systems to meet national standards and requires the states to monitor local water systems. Communities are expected to meet these standards even though federal financial help may not be available. Many small towns cannot afford to upgrade their water systems to meet these federal standards.

Congress has recognized the need for flexibility (so-called Reg-Flex) between federal regulators and small towns. Nonetheless, small towns continue to face financial and administrative difficulties in complying with federal requirements. Here, the planning process can help local officials to identify problems and reasonable solutions. Also, planning is helpful in applying for and obtaining federal grants for local projects to meet federal requirements. In this way planning helps to encourage public participation, which is so vital to the quality of life in rural and small town America.

A SHORT HISTORY OF PLANNING IN SMALL TOWNS

In the early 20th century, a strong community betterment movement arose in the United States to create a planning process that would address the changing needs of the local residents. This movement resulted in the appointment of official planning commissions, which were charged with producing a master growth plan for their communities. Planning commissions quickly understood that the planning process was more than drafting a new land use map each year. They would have to study the community and its region in a comprehensive fashion. Housing and transportation needs would have to be examined along with the local economy and growing municipal services. By the 1930s the practice of planning was well established as a way to accommodate change and promote community betterment, but most planning occurred in large cities and their suburbs.

Before 1950, few rural towns prepared comprehensive plans. Under the Housing Act of 1954, the U.S. Department of Housing and Urban Development made grants to small towns to undertake planning studies. But these 701 plans typically produced little more than data on local population and housing. The plans were not comprehensive, omitting most of the planning elements of a town: economic base, land use patterns, transportation, community facilities, and the built and natural environments. Nor did the plans lead to the creation of zoning and subdivision regulations, budgets, and capital improvements programs, which would put the plans into action.

Many small town residents felt that the 701 plans simply did not address small town needs. As a result, 701 plans were often put on the shelf, and the idea of planning as a practical, useful activity did not take hold.

In the 1970s, several small towns began to recognize the value of planning. These were often towns on the fringe of metropolitan areas that were experiencing the problems of rapid development and population growth: water pollution, traffic congestion, soaring public service costs and property taxes, and the loss of open space and rural character. Planning efforts, however, were usually begun after the damage had been done.

In more rural communities, planning was recognized as helpful in obtaining federal grants for sewer and water lines, roads, and public buildings, especially in the creation of industrial parks.

In the 1980s, the farm crisis and the recession of 1980–82 hit small towns particularly hard. High interest rates drove up borrowing costs, a strong dollar drove down exports, and the result was a sharp decline in the value of farmland. Many towns in the rural Midwest and South traditionally served as commercial centers for the surrounding farms. The downturn in the farm economy rippled through those communities that depended heavily on processing and transporting farm products and selling farm supplies. Manufacturing plants, which had sprung up in many small towns in the 1960s and 1970s, came under increased competition from foreign producers, who often enjoyed lower labor costs and relaxed environmental standards.

Meanwhile, retail sales in the rural Midwest and South were becoming more and more concentrated among discount chain stores, such as Wal-Mart and K-Mart. The discount chains targeted communities of 5,000 to

25,000 people having retail trade areas of 20,000 to 90,000 people. Studies show that those communities have generally benefited from the coming of the chain stores. Meanwhile, surrounding small towns have lost retail trade and have increasingly taken on the appearance of bedroom communities where people live but work and shop elsewhere.

Suddenly, economic development—attracting and retaining business to support the local tax base and provide jobs—became a popular activity in many communities. Town planning was recognized as an effective process for identifying problems, setting priorities, organizing resources, and applying solutions. And it became apparent that economic development efforts could not focus only on revitalizing downtown or promoting an industrial site; the whole community had to be involved. For example, it is essential for people in a small town to be able to earn a decent living, but the town must also provide a healthy living environment. A lack of good roads, sewer and water systems, health care, schools, and housing—all can seriously harm the ability of a community to grow or survive.

PLANNING CHALLENGES AND POTENTIAL

Small town people are often thought to be conservative and opposed to change. If conservative is defined as restrained or prudent, then the description is probably accurate. People who must work within very limited public budgets and live on the thin edge of economic survival do not have spendthrift attitudes. That small town dwellers are opposed to change is perhaps an unfair charge. Change is quite visible in rural communities. When the local bank collapses, it is very visible; the failure of family farms is highly visible; the regional consolidation of schools grabs everyone's attention. It is not so much opposition to change that characterizes the rural community as the need to control the rate and size of change.

Small town dwellers tend to have greater access to local government than urban people. This can be a great advantage, at least for the general public. Local officials are visible and known. In many one-party rural counties, local officials tend to become quite well known since election is tantamount to a life appointment. They can be approached at public meetings, on the street, and at their homes or businesses.

In small towns and rural counties, planning occurs mainly after dark, when planning commission and town council meetings are held. This format allows for sufficient time to examine issues and address local officials, all in an informal setting.

Small towns often can afford only limited professional planning advice. Three good sources of help are the regional council of governments (COG), the state land grant university, and the state government department of commerce or community affairs. A COG is a government-supported agency that offers planning and technical assistance for grant writing to small towns. Many land grant universities have departments of community planning and extension personnel who are able to provide planning studies or advice. State government is useful for obtaining information on grant programs and legal planning requirements.

Over the past few years, we have seen a change in local attitudes toward community planning. Previously, many smaller towns and counties refused to consider a staff planner or a shared community planner funded by a regional council of governments. Now, the question is can such areas afford not to have such professional advice available, at least part time? Mandated planning programs such as local emergency response, emergency services and rural addressing for the 911 program, the ever tightening availability of federal and state grants, and the Americans with Disabilities Act (ADA) are examples of some programs that require coordinated effort, financial resources, and planning expertise.

The biggest shortcoming that small towns face is limited financial and human resources. It is difficult to shift resources from one area to another, such as from repaving Main Street to building a new public swimming pool. Also, many small towns have limited public services, both in quality and quantity. Town services normally include fire and police protection; sewer and water distribution; trash removal; and library, recreation, and ambulance services. But towns below 1,000 residents usually lack public sewer and water and have only part-time police, fire, recreation, and library services. Towns above 2,500

people are generally considered full-service towns which provide a full range of public services.

Comprehensive plans and zoning and subdivision regulations will vary according to the size of the town. But the town plan, zoning and subdivision ordinances, capital improvements program, and other land use controls described in this handbook are designed to meet the needs of most small towns. Bear in mind that changes in planning methods must be made to reflect the size of the community. For example, in communities under 1,000 persons, a simple policy plan with general town goals and objectives may be more useful than creating an in-depth comprehensive plan.

The purpose of planning is to help decision makers arrive at informed and thoughtful decisions. Good information, which is the basis of good planning, helps decision makers to predict what might happen in certain situations. Planning helps ask the question "What do you want your community to look like and how should it function?" Ultimately, planning helps people to take responsibility for their community and mold it into the kind of place they want it to be.

Creating
a
Town Plan

CHAPTER

1

Why Plan?

Everybody plans! People make financial plans, travel plans, and work plans to help them achieve personal goals and objectives. Organizations and firms plan for strategic action and implement these strategies to help them gain a competitive edge. Plans help us to organize our time and to work toward our goals in a step-by-step fashion. Planning enables us to look before we leap and avoid costly and embarrassing mistakes. Through planning we come to understand where we are now and what must be done now and in the future to achieve our goals. Then we can put together a plan of action to accomplish tasks on time.

Planning makes good common sense. For a community, common sense involves striking a balance between being recklessly innovative and stubbornly conservative. Surprisingly, many small town dwellers display both traits. If a program works in one small town, other small towns often adopt it without examining the consequences. Alternatively, small town inhabitants may take an extremely conservative position toward pressing economic or social problems, hoping

that these problems will fix themselves or simply go away. In the end, the cost of the damage may greatly exceed a moderate, timely, and common sense expenditure to solve the problems.

Disorganized people have a hard time accomplishing much; the same applies for disorganized communities. We all know communities that always seem to act too late, never do things right, and stumble their way along with outdated programs and ideas. Planning forces us to think and organize our time, resources, and efforts. Planning makes sense for household budgets and for municipal budgets as well.

COMMUNITY PLANNING

Community planning begins with learning how to care for your town, its people, and those generations yet to be born. It is also learning to develop a respect for the limited world in which we live. Community plans and planning affect peoples' lives. Tough choices must be made about the natural, man-made, and financial resources in the community. Learning to care means that you have

1

adopted an attitude of fairness, that you listen to the opinions of others, and that you are willing to make compromises to ensure equal treatment.

Planning is also about learning how to share. This is no easy task. People in small towns often like to share their opinions with others but seem to have difficulty in sharing their community.

Exhibit 1–1
Good Planning Enables Us to
Look Before We Leap

A rural community recently spent $125,000 to purchase 120 acres adjacent to its existing sanitary landfill. The local officials felt that the acquisition was a well-timed, wise, and planned decision. The existing landfill had 10 years of remaining space and it was time to plan ahead. The timing was perfect; there was no public controversy, the soil conditions were excellent, and the price was right. Less than six months after the purchase, a planning consultant pointed out the existence of "Subtitle D" in the new state and federal landfill regulations. After assessing the financial impact of lining waste disposal cells, collecting leachate (liquid seepage), drilling water monitor wells, and other requirements, the community concluded that it would be more effective to contract with a commercial hauler to remove the solid waste to a regional landfill. The community thought that they were planning because they were looking ahead, seizing a strategic opportunity, and managing their decisions.

But looking before we leap requires that we understand where we are now, gather and assess all the relevant facts, and decide what we must do now and in the future to achieve our goals. Then we can put together a plan of action to accomplish tasks on time, in good order, and with the most complete information available.

Community planning is intended to serve the best interests of the community. Community planning does not attempt to replace market forces of supply, demand, and price but to shape and channel market forces by establishing certain rules for development and conservation. As a result, a community plan should foster "good growth," not "no growth." That is, growth should occur but not haphazard growth, which is unsightly and wasteful of space and results in sharply rising municipal service costs and property tax increases. Many small communities, however, are shrinking rather than growing. Planning offers a way to try to maintain a positive quality of life and revitalize the community.

A town plan shows the current positive and negative aspects of a community: the good, the bad, and the possible. What is good about the community should be carefully nurtured and protected; what is bad should be addressed and changed; what is possible should be sought after and attained.

A plan also offers priorities and guidelines for spending public money to improve the community's facilities and to specify where each type of private development should occur in order to make the community a better place to live.

Private development plans often run into conflict with community plans and desires. A major purpose of the community plan is to show private landowners and developers the location and type of development the community wants. In other words, a clear, concise community plan will save private developers considerable time and money in putting together their private plans. At the same time, a good community plan will help the community spend money wisely and effectively so that service costs do not result in a heavy tax burden on local residents. The community budget should be compared to the community plan to ensure that public money will be spent in accordance with the community's goals and objectives.

The community planning process also helps to educate us about ourselves, our attitudes toward others, and our willingness to share a sense of community. Planning is often promoted as a means of community decision making through public participation. But, planning also may involve conflict and friction because it may divide us into opposing groups. Some conflict in the planning process is good. It stimulates us to think and reminds us of the need to understand and tolerate, and even support, the opinions of others. A lack of conflict during the planning process might indicate poor public information and little citizen participation.

Many towns have functioned, and continue to function, without an official planning program or a comprehensive plan. Still other places have plans that are decades old and lie unused on the shelf. At first glance, several of these communities appear no different from those towns that have active planning programs. With or without planning, cities and towns can grow, change, prosper, and decline.

The key ingredient for small towns is local leadership. Good local leadership is essential for success. The absence of good leaders means that little will be accomplished in those communities and they will decline. Some towns have the gift of local leadership, many will develop it, but a few never will. Community size is not important, and financial resources are not an insurmountable barrier. Successful community planning depends

on local people. Planning without active local leadership is always uncertain, frequently disappointing, and generally fatal. For example, Ron Powers (1991, p. 5) describes the result of poor local leadership in his masterful account of change in two small towns:

> . . . In the meantime the town I had left began to wither, and to grasp at life. Like a son visiting a stricken parent, I journeyed back and watched some outside professionals try to restore my hometown to its former vitality. The professionals brought in scientific marketing techniques. Their plan was to reposition the town as a theme-park "attraction" based on its authentic past. The plan failed. The "attraction" became a gaudy parody, and then the parody itself faded. The town was left stunned and bitter, aware that it had participated in its own violation.

REASONS NOT TO PLAN

You should undertake a town planning effort only if you understand the purpose of planning. Keep in mind that a town plan should be:

1. Comprehensive in setting goals and objectives for all aspects of the community.

2. Part of a continuous planning process that is timely and responsive to the needs and desires of the townspeople.

3. The legal basis for land use regulations and a guide for a capital improvements plan for town budgeting.

Just as there are good reasons to plan, there are also valid reasons not to plan.

Do not expect a plan to produce immediate changes. In the short run, the changes brought about by planning may be small, and citizens and decision makers alike may become disappointed. Good planning takes a long time and involves trial and error, hard work, and attention to detail. Remember that a community does not gain its particular character in a few months, a year, or even a decade. The best planning usually takes place in communities that have been planning for a long time.

Also, be aware that a town plan is no substitute for action; a plan is useful only as a blueprint on which to base action. These actions come in the form of decisions on how to spend public money and where to locate different types of development.

Do not go to the expense of planning just because you have been told that planning will bring in those industries that have consistently passed over your community. Planning is neither limited to industrial development, nor can an industrial recruitment program serve as a substitute for sound, community-wide planning. It is important to understand two facts about industrial recruitment. First, the community may put all of its financial resources into industrial recruitment to the neglect of other community needs. This strategy may prove to be more harmful than beneficial to a community when a genuine opportunity for industrial development appears. Companies seeking locations for their manufacturing plants have become wary of communities that only plan for industrial sites and not for community facilities and homes for the plant managers and workers. Second, research indicates that effective industrial recruitment is tied to carefully planned community investments in infrastructure, education, and job training.

Do not plan merely because it is a popular thing to do at a particular moment. People must be convinced that a planning program is right for their community, and they must believe that there is a need for a continuing planning effort. Public officials often find that community support for planning declines as the newness of the plan wears off. Without a commitment from the community to carry on continuous planning activities, the community may find itself holding several hundred copies of a plan that never will be implemented!

Do not plan if you believe that what your community needs is zoning and that "planning is really zoning in disguise." An effective zoning ordinance is only one of the results of a comprehensive town plan. Beware that it is impractical and possibly illegal for you to zone first and plan later. The zoning ordinance should be drafted along with the zoning map after the town plan has identified where each type of development should go and at what density.

Some communities have hastily prepared a basic land use plan and then adopted a zoning ordinance to put the plan into action. But a carefully prepared comprehensive plan provides direction for the zoning ordinance to influence changes in housing, economic development, and other aspects of the community.

Do not plan if you intend to use the plan to stabilize ethnic groups (by concentrating them in redeveloped areas of town), to exclude mobile homes, to rid the community of existing junkyards or unsightly nuisances, or to protect certain individual interests. It will quickly become obvious that planning is not the proper tool to use for these ends. Above all, planning should not be used to put unreasonable restrictions on private property. Such planning activities are likely to get a community into costly legal trouble.

Do not adopt a comprehensive plan for limited or single purpose goals. Local management is much more effective than a planning program. For example, if your only concern is ridding the community of unsightly nuisances, then a single purpose ordinance is a better solution than a comprehensive plan and multipurpose zoning ordinance.

Do not plan if your real goal is to reform government. Planning is politics! But it is not a solution to bad politics. Successful planning cannot occur in a community with warring factions and unresponsive elected officials. All too often we hear the plea from townspeople that they need to establish a planning program because the politicians "won't do anything" or are defeating the best interests of the community. Citizen action is important, but it cannot defeat official action. Citizens must have the support and cooperation of elected officials. Poor government abounds and is surely one of the major reasons, along with typically poor voters turnouts, for the problems of small towns. The solution lies squarely within the political arena. Voters must elect candidates who will be receptive to a planning program.

REASONS TO PLAN

Do plan if you want to promote common sense and intelligent community thought. It makes good sense for a community to plan when change is occurring and the townspeople wish to have a say in shaping those changes. It makes even better sense in the communities where significant changes in business patterns, health care delivery, jobs, and services are rapidly occurring. Planning helps people to recognize local and regional changes and the impacts on the appearance, social life, and economy of their town. By planning, the community will come to realize that the economy, the housing base, the unique environment, and the historical characteristics are closely related to those annoying or pressing problems such as low water pressure, flooding, and the lack of adequate employment. Finally, planning is action, and it makes good sense for a community to anticipate change in order to shape it and to take action to solve problems before they become worse.

Do plan for community management. The main reasons for planning are to manage development and public infrastructure. Many local land use decisions are often uncoordinated because they are made over time by diverse groups—developers and builders; business people; church boards and school boards; local government; private individuals building homes; land speculators; and county, state, and federal agencies. An uncoordinated pattern of community growth will produce adverse effects on commerce, housing, streets, and public facilities. One of the most common examples of uncoordinated development is allowing elderly housing to be located where it is inaccessible from the rest of the community! Another example is when several small housing subdivisions are added onto the edge of town and a request is soon made for sewer and water connections and street maintenance. It does not take long for a community to realize that the entire process of providing services should have been discussed before approving those developments.

People may plan and build their homes only to find that within a few years they are neighbors to industrial or commercial uses that are not compatible with family living.

Also, some land may be developed before the community realizes that the land is subject to periodic flooding. All of these situations point to the need for planning to organize and manage community resources.

Do plan to encourage community participation. The aim of community participation is to build a consensus on local needs and desires. Planning should help draw people into policymaking through public hearings with public officials. The number of groups working toward some form of community betterment is often remarkable. Equally astounding is the amount of time and effort people spend in working at cross purposes for the same goal. In putting together a town plan, there is plenty of work for everyone who is willing to become involved. And the more that people take part in the planning process, the more they will feel that the final plan is their plan.

Do plan in concert with commercial and industrial development programs. Today, all reputable development programs feature strategic planning that meshes with an official community planning program.

Just as it is important to understand that industrial development is not the essence of a community planning program, it is equally important to know that a community plan is a crucial step in searching, attracting, and preparing for new businesses or the expansion of existing firms. A good community plan will indicate what types of business are needed and are a good match for the community. Planning can paint a picture of how much additional school space and how many recreational facilities would be needed if new businesses and industries were to locate in the community.

A plan can also show (1) whether or not the work force is sufficient to staff particular manufacturing jobs, (2) if the local transportation system is suited for industrial development, and (3) how to begin a grassroots information program that will lead to a public debate on the use of public funds for industrial development.

During the past 20 years, many practitioners and researchers have asked business people about their decisions to move or not to move to particular communities. The answers vary according to the special needs of the industry; but for most, the quality and size of the labor pool is important. For companies involved in the assembly of small component products, the answer is the right location, including easy access to a private parcel service. But in our experience the most common answer goes something like this: "We looked at your town plan. We were able to gain a good deal of information, and we were impressed that you had the foresight to examine a number of issues that are critical to our business and employee needs." Planning helps in convincing prospective firms that the community has considered the needs of the new employer and employees, not just the greater payrolls and property tax revenues.

Do plan to shape the physical appearance of your community. One of the important tasks of a community plan is to capture the community's sense of place that makes it special among the thousands of small towns. A well-prepared plan points to the need to protect unique physical resources and reinforces the fact that your area was shaped by development over a long period of time. Residents have no doubt that your town is distinct from other places, and to capture this feeling in your plan is a powerful argument in favor of planning.

In legal thinking, capturing this sense of place forms what the courts refer to as the *nexus* or connection between a plan and the ordinances or programs which are adopted to shape physical development. Although legal requirements vary from state to state regarding the role of the community plan, the most important consideration in making zoning and subdivision ordinances—other than good technical drafting—is a tight, logical connection between the ordinances and the well-reasoned goals and objectives of the town plan. These ordinances will assist the governing body and the planning commission in ruling on development proposals which would bring either small or large changes to the community.

Do plan to promote regional cooperation among towns and between towns and the county. A planning program will assist a community in thinking regionally. It is a rare community today that does not quickly abandon the notion that regional cooperation is somehow unconstitutional! Many small towns need to find regional solutions to providing health care and emergency services, siting landfills, submitting grant proposals, housing rehabilitation, protecting natural areas, promoting economic development, or sharing a professional planner. In some very small towns, local government simply can no longer afford to provide services for the townspeople. For example, state-approved jails with separate juvenile facilities and even local law enforcement officers are now too expensive for some very small communities and isolated counties.

Exhibit 1–2
Do You Need a New Town Plan?

Many existing town plans are out of date and do not represent current land use patterns or community goals. The following checklist is a useful guide to determine if your town needs a new plan or a plan update.

1. Is your town plan more than seven years old?
Yes   No

2. Are your town's public services able to meet current and projected future needs?
Yes   No

3. Does your town plan contain an economic base study?
Yes   No

4. Does your plan discuss current and future housing needs?
Yes   No

5. Does your town plan discuss community water quality and supply needs, and sewage and solid waste disposal?
Yes   No

6. Is your map of existing land uses up to date?
Yes   No

7. Does your map of future desired land uses agree with your zoning map?
Yes   No

8. Does your zoning ordinance further the goals and objectives of your town plan?
Yes   No

9. Does your town plan include an inventory of environmental features, such as natural areas, wildlife habitats, prime agricultural land, wetlands, natural hazards, and areas with development limitations?
Yes   No

10. Does your town plan include maps of community facilities and service areas?
Yes   No

Do plan to promote community pride and accomplishments. A main benefit of planning is the fostering of a caring attitude. Over the years, a community can take great satisfaction and pride in its accomplishments. Although much is said about the decline of rural America, we are impressed by the efforts and caring attitude of many small towns to preserve and maintain their physical and social character. Bill Bryson (1989, p. 196), in his entertaining and sometimes sarcastic commentary on small town America, reflects on a Wisconsin community:

> . . . Savoring the clean air and companionship, I was seized with a huge envy for these people and their unassuming lives. It must be wonderful to live in a safe and timeless place, where you know everyone, and everyone knows you, and you can count on each other. I envied their sense of community, their football games, their bring-and-bake sales, their church socials. And I felt guilty for mocking them. They were good people.

Do community planning programs make a difference, and do the preservation efforts reinforce the caring attitude of good, solid community leaders? The reviews, of course, are mixed. Some supposedly well-planned communities have inflicted shame on themselves by promoting glitzy, theme attractions designed to save jobs; but the results have been a loss of the very meaning of community. One need only visit Colorado and observe the recent drive in many towns for economic development through local casino gambling.

In the long run, the caring communities continue to have strong planning programs—and they work hard at it. They work hard to keep their streets in good condition, to place the Wal-Marts and K-Marts in their proper locations, to have travelers come in off the highways for food and a short visit, and ultimately to make their community a satisfying place to live.

2

The Planning Process and the Miniplan

Planning is an organized way of finding out a community's needs and then setting goals and objectives for future development in the community. Planning is a way of aiming for effective and efficient change that will make a community a better place to live. Above all, planning is a step-by-step process that can be used by small communities as well as large ones. This handbook shows how small cities and towns can develop and carry out effective plans that not only will express community needs, desires, and goals, but also will serve as a cornerstone for building a better community.

WHO MAKES THE COMMUNITY PLANS?

The group of people responsible for planning is known as a *planning commission*. This group is appointed by the town or county elected governing body; in a few instances the planning commission is elected directly by the voters along district lines. The five main purposes of a planning commission are (1) to establish a planning process; (2) to draft a community plan for future public and private development within the town or county; (3) to draft regulations on land use zones (residential, commercial, industrial) and the subdivision of land into new lots; (4) to draft a land use map showing the location, permitted uses, and densities of land uses within the community; and (5) to rule on new development proposals according to the community plan, the land use map, and the zoning and subdivision regulations.

Keep in mind that planning is an acquired ability. No planning commission is too isolated or resource poor to overlook training. Help is always available from a regional planning agency, the state land grant university, the cooperative extension service, or the state department of commerce or community affairs.

WHO APPROVES THE PLANS?

The planning commission is charged with making the town plan. Once the plan is approved by the planning commission, it is submitted to the town governing body for review and official approval. The governing body may not like the proposed plan and is free to suggest changes or may even refuse to adopt the plan. But, at some point, the governing body should give its approval. Otherwise, the town will have no plan and no direction.

An important purpose of the planning commission is to educate elected officials about the community plan and land use regulations, as well as the physical, economic, and public finance impacts of different kinds of development. But decisions made by the planning commission are only recommendations which the local governing body may accept or ignore in making the legally binding decisions on development proposals. But if the governing body ignores the town's adopted plan and planning commission recommendations, those elected officials usually weaken their ability as leaders.

Figure 2-1 The planning process

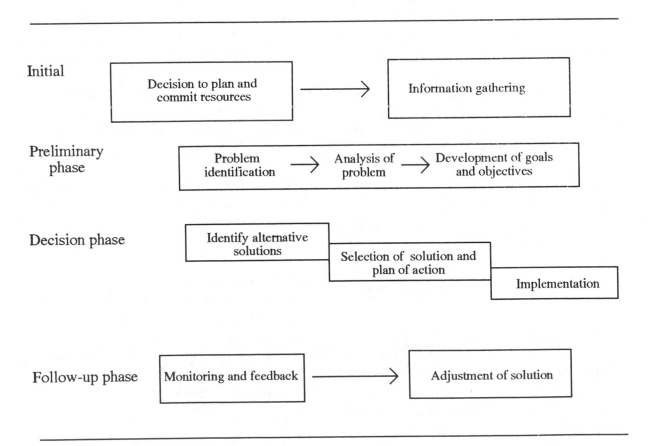

THE PLANNING PROCESS

To make the best use of this handbook, you must understand the connection between the community planning process (see Figure 2–1), the major plans, and minor plans. The planning process can begin in two ways. Often, town residents will become aware of a problem and decide on a strategy to solve that problem. In tackling one problem, townspeople may decide to develop a town plan as a way of handling additional problems both now and in the future. On the other hand, the planning process can begin when the governing body makes a commitment to plan. The planning commission gathers information which leads to an awareness of community problems. Next, the planning commission needs to analyze and understand the problems. Then the planning commission can develop community goals and objectives to address the problems and begin to discuss alternative planning solutions. The goal setting stage is also referred to as the mission statement or visioning process. This is where the planning commission tries to identify what changes should occur in the community and what should be protected, and how this change or protection should come about. By comparing the different alternatives, the planning commission is able to recommend what they consider to be the best or most workable alternative. Finally, a plan of action is chosen and implemented, followed by monitoring and feedback which provide information on how well the planning solution is working and what adjustments might be needed.

Plans are useless unless we can learn from them and make adjustments to improve their effectiveness. In planning we try to make in-telligent choices by getting all the facts first, determining goals and objectives, and then selecting solutions. In doing this we may encounter errors from old data, poor guesses, and changing economic and social circumstances. For example, many rural planning commissions in the 1960s were told to expect large amounts of urban migration to their areas. Several rural communities have spent the last 30 years adjusting to this often incorrect assumption. Today, most efforts go into creating plans that sustain rural communities rather than prepare them for urban-to-rural migration.

It is essential to keep the public informed and involved during each stage in the planning process. The planning commission should inform the public about the planning process and can use volunteers to help gather and analyze data. The public should be asked to respond to surveys, encouraged to offer their ideas and opinions on the plan, and invited to attend public meetings on the plan. Although there are some fine town plans in North America, the countryside is littered with the dead plans of communities that refused to take the time to prepare themselves, provide meaningful public participation, and offer assurances that a consensus of ideas and opinions would prevail.

THE STRUCTURE OF COMMUNITY PLANS

A small town or rural county often needs (or is required) to prepare a number of plans, which can be referred to as major and minor plans.

Major Plans

The major plan, commonly known as the comprehensive plan, master plan, or general plan,

Figure 2-2 Planning studies needed for a comprehensive plan

STEP 1   The community profile

- History
- General geography and location
- Natural environment

STEP 2   General studies

- Population
- Economic base
- Housing
- Land Use
- Transportation

STEP 3   Community - based studies

- Community human resources
- Community facilities and public needs
- Community restoration

STEP 4   Implementation elements

- Assessment of strengths and weaknesses
- Evaluation of opportunities
- Action elements

---

presents long-range goals and objectives for all activities that affect growth and development in the community (see Figure 2–2). The time range for the comprehensive plan varies from 10 to 20 years with suggested updating at 3- to 5-year intervals. The comprehensive plan serves to address the problems identified in planning studies (steps 1, 2, and 3 in Figure 2–2) of eight subject areas. The comprehensive plan then states community goals and offers recommendations for action for economic development, housing, land use, community facilities, the environment, and transportation. Thus, the comprehensive plan serves as a guide for public rulings on public and private development proposals and for the budgeting of public money. The comprehensive plan allows the community to compare how a town appears now and what it should look like in the future.

Minor Plans

Minor plans differ in scope and process from the major plans. One kind of minor plan is a shortened version of a comprehensive plan for a neighborhood or district rather than for the community as a whole. This concept is similar to a brief prepared by the legal profession. The brief or sketch does not cover the entire matter at hand, but rather presents the most important facts. Here, the minor plan offers an overview of the neighborhood's physical, social, and economic features and needs as a prelude to comprehensive planning for the entire community.

A second kind of minor plan presents a summary of the comprehensive plan in a series of maps and short narratives so that the future development of the community can be seen at a glance. The minor plan here depicts the changes that would most likely happen in the community, such as new community boundaries, the future transportation network, development of industrial sites, location of public facilities, new housing, and so on. This minor plan booklet is simply a handy device to illustrate the usefulness of the comprehensive plan.

Minor plans have also been applied to small communities that neither can afford nor actually need a full-scale comprehensive plan. Background studies, similar to those contained in a comprehensive plan, are undertaken, but in a shortened form. Community goals and objectives are determined, and then possible solutions and alternatives are sketched out in a number of drawings depicting the physical development of a community. A minor plan has a useful life of from four to six years, and updating is required about every year or two. This definition of a minor plan is quite similar to the eventual product of this handbook: The miniplan.

The Miniplan

The miniplan is a comprehensive plan for the community based on planning studies which present both historical and current facts and statistics together with estimates of future community activities. These studies are then used to compile a series of goals and maps for development strategies. The miniplan is flexi-

ble in that it may be changed to express new community goals or to present new strategies for achieving current goals.

The miniplan sets forth in a single document the public policies governing the future physical, social, and economic development of the community. The miniplan is middle ranged, general in perspective, yet comprehensive in scale. Middle range means that the plan is forward looking to the decade (5–10 years) rather than long range (11–20 years) or short range (2–4 years). General perspective means that the plan does not focus on small details that will detract from using the miniplan. Comprehensive scale means that the miniplan shows the relationships between those significant factors which affect the overall development and growth of the community. The structure of the miniplan is thus the same as for the comprehensive plan (see Figure 2–2).

The miniplan should clearly express the community's goals for the future development of the community. The miniplan is not a prediction of the future—although projecting probable trends into the future is a part of the process—nor is it a detailed program or schedule of activities. But, because the plan should reflect the best thinking of the townspeople, public officials, and the local governing body, all future proposals for development should be made with reference to the text and maps contained in the miniplan.

The miniplan is intended for use in communities with fewer than 10,000 people. However, due to a lack of community resources, communities of under 300 people may not be able to use the miniplan approach. Our experience, and comments given to us by users of the first edition of this handbook, indicates that preparation becomes increasingly difficult when community population is below 1,000 inhabitants. The miniplan approach may be useful for some communities of over 10,000 people. But these communities generally should be willing and financially able to develop long-range comprehensive plans with full-time professional planners on staff.

The first guideline for creating a miniplan is to establish a process that allows local citizens to prepare the bulk of their own community plan. Citizens should be encouraged to offer ideas at public hearings, and the miniplan should express a consensus of community goals and objectives. A professional planner may be helpful in preparing the miniplan, especially in the land use and housing sections. But there is no requirement that a professional must draft the miniplan. On the other hand, it is strongly recommended that the town employ the services of a professional planning consultant in drafting zoning and subdivision regulations. These regulations may be challenged in court someday.

The second guideline for the miniplan is that it should be reasonable and flexible. The plans must not advocate or result in the taking of private property without just compensation, according to the Fifth Amendment to the U.S. Constitution. The miniplan is flexible in that it may be changed to express new community goals or to present new strategies for achieving current goals.

The planning process and the amount of information to be included in the miniplan are flexible and need only serve the interests of the community and meet the basic legal requirements. Your community team must read and understand your state's statutes which govern planning activity at the local govern-

ment level. Foremost among these legal requirements is that the town plan should always include a land use plan and maps which show the present land use pattern and the future desired land use pattern in the community. Flexibility in preparation, however, should not be interpreted to mean flexibility in the final use. Too much flexibility in deciding on development proposals does not further the interests of the community or the leadership of elected officials. For a plan to be effective, officials must commit themselves to a regular and careful use of the plan as a basis for making development decisions. The most common failure in local planning is that once the final plan is published, it is filed and rarely referred to again. The plan is of no value as a mere document. The test of each proposal affecting community development should be the question: "Is it in accord with the policies and goals of the miniplan?"

The third guideline is that the plan must be a valid document on which to base (1) land use rules such as zoning and subdivision regulations; and (2) advance planning efforts to aid in the efficient use of community resources: that is, the capital improvement programs, central business district renewal, and housing plans.

The fourth guideline is that a small town plan should be reasonably inexpensive to prepare. The miniplan should probably be no more than 50 to 100 pages in length. The objective of this handbook is to produce a useful plan for under $10,000 exclusive of printing costs. The actual cost of the miniplan will tend to increase with the size of the town and the level of involvement by planning consultants. Generally, the smaller the town, the lower the cost of the miniplan because of fewer data sources needed. But, this is not a hard and fast rule. Many communities of less than 1,000 population do not have readily available data—and this can be expensive to collect. The handbook is designed to make use of local volunteer help whenever possible. On some issues, such as housing, land use, and solid waste, a professional planner may be needed for advice. However, before hiring a professional planner, a town should contact county, regional, and state agencies and the cooperative extension service of the state land grant university for planning assistance. Also, do not overlook the graduate and undergraduate programs in community planning at your state university. It is sometimes possible to arrange for a small team of students, under faculty supervision, to assist in preparing your plan. These public sources are often able to provide the necessary information at a much lower cost than a private consultant.

The fifth and final guideline is that a small town plan should be timely. The miniplan should be completed within a year to a year and a half, reviewed each year, and updated every three to five years. You should also be aware that the best time for preparing the plan, especially in communities over 2,500 showing active growth, is within the third to sixth year of each decade. This is because the plan relies heavily on data contained in the *U.S. Census of Population and Housing*. Preliminary census results are usually available one full year after the beginning of each decade. This data will remain useful for several years, but as time passes from the last census count, estimates and projections will be needed to update the data.

3

The Planning Commission

The miniplan handbook has been prepared especially for the local planning commission, planning students, and members of the public who wish to become involved in the planning process. A community must have a planning commission before undertaking the miniplan. No other official body, elected or appointed, can oversee the making of the miniplan. In the past, many communities have proceeded under the mistaken assumption that the governing body can serve in place of the planning commission.

Planning commission procedures are important for creating a legally acceptable miniplan. The planning commission adopts the written plan by either an ordinance, an order, or a resolution, which is then legally approved by the elected governing body. According to some state and local planning laws, however, the elected governing body may allow the planning commission to make the final legal approval of a plan.

The following discussion outlines the requirements and procedures for establishing a planning commission and the duties of a planning commission. Some states require that certain members, for example, those persons who hold an elective office, cannot serve on the commission. Often, there are minimum age and residency requirements. Therefore, along with this discussion, you should review your state's planning enabling laws. These laws describe the planning powers and requirements for a community and its planning commission.

TYPES OF PLANNING COMMISSIONS

There are four general types of planning commissions, and each is designed to meet different needs. Each of the four forms varies slightly in requirements, establishment, and membership.

Town or City Planning Commission

A town or city planning commission can exist

only in a place that has been incorporated. The town or city planning commission is created by an ordinance passed by the governing body. This ordinance also establishes the number of members, usually between 7 and 15. A new ordinance is needed to change the number of members on the commission.

County Planning Commission

Most of the nation's 3,104 counties have the power to plan and adopt land use ordinances. But in New England, New York, Pennsylvania, and New Jersey, county governments have very limited powers; cities and townships hold control over planning and land use matters. All land in a county is inside a city, a township, or a wildland tract. Many counties do not have a planning commission, and those county planning commissions that exist play an advisory role to municipal governments.

In the West, South, and in many parts of the Midwest, the county planning commission is established by resolution of the board of county commissioners and has between five and nine members. The county planning commission has jurisdiction over all lands within the county that lie outside the boundaries of incorporated cities.

Township Planning Commission

In the Northeastern states, county governments have very limited powers. Planning and land use controls are under the authority of city, town, village, and township local governments. These township governments are equivalent to municipalities, unlike Midwestern townships, which were created by surveyors and do not represent political boundaries. The township planning commission (often called the planning board) is usu-ally appointed by the elected township supervisors or selectmen and may consist of three to seven members. But in Maine, for example, state law allows some townships to elect planning commission members.

In the rural Midwest, the township planning body is often known as the zoning board. It is created by resolution of the board of county commissioners. The township zoning board drafts a land use plan and a set of recommendations for dividing the 36-square-mile township into zones and districts. In a county, there are usually dozens of townships. The designated township zoning boards do not have to develop a miniplan or a comprehensive plan. However, the zoning board may draft a plan and a map of the township outside the limits of any incorporated city. Members of the township zoning board are appointed by the county commissioners. There are usually seven members on the board.

Joint or Regional Planning Commission

A joint or regional planning commission offers many advantages for working on regional planning issues such as landfills, transportation, and large development projects. Several states allow a joint planning commission between (1) any two or more cities with adjoining planning jurisdictions, (2) any two or more counties with adjoining planning jurisdictions, and (3) a city and its county. A regional planning commission usually covers more than one county.

A joint or regional planning commission is created by an ordinance for each city involved and by a resolution of the county or counties. Take special note that in some states the agreement among the jurisdictions in the joint or regional area must be approved by the state's attorney general. This approval must be obtained prior to the actual establishment of the commission.

The number of members on the joint or regional planning commission is determined by the cooperating governments. Each government that enters into the agreement may also continue to have its own planning commission. Members of the joint or regional commission, whatever the number from each level of government, are appointed by the respective governing bodies.

PLANNING COMMISSION MEMBERS

State planning laws require that the planning commission members be appointed by the governing body. The following simple rules will help your governing body create a planning commission that is informed, dynamic, and concerned with the full range of community problems and circumstances. Members should reflect the population of the planning area; ideally, members would include different ages, sexes, ethnic groups, and occupations. Also, planning commission members should be selected from different neighborhoods within the community.

Many planning commission members are appointed because they are prominent in the community, which is fine in itself; but prominent people are also busy people. Members should be selected who can truly give of their time, who are competent, and who are willing to serve. A number of states prohibit more than two people with the same occupation from serving on a planning commission.

Planning is serious work, and during public hearings, it can be stressful. Not all people can handle stress and confrontation in a public forum. An ability to communicate with people is the most important qualification for a planning commissioner. Consider people who can be firm, reasonable, and courteous. Three types of personalities make poor choices for planning commissioners. The first type dominates meetings by talking incessantly or always having the last word. This behavior is not leadership and will only result in a power game at meetings. The second is the silent type. When this person talks, the questions may be quite good, but the person rarely talks. Conducting a hearing for a rezoning, for example, involves the art of conversation. Information is gained from questioning and listening. The final type cannot control his or her emotions, especially anger. People who often lose their temper have no place in a public zoning hearing. The hearing can be emotionally charged, but it is essential to have planning commissioners who can control their emotions and make objective decisions.

People with certain occupations are often included or excluded from service on a planning commission. Many towns seek architects, engineers, bankers, or builders because they know about the development process. On the other hand, real estate agents, attorneys, developers, general building contractors, or representatives of activist groups are often excluded from membership because they have a conflict of interest in the development process. That is, their fair judgment could be compromised because they stand to gain wealth or influence from their decisions. Attorneys are often excluded because of a fear that they will either dominate the process or introduce confusion through the constant need for legal advice.

It is our belief that no one occupation should be automatically included or excluded from serving on the planning commission. The governing body must conduct a careful screening of individuals, not their occupations. In addition to the personal qualities already discussed, people who have served effectively on public or private boards should be given priority. A well-crafted set of procedural rules for voting, conflict of interest, removal, and alternate members will definitely help screen out people with potential conflicting interests. Also, people with personal interests in a specific land use decision can be required to excuse themselves from participating in that decision.

DUTIES AND PROCEDURES

The planning commission is responsible for preparing a comprehensive plan for the community. In some cases, if the county does not have an official comprehensive plan, the plan may extend outside the boundaries of a community. The planning commission should make sure that the town plan is in accord with county plans, state planning requirements, and the plans of any special districts providing sewer, water, or school services to local residents. The planning commission must undertake or contract for studies of the past, present, and projected future trends in population, land use, housing, economic base, public facilities, transportation, natural resources, and possibly other community features. From these studies, the commission must develop general community goals and specific objectives for the development and redevelopment of the area within their jurisdiction. These goals and objectives are the heart of the miniplan.

Before adopting the plan, the commission must give public notice and conduct public hearings to solicit ideas from the citizens of the community and to hear specific complaints or recommendations for change. At the same time, the planning commission is required to coordinate its efforts with other governmental bodies. The proposed plan must be sent to the local governing body and county, state, and possibly federal departments for recommendations. After the plan is officially adopted by the planning commission and the local governing body, the commission should review the plan every few years and make recommendations for any necessary revisions. It is important to remember that if any of the above steps are neglected, or the sequence is out of proper order, the entire plan could be considered improper and without authority.

The planning commission conducts two distinct types of hearings—legislative and quasi-judicial. The *legislative hearing* indicates that the planning commission is making or revising plans or creating land development regulations. The discussion is informal, public hearings may have a loose structure, and the planning commission uses its own judgment to make plans or land development ordinances. The *quasi-judicial hearing* is frequently used when applications are filed for amendments to the zoning map or preliminary subdivision plats. The hearing involves a contest between two or more parties, one seeking a change and the other contesting the change. The planning commission assumes the role of a layperson's court and operates under rules of due process. The hearing structure is formal and the judgment of the planning commission is based on facts, and the planning commission must make findings of fact to justify its decision.

4

Determining Community Goals and Objectives

The purpose of this chapter is to help you draft goals and objectives for the community. Goals and objectives do not come from flashes of insight. Instead, they evolve from detective work, data gathering, and much discussion to determine how to maintain the community's good aspects and improve on its weaknesses.

The test of a community plan is how well it expresses the goals and objectives of the general public. Traditionally, the town planning commission is responsible for determining and stating these goals and objectives. The advice and opinions of elected and appointed representatives should be sought. But public participation—through public meetings, community education, and surveys—is necessary to identify goals and objectives that have broad public support. Public participation is also important if the townspeople are to become stakeholders in the planning process.

Goals are necessary to assure that the needs and desires of the community are understood. Goal statements cover a wide range of topics. On a personal level, they are like asking: "What do you want out of life?" Objectives are more specific and measurable tasks. They are like asking: "What will you do to achieve your goals in life?" Objectives may be long term, short term, or medium range, but they are tasks to be accomplished as part of attaining a stated goal.

The goals and objectives are statements of policy: recommendations of what needs to be done and how. The implementation of planning occurs when the governing body commits the town's money and personnel to carry out the goals and objectives set forth in the miniplan (see Figure 4–1).

CITIZEN INVOLVEMENT AND ACTION

Most people pay little attention to community planning until they are personally affected.

Figure 4-1 Managing the planning process

Action 1	Public and elected officials recognize the necessity for local planning
Action 2	Willingness to commit people and money to the planning process
Action 3	Appointment of a planning commission
Action 4	Public information and needs surveys General information gathering Form planning advisory committee
Action 5	General public participation: town and/or neighborhood or area meetings
Action 6	Form citizen's advisory committee
Action 7	Statement of general planning goals and objectives by the planning commission
Action 8	Approval or modification of general goals and objectives by the governing body and a firm commitment of budgeted resources to prepare and implement the plan
Action 9	Planning commission prepares a general work schedule and gives notice of working meetings

But this is not to say that these citizens do not care about planning in their community. It is the responsibility of the planning commission to encourage public participation in the planning process. For example, federal and state grant programs often have citizen participation requirements for local jurisdictions. Public participation is crucial to ensure that the goals and objectives statements in the community's plan represent the actual needs and desires of the community. When the town plan is based on a consensus of community opinion, there is a better chance of organizing resources, taking action, and achieving community goals.

PHASES OF PARTICIPATION

Citizen participation consists of two distinct phases—technical and general. The *technical phase* features gathering information, analyzing facts, and making estimates of future needs. During the technical phase, input from public officials and employees and planning professionals is assembled to study and analyze facts, not opinions or desires. Community officials should contact federal, state, and county agencies about existing regulations, available funding, and other future plans which may influence the community's choice of objectives.

Do not automatically assume that the planning process always begins with the collection of technical information. In a community of fewer than 500 people, the process of citizen participation should often precede all technical planning efforts. The public must look at the community and determine some broad goals. The most important of these goals is the survival of the community. In other words, what price will the public be willing to pay to continue living in their town? A public meeting or series of meetings is a good way to involve citizens and air their concerns. Such meetings are often the source of community planning action.

The *general phase* involves broad public participation. To stimulate interest, you should ask the local and area newspapers, or other existing media, to run a series of articles or discussions on planning both prior to and during the drafting of goals and objectives. Different sections of the miniplan, as they are completed and recommended by the planning commission, could also be published.

A town or neighborhood meeting can be an effective way to elicit public input. You should publish notice of any meetings well in advance. You may also want to send a letter about planning activities to each household in the community. Mailing costs can be saved by hand delivery through local youth or service organizations. Planning commissioners and the members of the local governing body should then hold neighborhood meetings (unless the town is very small and a single meeting will do) to receive citizen input and comments on the technical information that has been gathered.

After neighborhood meetings have been held, the planning commission should hold general public hearings. Notification of public hearings must meet all state requirements governing public notice. Notice should be published in newspapers at least three weeks in advance and each week thereafter until the meeting is held. In addition, ask that the general public planning hearings be announced at the regular meetings of any professional, service, or social organization. Announcement signs should also be placed at gathering places throughout the community.

GETTING STARTED

The most difficult phase in planning is getting started. Because there are many tasks to complete, it often is hard to know where to begin. Figure 4–1 shows the nine actions in managing the planning process.

A recognized need for planning begins with the public-at-large. Generally, the public must let the planning commission know that a town plan is needed or needs to be updated. Planning commissioners learn of the public's desires at planning commission meetings, at town or neighborhood meetings, and through informal conversation. It is important for commissioners to understand the subtle ways in which the need for a plan may be voiced. For example, the suggestion "Don't you think the school is getting overcrowded?" may indicate the need to plan for a new school.

Commitment

He has shown us how a few committed people with powerful and humane ideas can make things happen. . . .

David Johnson on Lewis Mumford

The planning commission then recommends that personnel and money be authorized to prepare a plan. But final approval of expenditures rests with the town governing body. It is important to obtain this approval before any planning studies are undertaken by the planning commission. It will cost about $5,000 to $10,000, exclusive of printing and distribution costs, to produce a useful plan. More funds may be needed if private consultants are hired. In addition, the local governing body must allow certain employees (the town assessor, for example) to devote time for gathering information for a town plan. The miniplan should be completed within one year, and the planning commission and governing body should agree to update the miniplan every three to five years.

At this point, actions 1 and 2—creating the planning commission and committing money and people—have been completed. Action number 4, information gathering and public participation, now becomes the primary task.

The planning commission then should draft a preliminary agenda of the actions needed to be accomplished to complete the miniplan. After reading this handbook, we suggest that you discuss and construct an agenda similar to the one presented in Figure 4–1.

Your preliminary agenda will be somewhat rough and subject to change as you work on specific tasks and data gathering. But the preliminary agenda is a good starting point because it provides a common frame of reference and sets some targets and deadlines.

ESTABLISHING A CITIZENS' ADVISORY GROUP

A citizens' advisory group can help the planning commission to shape the planning agenda. This advisory group may be organized along neighborhood lines or drawn from the public-at-large. Neighborhood groups tend to work best in ethnically diverse towns or in communities that have a range of incomes by neighborhood. The group should have between 15 and 25 people. Our experience is that the advisory group works best when drawn from the general public, resulting in a group of different ages, genders, ethnic backgrounds, length of residence in the community, occupations, and incomes. For example, men and women often have very different views of their community, and an effort should be made to include a good balance of both on the committee. Short- and long-term residents often have different perceptions of the community. It is also important to include a wide range of ages on the advisory committee. Remember that the under-21-year-old group can comprise a significant portion of the community and should be included. Business people, teachers, health care personnel, and a parent with young children are important members to select. So are representatives from service organizations, law enforcement, and town or county employees.

Always include a representative from the local newspaper for two reasons. First, all planning meetings are open meetings, and the press should always be notified. And, second, local reporters and publishers like to keep track of what is going on in the community. Finally, if this plan is being prepared for a town or village, you should be aware that a sense of community may not stop at the town boundary. Include people who live outside the town but consider it their home; you should especially include those involved in agriculture, ranching, fishing, forestry, or mining.

MAKING USE OF THE CITIZENS' ADVISORY GROUP

The citizens' advisory group should be appointed by the planning commission. Each member of the planning commission should be able to suggest appointments to the citizens' advisory group. Notice of the planning commission meetings with the advisory group should be published. Count on at least two meetings of no more than three hours' duration. All meetings should be tape-recorded or videotaped for later study and reference.

When meeting with the citizens' advisory group, the role of the planning commission is to listen and occasionally ask questions and clarify responses. It is often helpful to ask one person to run the meeting. This person serves as a *facilitator* (much like a talk-show host) to manage the flow of the meeting, not to participate in the outcome. If you cannot locate someone in your community who is qualified and willing to help, check in neighboring communities or with your county or regional council, or ask a city planner from a nearby area or perhaps someone from your state university.

The meetings must be well organized, although the format and atmosphere can be informal. A common approach is to have a member of the planning commission give a 10- to 15-minute presentation on the community planning process, the purpose of the meeting, and general introductions. An overhead transparency projector or large flip chart should be used to make key points for this presentation and throughout the meeting. The next phase of the meeting should be conducted by the facilitator, because only one

person can successfully direct and elicit conversation. Possibly the best method of directing the meeting is to use the SWOT approach, that is, gathering opinions about the town's (S) strengths, (W) weaknesses, (O) opportunities, and (T) threats. Carefully construct your questions around each SWOT category. Two scenarios commonly used by the facilitator to encourage comments are:

1. Facilitator: Assume that I am visiting your area to investigate the possibility of locating my small computer assembly plant here. I plan to bring about eight employees with me and hire about 10 part-time local workers. I have visited five rural communities in this region and will be making my decision within several months. What can you tell me about your area—strengths, opportunities, drawbacks, and challenges that might influence my decision?

2. Facilitator: I was born, raised, and have lived most of my life in rural areas and communities. I have very strong images of my community, some very positive and others not so pleasant. We often call it "the rural sense of place." What can you tell me about your sense of place in this community? What are some of your strongest images?

The role of the citizens' advisory group is to help the planning commission focus their thoughts before establishing goals and identifying action projects. Because the opinions of the citizens' advisory group are assumed to be representative of the community, it is very important that sufficient time be allowed to cover a broad range of issues, concerns, and community strengths. The discussion should include residents who have both short- and long-term memories of the community. Our experience shows that people who live in a town less than five years have very different perceptions than long-time residents. When drawing your own list of topics, do not avoid controversial issues, but at the same time, be aware that these issues should be approached in a sensitive manner. A general list of topics for discussion are:

- General economy and income levels.
- Employment opportunities.
- Attitudes toward growth.
- Satisfaction with local services.
- Educational assessment.
- Health care and social services.
- Police and Fire protection.
- Other emergency services.
- Condition of neighborhoods and the community.
- Arts and entertainment; cultural atmosphere.
- Opportunities for volunteerism.
- Safety and security.
- Availability and affordability of housing.
- Recreational opportunities for children and adults.
- Community attitudes toward local businesses.
- Opportunities for elderly citizens.
- General opportunities for youth.
- The visual appearance of the community.
- Stability of property values.
- Opportunities for tourism.
- The qualities that make this community unique.
- The reasons why people leave this community.

The final task of the citizens' advisory group is to help establish a list of priorities for community goals. At the conclusion of the meetings, there should be four sets of issues—community strengths to be reinforced, weaknesses to be addressed, opportunities to be sought, and threats to be examined—that can be used as the goal statements. One community's suggestions can be seen in Figure 4–2.

PREPARING A COMMUNITY SURVEY

Before drafting goal statements or initiating planning studies, the planning commission should conduct a *survey of community needs and desires.* Goal statements should express the wishes of the majority of people in the community. A survey of community needs can alert the planning commission to problems that should be addressed in the planning studies. Moreover, a community survey encourages people to become involved in the planning process and shows that the planning commission cares about individual opinions. The insights gained from the comments of the citizens' advisory group should be used by the planning commission to shape a community assessment questionnaire.

A written questionnaire is a much better way to identify community needs and opinions than a series of general public meetings. Although some communities may decide to forgo the questionnaire and use a series of public meetings to discuss issues raised by the citizens' advisory group, you should be aware of the limitations of public meetings. First, people have a tendency to attend public meetings only when they have concerns. In other words, there is a focus on threats and weaknesses, rather than strengths and opportunities. This reactive atmosphere is often counterproductive to the proactive discussion required for a serious planning agenda. Second, the opinions given at public meetings are likely to be less representative of the com-

Figure 4–2 Sample community survey topics

Evaluation topics

Local Government Resources

- Water supply and quality
- Solid waste collection
- Condition of streets
- Condition of sidewalks
- Fire services

- Police services
- Other utility services
- Customer service to the public
- Management quality of government
- Public transportation

Community Resources

- Primary schools
- Secondary schools
- Vocational Training
- Adult education
- General health care

- Hospital/clinic quality
- Physicians
- Dentists
- EMT service
- Specialized health care

Economic Development

- Adequate number of retail stores
- Attitude of merchants
- Variety of goods
- Parking for shopping
- Appearance of downtown

- Industrial development
- New jobs
- Wages and benefits
- Agricultural markets
- Current local industry
- Retail development

General Public Opinions

- Community appearance
- Entrances to community
- Housing appearance
- Adequate housing
- Community spirit
- Arts and entertainment

- Senior citizen opportunities
- Youth opportunities
- Recreational services
- Cultural opportunities
- New residents
- Entrepreneurship

munity at large than responses obtained through the privacy and unhurried pace of filling out a questionnaire. Finally, public meetings in rural areas, because everyone knows everyone else, tend to stifle frank and honest discussion of the real issues of community life. Public meetings are important for community planning. But, these meetings are best scheduled after the technical fact-finding phase.

Examples of the topics that might be investigated in a community assessment questionnaire are provided in Figure 4–2, and a model survey is shown in Exhibit 4–1. The planning

Exhibit 4-1 Sample community survey

Community survey

Instructions: This survey should be filled out by one adult in your household. However, please feel free to consult with other family members. To complete the survey please circle or check your response. Please do not write your name or address on the survey.

Demographics

1. Please indicate your gender?
   1. male
   2. female

2. What is your age?
   1. under 18 years   5. 45-54
   2. 18-24   6. 55-64
   3. 25-34   7. 65-74
   4. 35-44   8. 75 and older

3. Indicate the number of people currently living in your household, including yourself.

   1   2   3   4   5   6   7   8   9 or more

4. How many children under the age of 18 years live in your home?

   none   1   2   3   4   5   6 or more

5. How long have you been a resident of (community name)?
   1. less than 1 year
   2. 1-5 years
   3. 6-10 years
   4. 11-20 years
   5. over 20 years

6. What is your primary occupation? Check here ☐ if retired.

   1. agriculture   8. education
   2. finance   9. medical/health
   3. government service   10. clerical
   4. retail sales   11. utilities/communication
   5. personal services   12. construction
      (such as barber, waitress) 13. other trades
   6. management   14. other professions
   7. manufacturing   14. other (please specify)_____

7. What is the highest level of education you have completed?
   1. elementary   4. vocational/trade
   2. secondary   5. college
   3. junior college   6. post graduate

8. Where do you work?
   1. In (community name) or very close vicinity (within 2 miles)
   2. Within 2 - 10 miles of (community name)
   3. Within 11- 25 miles of (community name)
   4. Greater than 25 miles from (community name)

9. What is your approximate gross (before tax) annual family income?
    1. under $15,000
    2. $15,001-$29,999
    3. $30,000-$49,999
    4. $50,000 or more

Community facilities

On a scale of 1 to 10, with 1 being very satisfied and 10 being very dissatisfied, please circle your level of satisfaction concerning community services in (your community). If you do not know an answer, leave it blank. Feel free to make additional comments at the end of this section.

example: fire department service 1 2 3④5 6 7 8 9 10

	very satisfied				about average				very dissatisfied	
10. condition of community streets	1	2	3	4	5	6	7	8	9	10
11. availability of community sidewalks	1	2	3	4	5	6	7	8	9	10
12. quality of parks	1	2	3	4	5	6	7	8	9	10
13. accessibility of parks	1	2	3	4	5	6	7	8	9	10
14. water quality and service	1	2	3	4	5	6	7	8	9	10
15. sewer quality and service	1	2	3	4	5	6	7	8	9	10
16. gas and electric quality and service	1	2	3	4	5	6	7	8	9	10
17. fire department service	1	2	3	4	5	6	7	8	9	10
18. police department service	1	2	3	4	5	6	7	8	9	10
19. ambulance service	1	2	3	4	5	6	7	8	9	10
20. availability of general health care	1	2	3	4	5	6	7	8	9	10
21. quality of the elementary school	1	2	3	4	5	6	7	8	9	10
22. quality of the junior and senior high schools	1	2	3	4	5	6	7	8	9	10
23. quality of recreational programs	1	2	3	4	5	6	7	8	9	10
24. quantity of recreational programs	1	2	3	4	5	6	7	8	9	10

comments: (to continue, please use other side of sheet)

_____
_____
_____

25. Would you like to see a county public library in (your community)?
    1. yes
    2. no   [question from neighborhood meeting]
    3. no opinion

26. Would you like to see a swimming pool in (your community)?
    1. yes
    2. no   [question from neighborhood meeting]
    3. no opinion

27. Which, if any, new school facilities would you like to see located in (your community)?
    1. elementary
    2. junior high school
    3. senior high school
    4. no new schools are needed
    5. no opinion

Housing

28. Do you own or rent your residence?
    1. own
    2. rent

If you rent, what is your approximate payment per month (please check or circle).

Less $150 $200 $250 $300 $350 $400 $450   More

29. How do you feel about the overall appearance of housing in (your community)?
>1. generally, very good
>2. overall, about average
>3. poor
>4. no opinion

30. Compared to the region, do you feel the purchase price of housing in (your community)?
>1. very reasonable
>2. about average
>3. too expensive
>4. no opinion

On a scale of 1 to 5, with 1 being adequate and 5 being inadequate, circle or check your level of satisfaction concerning housing in [your community]. If you do not know an answer leave it blank. Feel free to make additional comments at the end of this section.

	excellent	mostly adequate	about average	somewhat inadequate	inadequate
31. quality of elderly public housing	1	2	3	4	5
32. availability of elderly public housing	1	2	3	4	5
33. quality of affordable housing	1	2	3	4	5
34. availability of affordable housing	1	2	3	4	5
35. quality of affordable rental housing	1	2	3	4	5
36. availability of affordable rental housing	1	2	3	4	5
37. quality of low income housing	1	2	3	4	5
38. availability of low income housing	1	2	3	4	5

comments:_____
_____
_____

39. What type of housing is most needed in (your community) ? Please circle all that apply.
>1. rental units   4. affordable housing
>2. public housing   5. higher income housing
>3. manufactured housing

Economics

40. Would you want to see more job opportunities in (your community)?
>1. yes
>2. no

41. If you answered "yes" to the previous question, what type of job opportunities/businesses would you like to see? Please circle all that apply.
>1. retail   8. restaurants   15. bar/tavern/club
>2. barber/beauty shop   9. video rental   16. laundry service
>3. finance   10. medical/health   17. appliance repair
>4. general industry   11. clerical   18. other_____
>5. car sales   12. light industry   19. other_____
>6. auto repair   13. pharmacist   20. other_____
>7. increased grocery service 14. hardware store

42. Which of the following does (your community) need ?
>1. economic development   6. jr. high and high school
>2. parks and Recreation   7. other_____
>3. swimming pool   8. other_____
>4. new medical facilities   9. other_____
>5. streets/sewer/water   10. none of the above

43. Would you support an increased mill levy for:
>1. economic development   yes   no
>2. parks and recreation   yes   no
>3. swimming pool   yes   no
>4. new medical facilities   yes   no
>5. streets/sewer/water   yes   no

44. Should (your community) provide additional resources (time, effort and/or money) to attract more businesses?
    1. yes
    2. no
    3. no opinion

45. Would you support a general obligation bond for an industrial park?
    1. yes
    2. no
    3. no opinion

46. Would you support a general obligation bond to construct a speculative building to attract a new industry?
    1. yes
    2. no
    3. no opinion

47. What do you consider to be the ideal population of [your community] in the next 25 years?
    1. smaller
    2. remain the same
    3. increase somewhat
    4. depends upon circumstances
    5. no opinion

48. Which direction would you like to see (your community) grow in the future?
    1. specific area or direction
    2. specific area or directoin
    3. specific area or direction
    4. specific area or direction

Community

49. When you shop in another community for items which are also available in your community, what are your primary reasons for doing so? Please check any that apply and list its order of importance.

	√ if important	rank order of importance
1. Prices	-----	-----
2. Variety of merchandise	-----	-----
3. Convenience of shopping	-----	-----
4. Quality of merchandise	-----	-----
5. Store hours	-----	-----
6. Merchant friendliness	-----	-----
7. Advertising	-----	-----
8. Frequency of items on special	-----	-----
9. Product service	-----	-----
10. Store policies on returns	-----	-----

50. Please list two reasons why you like living in (your community).

    1._____

    2._____

51. Please list two things you would like to change about (your community).

    1._____

    2. _____

52. Do you feel there is a strong sense of community pride in (your community)?
    1. yes   2. no

Please return your survey to the city office, Jones Discount Foods, or Security State Bank by
(date for return)

Thank you for supporting your community by
completing this survey!

Sample cover letter

To: City of [your community] residents.

Attached is a questionnaire designed to survey your opinions of [your community], and to determine the future needs of your community. This questionnaire was designed by the planning commission and an advisory board after many discussions with citizen groups. It is part of our on-going effort for community betterment.

Please take a few minutes to answer the questions in the survey and then return it to one of the following locations: [your community] city offices, [your community] Jones Discount Foods, or Security State Bank. We ask that only one person per household fill out the questionnaire, but please feel free to consult with all members of your household in forming your opinions.

The responses on the questionnaire will be tabulated by computer. No member of the community will take part in this tabulation. Only the final results will be presented to the public at large, the city council, and the planning commission. We assure you that the original questionnaires will be kept from public view and eventually destroyed. The information provided to us on individual questionnaires is anonymous and there is no way that anyone participating can be identified.

We hope that you will join us in the project and provide information to help guide your community through its next 10 years. We ask that you return the survey no later than (date for return).

Sincerely,

Julia Jackson, Chair of the Planning Commission

Grant Redstone, Project Coordinator

---

commission should use the issues generated by the citizens' advisory group to draft the community survey.

SOME BASIC RULES FOR CREATING A COMMUNITY SURVEY

Creating an opinion and needs survey is both an art and a science. We suggest that you follow a few simple rules in drafting your questionnaire.

RULE 1: You must guarantee that the survey is completely anonymous to ensure privacy and honest answers. It is a breach of public trust to attempt to identify questionnaires from specific respondents. Designate one or several trusted individuals to handle the questionnaires. All open-ended comments should be summarized and typed for final examination. An individual's handwriting can often be identified in a small community, and this may lead to a violation of confidentiality.

RULE 2: Questions that invade the right to privacy are another breach of the public trust. Do not force people to answer questions that they may consider to be an invasion of privacy. Always provide a "no opinion" check box or a "do not wish to answer" check box for all questions that may be sensitive. Probably the most sensitive question that can be included on a questionnaire is income. If you should decide to ask household incomes, be sure to follow the guides we have provided in the model questionnaire. You cannot, and must not, ask for a specific income figure.

Questions that relate to marital status or religious preference, target individual businesses, and request that specific persons be named cannot be used. Ethnic or racial identification is improper unless you have a compelling purpose and have been advised by a professional pollster.

RULE 3: Construct your questions carefully. Questions that are difficult to understand or that could be interpreted several ways are very frustrating to the respondent. You will receive poor responses to poor questions. Always test your questionnaire on a few people and make needed changes before distributing it throughout the community.

RULE 4: Always consult with your volunteers when you prepare the actual questions. If someone is helping you with computer tabulation of the results, that person should advise you whether the questionnaire is compatible with the available software.

Constructing the Survey

The survey questionnaire should be introduced by a cover letter on your town's official stationery. The letter should indicate the purpose of the survey and explain its importance to the community planning process. The letter should mention that the survey is an official project sponsored by the planning commission and governing body. The letter must explain that the survey is anonymous, that complete confidentiality will be maintained, and that the planning commission intends to use only the total responses from the questionnaires and not any individual questionnaires. Instructions should be given and repeated on the last page of the questionnaire about the deadline for returning the survey (generally, two weeks) and how or where the survey is to be returned. Finally, the cover letter should be signed by the chairperson of the planning commission and the governing body.

The first factor to consider in planning your questionnaire is the total length. Surveys that are too long frustrate the respondent, are time-consuming to tabulate, and cause extra expense. A questionnaire of four pages, including cover letter and instructions, photocopied front and back, is the maximum length. The recommended type size for the questionnaire is the standard character size on a typewriter (12 point or 10 to 12 characters per inch).

The questionnaire should begin with a short set of instructions for the respondent, explaining who should answer the questions in each household, and how to check, circle, or otherwise answer a question. If additional space for an answer is needed, then an additional sheet of paper or the margins may be used. A reminder not to write your name or any other identifying marks should also be added. We suggest that the survey be a household survey, sent to each residential address in the community. The instructions should indicate that only one adult person living in the household should fill out the questionnaire but that that person should be encouraged to consult with other household members.

Questions that will be used to cross tabulate the survey responses should come first, such as age, sex, family size, income range, place of work (inside or outside the community or county), and whether the household rents or owns the home. If the survey is being sent to people inside and outside the town boundaries at the same time, then a space should be included to indicate location, or else the survey should be color coded.

The remainder of the survey questions should be organized by specific categories. For instance, questions that seek to find opinions on public services should be grouped together, as should questions about shopping.

There are four types of questions that can be used in this type of survey. The *fixed response question* asks for a "yes" or "no" answer and possibly "no opinion" or "don't know." The fixed response question is limited to cases when there must be an absolute answer. For instance, a question designed to determine whether or not the respondent would support increased property taxes for a new swimming pool has either a yes or no answer and perhaps "undecided."

The *variable response question* allows the respondent to pick one or more appropriate answers to a question. For instance, a question designed to determine the overall visual quality of the community would generally include the choices "good," "average," and "poor." Frequently, a "no opinion" option or a blank space for the respondent to comment may be needed.

The *scaled response question* is used to find the rating, quality, or depth of feeling about an issue. Either a five- or a ten-point scale is typically used to rate the choice. Either a line or a matrix of numbers, as shown in the model survey, can be used to indicate a rating from very negative to very positive, or very poor to excellent. If a ten-point scale is used, then the number "1" is the most negative, "5" is about average, and "10" is the most positive.

EXAMPLE: Our community should establish and fund a permanent economic development commission.

Strongly Disagree	Disagree	Maybe	Agree	Strongly Agree
1 2	3 4	5 6	7 8	9 10

Comments or suggestions: _____

_____

_____

Finally, there is the *open-ended question*, which should be limited to questions aimed at clarifying a response or obtaining a written opinion. For instance, you might ask what is the most positive or most negative aspect about living in the community. It is inappropriate to provide a fixed response to this type of question because this tends to "lead" the answer. The respondent will need to write out a response.

EXAMPLE: Can you list any special qualities of this community that make it a good place to live?

_____

_____

_____

There are two general rules about using open-ended questions. The first is that leading words should not be used. They may lead the respondents to answer in a way that those who prepared the survey wish them to reply. For instance, if words such as "small town atmosphére" or "family values" were added to a question, this might lead the respondent to your conclusions rather than a well-considered answer.

The second rule is to mix questions that seek positive answers with questions that involve negative responses. This not only adds balance to the questionnaire, but also gives the appearance of fairness on the part of those who prepared the survey. For example, a question on "special qualities that make this community a good place to live" should be followed by a question which asks if there are any major aspects about the community that the respondents do not like.

After the questionnaire is written, several decisions remain on how it should be administered. The following guidelines have been very effective in small communities.

1. The surveys should be mailed or distributed (by local service groups, such as the Boy Scouts or Kiwanis) to all households in the community. Many communities choose to include the surveys with the monthly water, energy, or sewer bill. The community may include some people living outside the town's corporate limits if mailing lists or addresses are available. Surveys can be color coded to indicate the town returns as distinguished from those living outside the corporate limits.

2. You should provide a number of drop-off points where the questionnaires can be returned. Local government offices, banks, grocery stores, and restaurants make good

drop-off points. Make sure that each location is supplied with a covered box with a slit in the top for depositing the questionnaires. The questionnaires should never be handed directly to employees. Do not provide a pre-stamped return envelope with each survey. This is costly and not as effective as it might seem in a rural community. In fact, many people may resent the community spending the extra money.

A public hearing should then be held to announce the results of the survey. The general phase of public participation begins after the technical information and opinion surveys have been collected and analyzed and the community is prepared to begin the task of translating findings into policy goals and objectives. This phase of planning belongs to the people. Planning commissioners must never assume that what they believe is desirable and good is necessarily so! In the general phase of participation, neighborhoods, community groups, individuals, and special interests are all brought together to offer opinions and suggest goals and objectives. The formulation of goals and objectives is a public function, guided by the planning commission, with final selection and approval resting with the governing body.

Reconnaissance Survey. The planning commission should also conduct a preliminary reconnaissance survey of the community before drafting the goal statements. This survey will help the commission members to understand why the community is as it is, why it has developed as it has, and where it may go in the future. The reconnaissance.survey also helps to verify the results of the community needs survey and to indicate those needs that should be addressed in the planning goals. A suggested survey method is for the planning commission to (1) make a quick observation of the community by plane or car, (2) have small groups or individuals tour the community and record people's impressions of local problems, and (3) meet to discuss all findings. The field work should provide answers to the following questions:

- What is the physical character of the community and its surroundings?
  - How do people use the land?
  - How are people housed?
  - How do people get about?
  - What public services are available?
  - How do people make a living?
  - What are the characteristics of the people?
  - What are the planning resources?

Goal Statements. A goal statement should be developed for each functional area of the community so that a plan of action can be drafted for each area. Concise goal statements should be developed for the following topics:

- Economic Development: Commercial and Industrial*
  - Education
  - Environment*
  - General Government
  - Health Services
  - Housing*
  - Land Use*
  - Population
  - Public Protection
  - Recreation*
  - Solid Waste*
  - Transportation (roads, especially)
  - Water and Sewer*

These * work elements should be given immediate attention so that the time-consuming task of physical planning may begin.

Many planning programs feature a statement of an overall goal for the community. The following example comes from the Comprehensive Development Plan of Accident, Maryland, 1991.

The planning program of Accident is based on the overall goal of creating within the community a healthy, attractive, and pleasant living environment for its residents. This goal is the most significant element underlying the Comprehensive Development Plan.

Accident then lists a number of development goals or basic policies to guide the Comprehensive Plan:

1. Maintain the town of Accident as basically a rural community preserving its natural beauty and that of the surrounding countryside. Future growth should be concentrated within or immediately adjoining the existing built-up area. Population density should be maintained at a low to moderate level with the possibility of cluster development and multifamily units at appropriate locations.

2. Recognize the development potential of Accident in terms of its proximity to the Deep Creek Lake Complex, and with respect to the overall recreation/tourism potential of Garrett County.

3. Maintain Accident as a cohesive community and the focal point of the surrounding area.

Objective Statements. Each work element of the plan should include one or more objectives to achieve stated goals. The selection of objectives is one of the most critical steps in the planning process. Ideally, a number of alternative objectives should be discussed and

---

Athens, Texas, in its Community Development Plan sets forth a general goal for Public Safety:

Each citizen must be assured the opportunity to enjoy life in the community in peace and free from fear from criminal acts and preventable disasters. To meet constant challenges to public order and personal security inherent in rapid population expansion and increasing urbanization, the community should strengthen each of those agencies charged with the responsibilities of assuring public safety

---

then the most reasonable or feasible objectives selected.

Planning objectives are more precise than desired goals. Objectives are recommendations that, if followed, bring the plan to action and help to accomplish the goals. Objectives emerge after considerable study and the rejection of alternative actions that appear to be unfeasible or out of reach of the community. Objectives are not exact planning programs; objectives narrow the range of tasks to be accomplished. After objectives are expressed, then action plans can be drafted and money allocated to solve problems.

The following statements are examples of objectives that might be found in the transportation and utilities section of a comprehensive plan in a typical community:

- Extend the airport runway to 5,200 feet.
- Construct a loop road around the community to reduce traffic near the town square.
- Provide offstreet parking in the center business district.
- Provide for fire truck access to housing subdivisions on the northern edge of town.

Many methods can be used to select the most feasible objective that would accomplish a stated goal: for example, pick the objective with the lowest cost, choose by majority vote, select the objective that could be completed within the least time, or select the objective that is most consistent with the overall character of the comprehensive plan. There is no one best method for selecting or rejecting objectives; there are, however, at least two methods to be avoided:

1. If an objective is selected on the basis of lowest cost, it may not necessarily be the objective with the smallest initial price tag. For example, maintenance and operating costs can be much greater over time than the purchase price of a building or piece of equipment. Short- and long-range costs should be considered equally. Keep in mind that some small cost capital items may be expensive to operate and maintain and thus have a significant impact on future operating budgets.

2. Do not select ideal objectives that are unworkable. Objectives must be realistic; they must be attainable under the present financial resources.

Implementation.   Plan implementation occurs in two ways. First, the elected governing body must approve the miniplan for it to be a legal document. The governing body may modify the plan in the process, however. Then the governing body may create programs to carry out the goals and objectives of the miniplan. These capital improvements programs, such as a new school, a new sewer line, or street repair, become part of the town's budget. The governing body is responsible for deciding which projects have priority and how much money to spend on them. For example, after reading the miniplan, the governing body may decide that a new school is needed immediately to meet the projected future increases in school-age children. Similarly, the governing body may decide to spend money five years hence on a new fire engine.

The town planning process clearly aids in the town budgeting process. The extension, repair, and replacement of public facilities can be foreseen and town revenues allocated to meet those needs. Budgeting gives towns greater control over the cost of public services and over property taxes, the primary source of town revenues.

The second way plan implementation occurs is through the planning commission. The planning commission, with the approval of the elected governing body, adopts zoning ordinances, subdivision regulations, building codes, and other ordinances which determine the location, density, and type of development throughout the town. Many towns have wrongly assumed that planning is zoning and have enacted zoning and land subdivision ordinances without first creating a town plan. Some towns have had their zoning ordinances overturned in court because the ordinances were not based on a duly adopted town plan.

A town plan gives a legal foundation to zoning and subdivision regulations. It is very important to understand that zoning and subdivision regulations and other ordinances serve as the major means of carrying out the town plan. Thus, the town's ordinances should be drafted to reflect the goals and objectives put forth in the town plan. For example, if the town plan calls for maintaining a clean environment, but the zoning ordinance allows for toxic waste sites, then the purpose of the plan will be lost, and the town may develop in undesirable ways.

The planning commissioners should follow both the town plan and the town's ordinances when ruling on a proposed development. When a proposed development is presented to the commission, the commissioners must make a recommendation on whether the development is in keeping with the goals and objectives of the miniplan and the town's ordinances. For example, a proposed toxic waste dump may not be in accordance with the goal of a clean, healthy environment, even though it is proposed for land zoned for industrial use. On the other hand, a proposed electronics manufacturing plant offering 25 new jobs may meet the objective to diversify the local economy. Or a proposed development may meet some goals and objectives but not others. In this case, the planning commission may issue a conditional use permit allowing the proposed development to proceed if certain conditions are met (for example, adequate parking space will be provided).

The planning commission must maintain some flexibility in recommending whether a development is approved or rejected. The elected governing body, who ultimately will approve or deny a proposed development, must also have some flexibility in using both the miniplan and ordinances to judge potential developments. Yet, the planning commission and the governing body should try to keep their decisions consistent with the policies of the miniplan as much as possible. The miniplan is based on public needs and desires, and both the planning commission and the governing body are supposed to uphold the public trust.

This is not to say that a miniplan is set in stone. The miniplan will need to be updated every few years to reflect changes in the town's goals and objectives. This updating should consist of a review of new information about the town and new public needs and desires as expressed in a survey or at public meetings.

5

Information and Resources for the Miniplan

A community plan is no better than the information on which it is based. If a plan is constructed from unreliable or outdated information, then the plan itself will be of little use. The purpose of this chapter is to review resources and contacts that might be helpful in preparing a miniplan. Each of the following chapters suggests additional information sources for producing specific planning studies.

ORGANIZATIONAL RESOURCES

The planning commission will need to identify and assemble information sources before beginning the actual data collection and production of the miniplan. We assume that you intend to collect most of the data and produce most of the document rather than hire a professional planner to do the entire job. Before

you begin collecting information and enlisting volunteers, we have two suggestions. First, if you have a university in your state that offers a degree in community planning, contact the head of this department and ask if a student intern is available to work with your community on an extended basis. Second, contact a professional planner from your state, region, county, or nearby town and ask the planner to attend the organizational meeting for the miniplan. You should request that this person prepare a one- to two-hour presentation on the basics of community planning with a specific focus on the planning process.

Human Resources

A network of community volunteers is essential to the success of your planning process. In preparing the miniplan, you will need volunteer labor, local expert advice, and some technical assistance. Volunteers and experts alike should be cautioned to carefully check their sources and data. Although local needs will vary, you should at least prepare a network of the following types of volunteers that you can call on for occasional help and advice.

Technical Advice

- Someone involved in the upper management of a savings and loan or local bank to advise on the realities of local economics.
- A long-established businessperson who is active in local business associations to advise on area trade and sales.
- A local real estate agent who is knowledgeable about the housing market.
- A local merchant who has a clear understanding of the needs and conditions of the farm, ranching, mining, forestry or fishing community. Consider the manager of a farm implement sales firm, saw mill, or cannery.
- Someone who can speak for the elderly of your community.
- Someone who understands the value of racial diversity in the community and can speak about the needs of minorities.
- A person involved in the maintenance and installation of public facilities.
- A person skilled in communications, such as a newspaper editor.

Volunteer Labor

- A community historian.
- A person with good writing skills.
- A person with artistic ability who can produce simple pencil drawings of buildings and landmarks.
- A person with good public speaking skills.

- A person with experience in desktop publishing and database management programs. Even some high school students may have considerable technical skills in these areas.
- A person who has experience in preparing a written sample survey.
- A person with good photography ability.

Equipment

The minimum equipment needed to prepare the miniplan includes:

- A calculator with a memory function.
- A good typewriter, but preferably a personal computer.
- Access to a good quality photocopying machine with a reduction/enlargement feature.
- A camera.

A fax machine will pay for itself several times over in savings of time and travel. Searching your region and state for data can be expensive. A fax machine allows you to communicate quickly and cheaply.

We strongly suggest that you use a personal computer to organize information, store data, and publish the final document. You will need a word processing program or desktop publisher, a database manager, and a spreadsheet program. Typically, all three programs will be integrated into one package. The brand name of the program or programs is much less important than your experience with a particular program. Making or producing a plan is not the time to learn a new program. We have found that people have spent more time learning a program than they have in searching for data and undertaking the planning process.

A personal computer is not essential for preparing a miniplan. But it is an enormous help. A computer will vastly improve your organization of data and text. This technology, because of widespread interest and low prices, is now available in even the smallest, most remote communities in the United States and Canada. If your planning group, city hall, or county courthouse does not have access to a computer, a simple request to the local high school or the public-at-large is sure to bring offers of help. People with computer skills often like to share their talent with others. Any brand of computer is satisfactory; however, if you plan to produce spreadsheet tables and use computer graphics in your final document, you will need a computer with at least a 386DX processor.

A good printer is important for producing your final plan document. The plan is a means for community education and learning. Therefore, the document should be of high visual quality. Search for inkjet or laser printers or at least a letter quality dot matrix printer. As an alternative, you can rent a printer for a short period of time or have a business print the final document. If all you have is an older, low quality dot matrix printer, consider typing your plan and then pasting or taping your charts, graphs, or figures into the final document before photocopying.

INFORMATION TO COLLECT

Before you start to search for information, you should determine what types of data will be necessary to complete each planning study. You will often find that much important information is already part of the public record. The first step in collecting information is to contact the public officials and government employees of the community, county, and state. In the past, the resources and knowledge of these people have not been fully explored. Tax assessors and appraisers, building inspectors, engineers, surveyors, town and county clerks, and others keep large amounts of data on the day-to-day activities of the planning area over long periods of time. For example, you will find that records of deeds and the registration of mortgages will help to supplement information on new construction activities; and the town or county assessor can aid in locating different types of property.

Information Collected by Organizations and Firms

Public companies can be especially helpful in small towns where written records are scant. Accurate housing and population information can be gathered by asking the telephone, electricity, and natural gas companies for numbers and types of customers.

The private business sector can be of help if cooperation and understanding in the planning effort are secured early in the process. Insurance agents can often request from their companies any recent studies that might have been completed in the area. Many large retail outlets, such as supermarkets and discount chain stores, study a community when selecting a store site. The same is true for fast food franchises. Also, the large retail chains often conduct sales retention studies, and it is quite possible your particular community was included in a regional survey. This information can be especially useful in making population projections and in studying the community's potential for economic growth.

Perhaps the most underrated source of information are the local churches. Few people realize that most churches have large planning staffs at the multistate and national level. A simple letter of inquiry can determine if any population and socioeconomic studies have recently been undertaken in your area.

You should always contact the regional planning agency, if there is one, to determine the types and amounts of data it has collected. The regional planning agency may have statistical data at the state level for comparative purposes with other towns and regions. You should also contact individual state and federal agencies for data on special subjects, such as local soil and water quality.

Area newspapers can be highly useful to the planning effort. This is especially true when it comes time to identify local problems and conditions, since at some time these problems and conditions have been reported in the local newspaper. Newspaper editors and publishers are often strong resource contacts and promoters of community planning and development efforts. Also, newspapers can provide valuable publicity on community planning activities and keep the public informed.

Local and county historical societies are a valuable resource for examining past trends and conditions. Historical societies can usually be counted on to assist in the preparation of the plan, and they should be one of the primary contacts for issues concerning historic sites and historic preservation efforts.

The soil conservation service, located in almost every county, is always a worthwhile contact. The soil conservation service has proven most helpful in supplying information on the ability of soils to support development and on potential problems with soil erosion and water pollution. Many offices now have the capability to link to a national database via computer to obtain a complete assessment of soil types and development suitability. The cooperative extension service of your state land grant university and its county-level offices often have an abundance of information, too. Many states have created state data centers, often tied to the state land grant university, which can also be a ready source of useful population information.

A state's league of municipalities is an excellent source of technical assistance for compiling the miniplan. The league, in addition to having excellent files of technical information, can also help search for information contacts. As one of the first efforts in data collection, you should write your state's league and ask for the list of publications supplied at little or no cost.

Published Data

A surprising amount of published data exists for small towns, if you know how to search for it. The *Census of Population and Housing* for each state and other reports from the U.S. Bureau of the Census contain information on population, housing, and family income characteristics. This information is well detailed for communities of 2,500 or more residents. But census data includes some information on towns of 1,000 to 2,499 residents under the heading of Rural-Nonfarm. Detailed data profiles are available for all counties, census units (generally townships), and incorporated communities on CD-ROM from the U.S. Census Bureau. These CD-ROMs should be available at any mid-size library. The individual files for your community or county can be printed out or copied to files on diskettes to transfer to your computer as plain text files or imported to most spreadsheets. The U.S. Department of Commerce publishes information on business activity in places of 2,500 or more people. Most states publish a statistical abstract containing information on population, economic activity, health statistics, local finance, and school districts. If the census information is out of date, the state statistical abstract may be your single most important source of data.

The state department of health supplies summaries of births, deaths, and other related statistics on request to local agencies and governments. This department may also provide population estimates and projections by county and economic region.

State agencies often have large amounts of data on water resources, geological surveys, housing, natural resources, and environmental affairs. For example, the state water resources board has data on climate, water and soil, flood-plain hazards, and other water-related matters. State departments of natural resources often have available topographical and mineral maps of considerable detail.

Other important sources of published data can be obtained from:

- Your state association of counties.
- The National Association of Counties.
- The National Association of Towns and Townships.
- Your legislative research service.
- Your secretary of state.
- The government documents section of your state library.

Visual Data

Aerial photographs are always useful in the planning process, but they are generally expensive to take. Aerial maps are often available from several sources. You should contact the state highway department, the county office of the soil conservation service, and your county planning office. Since property reassessment is now widespread in the United States, most county assessors and appraisers have updated and comprehensive airphotos. The libraries of state universities and colleges and the state library are also excellent sources for this data.

Base Maps. Much of the data collected for the miniplan should be displayed in a set of community base maps. A *base map* is a representative drawing to scale of the community, depicting boundaries and major streams and rivers, streets, blocks, railroad tracks, and the location of community buildings. Either blank or partially filled base maps should be available and currently used for tax assessment, deed recording, subdivision, highway planning, and engineering surveys. All incorporated municipalities are required to maintain an official map of their boundaries, streets, subdivisions/additions, and lots. However, such requirements are often overlooked in small, rural communities and if for some reason a current and precise base map is not available, you should contact a planning or engineering firm and arrange for the drafting of such a map. Before preparing any new maps, however, you should contact the following sources for existing maps:

- County clerk.
- County engineer.
- State highway commission.
- State league of municipalities.
- State board of water resources.
- State division of recreation and parks.
- Soil conservation service.
- State department of economic development, planning division.

- Regional planning commission.
- Cooperative extension service.
- State library and libraries of the state universities.
- State conservation commission.
- Local abstract offices.
- Private engineering firms.
- Local surveyors.
- Local utilities; especially electrical/gas and telephone.
- Rural water districts.
- Regional federal census office.
- Local or regional library.

The scale for the base map is very important and will depend on the size of the community, the amount of reduction necessary to insert the map into the miniplan text, the types of information entered on the map, and the detail desired. In general, the scale should be in the range of 800 feet to the inch and one mile to the inch. Base maps should be kept rather small to make for easy handling.

Maps that are needed for the miniplan include the following:

1. *Housing base map* should show the location and quality of the housing stock. The map should include the following information:

- The concentration of housing districts throughout the community.
- Location of new housing subdivisions or additions in the past 10 years.
- The area in which dilapidated and substandard housing is located.

2. *Land use maps* show the current and future land use patterns of the community. The first map depicts the existing land use patterns of the community, and the second map indicates the desired location and density for future development. Both land use maps should indicate the town limits and include any developed areas just outside the town limits.

3. *Community facilities map* depicts the location of community facilities, including municipal sewer and water lines, parks and recreation areas, schools, major public buildings, and so on.

4. *Soil conditions map* illustrates the types of soils found in the community and indicates areas such as floodplains and steep slopes which have limited development potential.

5. *Transportation map* shows the major and minor streets and roads in the community and the location of rail lines, railroad stations, navigable bodies of water, docks, and airports.

6. *Flood plain maps* identify areas prone to flooding. These maps are available to most American towns and counties. They are supplied by the National Flood Insurance Program administered by the Federal Insurance Administration within the Federal Emergency Management Administration.

Generally, all of these maps can be gathered from the sources listed at the beginning of this section and from the following maps:

- Road maps.
- Air photo maps (for sale at U.S. Department of Agriculture Office in each county).
- Soil and ground cover maps (county office of the soil conservation service).
- Watershed district maps (county office of the soil conservation service).
- Public works maps (local and county).
- Engineering and utility maps (local and county; state highway department).
- Census maps (Bureau of the Census publications).
- County base maps (county clerk).

- Topography (U.S. Geological Survey, state geological survey).
- Area development maps (U.S. Army Corps of Engineers).

Making Your Own Maps

Most maps in the miniplan do not require extremely fine detail; they are meant to show information at a glance rather than at a minute scale. It is possible to produce a template of each base map on a computer program called a drawtool or, even better, a simple computer-aided design/drawing program (CADD). Once the template is produced, it can be used time and again to portray different information. Although the scale on the template will not be precise unless a computer-aided mapping tool is used, information such as generalized flood plains, prime farm soils, and future lands use designations can be entered on successive maps.

Another way to produce these maps, which does not involve the use of a computer, is to photocopy the base map and then cut and paste to create each map. The simplest way to make this map is to type out the text and paste it to the base map with a transparent tape or with white correction and coverup tape. Symbols and numbers can be placed on the map with the use of press-on letters. Thin plastic sheets with patterns or cross hatching can be cut and applied to fit certain areas on the map. These materials may be purchased at any office supplies or crafts store. Although this method is time-consuming, it is still common among surveyors and engineers for producing plats and maps.

The most common mistake in making your own maps is the size. Although photocopying technology now allows you to enlarge or re-duce nearly any size of map, it is still important to make the map no larger or smaller than about 30 percent of the size you intend to use in your document. Reductions or enlargements greater than this will cause problems. Too great an enlargement will cause lines, features, and text to appear grainy. Too great a reduction will produce letters too small and fuzzy to read, and you will not be able to distinguish between the different types of lines and symbols used in making the map.

OTHER INFORMATION AND RESOURCES

There are several resources that must be gathered or generated on the community level to aid in the planning process. Some of this data may involve the need for technical advice, while other resources will need to be produced exclusively for this plan.

Visual Aids

Good plans need pictures. Community residents relate very positively to photographs of landmarks, events, or people that invoke a strong sense of the town. A plan is a written and visual document; words convey meaning and context, but a visual image can often be more easily understood. Photograph monuments, historic homes and businesses, and significant architectural structures to help portray the built environment of the community. Take pictures of well-known community events or activities that relate to the human resources parts of your plan. These pictures can be photocopied directly into your plan to illustrate and reinforce the text. A black and white picture with the proper light and frame balance can be photocopied with near original quality. Better yet, ask your volunteer

Figure 5-1 Example graphic for document illustration

19th Century school house - Wheaton, Kansas   **Drawing by Elba Villazanna**

with artistic ability to make pencil line tracings of the original photos. After the line drawings are made on thin tracing paper, they can be reduced or enlarged by photocopying and pasted in the planning document before final reproduction.

Computer graphics and imaging can be used to place high quality photo images in your document. It is likely that a business or private person in your community has the necessary image scanner or video imaging capability to transfer your pictures to the plan document. The picture of the old rural school house in Figure 5–1 was taken from a black and white line drawing from a small town historic brochure. It was scanned on a 300 dot per inch scanner typically found in many business offices.

6

Community Profile, Geography, and History

Many plans begin with a brief profile of the community. This profile is optional, but we recommend it. It may be used in conjunction with a community history or it may comprise a small section of its own. The profile is recommended because it provides an excellent introduction to the miniplan and helps to summarize the physical, economic, and social changes that have occurred in the community. The profile also helps to build the interest of residents and nonresidents in the rest of the plan.

SUGGESTED OUTLINE FOR COMMUNITY PROFILE

The following outline will help in preparing the community profile; the outline should be expanded or reduced according to preference and judgment. Because the community profile is a summary section, it should be one of the last tasks accomplished in the miniplan process.

Community Profile Outline

I. General Information
    A. Descriptive names: town, city, county, region, state
    B. Descriptive location: geographical location of the town and county
    C. Growth or town size summary:
        1. County population 1990
        2. Community population 1970, 1980, 1990
        3. Decade population growth or decline by percent
        4. Minority population (by group if possible)
        5. Future population estimates

Exhibit 6–1
Sample Geographic Description

Hill County is located in the south central portion of Kansas. The town of Skyway is located in the southern section of the county 20 miles south of Hill City, the county seat. Skyway is located on a plateau at about 450 feet in elevation. The Cass River bounds the western edge of the town. Skyway is served by County Highways 14 and 58 which offer easy access south to Oklahoma or to Interstate Highway 9.

There are many organizations and institutions that should be able to supply information on physical features and location. The local chamber of commerce or any tourism group usually supplies this information for public distribution. The soil conservation service should also be able to assist in locating physical information. If more information is needed, contact the state fish and game commission, the area Army Corps of Engineers, or local colleges and universities. Also, be sure to consult your local library.

History

A community history may accompany the geographic information above or appear as a small section of its own. The history may be presented in either an outline or narrative form. An outline should include only the most significant dates and activities in the life of the community. Counties or towns which depend on their stock of historic areas and structures for a substantial portion of their livelihood will need to undertake a major effort in producing the history section. Rather than a simple summary, this section should take the form of an inventory and assessment of your stock of historic assets.

Exhibit 6–2
Sample History Outline

1859 Skyway settled by group of Swedish immigrants led by Alfred Skyway.

1867 Kansas Pacific Railroad comes to Skyway.

1882 Major flood of century destroys half of community.

1886 Skyway is rebuilt on higher ground and flourishes with the establishment of the New Colson Bible School; Skyway incorporates as a community.

1889 First factory built—Skyway Casket Company.

1911 Population of 3,400 was an all-time high.

1924 Major crop failures reduce population and resources of the community.

1931 Bible College closes; population is further reduced.

1942 Nearby Army Base established.

1943 Population of town increases to 3,300 with influx of Army families.

1947 Army Base closes; Skyway population decreases to 2,000.

1957 Kansas Pacific ceases scheduled runs.

1966 New agricultural industry makes home in Skyway.

1980 Population decreases to 1,810.

1990 Population appears stable at 1,750.

Exhibit 6–3
Sample History Summary

The Skyway area was inhabited by Plains Indians for centuries, and the Cass River was an important route for early Kansas traders. But it was not until the middle of the 19th century that any attempt was made at permanent settlement. Logging interests first moved into the area in the early 1850s and established several sawmills. In 1859, a group of Swedish immigrants arrived under the direction of Alfred Skyway. Skyway, the "City of Wood," was originally called Nelson Town and later Cassville until the formal incorporation of Skyway in 1886.

The Kansas Casket Company built its first plant in Skyway in 1889. This company, the town's major employer, was mainly responsible for helping Skyway get back on its feet after a flood destroyed half of the community in 1882. Skyway was moved to its present location up the river to higher ground during this period of rebuilding and has had no further flood damage. In 1886 the New Colson Bible College opened its doors to 180 theology students. In 1911, Skyway's population reached an all-time high of 3,400 inhabitants. But a regional crop failure in 1924 eventually led to the closing of the Bible College in 1931.

During World War II, an army base was established several miles from Skyway for training purposes. Once again, the community thrived with the influx of families and services. The base closed in 1947, but since then the town has been successful in attracting several small industries to stabilize employment and population.

Information for the history summary can usually be obtained from service groups, such as the League of Women Voters, who may have prepared programs on community history. The local or county historical society is also a valuable source of information and may even be willing to prepare this section under proper direction. Two additional sources of information are the local librarian and the newspaper. The librarian often is ready to accept research tasks and quite possibly can direct you to a previously written summary. The local newspaper files contain a rich source of information and should not be overlooked.

If the town is very small and only sketchy historical information is available, you should publish a request for assistance from any local resident who might have the records and knowledge to complete this section.

7

Population Estimates for the Miniplan

Population analysis and projections are the heart of a community plan; all other plan elements depend on the current and expected future population. Population information enhances the capability of the local government to prepare for the impact of future growth on land use and community facilities. In addition, most state and federal assistance programs rely on local population figures and projections.

The methods presented here are simple but should be sufficient to analyze a town that is experiencing normal population growth or moderate population loss. In a community undergoing rapid growth, it is difficult to predict the number of newcomers. Rapid growth communities are usually found on the edge of metropolitan areas and are in the process of changing into suburbs. In rural areas, boomtowns are often associated with energy, mining, and recreation or tourism development. Boomtowns typically experience cycles of in-

tense construction, a secondary expansion, and then stabilize or decline.

FINDING AND USING POPULATION INFORMATION

The U.S. Bureau of the Census

Gathering population data is an important yet time-consuming effort. The U.S. Bureau of the Census publishes a state-by-state summary of population every 10 years. The 1990 census of population and housing characteristics for your state shows the population numbers in even the smallest towns. Prior to 1990, the census contained detailed population figures mainly for towns of more than 2,500 people; the census also had some population data for towns of 1,000 to 2,499 residents.

For a town of 2,500 or more people, the U.S. Bureau of the Census publications are the only sources you will need to complete the projections presented in this section. Detailed publications on population characteristics are available at your local or regional library. You should look for 1990 CPH, which is entitled *1990 Census of Population and Housing: Summary Population and Housing Characteristics* (your state), and 1990 CP (your state) entitled *1990 Census of Population: General Population Characteristics*.

Information published by the U.S. Census for 1990 includes:

• The total number of people in your town.

• The total number of females and/or males.

• The number of people by race and Hispanic origin.

• The total number of households.

• Total number of people living in group quarters or institutions.

• Married couples/families.

• Average number of people/families per household.

• The median age of the population. (Note: the median age is not the average age. Half of the population is older and half is younger than the median age.)

• Persons by sex and age groups.

The Bureau of the Census also publishes detailed population information for rural communities, rural nonfarm areas, counties, rural census tracts, and townships. This level of information is normally available only on microfiche cards at the library of a state university, state library, or large regional library. You can either pay to make paper copies of the microfiche cards or have film copies made of the cards and use your own microfiche reader. Many counties make microfiche copies of critical information and are likely to have a reader and copier. An-

other source for the detailed population information on rural communities is available for the Census Bureau on CD-ROM (computer laser optical disk) at many regional libraries or directly from the Bureau of the Census, Data User Services Division. The individual files from the CD-ROM can be copied directly to a printer or transferred to floppy disk and carried back to your community for further analysis. These files contain complete demographic profiles of all communities regardless of size. A great deal of time and effort can be saved if you obtain either the microfiche or the CD-ROM files; and you can safely ignore the instructions that follow for converting age groups into standard cohorts for projection purposes. A sample of one page from the CD-ROM is shown in Exhibit 7–1 entitled "Sample of Profile Census Information."

Converting Population Data into Standard Cohorts

The publication entitled *General Population Characteristics* by the Bureau of the Census contains the number of people by age groups for all counties and all communities with 2,500 or more people. You need only copy the number of people in each four-year age group from this publication. Most of the census publications give the total population and then the number of females in each age group. The number of males in each age group must be determined by subtracting females from the subtotal of each group.

Information on age groups will be available (in most states) for all incorporated areas. If you are working in a town with a population of fewer than 2,500 people, you will find that the age groups are not reported in four-year

Exhibit 7-1 Sample of Profile Census Information Shown on Computer Optical Laser Disk, 1990 Census

1990 Census Of Population and Housing   Page 1
040   Kansas
160   Ness City city

URBAN AND RURAL RESIDENCE..
      Total Population... 1,729
Urban Population... 0
      Percent of Total Population... 0
Rural Population... 1,729
      Percent of Total Population... 100
Farm Population.. 20

SCHOOL ENROLLMENT
      Persons 3 years and over enrolled in school................... 405
Primary School.. 62
      Elementary or High School.. 310
Percent in Private School.. 23
College... 33

EDUCATION ATTAINMENT
      Persons 25 years and over... 1,729
Less than 9th grade.. 131
      9th to 12the grade no diploma.. 128
High School graduation.. 448
      Some college - no degree.. 270
Associate Degree.. 46
      Bachelor's Degree... 110
Graduate or Professional Degree... 46

SOURCE: 1990 Census of Population and Housing 3.282/2 CD 90-3 Computer Optical Laser Disk.

increments. Instead, the census uses the following categories shown in Table 7–1 entitled "Age Groups Shown in the 1990 Census for Small Communities." By contrast, the population information contained in the microfiche and CD-ROM is also shown in Table 7–1.

It is possible to convert these age groups to match the four-year data given for communities of 2,500 or more people. This conversion will require some judgment and a fairly good idea of the population structure of your county. Before you begin, compare your community's median age to the county's median age. (A median means that half of the population is younger than the median number and half is older.) If the two median ages are no more than two years apart, your final conversions probably will not require extensive ad-

Table 7-1 Age groups shown in the 1990 census for small communities

1 Shown in CP Printed Reports	2 Shown in CD-Rom and Microfiche	
Under 5 years	Under 1 year	21 years
Under 18 years	1 & 2 years	22 to 24 years
18-20	3 & 4 years	25 to 29 years
21-24	5 years	30 to 34 years
25-44	6 years	35 to 39 years
45-54	7 to 9 years	40 to 44 years
55-59	10 & 11 years	45 to 49 years
60-64	12 & 13 years	50 to 54 years
65 and over	14 years	55 to 59 years
75 and over	15 years	60 to 64 years
80 and over	16 years	65 to 69 years
Median age	17 years	70 to 74 years
	18 years	75 to 79 years
	19 years	80 to 84 years
	20 years	85 and over

Source: 1990 Census of Population and Housing, CP, Bureau of the Census and 3.282/2 CD 90-3 Computer Optical Laser Disk

justments. If the median ages are quite different, for example, a median community age of 41 years as compared to a median age for the county of 31 years, then you should seek expert help to determine which age groups are causing the differences.

Convert each age group for the county to a percentage. For example, if the total population of the county is 15,000 and the 0 to 4 years age population is 452, the percentage of the group to the total is 3 percent. If the total population of your community is 1,550 and the 4 years and under age group is 60 persons, the percentage is 3.87. There is some evidence that, at least among the very young, your community's age structure should be quite similar to the county's.

Since the under 18 years age group is reported for your town, this can be converted to a percentage and compared to the county's data. The 55–59 and the 60–64 age groups can be converted and compared, as can the age 65 and over, 75 and over, and 85 and over. By using the same procedure on your calculator or a spreadsheet, you can estimate all of the age groups with a reasonable degree of accuracy.

State and Regional Sources

For most towns with fewer than 2,500 inhabitants, you may be able to find data quickly and easily by contacting your state department of community affairs, state university, or regional planning agency. Many state agencies take the low level census details and compile the data into useable tables. Also, do not overlook major utility companies serving your town. These sources, notably energy and communications companies, often make population projections for towns and counties to predict their service needs. If the mini-plan is being prepared for an unincorporated area or township (in the Midwest or West) and only county population estimates are available, you can estimate your community's share of the county population by using the detailed census information for your county on microfiche or CD-ROM.

Local Information Sources

Do not overlook your own local sources for population information. First, check all county information sources. It is our experience that many counties collect yearly population data based on property tax receipts or motor vehicle registrations. Use these data carefully and understand how they are collected. Ask your county clerk, treasurer, or tax appraiser/assessor to explain the collection methods. Some of these data are quite good, but there is a danger of undercounting elderly people, military personnel, and those in poverty. Compare these data to other sources such as voter registration, county health department statistics, or social services information.

Second, visit the county (or equivalent governmental units in such states as Alaska and Louisiana) property tax assessor/appraiser to discuss the types of data that are being collected. In some states the county clerk is still in charge of assessing all property taxes. In recent years most states were forced to switch to state supervised assessment of real and personal property. Most of these assessments are now computer processed, and the amount and quality of population data are surprising. Even rural counties are now managing information under geographic information systems (GIS), and the quality of data is usually quite high.

On the local level, school districts can be very helpful sources of information. The local school district can supply you with information on the numbers and ages of people under 18 years old and may be able to give you population forecasts that they use in estimating future school enrollments. Because all school districts report their enrollments to the state school board or department of education, you should contact your state agency to obtain population and age data for nearby communities or counties so that you will have a basis for comparison.

Even the smallest communities can be good sources of indirect population information. For instance, most communities over 1,000 frequently use centralized computer billing for water, sewer, and even electric and natural gas use. A simple computerized sorting of this information will separate households from commercial and manufacturing users. Households not connected to services are generally easy to pinpoint, so they can be added into the population base. Compare the number of households (dwelling units) to the reported number of dwelling units in the 1990 census for your community. Adjust the discrepancy by accounting for new households or vacant structures since 1989 (the households for the 1990 census were actually counted in 1989 or earlier). Finally, divide the number of households by the median household size, which is available in the 1990 Census of Population and Housing. This should give you a reasonable estimate of the total community or county population.

A community may be small enough (under 600 people) so that you can construct population and age records from the property tax rolls, school enrollment, and other sources of public information. This is not an easy job or the preferred way. Rather, it is a last resort that will work in very small communities when no other data source is satisfactory. It requires an accurate block and lot map of the community to locate every dwelling unit. Some private consultants and regional planning agencies suggest that it might be necessary to use a questionnaire to obtain this information. We do not recommend this approach. A questionnaire is best used to obtain a sample of the population during the planning process. The aim is not to obtain data from the entire population; the objective is to gather data which is representative of the community. False or inaccurate information, combined with those people who will never reply to a questionnaire, make this an impractical method for collecting population data.

If you believe that a questionnaire is the only way to collect population information, then there are several important considerations. Rewrite the survey questionnaire provided in Chapter 4. Only one questionnaire should be distributed to the community during the planning process; multiple surveys are expensive and tend to make you look disorganized. Next, remember that this type of survey is not anonymous. You will have to know which households failed to return the questionnaire so that an accurate population count can be gathered by other means, probably door-to-door. This does not mean that the questionnaires are public information. They must remain confidential to protect personal privacy. Also, this questionnaire should be well publicized in the local media so that the townspeople are aware of the content and purpose of the survey. A cover letter signed by a member of your local governing body and planning commission chairperson should clearly spell out the purpose of the questionnaire and how vital it is that it be returned in a timely fashion.

COHORT-SURVIVAL POPULATION FORECASTS

Once information on the town's current population has been obtained, you should complete the following tables to estimate future population. Before starting, be sure to have a desktop computer available. Anyone in the community even moderately skilled with database management and spreadsheet computing will probably be more than willing to help with the population data. Also, computerized population information can now be purchased for your state and county from companies which specialize in providing detailed data from the census and other sources.

Estimating the Future Population

The method of population projection presented in this section is known as the *cohort-survival technique*. It is designed to determine the number of people in different age groups and then estimate the size of those age groups 10 years later. This method is recommended for several reasons. First, age groups are relatively easy to use and understand. Second, the data needed for analysis should be available in a small community. Third, the method is one of the few tools that can be used when no historical population information is available. Fourth, for the time and effort involved, the expected age group distribution provides the greatest amount of population information for future planning and development.

You should be aware, however, that the cohort-survival method does not account for in-migration and out-migration to and from the community. Migration is difficult to predict, although it may have major effects on the community's needs and goals. The analysis that follows is intended to indicate the general direction and size of change that is happening. Changes in the age distribution of the population should be viewed with the same importance as the total change in population.

Table 7–2, "Total Population by Age and Sex Group," shows the current number of town inhabitants according to age and gender. Using your census information, enter the number of females and males in columns 1 and 2 of Table 7–2. The numbers for female population in column 2 of Table 7–2 should then be entered in column 2 of Table 7–3 ("As-

Table 7-2 Total population by age and sex group

1 Age	2 Females	3 Males
0-4	( )	( )
5-9	( )	( )
10-14	( )	( )
15-19	( )	( )
20-24	( )	( )
25-29	( )	( )
30-34	( )	( )
35-39	( )	( )
40-44	( )	( )
45-49	( )	( )
50-54	( )	( )
55-59	( )	( )
60-64	( )	( )
65-69	( )	( )
70-74	( )	( )
75 +	( )	( )

Table 7-3 Assignment of survival rates for females

1 Age of Cohort	2 Present Number of Females in Cohort	3 Survival Rates of Cohort	4 Females 10 Years from The Present	5 Approximate Cohort in 10 years
0-4	( )	.99369	( )	10-14
5-9	( )	.99548	( )	15-19
10-14	( )	.99369	( )	20-24
15-19	( )	.99151	( )	25-29
20-24	( )	.98915	( )	30-34
25-29	( )	.98525	( )	35-39
30-34	( )	.97873	( )	40-44
35-39	( )	.96819	( )	45-49
40-44	( )	.95248	( )	50-54
45-49	( )	.93037	( )	55-59
50-54	( )	.89756	( )	60-64
55-59	( )	.84840	( )	65-69
60-64	( )	.77357	( )	70-74
65-69	( )	.66104	( )	75-79
70-74	( )	.50629	( )	80-84
75 +	( )	.21782	( )	85 +

Table 7-4 Assignment of survival rates for males

1 Age of Cohort	2 Present Number of Males in Cohort	3 Survival Rates of Cohort	4 Males 10 Years from The Present	5 Approximate Cohort in 10 years
0-4	( )	.99166	( )	10-14
5-9	( )	.99217	( )	15-19
10-14	( )	.98696	( )	20-24
15-19	( )	.98258	( )	25-29
20-24	( )	.98094	( )	30-34
25-29	( )	.97733	( )	35-39
30-34	( )	.96766	( )	40-44
35-39	( )	.94963	( )	45-49
40-44	( )	.92037	( )	50-54
45-49	( )	.87794	( )	55-59
50-54	( )	.82099	( )	60-64
55-59	( )	.74756	( )	65-69
60-64	( )	.65619	( )	70-74
65-69	( )	.52478	( )	75-79
70-74	( )	.40468	( )	80-84
75 +	( )	.18070	( )	85 +

signment of Survival Rates for Females"), and the numbers for males in column 3 of Table 7–2 should be entered in column 2 of Table 7–4 ("Assignment of Survival Rates for Males"). The simple assumptions in column 3 of Table 7–3 and Table 7–4 are the statistical survival rates compiled by the U.S. Bureau of the Census. The chances of a person surviving another 10 years are greater in the younger years but decline sharply in old age. This survival process can be illustrated by glancing at the first and last entries of column 3 in Table 7–4; the first entry shows that males aged 0–4 years as a group have a very good chance of surviving for 10 years (the entry .99166 means that the group stands a less than 1 percent chance of dying within the next 10 years). On the other hand, the last entry in column 3 of Table 7–4 illustrates that men now living who are 75 years and older

have a very slim chance of surviving another 10 years (the entry .18070 means that the group stands an 82 percent chance of dying within 10 years).

To estimate the age groups for women 10 years in the future, you should multiply each entry in column 2 of Table 7–3 by the corresponding survival rate in column 3 and enter the results in column 4.

To estimate the age groups for men 10 years from now, multiply each entry in column 2 of Table 7–4 by the corresponding survival rate in column 3 and enter the results in column 4.

Each entry in column 4 of Tables 7–3 and 7–4 is the estimated number of people by sex and age group that will survive 10 years in the future; column 5 shows the age group in which each current group will then be a part. In column 5, you can see that there are no estimates for the age groups 0–4 and 5–9. To es-

Table 7–5 Summary of childbearing females by age group

1 Age	2 Current Number of Females	3 Age	4 Current Number of Females
10-14	( )	5-9	( )
15-19	( )	10-14	( )
20-24	( )	15-19	( )
25-29	( )	20-24	( )
30-34	( )	25-29	( )
35-39	( )	30-34	( )
40-44	( )	35-39	( )
Total		Total	

timate these age groups, first take the current female age groups 10 to 44 from column 2 of Table 7–2 to fill in column 2 of Table 7–5. Next, take the current female age groups 5 to 39 from column 2 of Table 7–3 to fill in column 4 of Table 7–5.

Enter the totals from columns 2 and 4 of Table 7–5 in column 1 of Table 7–6, and then multiply the entries in column 1 by the figures in column 2 of Table 7–6. Place the results in column 3. Column 4 shows the age groups that are being estimated.

For example, using the number of current females aged 10 to 44 in Table 7–7, the total of column 2 in Table 7–5 would be 194. This would be the entry for the first two rows of column 1 in Table 7–6. When you multiply 194 by .20695, you get 40.15, which can be rounded down to 40 and placed in column 3 of Table 7–6. When you multiply 194 by .19914, you obtain 38.70, which can be rounded up to 39 and placed in column 3.

Taking the number of current females aged 5 to 39 in Table 7–7, the total of column 4 in Table 7–5 would be 209. When you multiply 209 by .20859 the male rate, you get 43.59, which can be rounded up to 44 and placed in column 3. When you multiply 209 by .20085 the female rate, you get 41.97, which can be rounded up to 42 and placed in column 3.

Table 7-6 Application of fertility rates

Totals from Table 7-5	1	2	3	4
Total of column 2		.20695		Males 5- 9
Total of column 2		.19950		Females 5-9
Total of column 4		.20859		Males 0-5
Total of column 4		.20085		Females 0-5

Table 7-7 Example of calculation spreadsheet

| | Present Population Cohorts | | | | | | | Future Population Cohorts | | | | | |
1	2	3	4	5	6	7	8	9	10	11	12	13
				Percent of all People		Percent of all People				Percent of all People		Percent of all People
Age	F	M	T	Females	Males		F	M	T	Females	Males	
0-4	35	30	65	3.5 %	3.0%	6.5%	42	44	86	4.3%	4.5%	8.8%
5-9	45	35	80	4.5 %	3.5%	8.0%	39	40	79	4.0%	4.0%	8.0%
10-14	30	35	65	3.0 %	3.5%	6.5%	35	30	65	3.5%	3.1%	6.6%
15-19	26	29	55	2.6 %	2.9%	5.5%	45	35	80	4.6%	3.5%	8.1%
20-24	23	27	50	2.3 %	2.7%	5.0%	30	35	65	3.1%	3.5%	6.6%
25-29	26	26	52	2.6 %	2.6%	5.2%	26	29	55	2.1%	3.0%	5.6%
30-34	29	29	58	2.9 %	2.9%	5.8%	23	26	49	2.4%	2.6%	5.0%
35-39	30	34	64	3.0 %	3.4%	6.4%	26	25	51	2.6%	2.6%	5.2%
40-44	30	35	65	3.0 %	3.5%	6.5%	28	27	55	2.9%	2.7%	5.6%
45-49	38	30	68	3.8 %	3.0%	6.8%	29	33	62	3.0%	3.3%	6.3%
50-54	44	38	82	4.4 %	3.8%	8.2%	29	32	61	3.0%	3.2%	6.2%
55-59	39	37	76	3.9 %	3.7%	7.6%	35	26	61	3.5%	2.7%	6.2%
60-64	37	33	70	3.7 %	3.3%	7.0%	39	31	70	4.0%	3.2%	7.2%
65-69	32	28	60	3.2 %	2.8%	6.0%	33	28	61	3.3%	2.9%	6.2%
70-74	28	22	50	2.8 %	2.2%	5.0%	29	22	51	3.0%	2.3%	5.2%
75 +	24	16	40	2.4 %	1.6%	4.0%	19	12	31	1.9%	1.3%	3.2%
Total	516	484	1,000	51.6 %	48.4%	100%	507	475	982	51.6%	48.4%	100%

Exhibit 7–2
A Note on Estimating Fertility Rates

The following method can be used to estimate the fertility rates listed in column 2 of Table 7–5. But birth rates currently are declining all over the United States, and you may need to verify birth rates from area hospitals. The calculations using sample data are as follows:

Step 1: (expected percent of live births male or female) × (the number of females in childbearing ages per thousand population—10 to 44 years) × (the survival rate for the age group 5–9)

Equation 1 (Males):
$$.51 \times 409/1,000 \times .99166 = .20695$$
Equation 2 (Females):
$$.49 \times 409/1,000 \times .99369 = .19950$$

Step 2: (expected percent of live births male or female) × (the percentage of females in childbearing ages per 1,000 population)

Equation 1: $.51 \times 409/1,000 = .20859$
Equation 2: $.49 \times 409/1,000 = .20041$

The projection for each of the age groups is now complete. The next task is a graphical representation of the current and the projected population data.

Take the numbers of males and females by the age groups given in Table 7–2 and enter these figures into columns 1 and 2 of Table 7–7. Next, add together columns 1 and 2 in Table 7–7, and enter the result in column 3. Then find the total of column 3 in Table 7–7.

Next, return to Tables 7–3 and 7–4. You will recall that these tables show the estimated population 10 years in the future when new births are not taken into account. To adjust for new births, simply take the information already calculated in Table 7–6, and add the new birth figures (male and female) to the 0–4 and 5–9 age groups.

After the new births have been included, enter the information in columns 7 and 8 of Table 7–7. Then add together the rows of columns 7 and 8, and enter each result in column 9. Total up the figures in column 9, and enter the result at the bottom of Table 7–7. The next sequence of calculations should be followed carefully:

1. Divide each entry in column 1 of Table 7–7 by the total of column 3 (1,000). Place the result of the divisions in each entry of column 4.

2. Divide each entry in column 2 of Table 7–7 by the total of column 3 (1,000). Place the results in each entry of column 5.

3. Divide each entry in column 3 of Table 7–7 by the total of column 3 (1,000). Place the results in each entry of column 6.

The same type of procedure must now be done for columns 7, 8, and 9 of Table 7–7:

1. Divide each entry in column 7 of Table 7–7 by the total of column 9 (982). Enter the results in column 10 of Table 7–6.

2. Divide each entry in column 8 of Table 7–7 by the total of column 9 (982). Enter the results in column 11.

3. Divide each entry in column 9 of Table 7–7 by the total of column 9 (982). Enter the results in column 12.

To aid in calculation, Table 7–7 has been filled in with sample numbers so that you can follow the chains of additions, multiplications, and divisions. You will need to round the percentages to add up to 100 percent.

The percentages of total population by age groups and by sex have now been calculated for both the present and projected future population. These percentages can

Table 7-8 Example pyramid graphing

Age	Graph 1 Present		Graph 2 10-Year Future		Graph 3 Total	
	Percent Female	Percent Male	Percent Female	Percent Male	Percent Present of Total	Percent Future Total
75 +						
70-74						
65-69						
60-64						
55-59						
50-54						
45-49						
40-44						
35-39						
30-34						
25-29						
20-24						
15-19						
10-14						
5-9						
0-4						
	5 4 3 2 1 0 1 2 3 4 5		5 4 3 2 1 0 1 2 3 4 5		5 4 3 2 1 0 1 2 3 4 5	

now be graphed into what are commonly known as population pyramids, as shown in Table 7–8.

To form the pyramids, take the percentages found in columns 4, 5, 6, 10, 11, and 12 of Table 7–7. Use these percentages to fill in the graphs in Table 7–8 in a horizontal fashion (bar graphs). Column 4 is barred on the left side of graph l, while column 5 is barred on the right side. Columns 10 and 11 in Table 7–7 are recorded on graph 2, while columns 6 and 12 are recorded on graph 3. As an example, notice that the percentages found in columns 4 and 5 of Table 7–7 for the 0–4 age groups are 3.5 percent for the females and 3 percent for the males. These percentages are graphed separately from the center line mark as shown in Figure 7–1. The next age group is graphed immediately above. For example, Table 7–7 shows that for the current population the 5–9 age group percentages are 4.5 percent for females and 3.5 percent for males. The 5–9 age group along with the 0–4 age group are illustrated in Figure 7–1.

Once the grouping of the three pyramids is completed, the present and future estimated age structure of the population becomes clear. This age structure is of little value unless

Figure 7-1 Bar graphing population pyramids

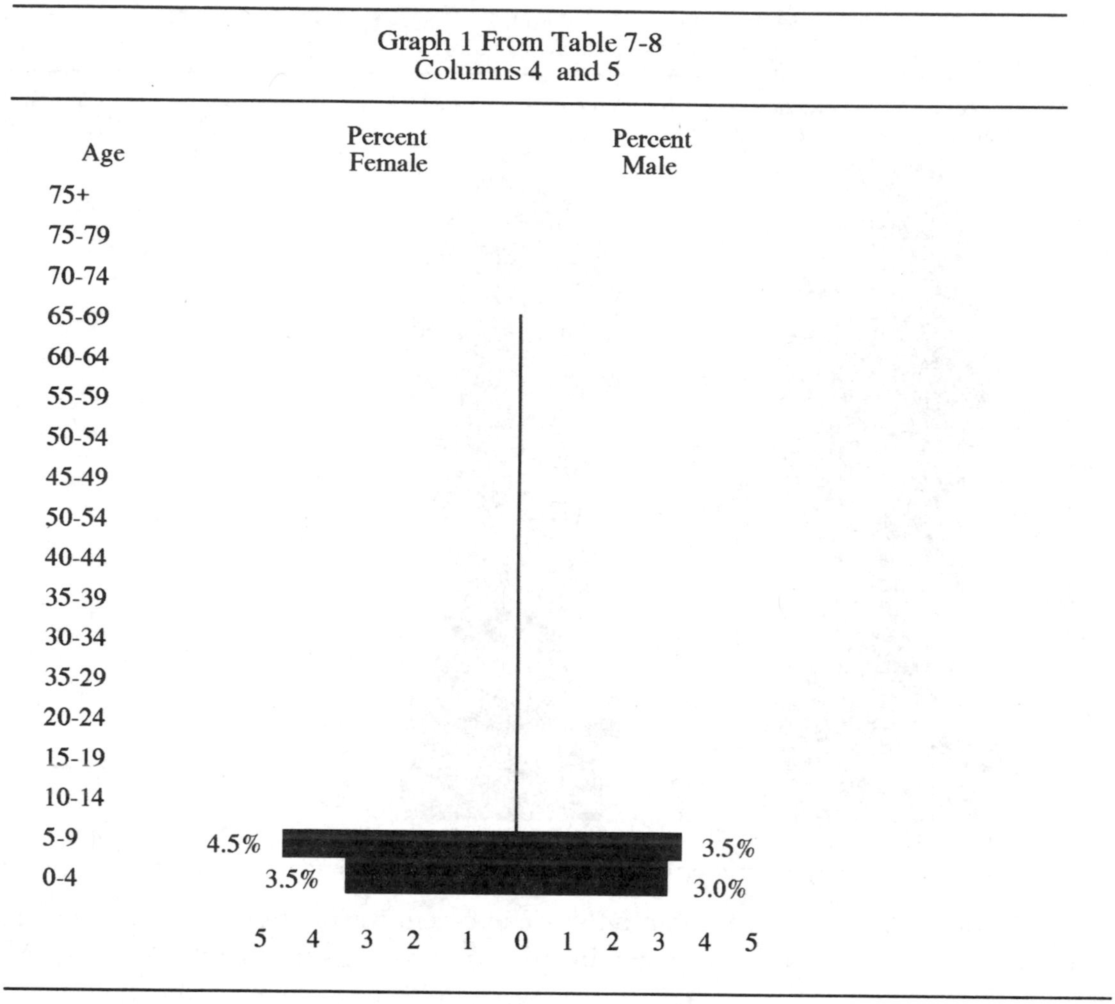

Graph 1 From Table 7-8
Columns 4 and 5

Age	Percent Female		Percent Male
75+			
75-79			
70-74			
65-69			
60-64			
55-59			
50-54			
45-49			
50-54			
40-44			
35-39			
30-34			
35-29			
20-24			
15-19			
10-14			
5-9	4.5%		3.5%
0-4	3.5%		3.0%

```
5   4   3   2   1   0   1   2   3   4   5
```

there is a background context from which to observe population trends over time.

Background Information

The following statements will help you to develop a population background of the community. These statements reflect general trends applicable to most small communities and thus provide a perspective from which to view the community population pyramid.

For example:

1. Most communities in the 1,000 to 2,500 population range in the past 30 years have had fairly constant population, with slight to moderate growth.

2. Rural towns and the surrounding farm communities in the Midwest and Plains states have been steadily losing population over the past 50 years. This decline will probably continue into the foreseeable future.

Figure 7-2 Median age for the community and the state

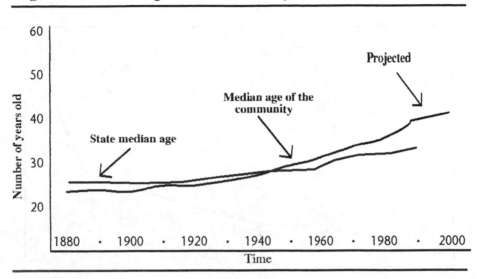

3. The number of jobs in rural communities is often limited. In other words, within the current structure of the local economic base there is a fixed number of jobs; if a person takes a job in a small community, she or he can expect to keep this job between 20 and 40 years, which is about twice the rearing time for children.

A limited economic base forces many younger people to leave the community in search of employment. This creates a long-term cyclical effect on the population structure of many communities. From the set of population pyramids shown in Table 7–8, the cycle of the median age of people in the community might appear as illustrated in Figure 7–2.

The cycle presented in Figure 7–2 would probably occur even if the community were experiencing mild growth and economic gain over time. But because of the nearly fixed number of jobs (as a ratio of the population), the age structure of many rural communities tends to fluctuate over time. Even so, many small towns have experienced an increase in the percentage of residents over 55 years old.

The usefulness of a population pyramid rests on two assumptions. First, the community exists for the needs of its inhabitants. These needs are provided by governmental or quasigovernmental agencies such as schools, roads, parks, and police protection; and by nonprofit organizations, retail establishments, services, health care facilities, and other businesses. The second assumption is that people have needs and expectations that change gradually as age increases.

Thus, the age cycle in the community might indicate that the community should adjust the type and amount of its public and private services as the population structure changes over time. As people age, for example, their service needs change, and this must be reflected in the miniplan.

For instance, a comparison of the median age in the community to the amount and type

Figure 7-3 Median age and doctors' patients visits per year

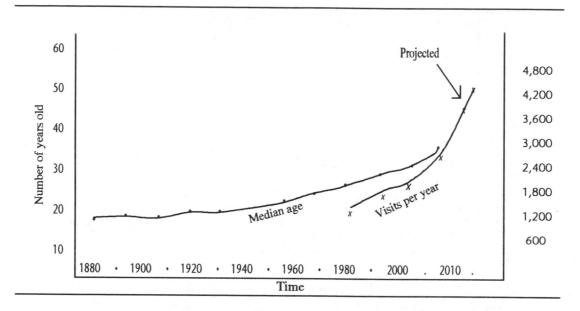

of medical services required could be illustrated as in Figure 7–3.

If the age structure of a community is changing, then both the public and private sectors in the community must plan for the future to provide the proper types and levels of service required by the inhabitants. The current population pyramid and the accompanying projection suggest only an approximation of the coming change, or lack of change, and local officials and business leaders must interpret the available information to plan for future needs.

ALTERNATIVE DATA FORMS AND POPULATION PROJECTIONS

If the community has a population in the range of 1,500 to 2,500, if there is an accurate census count from 1990, 1980, and 1970, and if there has been a noticeable growth in population—detected through increased manufac-

turing, business and trade, new homes and other building—then the age group projection method will probably not give you an accurate prediction of future population in the community. One reason is that the age group method does not take into account that people move in and out of a community as jobs and opportunities change.

To determine whether growth is taking place, you should plot the population trend on graph paper. Make a small table to compare population over time, as illustrated in Table 7–9, and then plot the population with the appropriate year as shown in Figure 7–4.

After the data points have been connected, as shown in Figure 7–4, the population trend will become apparent. You should fit or draw a trend line so that it passes equidistant between the data points. The trend line may then be extended outward for several decades to give an idea of future population. But you

Table 7-9 Sample historical population data

1	2
Total Population	Year
1,530	1950
1,720	1960
1,800	1970
1,880	1980
1,930	1990

should not assume that past or current population trends will continue into the future.

The data in Figure 7–4 show a moderate but healthy increase in population. The community appears to be gaining approximately 100 people per decade. But population growth

may be an indicator of new economic activity taking place within the community, not a direct result of excess births over deaths. You may want to consult a professional planner for more sophisticated techniques for estimating future population.

Many communities can use the simple trend line method rather than the cohort-survival approach to project population. The community must be small (currently about 1,500 people), showing either slow growth or decline for the past two to three decades, and located far from the metropolitan fringe and recreation areas. In using the trend line method, we simply assume that future population levels can be predicted from past trends. In other words, if the community has been slowly losing population since 1970, it is a fairly safe guess to assume that the community will either soon stabilize at the no-

Figure 7-4 Population trends

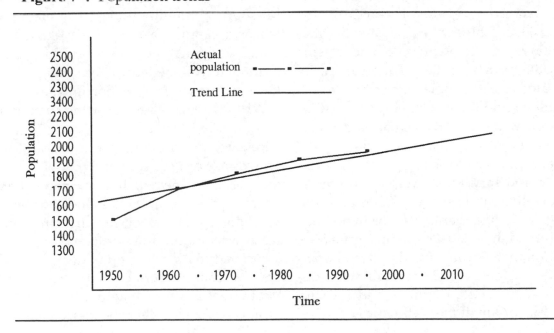

Figure 7-5 Population trend of a rural Nebraska community

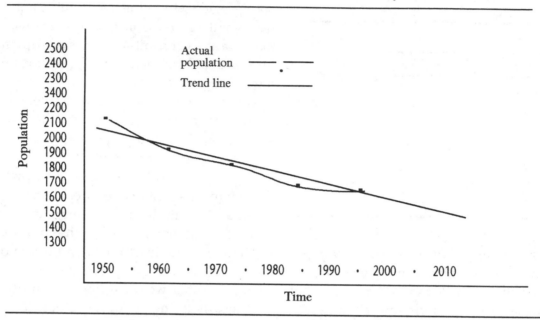

growth level or continue its slow decline for several more decades into the future.

Figure 7–5 gives the data and trend line for a rural Nebraska community. The trend line shows data from 1950 to the year 2010. The years 2000 and 2010 were estimated by finding the average decade change and placing these data points on the graph. A more sophisticated model, simple linear regression, is available to find the precise slope of the line. However, with only five actual data points and a fairly even increase or decline in the population each decade, using a simple average is satisfactory. Most computer presentation and illustration software programs will automatically find the slope of the trend line.

The trend line labeled A in Figure 7–6, "Two Common Growth Trends of Rural Communities," is an example of an Illinois community showing slow growth and stability since 1940. Again, if past influences continue

into the future, the population is relatively easy to estimate. If, on the other hand, the population had increased more rapidly as shown in the B trend, which shows a rural Missouri community undergoing metropolitan area capture, a simple averaging technique could not be used; neither could a cohort survival method, since in-migration is obviously driving population upward.

When we encounter a growing community as shown in trend line B in Figure 7–6, it is necessary to pinpoint the causes of the growth. We can project trend B by simply extending the connecting line or using a simple linear regression. But, this does not tell us anything about the events that are taking place in the community or its region that are associated with the population increases. Trend B could describe a small community located within the fringe of a metropolitan area. It could also describe an isolated com-

Figure 7-6 Two common growth trends of rural communities

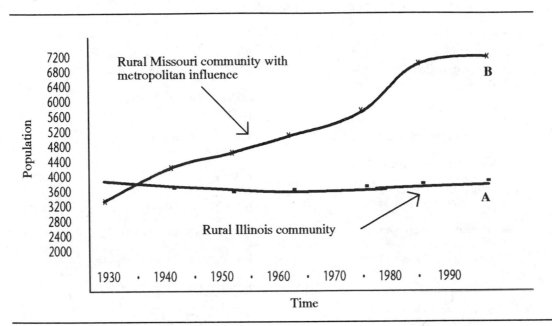

munity assuming a role as a trade center while the smaller communities within its region continue to decline. Understanding the situation is critical when final population estimates are prepared. A small town captured in the metropolitan fringe will continue to grow, quite possibly at accelerating rates well into the future. The isolated rural community will almost assuredly continue to grow at low or decreasing rates. As the population flows from the smallest communities in this isolated region to the community shown in trend B, there may be a point of near zero growth or minor decline for decades to come.

Table 7–10 lists the main reasons for growth and decline in small communities. Some of the sources of small town population increases are metropolitan overspill or in-migration, the increased exploitation of natural resources, and tourism. Each form of growth, though, has its benefits and drawbacks. Metropolitan-influenced growth can mean an economic boost from new families and firms. But growth can also mean social strife and conflicting values between newcomers and long-time residents. In remote areas, sudden upsurges in natural resources development can bring about rapid population changes, significantly greater tax resources, and a new community vitality. It can also create severe governmental and fiscal stress to provide new schools and infrastructure. Part of the stress is also due to anticipating when the bust period will follow the boom.

The causes of the decline of small towns are often more subtle than the factors promoting growth. There are some notable exceptions to this generality. The closing of a military base or a major employment firm is a rapid and

Table 7-10 Common reasons for population growth, fluctuations, and decline in rural areas and small towns

1. Change in regional economic structure	1. New technological shifts
2. Loss of natural resource base	2. Development of natural resources
3. Regional population loss	3. Metropolitan population overspill
4. Shift in trade area patterns	4. Tourism
5. Major changes in transportation routes and patterns	5. Gambling and gaming
6. Loss of major employer or gradual erosion of small businesses or firms	6. Recreational resources
7. Seasonal jobs	7. Environmental resources
8. Loss of community service capacity	8. New transportation patterns
9. Failure of leadership	9. New business patterns
	10. Regional growth and development

devastating blow to the small town, especially a single industry town. Other reasons for small town decline are regional economic restructuring, resource loss, and loss of historic importance. In most parts of the United States, small towns service large regions composed of farms and ranches, coastal villages, and even smaller towns. Economic downturns, long-term population out-migration, or the loss of banking and service firms in the region tend to restructure the economy of the trade area. The loss of forestry or fishery resources, shale oil, or coal over several decades frequently means a slow but sure population decline. Finally, many communities lose their historic importance. Some communities began life as mining centers, fishing ports, rail centers, cattle depots, or recreation facilities. Changing social habits, technology, and markets render these communities unable to retain population or generate a new community purpose.

You should not be left with the impression that all small towns are either growing or declining. Many small towns and rural areas maintain a birth to death rate and a migration pattern that allows them to stay nearly constant in size. There are two main groups of these sustainable communities. The first group periodically experiences growth or decline but then is able to maintain a level population over many decades. The second group exhibits very little population fluctuation over time. They are about the same size now as they were in the 1950s. Both groups of communities are in a *population corridor:* generally the upper and lower limits of this corridor are about 8 percent change. Both groups of communities display a healthy and normal but unremarkable population cycle.

Several optional tasks might be undertaken to help you understand population change in your community. To accomplish these tasks, you will need to gather data for your state and nearby communities, your county, or adjoining townships and then compare the population elements of your community with other places. The purpose of this exercise is to determine whether your community is diverging from or converging with certain trends. For example, examine the rates of growth or decline in other places. Use the figures in the 1950–90 publications to find total populations, ages, and household sizes. Pay special attention to the median age over the decades. Remember that the median age is not the average age. Rather, it indicates that half of the population is older and half is younger.

Figure 7–7 compares median ages in the town of Skyway in 1950, 1970, and 1990 to the median ages in the county (Hill County) and a neighboring town (Porterville). The figures show that Skyway's median age increased significantly from 33 years in 1950 to 44 years in 1990. Skyway's median age is much higher than the median age in the county and in the neighboring community.

CONSTRUCTION OF THE POPULATION SECTION

All population information and a written description should be presented in the population section of the miniplan. Consider presenting this section in three parts: (1) historic, (2)

Figure 7-7 Comparison of median ages - 1950 to 1990

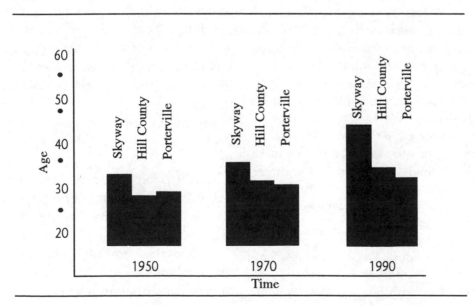

current, and (3) future population. You should make use of illustrations ánd descriptive tables, such as Figure 7–5 and Table 7–9. Make as many comparisons as possible among the three population parts. This will give the public a better understanding of population trends. Finally, you should present a summary of the major findings of the population study and the implications for future planning. A sample narrative appears in Exhibit 7–3.

Exhibit 7–3

Skyway had 1,750 people in the 1990 census, a loss of about 3 percent from the 1980 count. In 1980, Skyway had 1,810 people representing a loss of about 10 percent over the previous decade. The out-migration of people of working age and their families probably accounts for this decrease in population. In recent years, Skyway has lost residents while Hill County and the state of Kansas have gained population.

On a percentage basis, Skyway has a higher dependent population than either Hill County or Kansas. Approximately 47 percent of Skyway's residents are under 15 years or over 65 years of age, in contrast to about 37 percent of the population of the county or the state. A high ratio of dependent population requires many more costly services (such as public education and medical attention) than does a more balanced population.

The population in Skyway should remain stable or continue to decline unless job and housing opportunities increase within the town. Skyway has a large percentage of substandard dwelling units, which will increasingly dilapidate in the future. Unless these substandard units are repaired or replaced, people will be forced to find housing in other towns. Similarly, the lack of rental housing means that people wishing to live in Skyway must either build or buy a house. Finally, most residents work in central Hill County or in Hill City. Without additional job opportunities in Skyway, more people can be expected to move out of town into areas closer to employment centers.

The greatest potential for population growth comes from two sources: young people who grow up in Skyway and decide to remain here and older couples who live in other areas and choose to retire in Skyway.

POPULATION GOALS AND OBJECTIVES

Population goals and objectives are statements that address the strengths and weaknesses of the population base and what steps might be taken to capitalize on these strengths and overcome the weaknesses. These goals and objectives are very important in drafting the following sections on the economic base, housing, land use, and community facilities. Make sure that the goals and objectives of one section are consistent with the goals and objectives of the others. It makes little sense to advocate widespread new home construction if town goals aim to allow the population level to continue to decline slightly. On the other hand, new home construction will be needed and should be planned for if population goals include attracting new residents to the town. Be realistic; pursue goals that match your limited resources.

Towns that are concerned over population decline should discuss the following questions:

1. What happened in this community to cause the beginning of the population loss? Can we discuss any programs that might plug the leaks?

2. Does this community have any strengths that we might be able to exploit to slow down or stabilize population loss?

3. Are there any opportunities in the town or the county that we have not yet investigated? Could any of these opportunities help us with our goals?

4. What are the community weaknesses that contribute to population loss?

5. Looking at our region, what are the greatest threats to our community now and in the future?

While many communities will address the need to attract new people to the community to slow or reverse population loss, others must examine the need to manage population growth. These communities are influenced by metropolitan growth, tourism, or large-scale construction projects. You should be aware that it is illegal to exclude or discourage people from living in your community. The Fourteenth Amendment to the U.S. Constitution defends a person's "right of free travel," which means the right to live in any community. Population goals and land use controls that are aimed at zero population growth are likely to get the community into legal trouble.

The key to success in managing population change in a small town is *phased population control*, which matches the community's ability to grow to its ability to provide services. The adoption of land use regulations designed to punish newcomers will only succeed in creating bitterness, legal conflict, and costly delay. Be honest and clearly explain in your miniplan that change will be accommodated as quickly as possible. But, at the same time, make it clear that the new future population must bear their share of the increased costs which are caused by community change.

Growth costs money; new growth seldom produces gains in public finance in the short term. Today, growth in the small town, especially rapid growth, is often more damaging fiscally than it was in the 1970s or 1980s. The reform of property assessment laws and procedures throughout the United States no longer allows a community to capture increased property tax revenues from new construction while continuing to assess older structures at lower rates. In most cases growth results in higher property assessment rates for all, not just newcomers.

Each community must determine its own population goals and objectives. The following suggestions can serve as guidelines for a community losing population:

1. Goal: Promote a gradual increase in the number of townspeople.

2. Goal: Seek to attract young families with children.

3. Goal: Encourage young people to stay.

4. Goal: Encourage people of retirement age to move here.

5. Objective: Set aside land on the eastern edge of town for the construction of a retirement community.

6. Objective: Search for programs that will offer low-interest mortgages to young families willing to move to town.

SUMMARY

The population section sets the stage for the other functional sections of the miniplan. Information on current and expected future population is extremely important for planning future housing demand, land use patterns, economic development, and community facilities, such as schools. The population section will often be referred to as the miniplan is constructed. This section should be carefully researched and the population goals and objectives should be realistic. If data show that the town is growing rapidly, a goal of slow population growth will probably not be met. Similarly, if population is declining, a goal to promote rapid population growth will sound like nothing more than wishful thinking. For towns with populations between 2,500 and 10,000, the cohort-survival method is recommended because of the availability of census data. For towns of fewer than 2,500 residents, a simple population trend line may be sufficient. The biggest problem in accurately estimating future population is that in- and out-migration are often difficult to predict. This is particularly true in fast-growing communities and boomtowns.

8

Economic Data for the Small Community

The plans of many small communities do not include a section on economic activity other than a description of the major industries and employers and perhaps an inventory of businesses. This description typically summarizes the products manufactured in the area and the number and kind of manufacturing firms and commercial services. Businesses gained over the past decade are usually mentioned, and the future of the local economy is briefly discussed. Unfortunately, many larger communities include only a general discussion of the local economy in their comprehensive plans. An assessment of the local economy can be an important tool in educating the public and the foundation of local economic development efforts. For most small towns, an economic assessment should be an essential part of the miniplan.

If the community is below 1,000 people, a simple description is probably adequate. On the other hand, if the community is a retail trade center for the surrounding countryside and other smaller communities and is looking forward to future business and industrial growth, then the following approach should be adopted.

COMMUNITY ECONOMIC BASE

The purpose of an economic base study is to help a community create policies and programs which can lead to steady growth over the long run. First, a community must conduct an inventory of its economic situation and identify strengths and weaknesses, opportunities, and threats. The inventory reveals how people in the community earn a living and the kind of businesses and industries the community needs and could support. The inventory should also include projected increases in employment. This estimate can provide a useful benchmark for the community in planning for housing, schools, utilities, and other services.

The inventory will be helpful in putting together economic development strategies and programs to take advantage of opportunities and overcome threats (see Chapter 22). Economic threats include the loss of retail trade to larger communities, the departure of a major employer, the lack of labor skills, a small tax base, or a remote location. Opportunities will often depend on location and the natural setting. For example, a town within two hours of a major city and close to an interstate highway may be a good candidate for a branch manufacturing plant.

You should also compare your community's economy to your neighboring communities, similar-size communities, your county or region, and the state. Statistics and economic assessments are of little use to local decision makers unless they can determine how their community is performing compared with other communities.

Finally, a statement of economic goals and objectives summarizes the improvements that local residents would like to see. Economic goals typically focus on expanding the local property tax base and increasing incomes and employment opportunities by diversifying the local economy. In many rural communities a major goal will be to provide good jobs for young adults so that they do not have to leave the area to find employment opportunities. Economic objectives concentrate on specific incentives (for example, property tax breaks, public funding of sewer and water

lines) to attract and retain the kind of businesses and jobs the community wants.

THE ECONOMIC BASE STUDY

Outline of the Economic Base Study

The economic base study includes the following inventory:

I. Personal income of the local population
   A. Total income
   B. Income per capita
II. Labor force
   A. Number of workers and expected increase or decline
   B. Education
   C. Occupations
   D. Unemployment rate
   E. Average wages per occupation
III. Accumulated wealth
   A. Value of real estate (property tax base)
   B. Bank deposits
IV. Community finances
   A. Community budget
   B. Property tax rate per $1,000 assessed value
   C. Special assessment districts (sewer and water), if any
   D. Outstanding debts—bonds or loans
   E. Percent of bonding authority in use
V. Business and industry
   A. Export base businesses by size and type
   B. Secondary base businesses by size and type

Data Collection

If you have a computer, the most efficient way to organize the economic data for later use is to enter it in a spreadsheet or database program. This will enable you to analyze your data quickly and effectively and to produce small graphics and charts.

You should begin by collecting the standard information available to most every community. If there are banks or savings and loan institutions, call on them and ask for:

- Total savings deposits.
- Total checking deposits.
- The total amount of personal loans currently outstanding made to people in the community.

Next, the county and local assessors should be contacted and the following information collected:

- Assessed valuation of the community and of the school district in which the community is located. (Note: the boundaries of the town and school district[s] may differ.)
- Total population of the school district and your community's share of the school district population.
- Total indebtedness of the community and of the school district. Note that the total indebtedness may include both special assessments outstanding, general obligation bonds, no fund warrants, and revenue bonds.

Communities over 2,500 population can also find reliable information on economic activity in the socioeconomic characteristics of the *Census of Population,* published by the U.S. Census Bureau for each state. Communities under 2,500 population will have to make estimates for many of the economic assets or, when possible, collect the necessary information from firsthand sources within the community. You should be cautioned that the figures obtained from these estimates are only approximations and should be viewed only as general indicators of economic activity.

Every state publishes economic statistics in monthly, quarterly, or annual reports for their communities, counties, and the entire state. These statistics often include employment figures, construction activity, manufacturing, retail sales, and banking.

Estimating Community Income

Table 8–1 provides a useful worksheet for estimating community income. Column 3 in Table 8–1 contains a ratio of the community population to the county population. Equation 1 illustrates this relationship:

$$\text{Equation 1} = \frac{\text{Population of Your Community}}{\text{Population of the County}}$$

This ratio in column 3 will be a constant; that is, the same number is entered in all rows from top to bottom in column 3. The ratio in column 3 is given as a decimal. For example, if the population of the community is 1,000 and the rural nonfarm population of the county is 10,000, then the ratio to be entered is .10.

Table 8–1 Family income distribution income ratio

1 Dollars of Income	2 Number of Families in County	3 Ratio	4 Estimated Number of Families in the Community
Less than 1,000			
1,000–4,999			
5,000–9,999			
10,000–14,999			
15,000–24,999			
25,000–49,999			
50,000 and more			

Total Estimated Number of Families in the Community	_____
×	
Average Family Income	_____
=	
Total Community Income	_____

Enter the ratio in column 3 of Table 8–1, and then multiply each entry in column 2 by each ratio entry in column 3 and enter the result in column 4. The numbers in column 4, which are estimates of the number of families in each income level, should be rounded to the nearest whole number.

All entries in column 4 of Table 8–1 should now be added up to give the total number of families in the county. The sum of column 4 should be multiplied by the average income for all families. (Average family income can be estimated from the county average family income census figure, or by averaging the results in column 4, income group organized by the number of families.) The result is an estimate of the total income for the community.

Equation 2 = (Sum of Column 4) × (Average Income) = Total Income for the Community

Example: 1,420 × $20,000 = $28,400,000

You should note that, if the total number of families is known for the community and if each family's income class is known, you can simply fill in column 4 and leave columns 2 and 3 empty.

If each family's income class is not known, you can estimate it by using the number of families at the county level in each income class.

Work Force Characteristics

The work force is defined as the number of people in the community who are able to work. It is not the number of people who are employed at any one time. The work force may include some people who are still in school and some women who are at home raising children and may exclude some senior citizens who are able to work at least on a part-time basis. To estimate the work force characteristics, return to the section on population and add up the age brackets of the community's working population (ages 15 to 64) in either Table 7–2 or Table 7–7 in Chapter 7. Table 8–2 shows the age groups that are needed and then summarizes the results in columns 2, 3, and 4.

Table 8–3 presents an estimate of the educational levels of the community work force. Column 2 of Table 8–3 contains the number persons in the county aged 15 to 64 years old in each of the three educational levels, which is available from the census.

To complete column 3 of Table 8–3, take the total of column 2, the number of people in the county aged 15 to 64 years old. Divide this number into each entry in column 2 of Table 8–3. Enter the resulting percentages in column 3 of Table 8–3.

To complete column 4 of Table 8–3, return to Table 8–2 and find the sum of column 4,

Table 8–2 Characteristics of the work force

1 Age Brackets	2 Females 15 to 64	3 Males 15 to 64	4 Total Age 15 to 64
15–19			
20–24			
25–29			
30–34			
35–39			
40–44			
45–49			
50–54			
55–59			
60–64			
	TOTAL:	TOTAL:	TOTAL:

Table 8–3 Educational levels

1 School Years Completed	2 Number of Persons in County Aged 15 to 64 in Each Educational Level	3 Percent	4 Total Population 15 to 64 Years Old in the Community	5 Number of Persons by Educational Level in the Community Work Force
Elementary 1–8	1000	20%	640	128
Secondary 1–4	2000	40%	640	256
College 1–4 and more	2000	40%	640	256
Total	5000	100%	640	640

which is an estimate of the total number of persons aged 15 to 64 in the community. Take the sum of column 4 of Table 8–2 and enter it in each row of column 4 of Table 8–3.

Column 5 of Table 8–3 is found by multiplying each percentage in column 3 by each entry in column 4. The numbers in column 5 show the estimated number of people in the work force in each level of educational attainment. The procedure for the estimate is given in the example below.

Step 1

Number of persons in county aged 15 to 64 in each of the three educational levels—column 2 of Table 8–3 ÷ Total of persons age 15 to 64 in county = Percent in column 3

Step 2

Percent in column 3 of Table 8–3 × Total of column 4 of Table 8–3 (Total number of people aged 15 to 64 in the community) = Number of persons in community work force by educational level—column 5 in Table 8–3

The second part of the work force section deals with estimating the size of the labor force, sectors of employment, occupations, and the percentage of male and female workers.

The estimation procedure is divided into several different steps and should be performed in sequence. First, you need to estimate a *labor force participation rate*. This rate is usually higher for males than females, although women have been increasing their participation rate in recent years. A participation rate of .8 for men and .6 for women is a reasonable estimate. Place the participation rate percent for men and women aged 15 to 64 in the following equations:

Equation 3:

Male labor force partici- pation rate	×	Male population aged 15 to 64 from column 3 of Table 8–2	=	Active labor force of males aged 15 to 64

Example: .80 × 318 = 254

Equation 4:

Female labor force partici- pation rate	×	Female population aged 15 to 64 from column 2 of Table 8–2	=	Active labor force of females aged 15 to 64

Example: .60 × 322 = 193

Second, to estimate the number of unemployed people in the community, multiply the estimate of the male and female labor force by the percent of the unemployed male and female labor force. A county unemployment rate is published each month and should be available from your local newspaper, chamber of commerce, or state department of commerce. You can also use the latest annual average county unemployment rate.

Equation 5:

Female labor force aged 15 to 64	×	Female unemployed percent of labor force	=	Number of females unemployed

Example: 193 × 6% = 12

Equation 6:

Male labor force aged 15 to 64	×	Male unemployed percent of labor force	=	Number of males unemployed

Example: 254 × 5% = 12

To arrive at the estimated total employment of the community, subtract the estimated unemployed from the total male and female labor force.

Equation 7:

Labor force males	–	Unemployed males	=	Total males unemployed

Example: 254 – 12 = 242

Equation 8:

Labor force females	–	Unemployed females	=	Total females unemployed

Example: 193 – 12 = 181

Find the total employed by adding together the estimated number of males and females employed from equations 7 and 8 (242 + 181 = 423 total employed).

Table 8–4 shows the occupations of the labor force. Fill in column 1 of Table 8–4 from the number of rural nonfarm jobs by sector of employment provided by the U.S. Census for the county in which your community is located. Take each entry in column 1 of Table 8–4 and divide by the total employment 16 years and over for the county and enter the resulting percent in column 2 of Table 8–4.

Enter the figure from total employment in your community from equations 7 and 8 above in each row of column 3 of Table 8–4.

Table 8-4 Employment by sector

Employment Sector	Number for Nonfarm Rural County	Percent	Estimated Total Employment for the Community	Estimated Number Employed by Sector in the Community
Agriculture, forestry, fisheries	( )	( )	( )	( )
Construction	( )	( )	( )	( )
Manufacturing	( )	( )	( )	( )
Durable goods	( )	( )	( )	( )
Transportation, communication and other public utilities	( )	( )	( )	( )
Wholesale, retail trade	( )	( )	( )	( )
Personal services	( )	( )	( )	( )
Professional and related services	( )	( )	( )	( )
Other industries	( )	( )	( )	( )

Multiply each row in column 3 by column 2, and enter the results in column 4 of Table 8–4. The entries in column 4 are the estimated employment by occupation for the community.

Tables 8–5 and 8–6 give the number of female and male workers in different occupational groups. Divide each entry in column 1 of Tables 8–5 and 8–6 by the estimated total employment figures for males and females given above in equations 7 and 8. Each entry in column 1 of Table 8–5 is to be divided by the estimated number of females employed given in equation 8. Each entry in column l of Table 8–6 is to be divided by the estimated number of males employed as given in equation 7. Place the results of these divisions in column 2 of Tables 8–5 and 8–6.

To complete column 3 of Table 8–5, take the estimated number of employed females given in equation 8 and enter this number in each row of column 3. Do the same in column 3 of Table 8–6 by taking the number of estimated employed males from equation 7 and placing this number in each row of column 3.

Column 4 in Tables 8–5 and 8–6 is found by multiplying the percent in column 2 by the male and female employment figure in column 3. This result in column 4 of Tables 8–5 and 8–6 is the estimated number of males or

Table 8-5 Female occupations

Occupation Groups	Number for Nonfarm Rural County	Percent	Estimated Total Employed Females in Community	Estimated Females Employed by Occupation in the Community
Professional, technical and kindred workers	( )	( )	( )	( )
Managers and Administrators except for above	( )	( )	( )	( )
Sales workers	( )	( )	( )	( )
Clerical and kindred workers	( )	( )	( )	( )
Craftsmen, foremen, and kindred workers	( )	( )	( )	( )
Operators, including transportation	( )	( )	( )	( )
Laborers, except for above	( )	( )	( )	( )
Farmers and farm managers	( )	( )	( )	( )
Service workers, including private household	( )	( )	( )	( )
Total	( )	( )	( )	( )

females employed by occupation groups in the community.

This completes the estimation of the work force by education, sector of employment, and occupation for the miniplan.

Community Wealth

The ability of any community to sustain itself or to grow is largely determined by its economic assets. Every community, large or small, must continually invest in itself—both in the public and private sectors—if it is to remain a good place to live and work. Investment at less than normal maintenance will eventually bring about physical and social decay; investment above the maintenance level can generate economic growth and produce a feeling of community well-being.

The economic assets available to a community set a limit on the amount of possible

Table 8–6 Male occupations

Occupation Groups	Number for Nonfarm Rural County	Percent	Estimated Total Employed Males in Community	Estimated Males Employed by Occupation in the Community
Professional, technical and kindred workers	( )	( )	( )	( )
Managers and Administrators except for above	( )	( )	( )	( )
Sales workers	( )	( )	( )	( )
Clerical and kindred workers	( )	( )	( )	( )
Craftsmen, foremen, and kindred workers	( )	( )	( )	( )
Operators, including transportation	( )	( )	( )	( )
Laborers, except for above	( )	( )	( )	( )
Farmers and farm managers	( )	( )	( )	( )
Service workers, including private household	( )	( )	( )	( )
Total	( )	( )	( )	( )

investment; this is true even if the community intends to borrow money. The amount that any one community can borrow is limited by income and accumulated wealth (value of property) and often by state law. Any individual considering an investment must look at income and accumulated wealth to ascertain the feasibility of the investment; this same process is true for a community.

The assessed value of property, obtained from the local assessor, provides the first estimate of community wealth. Remember that real property is assessed at only a fraction of its market value so that the assessed value of all real estate must be adjusted to arrive at market value. To make this adjustment, you must find the assessment ratio. For a community assessed at one-third (assessment ratio of .3333), the adjustment must be made by taking the assessed value of all real estate times 3. Similarly, if community property is assessed at one-fifth value (.20 assessment ratio), the value of all that property is found by multiplying the assessed value by 5.

If for some reason the assessed value of property is not available (as might be the case in a very small community), it can be estimated by finding the school district in which the community is located and taking the ratio of the population of the community to the total population of the school district and multiplying this ratio by the assessed valuation of the school district. Otherwise, the county assessor should be able to estimate the assessed value for your community.

The type and availability of property valuation data is now much better in most states than it was only a decade ago. Sweeping changes in legislation which require frequent reassessment of property now means that highly detailed data are found in even the smallest communities. You should use this data to discover the source of your wealth, who pays the bills, and the cash flow from property tax revenues. We suggest that you prepare graphics and charts which illustrate:

1. Assessed or actual value of all real and personal property by the various classifications used by your state. In many cases, this will be:

- Urban and rural residential.
- Business or commercial.
- Manufacturing (various classes).
- Vacant land by classification (not agricultural).
- Agriculture.
- Public utilities (possibly state assessed).
- Exempt property.

2. The actual yearly tax revenue from each classification.

3. The percent or ratio of all urban to rural property value and income.

Figure 8–1 shows one possible method of illustrating how the property tax burden is shared in your community.

The savings of the residents are another important part of the community's total wealth. The savings calculations are presented below, assuming that there is a bank or savings institution in the community. If this is not the case, then there is no reliable method to estimate savings, and the only source of data would be to ask all banks in the county to calculate how many people have how much money on hand at a particular bank. This last piece of information is not feasible unless there is widespread agreement beforehand because the banks might run the risk of an unethical disclosure problem.

To estimate community wealth as a ratio of county wealth is not very accurate. Personal wealth is not distributed evenly across any county. Just because a certain community contains 10 percent of the county population does not mean that it will also contain 10 percent of the county wealth.

Assuming that there is a bank or a savings and loan institution in the community, you need only draw on the data already collected in this chapter to obtain a financial statement like the following:

Figure 8-1 Proportionate share of real property tax burden

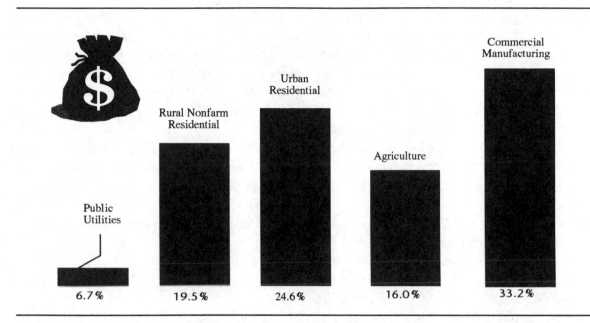

Public Utilities	Rural Nonfarm Residential	Urban Residential	Agriculture	Commercial Manufacturing
6.7%	19.5%	24.6%	16.0%	33.2%

Banks

Total Savings	$_____
Total Checking (average)	$_____
Total	$_____
Savings and Loans	
Deposits	$_____
Total	$_____

The borrowings of government agencies in a community is a matter of public record and can be obtained from the town or county clerk. This indebtedness is grouped by functional area: that is, general obligation bonds, revenue bonds, no fund warrants, special assessment and others.

Inventory of Local Businesses and Industries

A community's economy can be divided into two segments: the *export-base* and the *sec-ondary-base*. The export-base is made up of those goods and services that the community exports to other towns or regions in order to bring in money. A community grows mostly because it earns money from goods and services exported to other areas. These earnings in turn provide a community with the means to import goods and services. Export-base industries include most types of manufacturing, agriculture, mining, and forest products.

Secondary-base businesses provide the local community with day-to-day goods and services. Because the size of the community is often small, these local businesses are not likely to grow much. Secondary-base businesses usually include gas stations, grocery stores, laundromats, taverns, movie theaters, and the other retail establishments. The health of the secondary-base businesses is generally closely linked to the vitality and success of the export-base firms.

Export-base businesses have greater growth potential because they serve a broader market beyond the local community. As export-base businesses grow, they employ more people and attract new workers to a community. This increase in population and income has a *multiplier effect*, increasing the demand for the goods and services of secondary-base businesses. In turn, the secondary-base businesses grow and provide more jobs and income.

Communities have placed much emphasis on developing export-base businesses. Although these businesses are certainly important for economic growth, you should also try to determine what goods and services your community could produce that are now being imported. This development strategy, called *import substitution*, is aimed at retaining more economic activity within the local community by curtailing the export or leakage of consumer dollars out of the community. For example, energy conservation and alternative energy sources may be important in keeping money in a community. Small towns normally import most of their electricity, gasoline, and natural gas. Conservation efforts and the development of wood, hydroelectric, and solar energy sources can mean substantial savings as well as boost local economic development by making money which formerly left the town available for other purposes. The goal is to make your community more *sustainable*— more likely to survive and thrive in the future.

From an inventory of industries and businesses, and the past 10- to 15-year trends in their sales and employment, you should determine:

1. Is the economic base shifting from one industry to another?

2. What percentage of the economic base is export-oriented (goods and services exported outside of the region)? Has the region become more or less dependent on exports over time? Have income and employment in export-oriented businesses increased or decreased over time?

3. What kind of goods and services are imported? Has the value of these imports increased or decreased over time?

4. What are the trends in retail trade? Is there leakage to other towns or regions?

ECONOMIC GOALS AND OBJECTIVES

The economic goals and objectives should indicate where new businesses and industries should be encouraged, how public investment in infrastructure can induce private investment, what kind of new businesses and industries should be promoted, and specific recruitment efforts.

While each community must determine its own economic goals and objectives, the following recommendations can serve as guidelines:

1. Goal: Seek to increase employment opportunities and raise local incomes.

2. Goal: Attempt to diversify the local economic base by attracting new retail stores and manufacturing firms, while encouraging and facilitating the expansion of existing firms in the community.

3. Goal: Improve the mix of businesses on Main Street. Encourage new industries to locate in the industrial park at the south end of town.

4. Goal: Expand the local property tax base through increased economic development.

5. Objective: Obtain state or federal grants to improve local sewer and water systems in conjunction with the creation of a local industrial park.

6. Objective: Establish a low-interest loan pool with the help of local banks and businesses to aid in financing the start-up or expansion of local businesses.

7. Objective: Establish a nonprofit economic development corporation to recruit prospective new businesses.

The economic goals and objectives statements should indicate where new businesses and industries should be encouraged, how public investment in infrastructure can induce private investment, what kind of new businesses and industries should be promoted, and specific recruitment efforts and business retention strategies.

Economic development tools and strategies for small towns are discussed in detail in Chapter 22. You are strongly advised to read that chapter before drafting your economic goals and objectives.

A Note on Small Business and the Community

There is a strong temptation to think that economic development concerns only the recruitment of large, new firms into a community. Certainly this has been the focus of much community and chamber of commerce activity. But lately small local businesses have been the main source of new jobs. One of the most important objectives of any economic development plan should be the retention of businesses already located in the community.

Oftentimes the potential of existing firms is overlooked; many have the capacity to expand their operations and thereby increase jobs and the tax base. A thorough review of existing businesses should be done as part of the economic inventory process. An understanding of labor needs, space requirements, financing, and other factors related to possible expansion should be made clear. It is vitally important to put into place programs to keep good, productive businesses in the community and help them expand. A strategy for economic growth which promotes the creation of eight jobs here, six there, and another five elsewhere is usually more realistic and appropriate to the size and needs of smaller communities. There are just so many large firms looking to relocate to, or start-up new branches in, smaller communities. "A bird in the hand," in this case, may really be worth "two in the bush!"

SUMMARY

The results of the economic base study should be summarized by a discussion of the amount of private and public investment the community might reasonably be able to support on its own. This discussion should be general yet realistic. You will have to examine the types of capital investments (public improvements and large private investments) made in the community in the past, the extent of the property tax base, and the borrowing power of the local government. If there are any doubts about the interpretation of the economic base information, you should seek the advice of a professional planner. But, generally, local researchers should be able to present a clear picture of the local economy.

9

Housing

Shelter is the primary need of every community. When a community begins to lose sight of this fact, a slow process of decay will eventually result in dilapidated and inadequate living units and vacant businesses. A feeling of despair, evident in many depopulated small communities, can be brought on by the poor physical appearance of the community and its housing stock.

Much of the worst housing in America is found in rural regions and rural communities. In 1990, about one-fourth of the American people lived in rural areas, and they lived in about half of the nation's substandard housing.

The reasons for rural housing conditions are many and complex, including:

1. Much of the rural housing stock is old, probably built 40 to 60 years ago, and often not kept in good repair.

2. Few rural areas have adopted and enforced housing, building, plumbing, electrical, and fire prevention codes.

3. Many rural homes, especially in the South, still lack indoor plumbing.

4. Lending institutions generally prefer to loan money to individuals and development companies in larger towns, rather than in small towns.

5. Low family incomes, due mainly to poor economic conditions and limited opportunities, mean that many families cannot afford better housing.

6. Qualified builders and craftsmen are becoming very hard to find in some small towns.

HOUSING NEEDS AND HOUSING ANALYSIS

The 1990 National Affordable Housing Act and economic development programs in several states require communities to prepare an assessment of housing needs which describes the existing housing stock and identifies future housing needs. For communities with a population of 2,500 or more, excellent data are available from the U.S. Census Bureau. For communities of under 2,500, the following is suggested for the data collection phase of the housing plan.

HOUSING SUPPLY AND CONDITION

The purpose of the housing information phase is to determine the total number and quality of dwelling units in the community. The concept of dwelling units should not be confused with the words home, house, or structure. Each unit in which a household of one or more persons resides is classified as a dwelling unit. This means that each apartment in a private home, each unit of a duplex and each apartment within a complex is recorded as a separate and individual dwelling unit. There are several exceptions to this general definition: (1) a sleeping room for one person not provided with toilet and cooking facilities; (2) hospitals; (3) institutions for the care of the elderly or the treatment and care of patients; and (4) colleges, universities, or religious institutions.

Descriptive Housing Information

There are two alternative approaches for gathering data for a housing inventory: (1) using the information compiled by your local property assessor/appraiser and supplementing it with data from the 1990 Census of Population and Housing; or (2) conducting your own visual inspection. If the data from the local appraiser is computerized on a uniform system supervised by your state, this will probably be the best source of information for your plan. If, on the other hand, the data are on individual appraisal sheets (a file folder for each property), the best approach will probably be to conduct a lot-by-lot survey of all housing in the community.

The 1990 census contains housing profiles for all communities and counties regardless of size. This information is available from the Data User Division of the U.S. Bureau of the Census on CD-ROM at your regional library. This descriptive information will aid in understanding housing cycles and the characteristics of owners and renters in your community.

We suggest that you construct the following charts and graphs to help planning commission members and residents understand housing in your community. A graph such as Figure 9–1, "Decade of Construction of Existing Housing," can be constructed from data gathered from the U.S. Census and the local appraiser. The trend line shows the number of units in the present housing base and when they were built. The data show two upwards cycles. The first indicates that 550 units built between 1900 and 1910 are still in the serviceable housing base. The second peak indicates that the largest number of units in the housing stock, about 1,050, were built between 1970 and 1980. Figure 9–2, "Age of Housing as a Percent of the Total Housing Stock," was taken directly from the 1990 census. This bar chart shows that about 24 percent of the current housing stock was built before 1940, more than 50 years ago. Figure 9–3 indicates how long people have lived in the dwelling unit where they were residing in 1990. Finally, Figure 9–4 gives some idea of housing affordability in your community. This sample of homeowners shows a range of monthly mortgage payments for households in 1990. Notice that in this rural community about 60 percent of homeowners with mortgages pay between $300 and $700 a month.

Because property appraisal is now approaching some degree of uniformity throughout the United States, all the data necessary to complete the housing section of the miniplan may be available from local sources. Meet with

Figure 9-1 Decade of construction of existing housing

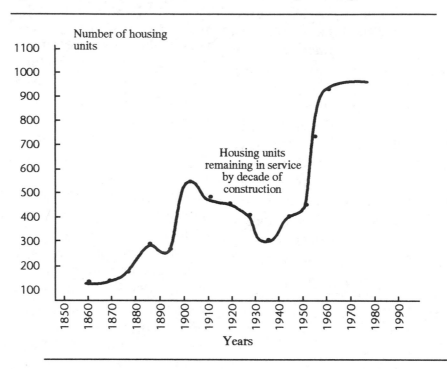

the local appraiser and discuss your needs. Explain that your goal is to obtain an assessment of housing conditions for the community. Before you request any information, you should understand that the job of the appraiser is to determine the value of property and not the ultimate condition of individual buildings.

It is likely that three (or more) separate factors that determine the condition of a dwelling unit are recorded on the appraisal sheets for each property. These factors are called (1) grade, (2) physical condition, and (3) condition-desirability-usefulness (CDU rating). These factors are somewhat intertwined and depend on the judgment of the person inspecting the properties. The criteria and scales used to obtain the different factors are shown in Table 9–1.

The grade factor of a building is normally associated with the quality of construction and design. The grade data are not directly related to the condition of the dwelling unit. But, a number of interesting inferences can be drawn by examining the numbers and percentages of units associated with each grade. For instance, for most rural areas we assume that if the majority of housing is in the lower grades C– and D, the greater will be your index of housing affordability. At the same time, large numbers of units in the lower grades can indicate that housing units may have less than normal useful lives.

The information on physical condition should be a reliable indicator of the interior and exterior quality of the dwelling unit. However, data collected by the appraiser

Figure 9–2 Age of housing as a percent of the total housing stock

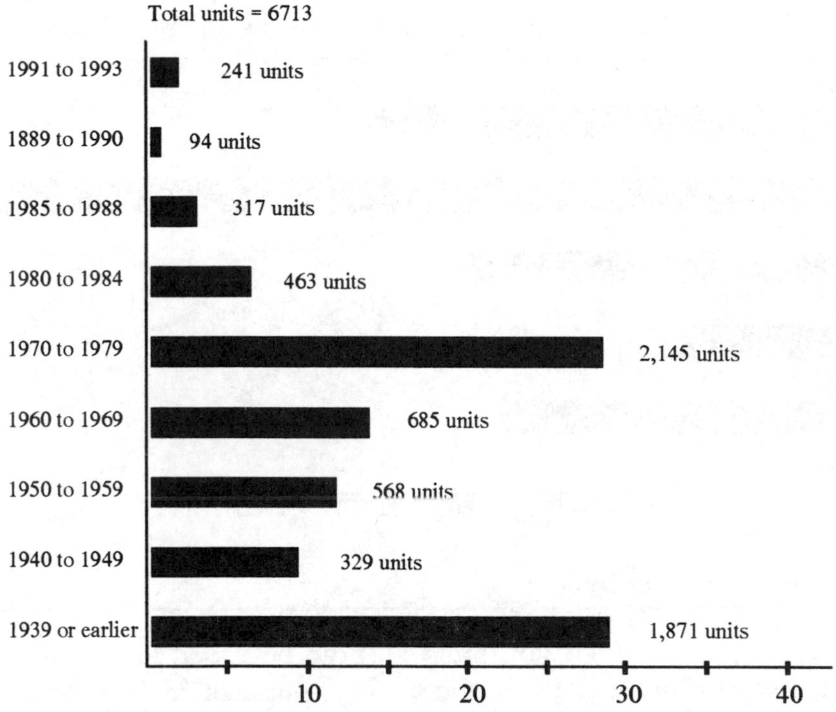

Total units = 6713

1991 to 1993	241 units
1889 to 1990	94 units
1985 to 1988	317 units
1980 to 1984	463 units
1970 to 1979	2,145 units
1960 to 1969	685 units
1950 to 1959	568 units
1940 to 1949	329 units
1939 or earlier	1,871 units

10   20   30   40

Source: U.S. Census of Population and Housing, 1990

often show far more or far fewer dwelling units in poor and very poor condition than indicated by a planner. Part of the difference may be due to the fact that the appraiser often is able to view the interior of a unit, whereas the planner seldom if ever has this opportunity.

The final factor is the condition-desirability-usefulness rating (CDU). This is a composite rating based on physical condition, grade, and a judgment of the local real estate market for a particular unit. The CDU ratings may be the most important information for determining both the affordability and the condition of housing in the community.

The probability is very high that if a significant percent of the housing in your area is ranked in the lower CDU ratings (see Table 9–1), improving your housing base should be one of the highest priorities in your planning process.

A visual inspection of the housing base may be required to clarify the appraisal data, or it can be used as an alternative step in the information gathering process. Remember that this communitywide visual inspection is required for several other studies in the mini-plan (especially the land use section). There is no need for several return visits if the trips are properly planned.

Figure 9-3 Tenure of owners and renters

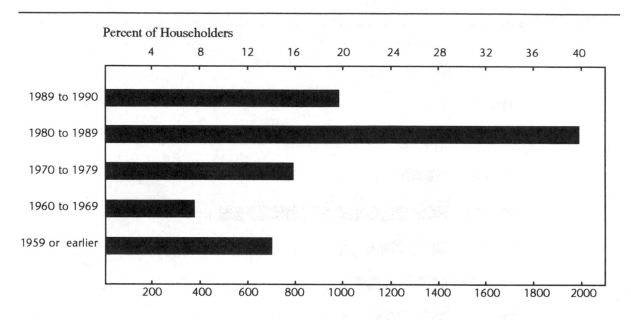

Source: U.S. Census of Housing, 1990

Before undertaking the survey, you must obtain the *block and lot map* for your community or the property owner's map for your township, county, or equivalent taxing unit. This map may be alternatively titled an assessor's map, official map, or property map. Regardless, it will show each separate lot, tract, and parcel in your planning area. You should drive or walk around each block in the community and record whether or not the property contains a dwelling unit, contains another type of structure or has a use that does not involve housing, or is simply vacant. Remember that many commercial buildings contain apartments. Each apartment needs to be located and visually inspected on the exterior. If a dwelling unit is on the property, note whether or not the dwelling unit is (1) standard, (2) substandard minor, (3) substandard major, or (4) dilapidated. A plus (+) or minus

(–) can be added to each to indicate a transitional phase of the structure.

Standard housing has no visible exterior defects, has solid construction that is obvious to the inspector, and is built to provide safe, healthy living.

Substandard minor housing has slight defects normally corrected during the course of regular maintenance but which require immediate attention. Defects might include:

1. Paint: cracks, peeling, missing.

2. Porches: slight damage such as rotting boards or cracked concrete.

3. Steps: slight damage such as sagging or cracked boards or concrete.

4. Windows: cracked or broken panes.

5. Exterior walls: (a) wooden: cracked or small amount of rotted boards; (b) brick, masonry: cracked or slightly worn brick, masonry, or mortar.

Figure 9–4   Monthly mortgage payments for sampled homeowners 1990

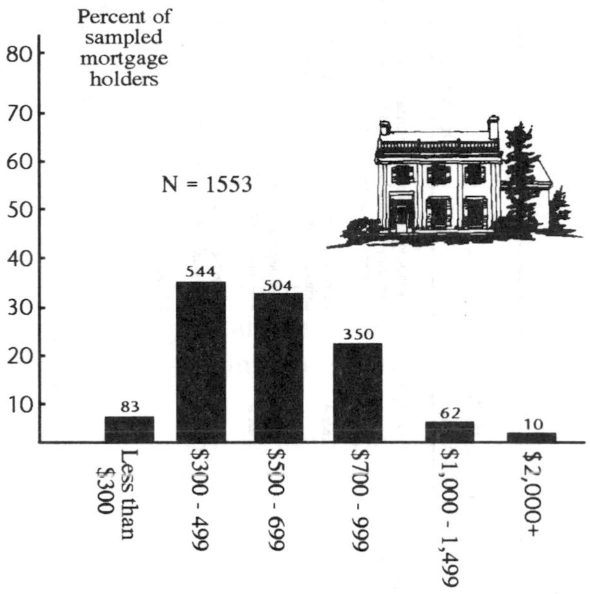

Percent of sampled mortgage holders

N = 1553

83	544	504	350	62	10
Less than $300	$300 - 499	$500 - 699	$700 - 999	$1,000 - 1,499	$2,000+

Source: U.S. Census of Housing and Population, 1990

6. Roof: few shingles missing or other minor damage.

7. Mobile homes: most of the above criteria apply; you should also look for rust spots and dents with cracks.

These defects should not in any way endanger health or safety. If a building has three or more defects in 1 through 7 above, then you should seriously consider classifying the dwelling unit as substandard major, due to the rapid increase in repair cost.

Substandard major housing needs more than regular routine maintenance. The essential need is not to bring the dwelling unit up to perfect shape but rather to make the structure safe and healthy for the occupants. Defects might include:

1. Porches: major damage such as broken or missing railings and supports.

2. Steps: major damage such as missing boards; large cracks and holes that have the potential to trip people.

3. Windows: missing panes, covered by boards; rotted or badly damaged frames and sashes.

4. Exterior walls: (a) wooden: extensive cracks and rotten boards; holes not over one foot in length, unless the damage extends to the interior wall; if so, classify as dilapidated; (b) brick, masonry: missing bricks and stones; holes not over one foot in length unless the damage extends to the interior wall; if so, classify as dilapidated.

5. Roof: many shingles missing; holes not

exhibits misuse, neglect, inferior materials, and severe structural defects. Unsound housing is unsafe and unsanitary for habitation.

Exhibit 9–1 is a sample housing data collection sheet that you can adapt to meet the needs of your community. In this case, the data were coded to enter on a computer spreadsheet to facilitate analysis and reports. If you decide to use a spreadsheet, a planning volunteer should aid in making the preliminary decisions about how to assign codes to properties during the visual inspection. A simple mistake that is often made is that pluses (+) or minuses (–) are entered in the coding cells. For instance, some physical conditions for property are often coded as A+ or C–. When the survey is finished and it is time to subtotal how many housing units are assigned to a property condition, the spreadsheet cannot calculate the numeric or letter values that have a plus or a minus.

How to Conduct the Housing Survey

It is best to assign the visual housing survey to a person who has some previous experience. Volunteers supervised by the local engineer or the assessor can be very helpful. But be careful when surveying and classifying housing conditions. *Do not disclose the street number or block location in the plan or at public meetings.* People do not enjoy sitting at a public meeting and having their home identified as very poor, substandard, or unsound. Rather, identify sections of the community that have a high ratio of dilapidated or substandard housing. As an alternative, divide the community into grids or quadrants and color or shade each according to the average quality of housing condition.

Take the information gathered from the appraiser or the visual survey map and construct your data similar to that shown in Table 9–2, "Sample Housing Conditions Data." Substitute your own language to indicate a set of ratings that best meets your needs. The information presented in Table 9–2 from a previous housing study cannot, of course, be included if such information is not available. Yet, many small towns have historical information on housing and housing conditions prepared by regional planning agencies during the 1970s.

HOUSING DEMAND

The expected future population of a community and the existing housing stock provide insight on the future availability of housing. If current housing is not adequate to meet future needs, then more housing will have to be built, or the increased demand will tend to drive up housing prices. Adequate housing is essential in supporting economic growth. To attract new businesses or industries, a community should be able to house new workers moving into the community. The demand for housing is also closely tied to future land use. If new housing needs to be built, where should it go and at how many dwelling units per acre?

A study of housing demand involves (1) expected future population, obtained from the population section of the miniplan; (2) current housing occupancy and types of housing; and (3) projected future housing. To prepare the table on housing occupancy and types you must determine whether the family unit rents or owns the property at its current address. Prepare the following information as illustrated in Table 9–3.

Exhibit 9–1 Example spreadsheet: Housing visual survey coding form

Estimated Separation
1. N = Feet of sideyard from nearest structure

Use
2. Residential
3. Institution
4. Commercial
5. Open space
6. Public
7. Industry

Additional Coding Notes

Street Condition
1. e = excellent
2. vg = very good
3. a = average
4. f = fair
5. p = poor

For Sale
y = yes
n = no

Dwelling unit
1. Single Family unit
2. Duplex
3. Triplex
3a. 3 apartments
4a. 4 apartments
5a. 5 apartments

Age
1. 1970 - 1993
2. 1950 - 1969
3. 1930 - 1949
4. 1900 - 1929
5. Before 1900

Parking
1. N = number of off-street spaces

General
1. r = recheck unit
2. v = zoning violation
3. x = over crowded

Structure Condition
a. Excellent
b. Standard - very good
c. Standard - good
d. Conservable - ave.
e. Conservable - fair
f. Deteriorating - poor
g. Deteriorating - v poor
h. Unsound - occupied
i. Unsound - vacant

4. xx = junk vehicles
5. m = mobile home
6. s = open storage
7. p = parking on lawn
8. z = abandoned

Environmental Conditions
1. Very Good
2. Good
3. Fair
4. Poor

Architectural Style
a. Bungalow
b. Ranch
c. Split level
d. Victorian
e. Old Style
f. Colonial
g. Cottage

9. q = Accessory building in poor condition
10. c = daycare on premise
11. zz = not sufficient parking for the use of the property

Notes
1. Poor weatherization
2. Detached garage
3. Home occupation
4. Additional out-buildings
5. Accessory apartment
6. No garage
7. Sign violation

Address	Lot	Use	For Sale	Dwelling Unit	Age	Structure Condition	Envr	Architectural Style	Notes	Estimated Separation	Parking	Side Walk
100 Allen Rd	13	2	n	1	1	a	1	a	4	20	1	4
104 Allen Rd	14	2	n	1	1	b	1	a	6	23	2	4
2109 Allen Rd	16	2	n	1	–	b	1	a	5	25	2	4
2111 Allen Rd	18	2	n	1	2	b	1	b	4	10	2	4
2117 Allen Rd	20	2	n	1	1	b	1	b	5	15	4	4
102 Griffith Dr	32	2	n	2	1	b	1	b	6	15	4	4
103 Griffith Dr	33	2	n	2	–	b	1	b	2	15	–	1
106 Griffith Dr	34	4	y	1	3	o	1	o	2	0	2	1
111 Griffith Dr	35	2	y	0	–	o	2	o	–	20	–	1
222 Griffith Dr	36	2	n	0	3	o	1	o	–	0	–	2
2208 Baker	43	6	n	4a	0	b	1	o	–	0	6	2
2209 Baker	45	5	n	3a	0	b	2	e	2	12	6	3
2211 Baker	47	2	n	1	2	u	2	d	2-4	14	5	3
2214 Baker	48	2	n	1	2	c	2	a	2	15	2	3
2216 Baker	49	2	n	1	3	d	3	a	–	20	2	1
2314 Baker	50	5	n	2	2	d	2	a	–	24	2	1
2316 Baker	55	5	n	2	2	e	4	b	4	12	2	1
2320 Baker	56	2	n	1	2	b	2	b	2	12	2	1
2205 Green	10	2	n	2	3	b	2	b	3	34	2	1
2209 Green	11	2	n	2	3	b	2	f	3	12	2	4
2211 Green	12	2	y	0	4	b	2	d	1	16	1	1
2218 Green	13	2	n	0	0	o	1	o	–	0	2	4
2222 Green	14	2	n	0	0	o	1	o	–	0	2	2
2226 Green	15	4	n	2	5	c	3	d	8	10	2	2
2229 Green	16	5	y	1	5	d	3	g	7	20	3	2
2310 Green	17/18	4	n	1	3	c	3	a	3	22	4	1
111 Popular	1/2	2/4	y	1	3	b	2	f	–	20	–	1
113 Popular	4	3	n	3a	1	d	2	b	3	20	2	4
119 Popular	5	2	n	2	1	b	2	b	–	11	2	4
620 Hanley	12/13	2/3	n	1	5	b	2	e	4	10	1	4
622 Hanley	11	2	n	1	1	e	2	c	2	12	4	4
711 Hanley	9	2	n	1	3	c	2	a	1	10	2	4
714 Hanley	7	4	n	1	3	c	2	a	–	12	2	4

Table 9–2 Sample Housing Conditions Data

Physical Condition Ratings	Past Housing Study		Present Housing Study	
	Units	Percent*	Units	Percent*
Total Units - Census	531		616	
Total Units - Local Data	571		622	
Total Units - Visual Survey	560		606	
Excellent	76	13.6%	68	11.22%
Standard	212	37.8%	254	41.9%
Very Good	167	28.8%	161	26.6%
Good	45	8.0%	93	15.3%
Conservable	154	27.5%	176	29.0%
Average	101	18.0%	122	20.1%
Fair	53	9.5%	54	8.9%
Deteriorating	89	15.9%	92	15.1%
Poor	61	10.9%	66	10.9%
Very Poor	28	5.0%	26	4.2%
Unsound - Inhabited	17	3.0%	12	2.0%
Unsound - Vacant	12	2.1%	4	0.7%
	560	100%	606	100%

*Totals do not add to 100% due to rounding

Table 9–3   Housing Occupancy by Status and Unit Type

Housing Occupancy	Units	Percent
Owner Occupied	155	89.0%
Renter Occupied	8	4.0%
Vacant (for sale or rent)	12	7.0%
Total Units	175	100%
Single Family	159	90%
Duplex	8	5%
Multi-Family	2	1%
Manufactured	6	4%

Information used in the vacant housing for sale or rent category can be obtained from local realtors. Housing types should be recorded when making the visual survey.

You should also prepare a narrative to accompany the data presented in the tables. For instance, Table 9–3 shows a high percentage of owner occupancy along with the fact that 90 percent of all dwelling units in the community are single-family residences. High rates of ownership, when accompanied by a general lack of vacant housing, place the community at a disadvantage in attracting new families who would generally prefer to live in rental housing during periods of high interest rates or until job stability and community ties are established. For a community which desires to attract young families or older retired couples, some form of rental housing must be provided to assure available living units. A vacancy rate of 5 percent or more is generally adequate to meet a short-term increase in housing demand.

The narrative might also mention, as would be obvious from Table 9–2, that the community has done a good job in house maintenance and replacement. A steady program of new home construction and existing unit maintenance speaks highly of the community's caring attitude, and this can translate into a major draw for new industry.

The next task is to project future housing needs, as shown in Table 9–4. The future demand for housing is estimated by comparing

Table 9–4   Housing Projections

Year	Housing Units Standard	Substandard	Total	Expected Families	Future Housing New	Upgraded	Total
1970	156	22 (12%)	178				
1975	166	15 (8%)	181				
1980	177	18 (10%)	187				
1985	193	18 (9%)	198				
1990	211	20 (9%)	211	103	31	8	40
2000				115	35	20	55
2010				152	46	5	51

the projected population growth (or decline) with the present stock of available housing and then estimating how many new dwelling units must be constructed to accommodate new families, and how many dwelling units must be restored or replaced to bring all dwelling units in the community up to standard quality. A professional planner or a knowledgeable volunteer should assist with the housing demand projection. Many pitfalls exist in oversimplifying housing needs. The accuracy of the data is especially important if your community plans to apply for housing assistance grants.

A professional planner or volunteer working with your community should examine and compare data on population and the economic base with the current and projected housing stock and prepare the following:

1. A schedule for upgrading currently dilapidated dwelling units or substandard dwelling units. An estimate of the average age of each type of dwelling unit and a schedule for upgrading and replacing those dwelling units which will probably become substandard or dilapidated over the next 10 years.

2. An estimate of the different types of new housing needed to accommodate the future population of the community: that is, elderly housing, multifamily units, mobile home units, or upgraded single-family units.

You should also prepare a list of recommendations to improve the community's housing stock. For instance, a typical recommendation would be that the community adopt and enforce a building code or improve the mix of housing to attract new residents. But make sure that the professional planner's recommendations are feasible and in line with community goals and objectives and that the possible effects of these recommendations, if adopted, are fully explored.

HOUSING GOALS AND OBJECTIVES

A community concerned enough to plan must concentrate on the quantity and quality of its housing stock. Adequate housing will probably determine the difference between having an effective town plan and attaining local goals or a static community which has only dreams of economic development. Housing goals and objectives will depend on the needs and desires of each particular town. The following suggestions can serve as guidelines for future housing development:

1. Goal: Provide sound, healthy, and affordable housing for all residents of all income levels.

2. Objective: Increase the number of multifamily housing units in the downtown area.

3. Objective: Provide space for the construction of new single-family houses at the north end of town.

Many alternatives for improving or modifying the community housing stock are possible. For instance, the community might want to investigate (1) a concerted effort at rehabilitation; (2) the feasibility of providing retirement villages for elderly to increase the amount of potential housing in the community; or (3) a search for federal, state, or local funds to construct housing for low- and moderate-income families.

Many communities encourage the construction of single-family homes on large lots and discourage or prohibit multifamily and mobile home development. To do so places a community at legal risk for not providing a variety of needed housing types. It is not the purpose of planning to exclude housing types or classes of people from a community.

SUMMARY

Available, affordable, and safe housing is a key ingredient in a community's appearance and ability to accommodate growth. The housing section provides an important link between town population goals and the economic development and land use sections. If a town wants to have population increases and economic growth, then housing will be needed for residents of differing income levels, single-family and multifamily, and for purchase or rent. The housing section presents a useful picture of the town's current housing capacity and location and what sort of housing will be needed and where it should go.

10

Land Use

The aim of the land use section of the miniplan is to compile an inventory of the existing land use patterns of the community and to recommend goals and objectives for future development that are compatible with the general character of the community. Planning will not enable you to completely avoid controversies over land use. An inventory of land uses and a discussion of possible future land use patterns should help to focus debate over how land is currently used and how it should be used in the future.

PURPOSES

The land use section of the miniplan is where you see how the town fits together and decide on how the land use patterns should change in the future. The first task is to inventory and describe the existing land use patterns of the community on a current land use map. Once you have evaluated the current land use patterns, examine the population projections, housing needs, economic base, and community facilities. Then decide on a land use pattern for future development

which is compatible with the general character of the community. This desired land use pattern is shown on a future land use map.

The land use section serves as a guide for the planning commission and the elected governing body when they review private development proposals and make decisions on the location of public facilities. The land use section also lays the foundation for zoning and subdivision regulations and the capital improvements program, which put the goals and objectives of the land use section into action. For example, the zoning map should reflect the land use patterns of the future land use map and enable those desired patterns to occur.

The land use section is where the community presents its vision for the future. For example, do the townspeople want to see commercial development occur in the downtown, or out along a commercial strip? Deciding to favor the traditional downtown location may provide access for local residents, but the commercial strip option may serve to capture a larger share of passing motorists. Poor planning often comes about when townspeople cannot think ahead to see what they want the town to look like and how it will function as a place to live, work, and play. A sound, realistic vision gives the community an overall land use pattern to work toward. Land use decisions based on this vision will affect the design of the community for years to come.

It is often helpful to visit small communities that had a clear vision of how they wished to develop and maintain their towns. Places within the town are accessible. Elderly housing facilities are found in a central location rather than across a highway with no opportunity to reach the main town except by automobile. There are public spaces for people and they feel welcome in these spaces. New residential additions to the town fit into the existing pattern, rather than lie hidden away from the town.

The planning and zoning enabling legislation of many states requires either a land use plan or a comprehensive plan to be prepared and properly adopted prior to the drafting of zoning and subdivision regulations. In addition, zoning and subdivision regulations are assumed to be consistent with an adopted land use plan or comprehensive plan that includes a future land use map. This means that the map will be an important factor in any legal dispute over a particular zoning or subdivision provision or procedure.

COMMUNITY LAND USE PATTERNS

The tasks for this section are (1) data collection, (2) interpretation of the data, (3) setting goals and objectives for the type and location of future development, and (4) drafting land use maps indicating the type and location of current land uses and desired future development.

Data Collection

While data collection can be accomplished by several volunteers from the local community, interpretation of the data and the implications for future development must be done by a professional planner. State planning enabling laws require that a community prepare and adopt a land use plan or a comprehensive plan which includes land use maps, if the community wishes to enact land use regulations or annex land into the town boundaries. Because of this legal requirement, it is important that the land use section of the miniplan be prepared by someone skilled in community planning. It is highly likely that the community's zoning ordinance will eventually be challenged in court; and if the land use plan is not technically correct, the community can expect costly trouble.

Drafting the Current Land Use Map

A working reference map is the first task. Use the official town map and include an area of about one-half mile beyond the corporate boundaries. If your town does not have base maps available through a computer aided design (CADD) file or geographic information system (GIS), locate the most current base map of the community depicting the corporate boundaries, blocks, lots, and public streets. The town, county, or consulting engineer will be able to aid in drafting and updating this map; also, the assessor should be able to supply you with an accurate tax map. In addition, you should also obtain a reasonably current air photo map of your area. This will be necessary to make accurate judgments when buildings are located on more than one lot, for showing flood plains, and for a town overview.

Make several copies of the reference maps at different scales. Use one map to cut in pieces and use photocopying enlargements. Each piece should represent a block with lot numbers for a town or other, larger individual land holdings.

Using the base map, you should conduct a reconnaissance survey. The housing condition survey should be completed at the same time to avoid returning to the same area. Either walking or driving, you should inspect each block and lot of the community and mark on the map the type of land use on each property. Larger communities typically use the Standard Industrial Classification (SIC) number system to classify land use. For a small town or rural survey, however, the following categories should be adequate:

  1. Residential.
    • Single-family.
    • Duplex (two-family, three-family, four-family).
    • Multifamily (more than four families).
    • Mobile home.
  2. Commercial.
  3. Warehouse, transportation or storage.
  4. Industrial, manufacturing, processing, fabricating.
  5. Institutional (Example: school, church, hospital).
  6. Public/governmental (Example: city hall, parks).
  7. Farm and forest land, vacant land.
  8. Mixed—such as commercial and residential on the same lot or within the same structure.

Each land use type on the map should be coded according to a color scheme or keyed to a numbering system. The coding system should be carefully organized prior to undertaking the survey if the data are to be entered in a computer.

Special classifications should be devised to handle the uses that do not fall into one of the functional areas listed. For instance, some buildings may have both a residential and a commercial use, and some buildings may have commercial and manufacturing uses.

While conducting the land use survey, you should consider collecting data and observations that can be used to prepare a conflicts map and report. Mark on a base map the obvious and significant conflicts that you observe during the reconnaissance. This sketch map with your notes will be very helpful when land use goals are debated by the planning commission. Common examples of conflicts are:

  • Dangerous or crowded intersections.
  • Poorly signed streets or railroad crossings.
  • Lack of sidewalks that force pedestrians into the streets.
  • Lack of screening for unsightly outside storage.
  • Inoperative vehicles.
  • Needed crossings for schoolchildren.
  • Poorly kept structures that obviously detract from the neighborhood.
  • Poorly kept sidewalks and streets.
  • Poor motor vehicle vision on streets or intersections.

After all of the information has been gathered and placed on a map (see Figure 10–2, "Current Land Use Map"), you should return to the base map and, with the aid of a calculator, computer database, or spreadsheet, calculate the land area in acres for each land use

Figure 10-1 Reconnaissance map for community conditions

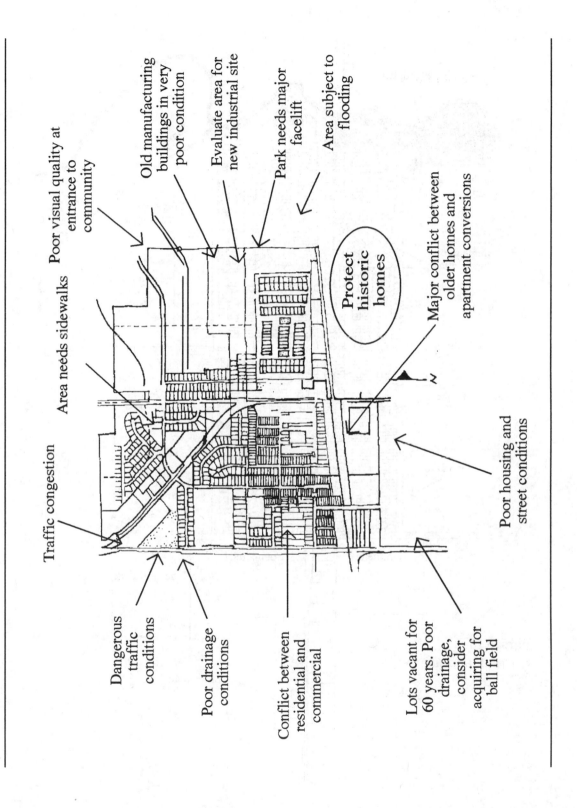

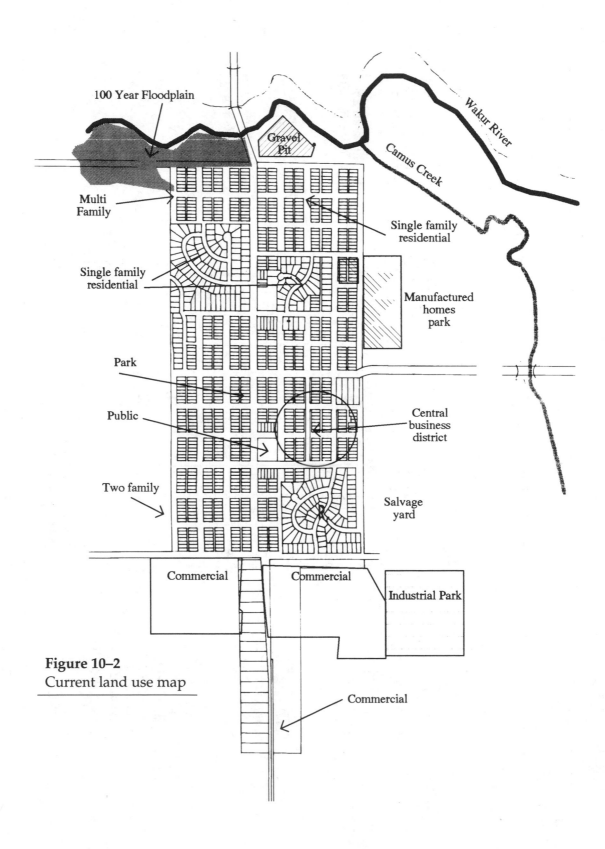

100 Year Floodplain

Multi Family

Single family residential

Park

Public

Two family

Gravel Pit

Wakur River

Camus Creek

Single family residential

Manufactured homes park

Central business district

Salvage yard

Commercial

Commercial

Industrial Park

Commercial

Figure 10–2
Current land use map

Table 10-1 Sample land use classifications and areas

Land Use Classification	Acres
Residential	45.5
Commercial	11.5
Industrial	8.7
Public	15.0
Buildings	3.0
Parks	10.0
Other	2.0
Institutional	14.0
Private	1.2
Schools	13.8
Unclassified	14.0
Total Developed Land	138.7
Vacant Land	12.0
Incorporated Town Area	150.7

category. This can be done by using the scale indicated on the base map and a ruler or by several instruments especially designed for this purpose such as an area overlay or a planimeter. You should then organize the data according to the example given in Table 10–1.

Another important factor to consider in developing the land use maps is the suitability of land for different types of uses. As part of the natural resources inventory, discussed in detail in Chapter 11, you should collect information on soil types and topography for all large tracts of vacant land in the community and those parcels immediately adjacent to the community boundaries. Topography—contours, slopes, grade, and drainage—will help to determine sites that are easy to develop, sites that will require moderate to extensive improvement for safe construction, and sites that cannot support buildings. Soil types will yield a wide range of information for the land use plan. Some soil types may drastically limit the capability of septic tanks, thus indicating the need for community sewer lines prior to development. Other soil types may prohibit metal water pipes because of corrosiveness. Soil types that have severe limitations for buildings and dwellings can be designated for uses that are appropriate to the particular conditions, such as sanitary land fill, parks, wildlife habitat, agricultural production, or cemeteries. Also, you should identify any environmental constraints imposed by federal, state, or county governments, such as wetlands, wildlife habitat areas, and coastal dunes, among others.

The next task is to overlay the flood data on your land use map. Information on the actual flood zones and the 100-year and 500-year floodplains should be transferred from the flood insurance rate maps to your current land use map. The floodplain information was originally developed using air photo maps; it should be an easy task to find the proper scale for making the overlay to the land use map.

Information on soils and topography can be obtained from the soil conservation service in your county. Some areas may not have been fully surveyed or do not have published maps, but the county soil conservation service representative should be able to help you. Flood insurance rate maps are available from local governments (presuming they participate in the federal flood insurance program) or from the closest Federal Emergency Management Agency office.

If your town expects to annex additional land in the next five to ten years, you would be wise to compile an inventory of land uses up to two miles beyond the town boundaries. This will help determine what lands the town may want to annex, what uses various lands are able to support, and how the additional land will fit in with the town's overall patterns of land use and public services.

Water and sewer facilities are two of the most important considerations for future development. Sketch in or overlay the water and sewer lines in your community. Either show the direction of flow or the land contour and depth of lines to illustrate which areas can be linked to the treatment plant or the water supply. Replacing smaller lines with those of greater capacity is an expensive proposition. But, it is even more expensive to allow a subdivision to develop near a community only to discover that the sewage must be pumped to reach the treatment plant.

Work sessions should be scheduled with city, county, or water/sewer district officials in an effort to assess the present condition and future capacity of your water and sewage treatment and distribution system. The goals for these work sessions are:

• To determine the approximate capacities of the treatment and distribution systems.

• To examine the water supply.

• To discuss which areas are relatively easy or difficult to service.

• To estimate, generally, the serviceable life of your treatment and distribution systems.

• To discuss the overall trend of costs involved in treating sewage and delivering water to your area. You should determine if some areas are much more difficult and costly to service than others, then the land use plan must include policies that discuss a fair method of cost sharing for new additions to your service area.

Finally, you should contact federal, state, and county agencies to learn of any planned projects that may affect land use in your community. For example, the state highway department may be planning to build or widen roads in your community; the county may be considering the approval of a large residential development in an unincorporated area adjacent to your community; or the federal government may be interested in building a dam on the river that flows through your community. In short, the more information you can gather about the other plans affecting your community, the more realistic your own land use plan will be.

Data Interpretation

Both planning professionals and knowledgeable volunteers will be needed to help with the task of interpreting the data. The following steps must be accomplished:

1. The creation of a soils, terrain, and flood areas map to determine which vacant lands will best support new developments.

2. A projection of the future demand for land in acres based on population growth, land needed for roads, land needed for new housing, and land needed for community facilities and institutional needs.

3. An examination of the future demand for commercial and industrial uses and the community goals for the expansion and location of these uses.

4. An analysis of the goals of the community concerning the future desired type and density of development. For example, goals must indicate whether future commercial development should remain in the central business district or be placed on the edge of the community.

5. Preparation of the proposed future land use map.

The planning consultant or knowledgeable volunteer team should prepare all necessary maps and future land use projections, along with a description of the land use patterns in the community. All maps and charts should be kept to an easily understood size and scale and included in the miniplan document.

Information Needed in Drafting the Future Land Use Map

A working reference map is the first task. If your planning district is a community, then consider using the official town map and include an area equal to about one-half mile past the corporate boundaries; air photos are even better. If the planning district is a county, then enlarge the official map and divide it into townships, groups of sections, census tracts, or other logical pieces. The information that must be included—overlaid—on the map is discussed earlier.

Exhibit 10–1
Environmental Features to Be
Shown on Land Use Maps

Natural Environmental Features
1. Floodplains, streams, greenbelts.
2. Aquifer recharge areas.
3. Soils.
4. Slopes.
5. Vegetation (tree cover, prairie, etc.).

Man-Made Environmental Features
1. Water system.
2. Sanitary sewer system.
3. Storm sewer system.
4. Transportation system.
5. Commercial land use.
6. Industrial land use.
7. Residential land use.
8. Vacant developable land.
9. Agricultural land.
10. Forest land.
11. Parks and recreation areas.
12. Historic sites.
13. Schools and school district boundaries.
14. Landfills.
15. Public buildings and land.
16. Government restricted areas.

The Future Demand for Land—Housing and Public Facilities

The data and the projections prepared in the population, economic base, and housing sections must be closely examined to estimate the future need for land over the next 10 years. This is a difficult task even for professional planners. For the miniplan, the future demand for housing and public facilities is based on past trends and population projections. You must decide on the increase or decrease in population that can reasonably be expected over the next 10 years.

Divide the projected total future population by the average household size. This household size will generally range from about 2.5 persons per unit to approximately 3.8 persons per unit in rural areas. A good benchmark is 3.5 persons per unit. The result is the total number of housing units needed over the lifetime of the plan. Remember, the plan must be updated frequently to be useful to the community, so there will be adequate opportunity to make adjustments to this estimate.

Next, estimate the number of residential units that must be replaced from the existing housing stock. This estimate can be no more than a reasonable guess. The housing condition survey, the U.S. Census of Housing, and your own appraisal data will yield the best evidence. Those dwelling units rated as very poor or dilapidated should be counted as units that must be replaced during the lifetime of the miniplan.

The total number of new dwelling units needed from new growth plus those units that must be replaced equals the total housing demand over the life of the plan. A check for consistency should be performed by comparing your totals with the U.S. Census of Housing data for 1990. The information in the census will indicate the age of dwelling units and thus give you a good idea of the number of units constructed over the past 25 years.

The next task is to translate the housing demand into land required for future building purposes. A simple approach is to assume that a house, along with the necessary easements and rights-of-way, will require approximately a half acre of land. Be aware that the average amount of land required for one new dwelling unit can vary tremendously. The nationwide trend is smaller lots, fewer easements, and narrower streets; though this trend has not significantly affected the more isolated rural areas. Lot prices and land preparation costs are significantly lower in rural areas than in urban areas. A lack of public sewer and water, and even the perceived need for more space, means that rural housing lots frequently begin at two units per acre and range upward to four acres per unit. Even rapidly growing suburban communities that were once small towns allow some subdivisions to develop without public sewers. A reasonable assumption for the minimum space required to treat sewage on an individual lot is one acre per house. It is important, however, that you check with local, county, and state officials regarding minimum lot sizes required for on-site sewage treatment. A minimum of two acres is even better, given the likelihood of having to move a leach field sometime during the life of the septic system. Also, if an on-site well is used to provide water, the greater distance between the well and the septic system the better.

Land required for public spaces (such as parks and recreation), governmental institutions, schools, or for the expansion of public facilities (including your sanitary landfill) should now be added to the total demand for land. The best sources for most of this information are your public officials and the local engineers or consulting engineers who design and plan public facilities. School district officials, using national and state standards, will be able to supply estimates of the total land needed for future additions and improvements. National recreation standards, available in most basic civil engineering, planning, and landscape architecture handbooks,

Table 10-2 Sample land use classifications and areas

Land Use Classification	Current Acres	Additional Acres of Land Needed by the Year 2000	Additional Acres of Land Needed by the Year 2010	Total Additional Acres of Land Needed
Residential	45.5	12.0	12.0	24.0
Commercial	11.5	16.0	5.0	21.0
Central business	----	7.0	3.0	----
Service business	----	9.0	2.0	----
Industrial	8.7	44.0	10.0	54.0
Light	----	36.0	10.0	----
General	----	8.0	----	----
Public	15.0	19.0	4.0	23.0
Buildings	3.0	1.0	3.0	----
Parks	10.0	18.0	1.0	----
Other	2.0	-----	-----	----
Institutional	14.0	22.0	1.0	23.0
Private	1.2	-----	1.0	----
Schools	13.8	22.0	----	----
Unclassified	14.0	9.0	3.0	12.0
Totals	138.7	122.0	35.0	157.0

should be used to estimate space required for parks, playgrounds, and sports facilities.

The estimates can now be assembled into a chart similar to the one shown in Table 10–2.

The Future Demand for Land—Commercial and Industrial

Towns near metropolitan areas have a definite advantage in estimating the amount of land needed for future commercial and industrial growth. Employment forecasts and market expansion estimates are commonly available and are reasonable indicators of future land requirements.

But most small communities and rural areas exhibit a rather slow change and low demand for new commercial space. Towns with respectable growth rates can sometimes estimate the future demand for commercial space by finding the ratio between total population change and new commercial square footage over the past 5 to 10 years. Usually, it will be necessary to use a common sense approach for these estimates. Before proceeding, you should be aware of some nationwide trends in rural areas.

1. The demand for new or converted space for business and professional offices may be weak in rural areas, but it is not dead. New markets continue to develop or reform in rural areas and are not necessarily dependent on increased population growth. Fast food restaurants and convenience stores now actively locate new operations in rural communities, whereas, at one time, only communities with 50,000 or more people were targeted. Warehouses, factory stores, and outlets are now frequent in rural communities with access to busy interstate traffic.

2. Discount retail stores and bulk groceries are now common in rural areas. These businesses thrive not because of rural population growth but because they can capture large market shares from stable or slowly declining populations. Even moderately sized discount stores in rural areas attract additional businesses hoping to capitalize on the concentration of shoppers. New restaurants, fast food chains, and smaller volume outlets follow the discount stores.

3. The new rural enterprises continue to avoid the older central business districts in favor of highway sites or cheaper locations.

4. Conversions of older homes to commercial uses were once rare in rural America. Today, because of the public demand for alternative lodging (bed-and-breakfast), crafts, antiques, and second-hand items, conversions are frequent.

5. The oversupply of professionals in many careers in big cities means that professional opportunities in small towns are becoming attractive. Because many professionals wish to avoid high start-up costs, there will continue to be a demand to renovate old buildings in small towns into office space.

All of these trends do not necessarily point to a small town economic resurgence. But they suggest that there may be additional commercial and even industrial land use needs in rural communities.

Common sense methods for estimating future commercial, professional, and other office space are given below. All nonindustrial firms such as restaurants, private hospitals, motels, and business offices should be included. Remember that estimates must include total space, not just the building area. Parking space and the remaining open space within individual lots are important also.

- **Example 1:** Estimate the current amount of space in square feet used by nonindustrial firms in your planning area. Find the ratio of the current population to the current square footage—in other words, the square footage per person. Assume that the need for new space per person will increase at the same ratio throughout the planning period. If the current ratio is 480 square feet per person, and the total expected number of additional people by the year 2020 is 840, then the need for new commercial space will be 840 × 480: approximately 403,200 square feet.

- **Example 2:** Estimate the amount of new commercial space built or converted outside the central business district during the past 20 years. Assume that approximately half the same amount of space must be made available over the next 10 years.

- **Example 3:** Ask the experts—the people who operate the businesses within your community! Use your local chamber of commerce or similar organization, or survey all your firms about plans for expansion within the next 5 to 10 years.

- **Example 4:** If your community has accurate records of building permits, you can construct a trend line or a bar chart showing the amount of new commercial space added over the past two decades (see Figure 10–3).

In a typical small town, between 15 to 18 percent of all land (including the structures and the lots) is used for commercial purposes. This formula may serve as a benchmark for the unexceptional, isolated, stable small town with a population base of approximately 2,500 persons. The problem is that small

Figure 10-3 Square feet of commercial and industrial space by building permits 1970 - 90

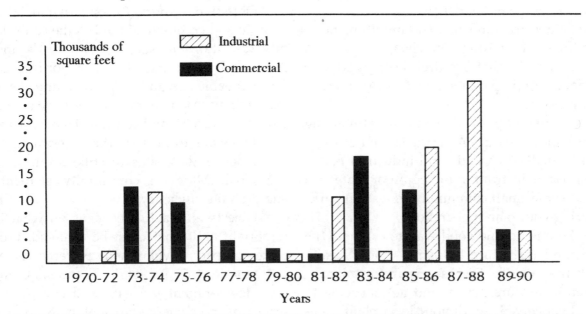

towns exhibit wide variations in their actual uses of commercial space. Many small communities, which serve as trade areas for large regional territories, need large amounts of commercial and professional space. On the other hand, many small, rural communities, with their low density housing patterns and compact town design, have a small ratio of commercial uses to the total town area. This is especially true if the community is not located on a major highway.

You should also estimate the demand for industrial land, using the current ratio of population to industrial acreage to project future needs as your population increases. If an industrial park has not been established in your community, you should turn to Chapter 22 on economic development and carefully consider your options. If you do not have an area set aside for industrial relocation, expansion, or attraction of new firms, then the general rule will almost certainly apply to your community. Unless you prepare, you will find it difficult to participate.

Industrial firms are not willing to relocate or expand unless a community can provide accessible, reasonably priced land with public sewer and water. Planning for industrial development requires a long-range vision. Once investments are made and land is assembled, there is very little opportunity for change. For the land use plan, a minimum of 40 contiguous acres should be designated for an industrial expansion area. The purchase of an additional 40 contiguous acres for long-term future growth is recommended. There are four essential criteria to bear in mind for planning purposes.

• Ease of access is very important—lack of accessibility is fatal.

• Infrastructure (roads, sewer, water) and public services are crucial to the long-term success of the industrial area.

• New firms in small communities thrive on low-cost buildings and cheap preparation costs. A site that requires even moderate amounts of preparation may frustrate most of your plans.

• Consider your options before finalizing your plans! North America is well stocked with small town and rural industrial parks. Ask for help from your region or state and visit some small community industrial parks during your plan preparation.

There is no one good way to estimate the demand for future industrial lands. Again, ask the experts. Discuss expansion plans—even if they are distant and not particularly well conceived—with your local plant managers and owners.

Land Use Goals and Objectives

The land use patterns of a community have a major influence on transportation, energy consumption, property taxes, compatible or conflicting adjacent land uses, and possibilities for future growth. The community's land use pattern and subsequent vision of the future are major components of what is commonly referred to as the image of place. These images can range from the forgettable to the essential. The basic purpose, therefore, of land use planning is to maintain the essential and change the forgettable. This is fostered through a community's visioning process—its goals and objectives. While each community must determine its own goals and objectives, the following recommendations can serve as guidelines for future development:

1. Goal: Develop a land use plan consistent with the community's ability to service existing and new development.

• Objective: Provide for only as much industrial and commercial land as the community can afford to service with roads and sewer and water lines. In other words, plan for reasonable demand rather than unrealistic expectations. Many communities have zoned land for industrial and commercial uses without the means to provide the necessary services; most of these sites are still vacant.

2. Goal: Maintain community elements and promote efficiency.

• Objective: Reach consensus on what is important and what must be changed. Promote compact development patterns, especially for new residential development. Compact development is easier and cheaper to service, is more energy efficient, helps to preserve open space, and encourages a greater sense of community.

3. Goal: Cultivate an attitude of area-wide thinking for land use planning.

• Objective: Develop an annexation policy! If the community foresees annexing lands or developments in unincorporated areas, these lands or developments should be immediately adjacent to the town's boundaries. To annex lands and developments a mile or more from the town's boundaries invites spread out development that will be difficult, expensive, and generally impossible to service.

4. Goal: Lessen conflicts.

• Objective: All land users have different expectations; where quiet is a common expectation in residential areas, intense activities and unfettered working habits are expectations among our agricultural lands. Conflicting land uses require modifications, intelligent forethought, and the maximization of separations and buffers. Effective site planning is a necessity for community balance, not a luxury.

5. Goal: Consistency.

• Objective: Land use goals and objectives must be consistent with the goals and action initiatives and objectives of the other functional areas of the miniplan. Be sure to check the sections on population, economic base, housing, community facilities, natural environment, and transportation. These functional areas are especially important in drafting the land use map.

The Future Land Use Map

The land use section must contain an official map entitled the *future land use map* (see Figure 10–4). The map is both the community's statement of a desired future and a precise guide to land use consistency and change.

Consistency. The official zoning map and ordinances, discussed in Chapter 16, must be consistent with the future land use map and land use goals and objectives of the land use section of the miniplan. The land use categories shown on the future land use map should be consistent with the different zones shown on the zoning map.

Change. The land use section and future land use map give direction to the planning commission in reviewing development proposals. Future changes in zoning or subdivision polices must be based on the land use patterns shown on the future land use map. The zones, districts, development policies, and subsequent changes used to implement the plan are based on the land use section and the future land use map. The future land use plan should also be used to guide public improvements through the capital improvements plan. In short, the land use goals and objectives and the future land use map are the basis of rational action so important to good community planning.

The larger the planning area, the broader and less defined will be the future land use categories. The smaller the area, such as within the boundaries of a small municipality, more specific land use categories are needed. For example, areas desired for residential use should indicate both the land use and density level. The map must differentiate between traditional single-family, multifamily, and perhaps mobile home parks. The map must also indicate the difference between light or moderate use fabrication and heavy industrial activities. Commercial activities have a wide range of use intensity. There is a big difference between a small antique shop in a converted residential structure and a regional farm implement dealership.

County and regional land use maps tend to show large and generalized areas where residential, commercial, and industrial uses may be acceptable. These maps commonly include a good deal of resource data (floodplains, prime farmlands, sensitive environmental areas) as a guide to which lands should not be open for development. The following land use categories can be used to complete the future land use map for a small town with the power to plan for adjacent lands and for larger planning areas, such as a county, parish, or township.

Large Area Planning—Such as a County, Parish, or Township

1. Resources protection "RP" to indicate those lands used for forestry, mineral extraction, or agriculture, which require special conservation measures.

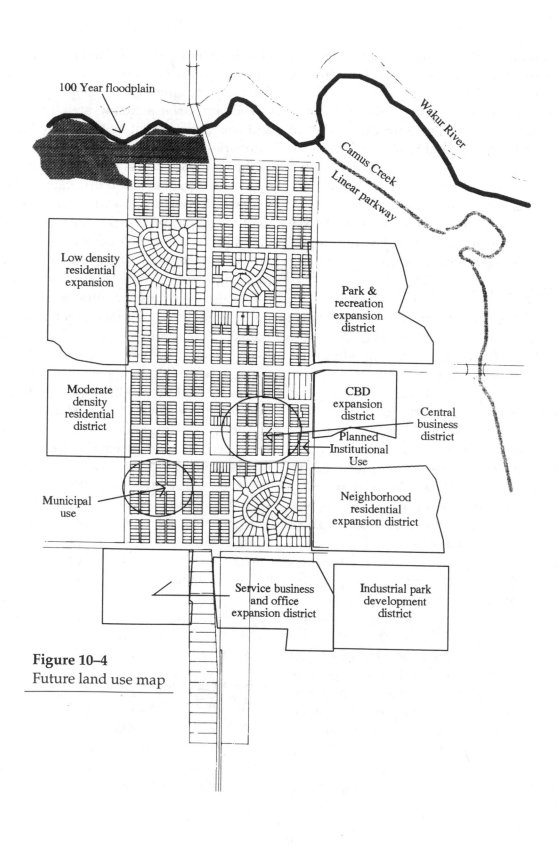

100 Year floodplain

Wakur River

Camus Creek
Linear parkway

Low density
residential
expansion

Park &
recreation
expansion
district

Moderate
density
residential
district

CBD
expansion
district

Central
business
district

Planned
Institutional
Use

Municipal
use

Neighborhood
residential
expansion district

Service business
and office
expansion district

Industrial park
development
district

Figure 10–4
Future land use map

2. Residential "RLD" to indicate rural low density.

3. Residential "RMD" to indicate rural moderate density.

Rural low density generally includes areas suitable for scattered or individual residences on large tracts, especially lands with steep slopes and other development limitations or in accord with a rural preservation plan such as one nonfarm residence per 20 or more acres. Residential moderate density generally includes sites suitable for multifamily housing, housing developments, and scattered residences with small lot requirements. These areas are usually located in rural water and/or sewer districts, along major roads, or within the future service areas of small communities.

4. Commercial "L" to indicate local service commercial.

5. Commercial "G" to indicate general service commercial.

The commercial local service area includes low-activity firms that sell and/or store goods, provide personal or professional services, and require few employees. The rationale is that most activity, except for parking, occurs within buildings. General service commercial encompasses a wide range of more intense activities which require distance separation from rural neighborhoods.

6. Industrial "LA" to indicate low activity industrial.

7. Industrial "GA" to indicate general activity industrial.

Industrial firms which conduct all, or nearly all, of their activities within enclosed buildings in rural areas are usually considered to fall within the light activity range. Firms which conduct a reasonable share of their activity outside of buildings and produce glare, noise, and odor beyond their lot lines can be considered as general activity industrial uses. Rural areas offer an above average temptation to those firms which seek isolation from all surrounding uses and to those industries which process natural resources. Rather typical examples are hazardous waste storage, electrical power generation or natural gas compression and transmission, cattle feedlot operations, auto race tracks, and asphalt or concrete mixing plants.

8. Public "P" to indicate public land owned by any level of government.

9. Flood protection "FP" to indicate flood protection zones at the 500-year level and below according to your area flood insurance rate map.

10. General overlays (XO) to indicate a particular overlay area.

An overlay on the land use map indicates that there is an additional resource or caution to be taken into account during the final zoning and land development process. An overlay needs to be named and could indicate special cautions or protection for historic structures or areas, lake or shoreline protection, wetlands, prime agricultural land, or even areas subject to dangerous subsidence. Flood protection areas can also be indicated as overlays.

Small Town Settlement or Incorporated Areas

1. Residential "RS" to indicate single-family residential.

2. Residential "RM" to indicate multifamily residential—typically structures which contain three or more housekeeping units.

3. Residential "MH" to indicate certain types of manufactured housing.

Historically, small communities set aside land for detached housing. Some limit this to single-family (single housekeeping unit), but commonly this designation also includes two-family detached units (duplex or a rental unit incorporated in the traditional detached home). Another designation is used for multi-family housing. Uses range from attached assisted housing to small apartment buildings. In addition, nearly all small communities contain an area of larger, older homes that have been converted to three or more rental units.

4. Central business "CB" or commercial to indicate the uses to be included in your central business district.

5. Neighborhood service "NS" business or commercial to indicate those activities which are acceptable in or near residential neighborhoods.

6. General service "G" business or commercial to indicate the land uses which are too intense for or not acceptable to either the central business district or neighborhoods.

Small towns need at least three commercial land use designations: central business, neighborhood service, and general service. Most towns are planned around a central business district. Although retailing and financial services have undergone massive changes in the past two decades, the need to sustain a coherent, well-structured central business area remains high on the planning agenda for most communities. Especially if your town tries to integrate a wide range of uses within the existing central business district, the town should strive to protect the essential character of this district. Noisy and distracting occupations should be discouraged, as well as any use which exhibits a marked or excessive difference from the existing pattern of commerce, government, and professional services. Neighborhood service is based on the idea that a limited range of businesses, offices, and professional services can be offered outside of the central business district to service residential neighborhoods. Their main characteristics are small scale, low activity and intensity, and integrated design. The general service district, often located along major travel routes, is the land use designation for intensive commercial activities.

7. Light industrial, fabrication/manufacturing "I1 or M1" to indicate a general class of manufacturing activities that carry out their occupations within buildings.

8. General industrial or manufacturing "I2 or M2" to indicate those types of firms that carry out their activities to the exterior of buildings; generate noise, excessive glare or light, or odor; or perhaps have extended hours of operation.

As with most land use classifications, the range of manufacturing or industrial activity is quite variable. You are equally likely to find a small assembly firm in a new metal building as you are an older trailer manufacturing plant with all its noise, glare from welding, and strong paint vapors. Rural communities, at a minimum, require two different industrial zones. The first would permit firms that can contain all or most of their side effects within their buildings, and a second for firms that cannot control the side effects of their activities.

9. Public use, parks, and recreation "P" to indicate public open space or recreation areas or open land owned by any level of government.

10. Floodplain protection "FP" to indicate flood protection zones at the 500-year level and below according to your area flood insurance rate map.

11. General overlays (XO) to indicate a particular overlay area.

An overlay on the land use map indicates that there is an additional resource or caution to be taken into account during the final zoning and land development process. An overlay needs to be named and could indicate special cautions or protection for historic structures or areas, a special sign or design control area in the central business district, or even planned unit development overlays indicating where higher density or mixed used development is appropriate in the community. Flood protection areas can also be shown as overlays.

SUMMARY

The land use section is very important for directing future public and private development in the community. This section should be referred to by both public officials and private developers in making decisions on the type, density, and location of development. The land use section will be one of the last tasks completed in the miniplan because it ties together all of the functional-area sections and gives an overall picture of the community now and in the future. The land use goals and objectives, along with the land use maps of current and future development, are necessary to draft zoning and subdivision regulations which put the land use section of the miniplan into action. Once these regulations have been approved by the planning commission and elected governing body, the particular zones should be shown on the current land use map. The land use section will also be useful in creating a capital improvements program which determines the future pattern, extension, and upgrading of public utility, transportation, and recreational facilities. When, where, and how many capital improvements are made will have a major impact on private development, public finances, and the overall pattern of land use in the community.

11

Community Resources and Public Facilities

Community facilities are buildings, lands, and services which serve the public. Examples of community facilities include hospitals, schools, parks, and police and fire protection. Other public facilities comprise the essential skeleton for servicing the community—water, sewer, power generation and distribution, communication, and transportation. Together, community facilities are known as the *infrastructure* of the community. The planning commission does not have decision making power over some community resources, such as police and fire protection. The elected governing body does have control, especially in allocating town revenues among different public facilities and personnel.

THE NEED FOR COMMUNITY FACILITIES

The need for community facilities depends on the size of the planning area, population numbers and density, expected growth, local wealth, and the capacity of existing facilities.

In addition, many families, businesses, and industrial companies look at the availability of these facilities as an important factor in deciding where to locate. Because private development tends to follow the location, quantity, and quality of public services, advance planning of community facilities should be coordinated with economic development, housing, transportation, open space, and land use objectives. Such an effort will help to determine community facility needs now and in the future, set priorities and timetables for projects, aid in financing projects, and identify desirable locations for facilities (see Chapter 18).

HEALTH FACILITIES

Access to quality health care is essential for the survival and growth of a small town. A lack of health care facilities and personnel will discourage new businesses from moving to the community and may force some existing businesses to leave. For the small community, the major problem is a lack of trained medical personnel. Also, many rural hospitals have recently been hard pressed to show a profit.

Description of Health Facilities

The section on health facilities should include a narrative together with tables and graphs on the following types of information:

General medical personnel

1. Number of practicing physicians per 1,000 community residents.

2. Number of practicing physicians per 1,000 county residents.

3. Number of practicing dentists per 1,000 community residents.

4. Number of practicing dentists per 1,000 county residents.

5. Number of registered or licensed nurses in the county and community.

General medical facilities

1. The number of professional clinics, either medical or dental.

2. The number of hospital beds in the community.

3. The number of hospital beds in the county.

4. A description of available medical facilities in both the community and county in terms of the adequacy of buildings, equipment, and staff.

5. Ambulance services.

6. Description of large regional facilities—their capabilities and service area.

Rural Health Personnel

More than 1,300 rural counties have a shortage of doctors. The lack of medical services can threaten the quality of life and economic growth of a small town. Because many towns have large elderly populations, a shortage of medical services puts these people in particular in jeopardy. Without medical services, new businesses might not come to the community and existing firms might move away.

How does a community go about attracting medical personnel? Can the miniplan help accomplish this goal? Have other communities of the same size tried this before? The answer to all three questions is yes. In examining plans from small communities all over the United States, we found that (1) most small communities devote a large amount of space in their plans to explain their need and desire for medical practitioners, and (2) most communities feel that the miniplan is a good place to express the health care desires of the citizens.

To attract medical personnel, many planners suggest that a community consider the following:

• Contact and work with local, county, regional, and state chapters of the American Medical Association, the American Dental Association, and other organizations of doctors, dentists, and nurses.

• Contact the state and regional medical schools and become familiar with the programs and procedures for employing doctors, dentists, and nurses. Ask for a list of professional journals and publications in which many towns advertise for medical practitioners.

• If the need is particularly acute, have local officials contact state representatives and members of Congress and ask them to aid in the search. For example, the National Health Services Corps has placed health professionals paid by the federal government in medically underserved areas.

• Explore the possibility of providing financial aid to students in medical or dental school in return for having them serve in your community after graduation for a specified amount of time. This could be rewarding if it is a well-planned program. Some communities have experimented with a program of awarding a grant to a local outstanding college student to continue his or her education in medical school. If the student continues in medical studies and performs satisfactorily, the stipend can be increased to cover all expenses in return for medical services in the local community for up to five years after graduation.

• Some communities are finding alternative health providers, such as nurse-practitioners, an effective way of addressing their immediate health needs and concerns. Such professionals, often working in connection with physicians, can help create a primary health care system that is adequate for the needs of many smaller communities.

• Some communities have placed large and skillfully worded signs at their town limits advertising the need for medical personnel.

• Some communities have even built offices or clinics to attract medical personnel.

The miniplan can be used to inform and advertise for medical personnel. The plan should contain information such as the following:

• Available medical facilities in the community ready for use by doctors and dentists. The community might also survey its citizens to determine the approximate number of trained medical technicians and nurses.

• Descriptions of cash or benefit incentives for medical professionals, available regional medical facilities, and regional facilities that are planned or contemplated.

• Prevailing need for type of practice (general practice, geriatrics, ob-gyn, dental).

• Extent of the area that would be served if a medical professional were to practice in the community.

• Available emergency medical services, either locally or on a regional basis.

• Number of nurse-practitioners in the community. Nurse-practitioners are becoming a popular way of meeting many small town medical needs, particularly for the elderly.

POLICE PROTECTION

Information concerning police protection should be collected and presented by the local police department. A narrative should be written for this section and included in the miniplan (see Exhibit 11–1).

Exhibit 11–1
Sample Police Protection Narrative

Skyway relies heavily on a resident state policeman who is augmented by night constables. The resident state policeman is on call 24 hours. The community is covered by the state police from "Troop C" in Hill City with offices in the town hall. As the community grows, Skyway could request that a second state policeman be assigned to meet its needs. As an alternative, the community could hire a full-time marshal to direct the constables. With either arrangement, the community could be protected unless the population exceeds 3,500 people. Above this population figure, the community will find it necessary to make a transition, if the experience of our neighboring towns is any indication, to a community police force entirely responsible for the public safety. One of the pressing needs of Skyway is to enter the 911 system or the 911 enhanced emergency system. The community will need to join with Hill City and the county to obtain 911 service.

The miniplan might also include:

• The total number of phone calls per year requesting assistance.

• The total number of criminal investigations conducted in the past three years for each year.

• Percent increases or decreases of the above.

• Detailed crime statistics by type and number for the past year.

• A description of the present physical condition of buildings and equipment devoted to law enforcement.

• The number of full-time people employed in law enforcement.

• The number of part-time people employed in law enforcement.

FIRE PROTECTION

A community plan must always discuss fire protection, because as the town grows and equipment wears out, the need for quality fire protection service grows. You should develop a narrative on fire protection using the following outline for direction. In addition, you

should include a small map of the areas served by the community water system.

Outline for Developing Fire Protection

• The location of the fire company and any substations.

• A list and description of all fire-fighting equipment in each fire house.

• Discuss any present or future plans to replace old fire-fighting equipment or acquire new equipment.

• Discuss any shortcomings of the water and hydrant system.

• Discuss alternatives for developing a water and hydrant system for meeting present or future demands.

• Number of full-, part-time, or volunteer firemen.

• Area served by the fire department.

The National Board of Underwriters recommends a maximum four-mile radius for a fire-fighting district, but different standards exist. You can also evaluate the community's fire protection services in light of the standards given in Table 11–1. You should also de-

Table 11-1 Recommended distribution standards for fire protection

Type of Land Use	Suggested Service Radius	
	Engine or Pumper Company	Ladder Company
1. Commercial/industrial	.75 - 1.0 mile	1.0 mile
2. High to medium density residential	2 miles	2.0 miles
3. Scattered residential	3 - 4 miles	3.0 miles
4. Rural low density residential	4 - 6 miles	---------

Table 11-2 Total fire department calls

Calls	Weekday			Weekend (Sat/Sun)			
	7 am - 3 pm	3 pm - 11 pm	11 pm - 7 am	7 am - 3 pm	3 pm - 11 pm	11 pm - 7 am	Total
Emergency Calls							
Fires	75	36	61	60	44	37	313
EMS	125	47	98	91	65	42	468
False Alarms	60	14	39	31	26	55	225
Good Intent/Scares	50	15	66	14	11	12	168
Other Emergencies	25	22	43	19	10	4	123
Non Emergency Calls	12	6	9	8	7	3	45
Annual Total	347	140	316	223	163	153	1,342

termine the number of responses made each year by the fire company. Table 11–2 uses data from 12 rural volunteer fire departments and three small municipal departments over one year in a county of 19,000 people. This information is taken directly from each fire company's log book by the time of day the call for help was made.

When residential buildings have an average separation of less than 100 feet, the area is considered closely built; when average separation is predominantly greater than 100 feet, the area is considered scattered residential. You should also note that if a railroad cuts through a town, a substation may be needed if trains periodically block the crossings and if growth occurs on the side of the tracks opposite the main station. In addition, you should find out your community's fire insurance rating and how you might lower the rates the community pays.

Using the standards and information provided earlier, you should be able to complete this section by (1) discussing fire protection needs in areas of potential future growth as indicated in the land use portion of the mini-plan and (2) examining current fire protection needs in built-up areas of the community.

SOLID WASTE DISPOSAL

You should describe the present facilities used by the community for solid waste disposal. Because of the technical aspects of solid waste disposal, you should seek assistance from the town or county engineer, regional planning agencies, or professional planners. Increasingly, solutions to solid waste disposal problems can be found through some form of regional integration of facilities and services rather than each community going it on its own. A description of solid waste facilities should include (1) a map showing the locations of landfills; (2) the expected life of the present landfills; (3) the disposal area, in acres, at the time the site was opened and at the present time; and (4) the condition of the disposal site and any problems that are experienced.

Also, you should explore the creation or expansion of the recycling of glass, paper, plastics, and aluminum products. You should ask citizens what kind of recycling they are willing to support. In some states, such as Pennsylvania, recycling is mandatory. Recycling will tend to increase the useful life of your landfills and may result in some new businesses.

Any hazardous waste sites should be identified. The regional office of the Environmental Protection Agency or your state department of environmental resources should have information on the location, size, contents, and potential dangers of these sites. Hazardous waste sites preclude any kind of development both on the site and nearby. Hazardous waste can leach into the groundwater and contaminate neighboring groundwater supplies.

WATER SUPPLIES AND SEWAGE DISPOSAL

Many small towns have recognized that safe, reliable water and sewerage systems are necessary to attract industry. Many federal laws require that water quality be maintained and that polluters pay fines. No industry wants to be charged with polluting water, nor does a community want to endanger the health of its citizens.

A public water supply is a network of storage, filtration systems, pumping facilities, and distribution pipes. Wastewater treatment systems consist of sewage pipes for collection, storm sewers, and sewage treatment facilities. Over half of the small towns in America have public water service, but fewer than one in three communities has wastewater treatment facilities. Towns of under 2,500 people are especially lacking in public

sewage treatment because the cost of a public sewage system would be very expensive.

Even with the spread of indoor plumbing, small town residents generally use septic tanks and leach fields, not municipal sewerage systems. Recently, many small communities have created sewage lagoons to dispose of wastes. These lagoons are shallow ponds that hold wastes so that they can decompose naturally. The lagoons require generally impermeable soils so that sewage will not leak out in a quantity that would pollute groundwater. Occasionally, liquid waste will be pumped out and sprayed on nearby land and sewage sludge at the bottom of the lagoon must be dredged out and spread on land. For more information on sewage lagoons, contact your county engineer, county health department, or state department of community affairs.

Historically, small town families and businesses have obtained their water from wells and cisterns. Information on the location, size, and quality of underground water and surface water supplies can be found by contacting the state geologist, state water resources department, or geology department at your state university.

A shortage of clean water will be a hindrance to economic development and even to the survival of the community! Groundwater pollution is a serious and growing problem in many rural communities. Once groundwater becomes polluted, it is very difficult to clean up. Pollution can be caused by poorly maintained septic systems; excessive applications of pesticides, herbicides, and fertilizers on lawns and farmland; the injection of waste into wells; leakage from landfills and underground gasoline storage tanks; run-off from feedlots; and so on. A safe rule of thumb is that there should be about two acres for each on-site septic system. During the life of the system, it will be necessary to dig up and move the leach field. Also, a septic system should be pumped out at least every 18 months. Some towns have even adopted ordinances requiring periodic pumping of septic systems.

Each state now has a well-head protection program, approved by the Environmental Protection Agency, which serves as a guide for local governments to keep away land uses that would pollute wells. Most wells are drilled about 150 to 200 feet deep. Some new developments, such as car washes and feedlots, should not be located near wells. Nor should the use of injection wells be allowed for disposing of industrial and commercial waste. Soil information from the land use section will help determine the ability of different lands to absorb waste from different types and densities of development without causing water pollution. Above all, your community should set an objective for the regular testing of town water supplies and encourage testing for private wells.

If your community has a municipal sewer and water system, you should determine (1) the capacity of the system, (2) the current levels of use, (3) the location of sewer and water lines, and (4) the age and condition of the system. This information will be useful in evaluating the ability of the present system to support future development and in estimating the cost of expanding the system to service new growth.

If your community does not have a municipal sewer and water system, you should use the information from the housing section to identify dwelling units that do not have adequate plumbing. You may also want to explore the creation of alternative community wastewater systems such as spray-irrigation or lagoons.

Towns with more than 2,500 inhabitants may want to explore the possibility of a municipal sewer and water system by contacting the following federal agencies: the Department of Housing and Urban Development, the Environmental Protection Agency, and the Farmers' Home Administration. The Farmers' Home Administration offers water and wastewater disposal loans and grants for rural communities of fewer than 10,000 inhabitants. The Environmental Protection Agency has a construction grants program for safe drinking water supplies to help communities meet the provisions of the Clean Water Act and the Safe Drinking Water Act. Identifying these funding sources will be helpful in putting together a capital improvements program for the town (see Chapter 18). Your community may also wish to explore the creation of a regional water authority with other towns.

LIBRARY FACILITIES

Library resources are an important part of the community base. No exact standards can be applied to any one community as the needs and desires of citizens vary widely. In addition, several alternatives to the traditional town or county library are now in widespread use across the county: for example, bookmobiles, regional depositories with local library stations, and joint resource libraries of school districts and the local community.

Library statistics should be compiled by the local librarian. Examples of the type of statistics needed include:

- The total number of usable volumes.
- The total number of reference volumes.

• The total number of volumes purchased in the previous three years.

• A breakdown of the preceding year's book checkouts in the following classifications: children, young adult, adult.

• Any area library resources available and commonly used by the citizens.

Table 11–3 may be used as a model for classifying standards for the library system of a community.

EDUCATION

You should ask a representative of the local school district to prepare the education section of the miniplan; quite possibly, most of the information and estimates needed have already been developed. You should be aware that local school districts are separate units of government in some states and may cover different territory than the town boundaries; this is particularly the case in Midwestern and Western states. The education section should at least contain the following information:

• A current listing of public and private schools; the locations, current enrollment, and maximum capacity enrollment of each school.

• The physical condition and useful life of all buildings and facilities.

• A 10-year estimate of future enrollment for the community and the school district (if they are not the same).

• An estimate of future school expansion or renovation needed to accommodate the future school-age population.

In a brief narrative, a representative of the school district should evaluate the school buildings and interior physical facilities, the

Table 11-3 Model library holdings and size assessment

		Size of Library Holdings		
Population of Service Area	Population of Town or County	Per Capita Recommended Volumes	Existing Volumes	Deficiency From Standards
100 - 500	450	5	( )	( )
500 - 1,500	800	6	( )	( )
1,500 - 2,500	1,000	6	( )	( )
2,500 - 5,000	2,500	7	( )	( )

		Size of Library Building		
Population of Service Area	Population of Town or County	Per Capita Recommended Number of Square Feet in Building	Existing Size	Deficiency From Standards
100 - 500	450	1.00	( )	( )
500 - 1,500	800	0.85	( )	( )
1,500 - 2,500	1,000	0.90	( )	( )
2,500 - 5,000	2,500	0.90	( )	( )

Source: Coleman and Granito, *Managing Fire Services*, Washington, DC: ICMA, 1988 page 155

overall teaching program in terms of strengths and weaknesses, and the adequacy of the administrative and teaching staff in relation to the present school-age population. The educational representative should also explain the plans for future facilities relative to the future projected population of the school district. Estimates of future facilities and future population may reveal increasing or decreasing future cost per pupil. For example, an increase of 100 school-age children in the community does not necessarily mean that it will cost more than the current dollar average per pupil to bring the district up to standard. All estimates of educational resources and needs should be based on areawide or state standards. Your state department of education should be able to provide you with these standards.

This section should also discuss how local post-secondary educational institutions—colleges and universities, community colleges, and vocational educational centers—play a role in the life of the community. A forward-looking educational plan should also address technology needs, such as computers and telecommunication facilities, since these are rapidly becoming necessary for small communities.

PARKS AND RECREATION

Parks and recreation are major community concerns. Parks provide open space for residents and visitors alike and enhance a town's appearance. The amount of park land needed or desired will vary widely from town to town. You should determine the number of acres of park land and show the parks on the land use base map. In addition, you should describe the type and condition of the recre-ational facilities available at the parks and public schools. These facilities might include playgrounds, swing sets, tennis courts, bicycle paths, swimming pools, baseball and softball diamonds, basketball courts, picnic areas, and nature trails. Finally, you should estimate how often the parks are used and by how many people. This will give you some idea of whether new park land and associated facilities are needed.

COMMUNITY RESOURCES AND PUBLIC FACILITIES GOALS AND OBJECTIVES

Specific goals and objectives should be developed for each of the community facilities discussed in this chapter. The goals and objectives will be closely related to the population projections and expected economic growth. The number of townspeople will determine the demand for community facilities and economic growth will help pay the cost.

The following recommendations for goals and objectives are intended to serve only as guidelines. Individual community needs and desires will vary widely.

1. Goal: Increase the number of medical personnel in the town.

2. Goal: Provide sanitary disposal of solid waste.

3. Goal: Provide reliable fire and police protection.

4. Goal: Provide safe drinking water supplies.

5. Objective: Purchase park space through local fundraising.

6. Objective: Expand the local high school, given the expected increase in school-age children.

7. Objective: Seek the construction of a municipal water system with the help of federal grants.

8. Objective: Expand local recycling efforts.

9. Objective: Develop a well-head protection program and regular testing of wells.

SUMMARY

The effort spent on this section may return benefits far beyond the investment in time and money. An honest and clearly written evaluation of current community facilities and future needs can bolster cooperation in the community. Current and potential industries, businesses, and residents have a deep interest in the quality and quantity of community services. A community's quality of life and ability to attract and retain economic growth often depend on the quality and quantity of community services. People usually are not attracted to a community solely because of a quality transportation network or an expanding population base. Individuals and families are attracted to a community (provided a minimum number of jobs are available) because of their desire for quality education for their children, because they wish to have a sense of safety in their property, because they enjoy the refreshing openness of parks and recreational areas, and because they can obtain medical services and other amenities which give their lives a feeling of security and growth.

12

The Natural Environment and Community Preservation and Restoration

A study of the community's natural and physical environment is an essential element of the miniplan. Even small communities can plan for many aspects of protecting natural areas and upgrading buildings without the aid of planning experts or environmental specialists.

The following section is divided into two parts. The first part describes the physical and historical character of the community, while the second discusses the larger area of ecology, the plant and animal systems found in the community. You should note, however, that there are serious limitations for large-scale ecological studies and programs in the small community. The most common limita-

tion is enforcement capability. Smaller jurisdictions simply do not have the equipment and personnel needed to enforce all of the environmental standards governing air and water quality or noise abatement, for example. The most pressing environmental concerns in most small communities are (1) the preservation of the rural character, (2) the segregation of agricultural uses from residential development, (3) water quality, (4) protection from floods, and (5) the preservation of open space and unique sites.

RURAL CHARACTER

Open space and small-scale buildings are the two hallmarks of rural character. Rapidly growing towns lose open space as they sprawl out into the countryside. Commercial strip development, common to suburban America, tends to look out of place in small towns and draws economic vitality away from the downtown business district. Large new buildings for residential, commercial, or industrial uses can dominate a town's appearance. Some towns have adopted design review ordinances to control the appearance of new buildings so that they will fit in with the surroundings. This is especially true in towns with many older, yet well-maintained buildings and historic districts. The visual character of a community leaves an impression on residents and visitors alike. This impression suggests a quality of life and a community attitude which may or may not be positive. The physical design of small towns is discussed in detail in Chapter 21.

AGRICULTURAL LANDS AND COMMUNITY DEVELOPMENT

Many people view agriculture as a key component of rural character. Yet, it is not widely understood that modern agriculture is an industrial process, using chemical fertilizers, herbicides, pesticides, and heavy machinery. Although farmland is pretty to look at, farmers and nonfarm residents generally do not make good neighbors. Farming generates noise, dust, odors, chemical sprays, and slow-moving machinery. Manure runoff and fertilizers can raise nitrate levels in nearby groundwater and surface water above federal safety standards. In turn, farms are subject to trespassing, vandalism, and complaints from nonfarm neighbors.

Some conflict commonly exists between traditional crop farming and residents at the edge of the community. But very intense con-

Figure 12-1 Land use character

Positive Aspects of Rural Character

Wooded areas	Fence lines	Forests
Rivers	Open range	Storage elevators
Coastlines	Mountains	Historic sites
Open fields	Water	Low activity
Trees along roads	Farm residences	Quiet
Two-lane roads	Prairies	Ravines and bluffs
Wildlife	Architecture	Simplicity
Farm animals	Vistas	Imagery
Planted fields	Nurseries	Wetlands

flicts often occur because of the strong odors produced by agricultural processing plants or commercial livestock feedlots. Many legal battles have been fought between community residents and the owners of livestock enterprises or grain and fertilizer plants over health concerns and objectionable odors. The controversy is basically at a stalemate and promises to remain so in the foreseeable future. Many states allow only the use of subdivision regulations to prohibit or restrict agricultural uses outside of municipal boundaries, particularly if the agricultural use predates a neighboring residential use. Agricultural development generally is allowed to occur and continue near community boundaries.

On the other hand, communities have felt the need to expand outward from their municipal limits, yet have found large areas of land undevelopable because of conflicts with nearby agricultural uses. The communities have opposed these agricultural uses on the grounds of the *nuisance doctrine.* This doctrine allows for legal action against any use which affects surrounding land through the discharge of objectionable and unhealthful odor, light, heat, dust, vibration, or glare. Nuisance litigation to restrict standard farming practices has not been successful in most cases and the controversy continues. Nearly all states have attempted to protect farming from nuisance litigation by passing right-to-farm laws, which grant farmers immunity from nuisance ordinances for standard farming practices. But right-to-farm laws do not protect farming practices which threaten public health or cause environmental damage in violation of state or federal laws. Each community should determine if its state's right-to-farm law is applicable to a particular situation.

To avoid conflicting land uses and to preserve the environmental quality of the community and the surrounding area, you should work closely with county, state, and local agencies to devise safe areas (probably zoned agricultural/industrial or agricultural support district) in which new, potentially objectionable agricultural uses may locate. Since most of these conflicting agricultural uses occur outside the town boundary lines, the only means of effective coordination is through joint action between towns, or between towns and surrounding townships, or between the town and county in making land use plans and land use regulations. In some states, municipalities have extraterritorial power, allowing them to control land uses for up to two miles or more outside of the community boundaries. And in the Northeastern states, township governments each have planning authority over several thousand acres, including most villages. Otherwise, written agreements between towns, between towns and townships, or between towns and counties can clarify what agricultural and community developments will be allowed and where they will go.

The method of extending planning power will depend on local conditions and judgment. It is important that one of the above methods be selected. If the planning jurisdiction remains inside municipal boundaries, little or nothing can be accomplished in avoiding future conflicts. Once cooperative or extended planning is agreed on, sites that are particularly suited for farming or agricultural processing activities should be identified. Special consideration should be given to the natural and man-made characteristics of all open sites surrounding the community for up to three miles including soil types and runoff patterns, prevailing climate conditions, and topography. Areas that are particularly unsuited for community development, but are compatible with agricultural uses, should be given the highest preference.

For information and assistance in planning for agricultural uses, contact the U.S. Department of Agriculture, your state farm bureau chapter, the soil conservation service, cooperative extension service, or your state department of agriculture.

You should also be aware that farmers may take advantage of state differential property tax programs for farmland. This reduces the amount of property taxes that farmers pay and could have a fiscal impact on the community by shifting tax burdens to nonfarm property owners.

NATURAL RESOURCES INVENTORY

Natural resources are an important part of a town's character and appearance. Natural resources include the soils, water, forests, minerals, geologic formations, and plant and animal species found within the planning area. An inventory of the quantity and quality of natural resources can help the community to identify areas of the town that are suitable for development, other areas that can support only limited development, and, finally, areas that should be protected from development. One challenge in putting together a natural resources inventory is that towns have political boundaries that are likely to differ from geologic or ecological boundaries. For example, the town may be part of a river basin or wildlife migration route. The danger is that the town may plan to conserve and protect natural resources which really depend on regional cooperation.

The inventory should include information on specific sites and land ownership patterns. Ownership patterns show who owns the natural resources, the number and size of land parcels, and how close these resources are to built-up areas. Land parcels can be identified from local tax maps. Identifying the landowner may eventually prove helpful for negotiating conservation restrictions or for general education about management and protection.

The natural resources should be rated in priority for protection as follows:

1. If the resource is renewable or irreplaceable; if irreplaceable, the resource is more valuable.

2. The rarity of the site; the less common, the more valuable the resource, particularly in the case of rare and endangered plant and wildlife species.

3. The size of the site; generally, the larger the site, the more important it is.

4. The diversity of plants, wildlife, scenic views, and other natural features; the greater the diversity, the more important the site is.

5. The fragility of the site, including the quality of the undisturbed site and human threats to the site. For example, at higher elevations, soils are likely to be thinner, more erosion-prone, and more vulnerable to human activity.

These resources should be presented on a series of maps along with a brief narrative description. These maps are especially helpful in putting together the maps of current land use and desired future land use in Chapter 10. A town should be careful not to put too much information on maps. But the more comprehensive the maps are, the better the chances are of discovering problems or planning solutions. Also, enough information should be mapped to help evaluate the impacts of proposed developments on the environment.

A planning professional should be contacted to evaluate (1) wildlife habitat and environmentally fragile areas where development would be especially damaging; and (2) the *carrying capacity* of the community, that is, how many people and how much development can the community support before serious negative impacts on the natural environment would occur. You can think of carrying capacity in terms of overload, such as when too many withdrawals of groundwater will exceed the water supply (carrying capacity) and result in saltwater intrusion in coastal areas or the depletion of an aquifer as in much of the Great Plains.

NATURAL RESOURCES INVENTORY ELEMENTS

1. Soils: slope, erosion potential, permeability, depth to bedrock, prime agricultural soils, forest soils.

2. Water: groundwater, surface water, wetlands, floodplains, drainage.

3. Wildlife: animal and fish spawning grounds, vegetation, rare and endangered species.

4. Geology: mineral and aggregate deposits, unique features, topography.

The value of the natural resources inventory is far-reaching. While it is essential for people in a small town to be able to earn a decent living, the town must also provide a healthy environment. For example, hunting and fishing may be important to the local economy as a source of food, recreation, and employment. In this case, it makes good sense to identify wildlife habitat and estimate wildlife numbers.

Soils

Soils information indicates the ability of a parcel of land to support buildings, absorb water, and grow plants (see Table 12–1). Soil surveys and maps produced by the U.S. Soil Conservation Service contain detailed descriptions that show potential limitations to development. Steep slope, shallow depth to bedrock, poor drainage, and wet soils can hamper the construction of sturdy buildings. Sewage disposal by on-site septic tanks and leach fields may pollute water supplies, cause a public health hazard, and reduce wildlife in nearby natural areas.

Water

Information on the town's water resources should include maps showing the location of public water supplies, groundwater aquifers, and recharge areas in relation to developed areas. For example, an intensive development on poor soils near a public water supply suggests a likelihood of soil erosion and runoff from sewage systems and a threat to the public water supply.

The quality of water resources should also be noted (see Table 12–2). Only about half of all small towns have public water supplies, and most towns depend on groundwater for drinking. Groundwater, once polluted, is very difficult to clean up. A reduction in water quality means greater risks to human health and the need for costly water treatment systems or inconvenient boil water orders. An inventory of water quality often provides insights into the effects a development may have on water quality. This information can be helpful in drafting regulations on the siting, density, and design of new de-

Table 12-1 Soils capability ratings of the U.S. Soil Conservation Service

Soils Class	General Slope	Erosion Factor	Limitations
Class I	Slight	Slight	Few limitations that would restrict use
Class II	3 - 8%	Moderate	Some limitations; use conservation practices
Class III	8 - 15%	High	Many limitations; use special conservation practices
Class IV	15 - 25%	Severe	Many limitations; very careful management required
Class V			Very low productivity: pasture, range, woodland, wildlife
Class VI			Severe limitations; few crops, pasture, woodland, wildlife
Class VII			Very severe limitations, no crops, use for range, pasture, wildlife
Class VIII			Most limitations; use for range, woodlands, wildlife, aesthetics

Source: USDA Soil Conservation Service

velopments. Also, several communities have drafted well-head protection ordinances to ensure that drinking water supplies are not polluted.

Wetlands have become a controversial issue. On the one hand, wetlands perform three important functions: (1) wetlands are a water filtration system, absorbing pollution; (2) wetlands moderate changes in water supplies; they store water in dry periods and catch and hold water during floods; and (3) wetlands are major breeding and feeding grounds for wildlife and may contain a variety of rare and endangered plant and animal species.

On the other hand, wetlands have been filled by farmers and developers who see wetlands as potentially productive for growing crops and building sites. State and federal regulations on the filling and development of wetlands have changed often, and it is a good idea to identify and map wetlands.

Wildlife

Local governments have a major responsibility for the protection of wildlife. The main cause of the loss of wildlife is the destruction of their nesting and breeding grounds. Animals are often vulnerable because they are concentrated in a small area.

Although it is often difficult to count wildlife because they move over a wide area, it is possible to locate and protect spawning grounds, nesting areas, and feeding spots. Wildlife habitats can be identified by knowledgeable local volunteers and personnel from the state university and state fish and wildlife

Table 12-2 Water quality and stream order ratings

Water Class		General Use	Typical Depth	Typical Width	Limitations
Water Quality					
Class A	Excellent quality	Public water supply			None
Class B	Good quality	Recreation, wildlife, water supply and irrigation			Filtration and disinfection for drinking
Class C	Fair quality	Some irrigation, re-creation, wildlife, in-dustrial purposes			Irrigation of crops not used for consumption without cooking
Class D	Poor quality	Certain industry, navigation, hydro-electric power			Not for food purposes
Class E	Unfit	Wastes; typically unfit for use.			Unsafe for body contact, fishing or boating
Stream order					
First order		Intermittent, bare or grassed swales for water runoff	to 1.5 ft.	1 - 5 ft.	Natural, aesthetic, marginal barriers
Second order		Intermittent or perennial water and storm runoff	1 -3 ft.	3 - 12 ft.	Natural, aesthetic, fair barriers
Third order		Low order stream flow is continuous	2 -5 ft.	10 - 25 ft.	Aesthetic, good linear parks and walking trails
Fourth order		Moderate order stream flow with slight channel	3 - 6 ft.	20 - 40 ft.	Canoe, guarded walking trails, some fishing
Fifth order		Continuous flow with shifting channels	1 - 10 ft.+	50 - 200 ft.+	Recreation, boating, fishing

Source: Adapted in part from Bureau of Water Protection, State of Kansas - Department of Health and Environment, Information Panel 642, 1988.

department. Habitats should then be mapped and rated for importance.

Geology

The geology of the town includes the rocks and soils which underlie the community. The geology will show areas with shallow depth to bedrock which are not capable of supporting on-site sewage disposal. Also, there may be underground faults which could lead to landslides or earthquakes. These should be identified and mapped. There may also be unique geological features such as hills, mesas, and rock outcroppings which should be protected.

FLOODPLAINS

Each year floods destroy millions of dollars worth of property throughout rural America. Unfortunately, many millions of dollars worth of property will be destroyed in the future as a result of short-sighted planning and the desire for short-term profit taking by private landowners.

One of the most important tasks is to investigate the occurrence of flooding and the potential for damage within the town boundaries and extending outward for a safety margin of at least three miles.

You should first contact the state division of water resources or the Federal Insurance Administration of the Federal Emergency Management Agency to request information on floodplains. These agencies will mail out a packet of data with floodplain maps, officially called flood insurance rate maps. These maps show watercourses, the flood risk, the likely extent of flooding, and the destructive force of the flood waters. Using this information and a model supplied by the Federal Emergency

Management Agency, your community can develop floodplain management regulations for both new and existing structures.

A floodplain, called a special flood hazard area, includes land adjacent to a waterway that has at least a 1 percent chance of being covered by a flood in any one year. Stated another way, these lands have a 100 percent chance of flooding within a 100-year period. This is the national standard on which all flood management programs are based.

Figure 12–2 illustrates this three-part breakdown in a slightly different manner. The channel of the waterway and the normal area of a 1 percent flood is termed the *floodway*. This is the danger zone where experience and statistical probability indicate that destructive flooding will most likely occur. The perimeter zone corresponds with the flood fringe district in the classification above. Again, both historical evidence and statistical probability should indicate that the perimeter zone will be subject to backup water or occasional moving water. The miniplan adds one additional zone to the traditional floodplain concept: *flood warning district*. On a base map, this warning area should include land immediately adjacent to the flood fringe. The warning area should be used to alert residents, potential subdividers, or home buyers that the land may experience backup water during a higher than normal flood. The warning zone may also be used to indicate that there is a less than 1 percent chance of flooding in any one year.

The purpose of the floodplain study is to advise the planning commission and the governing body of the possible danger of flooding to existing and future development. Once advised, local officials should begin to devise

Figure 12-2 Example flood information

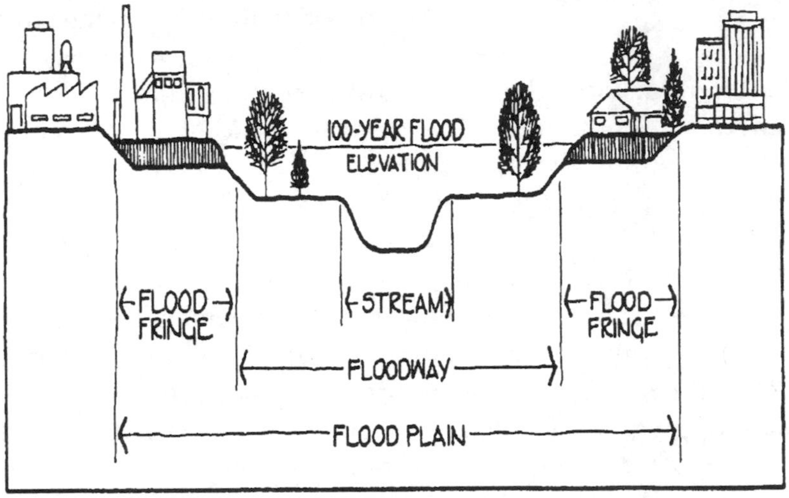

Source: Federal Emergency Management Agency, "Types of Maps," publication SM-3-37, 1993.

and implement one or more of the several methods available for flood protection. In general, these protective measures are divided into two groups—(1) structural and corrective or (2) nonstructural and preventive. Structural measures include reservoir construction and operation, levees and bulkheads, and channel alteration. Some buildings may also be flood-proofed to reduce or eliminate flood damage. Nonstructural or preventive measures involve keeping people and damage-prone property out of the floodway and regulating uses in the floodway to minimize destruction when flooding occurs. These regulations are normally accomplished through zoning and subdivision ordinances.

Regulations for flood control must be based on realistic appraisals of flooding threats. The flood hazard at a particular site usually cannot be estimated by the average citizen using the naked eye. Factors influencing flood hazards are often difficult to iden-

tify. Engineers will examine soil, topography, vegetation patterns, and physical evidence of flooding to determine flood velocities, duration, and frequencies.

Finally, you should be aware that most insurance companies do not offer flood insurance. In order for residents and landowners in the floodplain to be eligible for inexpensive federal flood insurance, the community must plan for and implement measures to reduce or eliminate flood hazards. These measures must meet specific federal standards. For more information, you should contact the Federal Insurance Administration of the U.S. Department of Housing and Urban Development which oversees the National Flood Insurance Program. The Federal Insurance Administration is responsible for identifying flood-prone communities and determining the boundaries of floodplains with special flood hazards. The agency also makes available low-cost federal flood insurance for communities that have undertaken planning to minimize potential damage from floods.

SCENIC GREENBELTS AND OPEN SPACE

The creation of scenic greenbelts, buffer strips, and open spaces involves planning for the protection of land adjacent to both natural and man-made sites, for scenic enjoyment, and for the protection of community residents.

Greenbelts are parcels of land that are adjacent to roads, lakes, parks, streams, or rivers. Within the greenbelt, signs and buildings are generally discouraged. Farming, grazing, recreational areas, and grassland management are normally allowed within the greenbelt, as are rights-of-way to private property.

Buffer strips are useful in providing an open area of transition between adjacent properties. Buffer strips help to reduce spillovers of noise, odors, and visual impact from one property to another. Although buffer strips can be found between public and private land uses, these open spaces are often located between private properties (see Performance Zoning in Chapter 16).

In undertaking greenbelt planning, you should begin by working with local citizens and groups to establish objectives. Also you should determine what areas would best benefit from protection with greenbelts. Excessive use of the greenbelt concept, if implemented into a zoning plan, would not be looked on with favor by the courts. This would constitute an unreasonable restriction of private property for aesthetic purposes. Moreover, too many greenbelts may seriously restrict the amount of land available for community growth and development.

A second step in greenbelt planning is to achieve an areawide perspective by working together with the county and neighboring communities through a joint or regional planning commission. Although limited greenbelt areas can be established within the town boundaries, a greenbelt is likely to be more useful if extended beyond the local jurisdiction. For example, if your town creates a greenbelt along a river, but towns upstream do not, your town may not benefit as much as if all towns along the river agreed to create greenbelts to protect floodplains and reduce water pollution. Without such coordination, a town might try to create greenbelts of differing widths and uses along a single road or river course. But an uneven greenbelt can bring needless confusion to the appearance of an area and adversely affect future development possibilities.

A third phase is to determine what areas are most suited for greenbelts. Prime candidates to consider include (1) areas along major highways or particular scenic routes; (2) floodplains and flood hazard districts; (3) areas adjacent to small streams and rivers; (4) the edge of lakes, reservoirs, and wetlands; (5) lands near parks and recreational districts; and (6) the edges of industrial districts. Examples of greenbelts and other open space areas are shown in Figures 12–3, 12–4, and 12–5.

Greenbelts and open space preservation techniques along highways are accepted practices in the United States. Development tends to follow roads and highways—both in town and in the countryside—rather than force its way through open land that is not served by transportation links. The use of greenbelts will not itself stop this strip development. But, if properly applied, greenbelts

Figure 12-3 Riparian greenbelt

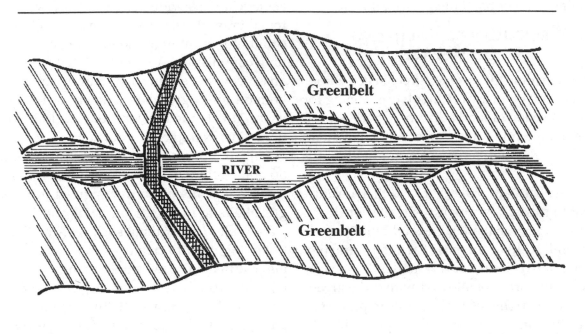

should encourage all buildings and signs to move back a few hundred feet from the road. The community can then require creative landscaping, such as trees and shrubs, to result in attractive open space management.

Greenbelts along highways can also protect public health and safety. Public safety is enhanced by the removal of development immediately adjacent to the roadway—thus providing greater freedom from distractions. Public health benefits from the absorption area created by the open space belt and landscaping with trees and plants. Within this absorption area, sound and noise from traffic is greatly reduced as is the buildup of fumes from cars and trucks.

Greenbelts are also commonly used in conjunction with designated floodplains. Picnic and recreation areas that are allowed to remain in their natural state may easily be used during the warm weather season when there is little danger of flooding. Many of these areas, however, may not be well suited for recreational use because of insect infestation; the county or local health planning authorities should be contacted to assist in this matter.

Greenbelts are especially useful for preserving the shoreline and cove areas of a lake. Because septic tanks are generally incompatible with lakefront development, due to sewage percolation through the soil and high water tables, shoreline greenbelts can provide valuable environmental protection.

A final step in greenbelt planning is implementation. Both zoning ordinances and the subdivision regulations should recommend development standards within the greenbelts: for example, width of the greenbelt, setback requirements, permitted uses, and so on.

Figure 12-4 Highway greenbelt

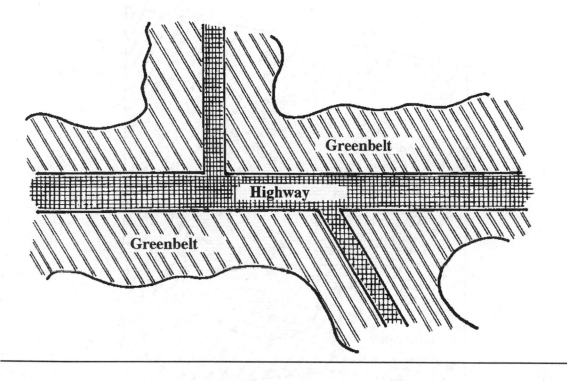

PRESERVATION OF SPECIAL AREAS

Many communities contain one or more areas that are special to the local or regional environment. Whatever the particular circumstances, it is important that the community as a group decide on what constitutes a special area.

Special areas, such as greenbelts, can be designated for protection and/or eventual acquisition by the public. In this section of the miniplan, you should list the unusual sites, describe their characteristics, and discuss the possible benefits to be gained from preservation.

For instance, some Kansas communities have designated certain open space sites where the Oregon or the Sante Fe trails once passed. Other communities, usually in con-

junction with the county, have preserved marshland and grassland, and even scenic vistas.

The decision to preserve certain sites on the basis of their natural appeal must be an official act. American planning law does not allow governments to restrict the development of private property because of the appeal or uniqueness of an area unless a reasonable economic use of the land remains. The courts have interpreted a *reasonable economic use* to include farming, forestry, and other similar uses. Some form of agreement, whether by easement or outright purchase, may be negotiated between the governing body and the landowners as an alternative to zoning restrictions. To acquire private property without paying compensation would constitute a confiscation of private

Figure 12-5 Lake protection greenbelt

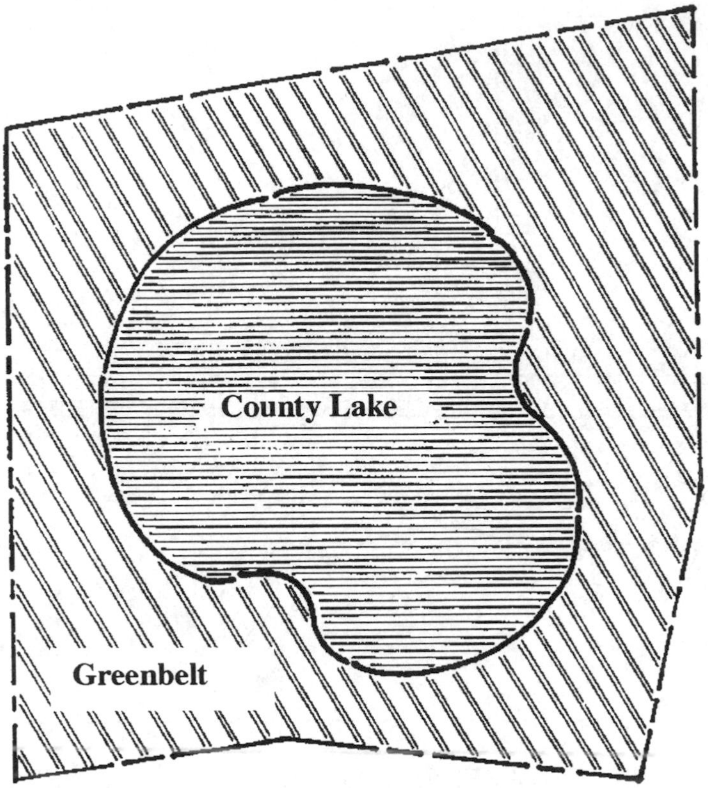

property—something that is not permissible even for the most extraordinary natural sites. Some communities have found it useful to work with a private land trust, of which there are nearly 1,000 nationwide, to reconcile the interests of the community and the landowner. A landowner may voluntarily sell or donate a conservation easement to a land trust or local government. The conservation easement may restrict the use of land to open space, agricultural uses, or limited development.

HISTORIC PRESERVATION

For this section of the miniplan, you will want to contact local, county, and state histor-ical societies and the state historic preserva-tion office for information on important sites and structures. The local chapter of the American Institute of Architects and local university architecture schools may also be helpful. A map should be used to indicate the location of these sites and their relationship to present development. A narrative should explain the importance and the history of each site or structure. You should also include recommendations for future action, such as use for public display, museums, cultural center, gallery, and so on.

When possible, the sites should be ranked according to the historic importance and benefit of each site to the community. This priority ranking should be used for future policy-making by the planning commission and governing body. As a suggestion, the following priority ranking scale is offered: (1) critical, (2) essential, (3) desirable, and (4) future action.

Critical rankings indicate that an important historical site is in danger of destruction. An *essential ranking* shows that an important historical site would benefit the community if immediately protected. A *desirable ranking* signifies that the historical significance and worth of a site has been documented and that the site should be protected as time and financial resources permit. A ranking of *future action* means that a particular site is in the process of being studied.

Courts throughout the United States have long recognized the need to preserve our links with the past. It is generally permissible for a planning commission or elected governing body to establish zoning standards in historical districts or for individual sites. Such standards could exclude certain commercial and industrial uses which would tend to detract from the district or site.

Another area of interest is business district and storefront renovation. Several *Main Street programs* have been undertaken throughout the United States to assist small community merchants in making their business district a more attractive place in which to shop. Federal investment tax credits are available for renovating commercial buildings which are historically significant or are on the National Register of Historic Places. For more information, you should contact your state historic preservation office, the National Trust for Historic Preservation in Washington, D.C., or

a regional office of the National Trust. Historic preservation tools and techniques are discussed in detail in Chapter 21.

NATURAL ENVIRONMENT AND COMMUNITY PRESERVATION GOALS AND OBJECTIVES

A town's natural environment and buildings determine the town's appearance and image as a place to live, work, or visit. Each town will have a somewhat different geographic setting as well as different condition of buildings. Some New England townships have appointed conservation commissions to advise the governing body on the impact of proposed developments and ordinances on the natural environment.

The following suggestions can serve as guidelines, depending on the needs and desires of each town:

1. Goal: Preserve the rural character of the town.

2. Goal: Separate agricultural uses from community development.

3. Goal: Protection from floods.

4. Goal: Improve the appearance of downtown.

5. Objective: No new buildings of over three stories in the downtown.

6. Objective: Zone agricultural land for farm use.

7. Objective: Zone flood plains so that no new dwellings can be built.

8. Objective: Develop a small fund for the renovation of downtown building fronts.

SUMMARY

Planning policies and objectives for preservation and restoration can be rewarding experiences for the small community. Unlike some of the other studies in the miniplan, the studies presented in this section are usually highly visible and indicative of community concern. The only word of caution involves the interpretation of this visibility. Too many times in the past a small community has undertaken a comprehensive plan only to find that, because of the great interest in historical preservation, beautification, or tree replanting projects, there was little time left for other planning concerns. These projects, although commendable, are only part of community planning and should be considered secondary to the purpose and goals of the entire planning process.

13

Transportation and Circulation

Transportation networks tie a community together and link it to the outside world. Local streets and roads should provide safe, reliable access to work, schools, shopping, and residences. The livelihood of a community also depends on how goods and services are imported or exported. The location and size of a community will often affect the modes of transportation available for traveling long distances. For example, in the past 30 years, proximity to an interstate highway has brought growth to many rural cities and towns. Likewise, distance from a major highway has meant that some towns have been bypassed by growth and development. Increasingly, the absence of regional airport facilities is creating a barrier to the survival of more remote small towns. The transportation and circulation section of the miniplan should address the condition of both local circulation networks and the types of transportation connecting the community to the outside world.

Transportation networks to the outside world are important to the economic growth of a community in providing needed access to markets and to goods and services not found in the community. Four modes of transportation may exist: (1) roads, (2) railroads, (3) aircraft, and (4) boats. An inventory of each mode should be conducted and a summary included in the miniplan.

Roads into and out of a community are the main mode of transportation in nearly all rural areas. The condition of these roads should be noted in the plan. Lately, many state governments have realized the great expense involved in maintaining the interstate highways. State highways and bridges often receive only secondary attention. If the condition of the local state highway is inadequate, then the community should make its needs known to the state highway department and state representatives. Similarly, some roads come under county, township, or town control. The condition of these roads should also be assessed.

The deregulation of bus and trucking companies has led to the abandonment of bus and trucking services to many small towns. The stability of these services should be evaluated in terms of (1) the frequency of arrivals and departures and (2) freight and passenger rates to several destinations. Also, the deregulation of railroads and the abandonment of spur lines since World War II have left many rural towns without rail service. Train transportation for both passengers and freight should be noted.

By contrast, the deregulation of the airline industry has resulted in the expansion of small regional airline companies to service more rural areas. Distance to the nearest public airport and the size of that airport should be determined. Any public airport within the town limits should be noted and adjacent lands should be planned for compatible uses.

Water transportation is used almost exclusively for shipping freight. The availability of public docks, frequency of service, and freight rates should be described.

ROADS

An adequate road system is essential for a reasonable flow of traffic and accessibility to all parts of the community. You should first prepare an inventory of streets and roads. In compiling this inventory and in developing goals and objectives for the transportation plan, you should keep in mind the following general purposes of transportation planning:

• To move people and goods with minimum interference to residents and commercial activities.

• To enable residents to move safely and easily from one part of the community to another.

• To develop a street system that leads into the regional highway system.

• To develop a local street system to provide adequate internal circulation.

• To develop a street system that will encourage the separation of through and local traffic.

• To minimize pedestrian-vehicular conflict points.

• To improve existing street conditions.

There are three kinds of roads and streets, each of which has a different function:

• Local streets—provide access to property.

• Collectors—conduct traffic from local streets to arterials.

• Arterials—carry traffic into and out of the town.

Local and collector streets usually comprise the entire circulation system of a small community with the exception of one main arterial running in and out of town. Aside from providing access to property, local streets also serve as an easement for all types of utilities, provide temporary parking space, separate land development so as to provide light and air, and act as a fire preventative. In residential areas the common right-of-way in local streets may vary from 40 to 65 feet with a street pavement width varying from 26 to 48 feet. The right-of-way width will be greater in commercial areas, usually from 60 to 100 feet, depending on parking requirements, sidewalk widths, and community layout.

The collector street gathers traffic from local streets and conducts it to main sections of the community. In most small communities

Figure 13-1 Street classification system

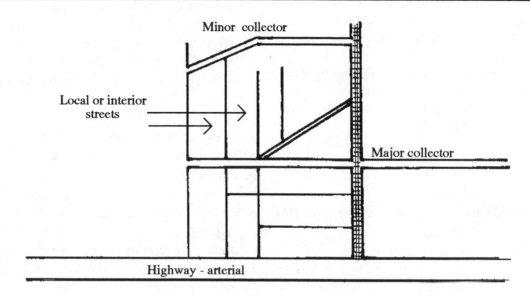

there will probably be a few collectors with most streets classified as local. Access to individual properties is a secondary function of the collector street. The right-of-way of the street should vary between 60 to 80 feet with the pavement width of 30 to 80 feet.

You should present a written description of the community street system using the above categories. The sample narrative in Exhibit 13–1 can be used as a guide.

Exhibit 13–1
Sample Narrative of Community
Street System

The city of Skyway is small enough not to have any collector streets. The numbered highways (Kansas 14 and U.S. 58) can be considered arterials, while other streets within the community can be considered local.

All traffic is funneled into the center of town, where it must go around the courthouse square. Except for large trucks, this system appears ade-

quate for current loads. According to the state highway commission, the widening of Highway 14 through the town is classified as noncritical, which means that nothing will be constructed for at least 10 years. In addition, it has not yet been determined if there will be a bypass to the east or west of Skyway or if U.S. 58 will continue to run through the edge of the community.

Most roads in the community, other than the arterials, are in need of repair. There are large potholes as well as drainage problems along most roads. The county engineer has been contacted about the drainage problem. The state highway commission receives motor vehicle revenues from Skyway. Drawing on these funds, the highway commission gives Skyway and other towns a set amount of money for each mile of local roads the jurisdiction agrees to maintain. This means that repairing and maintaining local roads is the town's responsibility.

Sidewalks run along most of Kansas Highway 14 and for a short distance along Snow Street—the major local street in the community. No other part of town has sidewalks. Eventually, it is hoped that sidewalks can be built throughout the entire town from special assessment revenues. This will be especially important for children on their way to and from school.

New roads are needed in the community if new housing or industries are to be built on the vacant lands in the northern parts of Skyway. These areas now have no interior streets.

As part of the narrative on transportation, you should survey streets and roads for the following information:

1. The total number of miles of streets.

2. The surface cover of streets in miles according to the following classifications:

- Dirt surface (number of miles).
- Rock and gravel surface (number of miles).
- Mixed bituminous (number of miles).
- Concrete (number of miles).

3. A list of all streets in the community accompanied by a condition report of each in terms of the following classifications:

- Poor: Needs major construction.
- Fair: Extensive repair of old surfaces.
- Good: Only normal maintenance needed.

In addition to this survey, you should gather information on traffic counts and trips per day in certain areas of the community. At the very least, traffic should be counted on the main road of the community that leads in and out of town. You should, however, check with the state highway commission before undertaking any counts as the commission usually has up-to-date information for most communities. On the major internal streets, traffic counts will have to be performed locally. The same street should be counted at least twice on different days of the week (Monday and Friday are often best) and an average number of trips per day should be estimated. Select the streets which have the most obvious traffic flows (collectors and arterials). Do not count traffic on short local streets.

Next, you may wish to survey the community residents to find out who travels where and for what purpose. This survey may either be mailed or conducted from door to door by volunteers. In either case, the survey should be given advance publicity in the media and a copy of the survey should be published. A suggested questionnaire is given in Figure 13–2; it was used by the Wichita-Sedgwick County Metropolitan Area Planning Department. In the comments section, the purpose of the trip, the mode of travel, and other similar information should be given.

As a final task, you should prepare a base map of the community which outlines the transportation network. Any collectors or arterials should be clearly distinguished from local streets on the map. In addition, you may wish to identify the more heavily traveled streets and, possibly, those streets which are in poor, fair, and good condition. Also, it is good practice to place the outline of any proposed streets on the map.

TRANSPORTATION AND CIRCULATION GOALS

The number and condition of local roads vary widely among small towns. Similarly, other means of transportation in and out of town will depend on public transportation and proximity to an airport, railroad, or navigable water. The following recommendations are

Figure 13-2 Sample survey question for commuters

Instructions: The purpose of this questionnaire is to determine the commuting pattern in our community. If you work outside Skyway, or generally travel to another community on a daily basis, then please indicate the average daily mileage for the driver of each vehicle.

1. Number of automobiles _____;   number of motorcycles _____
2. Number of drivers in household _____

The following should be answered by each driving family member whose primary place of employment or destination is not in Skyway. Please use the box provided to indicate if the primary destination is in Hill County or another county.

	☑	Hill County	Other County
Driver 1: My average workday driving mileage is _____		☐	☐
Driver 2: My average workday driving mileage is _____		☐	☐
Driver 3: My average workday driving mileage is _____		☐	☐
Driver 4: My average workday driving mileage is _____		☐	☐

intended to serve only as guidelines. Specific needs and desires will be different for each town.

1. Goal: Provide safe, reliable circulation within town.

2. Goal: Improve transportation links with the outside world.

3. Objective: Repair the bridge at the north end of town.

4. Objective: Add a traffic light at the corner of Main and Elm Streets.

5. Objective: Increase bus service to and from town.

6. Objective: Upgrade the local airstrip.

SUMMARY

A safe, efficient transportation system is essential to the smooth functioning of a community. The location and quality of the local street system will have a major impact on where future growth is likely to occur. Transportation links with the outside world greatly influence the potential for economic growth. Transportation costs are an important factor for new businesses and industries searching for a location. The transportation studies in this section provide a town with an assessment of how easy or difficult it is to move within town and to and from the outside world.

14

Printing and Publication of the Miniplan

The miniplan will probably go through more than one draft before it is approved by the planning commission and the governing body. An effective method of keeping the public informed and soliciting public comment is to publish a draft of the plan for widespread circulation. Ideally, this draft shows the public that its desires for the community were considered and included in the miniplan. In short, the miniplan is their plan!

An inexpensive way to publish a draft of the miniplan is to use a tabloid style on newsprint. Check with your local newspaper, commercial printers, or even local colleges about printing services.

Once the miniplan has been written and approved by the planning commission and the local governing body, you will need to publish several copies for reference and for the public.

This chapter presents advice on how to publish a town plan. After reading this chap-

ter, you should check with local sources on the cost and possible alternatives for printing the miniplan.

PRINTING AND PUBLICATION

The cheapest and most efficient way to publish the final plan is by photocopying. Check with the nearest commercial printer or duplicating service. Always quote the number of copies to be printed and the total number of pages to be duplicated when requesting price quotes because the cost per copy should decrease as the number of copies requested increases. As of early 1994, commercial photocopying costs were 3 to 4 cents per single page and 5 to 6 cents for two-sided reproduction. Color photocopying ranged between $1.00 to $1.50 per page depending on the quantity printed.

Offset printing may be used, but it is more costly. Although offset printing generally produces a higher quality publication than photocopying, the difference in quality often does not justify the extra cost. For offset printing, check with the nearest newspaper publisher, and then compare prices with other sources such as the nearest college or commercial printer. Commercial printers usually charge almost twice as much as colleges and newspapers, but the quality of work tends to be superior.

If you have compiled the miniplan on a personal computer, you may want to produce several copies on a printer. Only a 24 pin letter quality dot matrix printer, an ink jet, or a laser printer should be used; lower quality printers are only acceptable for draft copies. At least one copy should be produced by the printer and retained as the official copy.

One of the primary objectives of this handbook is to keep all costs to a minimum. All typed pages should be in large, clear letters, and all maps or illustrations should be drawn in black and white. Color reproductions certainly enhance the visibility of the plan, but they are costly to make. Black and white line drawings, when done with a degree of artistry, can be the equal of color reproductions.

Deciding on the number of plan documents to print is crucial. Copies to be distributed or sold to the public must be available through the town or county clerk or zoning administrator. Each elected official, planning commissioner, and economic development council member will need to be given a copy. Many state statutes require that a certified copy be sent to neighboring communities within the same county. There is no reason for an oversupply. Print only 30 to 40 copies for a first try; if an offset method is used, additional copies can always be printed in a week or so as the need arises. Do not make the mistake that so many towns do and end up with hundreds of copies of a 10-year-old plan. Since the miniplan must be updated at three- to five-year intervals, it is best not to hold a large number of copies on hand.

Also, it is advisable to put copies of the plan into loose-leaf binders for use by the planning commission and governing body. This will make revisions to the plan easier to do and will allow for the creation of a few new pages, rather than printing entire new copies.

Finally, remember that in addition to serving as a guide to planning commission members and elected officials, the plan has a variety of uses. The plan is also an instrument for community education, economic promotion, and public relations. Therefore, appearance and presentation are important. Ask a volunteer to sketch a local landmark that can be incorporated into a cover design. When possible, use color on the cover. This will noticeably enhance the appearance of the final plan document.

15

Miniplan: Procedure, Information, and Management

The four main ingredients in creating a useful miniplan are an open and organized process, strong community leadership, good information, and careful management of public expenses. These four ingredients are also the keys to successful town government.

How a miniplan is compiled and then put into action says much about a community. If citizen involvement is widespread and enthusiastic, chances are that the planning commission, local planner, and governing body have encouraged public participation and want to draft a miniplan that reflects public desires. On the other hand, if there is little public involvement and a lack of cooperation between the planning commission and others in town government, then the miniplan will probably not be a strong statement of the community's needs and goals.

Good planning requires a commitment to partnership! In short, everyone needs to feel that his or her voice can be heard and that the town government is genuinely committed to producing a plan that will help to make the community a better place to live. To earn this trust, local leaders must recognize that planning is vital to the community's development.

Good information is essential for a town to know where it is and where it is going. The quality of the information gathered and the time involved often depend on how many people are willing to volunteer to help. If the planning process is open to the public, then there will probably be many volunteers. These volunteers should work closely with the planning commission or the town planner (if there is one). Volunteers can also help save on the cost of the miniplan. If pointed in the right direction, volunteers can locate equally as good information as a private consultant can.

The analysis and evaluation of the information should be done by the planning commission, town planner, or, in some cases, a professional consultant. Understanding what the data say is extremely important for drafting accurate town goals and objectives. Moreover, the townspeople should be able to see how the data support the goals and objectives of the miniplan.

The plan management stage is where the plan truly comes to life both in terms of the town budget and in decisions on whether to allow certain proposed developments. Here, the success of the plan depends on how well it is implemented by the planning commission and, more importantly, by the town governing body. Public participation is needed to see that budgeting and development decisions are meeting the public goals and objectives spelled out in the plan. Also, town officials and the public must evaluate how well a plan is working and what adjustments might need to be made.

Planning procedures, information, and management are closely linked. Even though

> Planning is more than a tool or a technique; it is a philosophy for organizing action that enables people to predict and visualize their future.
> Frederick Steiner
> *The Living Landscape*, p. 24

this handbook covers planning information and procedures in detail, plan management depends on the quality of the miniplan, leadership, and the degree of public participation in each individual town. If the miniplan has been put together in an open and organized fashion with well-researched and carefully analyzed information, then the management of the plan should become somewhat obvious. Good town management requires strong leadership and a willingness to act according to a public consensus. An important part of this leadership style is persistence. Leaders must show a long-term commitment to planning, thus guaranteeing continuity and an open planning process. Both the creation of a town plan and its management should increase the level of public involvement. This, in turn, should generate a greater sense of pride and caring in the community. And the more people care about their town, the more they are determined to make it a good place to live and work.

Putting the Town Plan into Action

16

The Zoning Ordinance

The zoning ordinance, along with other land use regulations and town spending programs, serves to put the town miniplan into action. This chapter provides a guide for local officials and planning commissioners in drafting zoning regulations and evaluating development proposals. The chapter explains the purpose of a zoning ordinance and the use of zoning regulations by the planning commission, the governing body, and small town residents.

The material in this chapter rests on the assumption that your town has drafted a plan. The plan provides the basis for making your zoning regulations. If a town has a zoning ordinance but no town plan, the ordinance or decisions on development proposals may be declared invalid by the courts. Although this chapter and the following chapter on subdivision regulations offer some guidelines on how to avoid serious legal challenges, the authors do not presume to give specific legal advice. You should always consult with your town attorney or a private attorney on legal procedures and points of law.

As part of the miniplan, inventories have been made of the town's land use patterns, housing, natural environment, and public facilities. In addition, the miniplan includes a forecast of future population, economic activity, public capital improvements, and land use needs. The inventories and forecasts paint a picture of the internal and external forces which bring about change in the community. We recommend that a town adopt and implement a zoning ordinance that fits its particular needs. The role of the zoning ordinance is to shape change into orderly land use patterns and to promote healthy, manageable growth. The benefits of a zoning ordinance include minimizing incompatible land uses, economizing on the extension of public facilities, maintaining an attractive community, and encouraging economic development.

A community must be careful in adopting the form and content of a zoning ordinance. State planning and zoning enabling laws, which authorize the use of zoning on the local level, vary from state to state. Some rural governments, notably townships outside of the Northeastern states and counties in the Northeast, do not have the authority to adopt zoning regulations. However, most rural governments may enact zoning if they choose to do so; still others may be required by state law to adopt a zoning ordinance.

WHAT IS ZONING?

Zoning is the most common means of regulating local land use in the United States. Zoning gained popularity in the 1920s when many states passed planning and zoning enabling legislation, allowing cities, towns, and some counties to enact land use plans and zoning regulations. Zoning has three main purposes: (1) to separate conflicting land uses, such as industrial and residential; (2) to ensure that new development is located according to a general community plan; and (3) to promote quality development which will not harm the health, safety, and welfare of the public.

Zoning represents a balance between the right of the property owner to use land and the right of the general public to a healthy, safe, and orderly living environment. Zoning must have a tight, consistent connection to real community goals and objectives, not vaguely perceived needs. The right of the public to restrict the use of private property must be based on a well-reasoned, desired future community, as shown in a community plan.

Zoning involves separating the town into land use zones and districts. Typical zones are R-Residential, I-Industrial, C-Commercial, and P-Public. Districts refer to specific kinds of zones such as R-1 Single-family Residential and R-2 Multifamily Residential. In each district, certain land uses are permitted outright or may be permitted as conditional uses; other uses are prohibited or not listed. For instance, in a residential zone a single-family home is permitted outright, a daycare center in a single-family home may be permitted conditionally if it does not change the character of the area, but the construction of a tire sales and repair business (an intense commercial use) is likely to be prohibited.

A zoning ordinance consists of two parts—a text and a map. The text explains the different land use zones and districts, including permitted and conditional uses, minimum lot requirements, some general development standards, and how the zoning process is to be administered. The zoning map reflects the future land use map of the miniplan and shows the location of the zones and districts for different types of land uses, such as agricultural, residential, commercial, industrial, public, and conservation. Ordinances or resolutions adopting zoning refer to both the text and the map.

A zoning ordinance does not normally include nuisance regulations. A *nuisance* is a use of land that brings harm to adjacent owners or the public in general or destroys a neighbor's enjoyment of his property. Zoning was

---

Zoning reached puberty in company with the Stutz Bearcat and the speakeasy. F. Scott Fitzgerald and the Lindy Hop were products of the same generation. Of all these phenomena of the twenties, only local zoning has remained viable a generation later.

Richard Babcock, *The Zoning Game*, page 3.

originally designed to prevent such land use conflicts. But, zoning has limited ability to improve the situation once conflict is underway. A simpler solution to small town land use conflicts that lead to harm or aggravation is to adopt a set of general nuisance provisions and place them in your town ordinances. Common examples would be prohibiting vehicles with a weight of greater than one ton from parking on residential streets or forbidding the accumulation of inoperative vehicles in residential driveways. Also, most states offer communities legal support to control a wide array of nuisances such as noise, air pollution, and dangerous structures (see Chapter 19).

Zoning has not been successful in reshaping land uses and growth that have occurred in the past; this is a disappointing lesson learned by rural communities that adopted zoning regulations to deal with already existing land use problems. Typically, small towns enact zoning ordinances in reaction to some undesirable development or series of events. These developments may be manufactured homes moving to vacant lots in a neighborhood of single-family houses or the new homeowner disrupting a nearby farmer's normal operations. If your community is reacting to an event rather than moving to establish consistent quality standards for development, the problem may have a solution other than zoning. For example, a right-to-farm ordinance would protect the farmer from neighbors' nuisance suits. Nonetheless, zoning can often prevent land use problems from becoming worse.

Although zoning is not generally aimed at controlling land uses that legally existed prior to the adoption of land regulations, the ordinance can be used to prevent *nonconforming uses* or structures from being rebuilt if they are destroyed, or from being converted to another nonconforming use. For example, suppose a grocery store in a residential zone was considered a nonconforming use. If the grocery store were to burn down and the owner proposed to build a new one on the same site, the town government, under the zoning ordinance, could legally deny the owner the chance to rebuild the grocery store.

Zoning has a long history of controversy in rural America. Zoning directly affects property, and property is tightly woven with personal enjoyment, profit, and perceptions of basic rights. For many Americans, a house, business building, or land is the single largest and most important investment they will ever make. Hence, the future expected value of that property is of utmost importance. Because zoning allows certain uses on some land and not on others, zoning can bestow economic benefits, or *windfalls,* to some property owners and impose economic losses, or *wipeouts,* on others. For example, a landowner in an industrial zone can sell land for a new factory and make a substantial profit. On the other side of town, another landowner in a residential zone cannot sell land for a new factory but only for new housing and thus cannot make as much profit as the first landowner.

Zoning has been accepted by the courts as a valid use of the police power of government, because by separating potentially conflicting land uses (such as heavy industrial and residential), zoning is intended to protect the public health, safety, and welfare. However, this does not mean that every specific zoning provision will withstand a legal challenge. For this reason and others, the planning commission should be encouraged to attend seminars and training sessions which discuss legal challenges to zoning and basic zoning procedures.

There are four major areas of legal concern for any community involved in zoning. The first concern is that the zoning ordinance might run afoul of constitutional right to free speech found in the First Amendment. Provisions adopted to control aesthetics, especially sign regulations, are particularly vulnerable. Advertising and appearance are forms of speech. Challenges frequently arise when a regulation goes farther than what is reasonable or necessary to obtain a consistent standard of community appearance or behavior. For example, a community might attempt to tightly regulate business or roadside signs but be lenient toward political, religious, or popular protest signs.

The second area of legal concern centers on what is commonly called the *taking issue*. The Fifth Amendment prohibits government from taking private property unless it is for a public purpose and just compensation is paid. Normally, we assume that when private land is taken for a public purpose, such as a road or park, the landowner will be fairly compensated. However, a taking may arise from land use regulations that deprive a property owner of virtually all economic value of the property.

Two more areas of concern stem from the Fourteenth Amendment to the U.S. Constitution. One is called *due process*, which governs the substance and conduct of all government regulations. Due process requires that governments treat people fairly and reasonably. The restrictions imposed by zoning regulations must be reasonable; they must be based on actual needs and not on arbitrary or unrealistic standards. In administering the zoning regulations, the local government must treat people fairly; likewise, the planning commission must hold fair hearings. Failure to give proper notices of hearings or failure to follow procedures set down in enabling statutes are examples of violations of due process.

The final legal concern is grounded in the *equal protection clause* of the Fourteenth Amendment. This clause requires that governments treat all people the same unless there is a valid purpose for dissimilar treatment. The equal protection clause is especially stringent when it comes to prohibiting discrimination by race, creed, color, disability, national origin, or gender.

The first major constitutional challenge to a local zoning ordinance came in a case heard before the United States Supreme Court: *Village of Euclid, Ohio* v. *Ambler Realty Co.* [272 U.S. 365, 1926]. The village of Euclid was a small town in the early 1920s but was feeling development pressure from its urban neighbor, Cleveland. Ambler Realty owned a tract of land in Euclid near a railroad. This company planned to use the property for industrial development, but the district zoning regulations restricted the property to residential structures. Ambler Realty argued that, contrary to the Fourteenth Amendment, Euclid's zoning ordinance unlawfully restricted the use of the land, and it confiscated and destroyed most of the value of the property. In response, the U.S. Supreme Court reasoned that the zoning restriction on private property was justified as a legitimate use of government police power to protect the public welfare. The zoning ordinance was reasonable and was not an arbitrary rule.

CREATING A ZONING ORDINANCE

The elected governing body must start the process for creating a zoning ordinance, just as the governing body must approve the effort to create a town plan (see Figure 16–1). The governing body first appoints a planning commission to oversee the drafting of the plan. The planning enabling legislation of your state requires that the planning commission be properly appointed (and in some cases elected) before the zoning ordinance is prepared. The planning commission will have the power to draft or supervise the drafting of the zoning ordinance and will make recommendations on the ordinance to the governing body. The main difference between developing the town plan and the zoning ordinance is that the town plan can generally be researched and written by nonprofessionals, whereas the zoning ordinance should be written by a professional planner.

At the very least, a professional planner should read, comment on, and make final corrections to the draft ordinances. An attorney should be asked to review the final draft and examine the procedures used to adopt the zoning ordinance.

If a planning consultant is hired to prepare the entire zoning ordinance, costs may range from a few thousand dollars to tens of thousands of dollars depending on (1) the size of the town, (2) how much information must be gathered, (3) the size of the consulting firm hired (large firms tend to have large overhead costs), and (4) whether the consultant will be asked to attend all meetings involving the review and adoption of the zoning ordinance.

Charges for reading, reviewing, or revising the zoning ordinance should be considerably less, depending on the amount of change necessary (see Exhibit 16–1).

The planning commission can recommend the hiring of a planning staff or a professional consultant to the governing body, but the governing body has the final say on who gets hired and for how much money. The smaller the town, the less need there is for a full-time planning staff. Generally, towns of fewer than 2,500 people do not need a full-time planner but can rely on planning consultants or planners in government agencies as the need arises.

One excellent method of obtaining a staff planner is the circuit rider or shared staff. Two, and possibly three, towns or even counties can share the cost of a staff planner. This individual then allocates time based on the cost share of each government. The shared planner attends the planning commission meetings of each jurisdiction, helps with the preparation of land regulations and amendments, and prepares reports and recommendations for each planning commission.

The planning staff or consultant prepares a draft of the zoning ordinance and submits it to the planning commission for public review and comment. The planning commission may make changes to the zoning ordinance and recommend approval or rejection of the ordinance to the governing body. The governing body will study the ordinance, hold a public hearing, and may make changes to the ordinance. Finally, the governing body officially adopts the zoning ordinance and zoning map, and publishes them, and they become law.

Figure 16-1 The process for creating a zoning ordinance

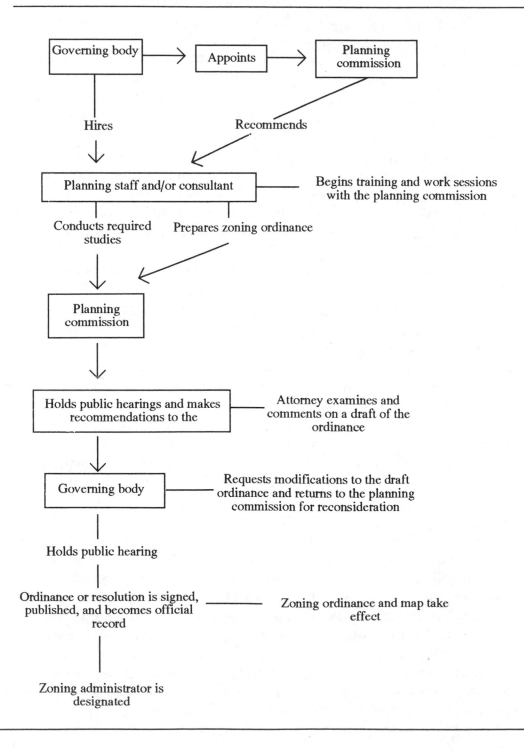

Resources You Will Need

We realize that a planning commission may want to help write its own zoning ordinance. The planning commission is the board that will be working with the zoning regulations for decades to come. From this standpoint, it is better to have the opportunity to correct your own mistakes than to live with the mistakes of someone who will have no connection with local planning and zoning. Finally, the planning commission needs to understand how the regulations are created, administered, and defended. The planning commission drafted the town plan and will be most closely involved in implementing the plan through the zoning regulations.

Three resources are needed to produce a zoning ordinance: correct statutory authority; an example of a good zoning ordinance; and a way to publish the ordinance for review, distribution, and amendment.

First, obtain a complete set of your state's enabling statutes on land development regulations. These will include all the statutes (annotated version) on zoning, subdivision, roads, plats, and mandatory planning requirements. Often, all the land development statutes are published together in adjoining chapters or articles, but you may encounter situations where they are spread throughout the statute books. Remember that statutes are frequently revised, so be sure to check in the supplemental or pocket part versions of the statutes for recent changes or additions. The state law books can almost always be found at the town hall, the county courthouse, or the regional public library. State laws have never been known for their readability, and it is advisable to obtain a reorganized, anno-

tated, and even illustrated copy of the state zoning enabling law. Such a copy is available in each of the 50 states, most often from the league of municipalities, the state chamber of commerce, and the state chapter of the National Association of County Governments. Other sources for state zoning enabling legislation include the cooperative extension service, the state legislative research department, the regional planning agency or council of governments, the local bar association, the district state's attorney's office, local or state real estate associations, and the nearest city planning and zoning department.

Land development statutes are commonly republished as a group by state planning agencies, the state league of municipalities, association of townships or counties, and professional societies such as your state's chapter of the American Planning Association. Make a photocopy of all statutes for each member of the planning commission and anyone else involved in drafting the zoning ordinance.

The next assignment is to read the state statutes. This will be your guide to who does what, when, how, and where. The statutes leave little room for interpretation; if it does not say that you may do something, then you must assume that it is not authorized. If your state grants broad home rule powers to local governments, then you should have your attorney explain to the planning commission about the use and meaning of home rule procedures.

All state enabling legislation will contain some variation of the following:

Entitlement. State zoning enabling legislation defines which local governments have the authority to enact zoning regulations. Nearly all cities, towns, and counties (including boroughs and parishes) may enact zoning regulations. Generally, townships (except in the Northeastern states) and other forms of local government, such as special districts, may not adopt zoning ordinances.

Studies. State zoning enabling legislation commonly requires that a jurisdiction complete and adopt a land use study and/or a comprehensive plan before drafting a zoning ordinance. In certain states, Florida and New Jersey for example, the plan must be consistent with the goals established by the state. You should find out whether a study or plan has been completed and whether it was adopted by a resolution of the governing body. A study or plan is not a law but either one must be formally adopted to be deemed official. Failure to have an officially adopted plan or a study will place the entire zoning process in jeopardy. A competent attorney will ask for a copy of the plan or will study the adoption resolution (properly dated and certified) as a first step in challenging a zoning regulation. If the adoption resolution for the town plan or study does not exist, the zoning regulation may be declared invalid by the courts.

In addition, there must be proof that the town planning commission has been properly created. In nearly all states, planning commission members are appointed by the governing body for a certain period of time. Many states have legislation limiting the number of members on a planning commission who have the same occupation. Usually a planning commission member must reside in the jurisdiction which is enacting the zoning regulations. However, it is not uncommon to have one or two residents from the county serve on the town planning commission. All

The Attorney

Ask the governing body to make an attorney available while you are preparing the land development regulations. The planning commission will benefit when you schedule several informal work sessions with the attorney.

Very few attorneys have expertise in land development regulations—many know less about drafting these regulations than a good planning commissioner with a few years of experience. But, attorneys are helpful when specific language or interpretation is at stake. Many state planning and zoning enabling statutes are ambiguous and require explanation. Also, land regulations may conflict with common due process requirements, property rights, and civil rights. Advice on how to minimize these conflicts is the domain of the attorney.

commission members must be from the proper jurisdiction, the term of their appointment must be current, and there must be resolutions of the governing body attesting to these facts.

Although the planning commission should be cautious about using the zoning regulations of another town, there is no substitute for a good working example. Some state planning offices have model zoning ordinances available; the state association of cities and towns may also be of help. The planning commission should try to obtain current zoning ordinances from other towns or counties. Generally, avoid using ordinances that are more than 10 years old and try to obtain ordinances from towns that are about the same size as yours. A town of 2,000 residents has little use for the regulations of a city of 50,000. Gather several zoning ordinances and compare different sections of the ordinances with the requirements of the state zoning enabling legislation. The purpose of obtaining these sample regulations is twofold. First, it is difficult, if not impossible, to produce a zoning ordinance until you see an actual well-drafted ordinance. Second, a good example will show you how to organize, illustrate, and structure your ordinance. The purpose is not to copy the zoning regulations of another municipality. You should draft a zoning ordinance for your community that meets local needs.

You will need a good word processing program and someone who will type all of your drafts and the final zoning ordinance into a computer. Constructing zoning regulations typically involves many drafts and changes. Working copies need to be sent to your attorney, governing body, and other public boards and agencies. In addition, the zoning ordinance is a living document that will need frequent changes and amendments even after it has been formally adopted. This is exactly the type of work where a computer is helpful.

Many local governments that use zoning have some desk references or subscribe to zoning periodicals. These references are further described in the bibliography at the back of the handbook. Four excellent reference books on zoning are *The Practice of Local Government Planning* (especially Chapter 15), edited by Frank So, Israel Stollman, Frank Beal, and David Arnold; *Winning at Zoning* by Dudley Hinds; *Strategy and Tactics in Municipal Zoning* by Clan Crawford, Jr.; and *The Zoning Board Manual* by Frederick Bair. *Zoning News* is a monthly report of the latest zoning techniques available from the American Planning Association. *Land Use Law and Zoning Digest*, also available from the American Planning Association, is an excellent source for

legal cases involving zoning, especially for larger towns. Another excellent source for the latest in zoning cases and techniques is the *Zoning and Planning Law Report*, published by the Clark Boardman Company. This is available both monthly and as a summary of yearly events. Many of the topics deal directly with small town planning and zoning issues.

If the state university or a nearby private university has a department of community planning, the planning commission should call and ask if help is available for the preparation of a zoning ordinance. Community planning departments commonly require their students to prepare town plans, land use ordinances, and studies (under instructor supervision) as part of their degree program.

Another possible source of assistance is the state chapter of the American Planning Association. Some state chapters will help small communities as part of their service programs. In the Western states, the Western Planners Association is quite active in providing small towns with planning assistance. Many states also have an association of zoning and building code administrators which can lend valuable technical advice. Any of these associations can be located by calling the nearest large community with a city planning department.

The planning commission should also contact the department in your state government in charge of community planning and development to find out if help is available for preparing zoning regulations. If formal help is not offered, the planning commission should at least request that a state employee visit the community and speak to the commission and governing body about the use of zoning, different experiences with zoning throughout the state, and additional resources that might be useful. The regional council of governments and county planning office may also be helpful.

Exhibit 16–1
A Note on the Use of Planning Consultants

Planning consultants can be of great help to a town by drafting plans and ordinances and preparing grant applications and technical documents. Planning consultants are often associated with architectural or engineering firms. Every state, however, has small firms which specialize in planning for small towns and rural areas.

There are no state or national standards for planning consultants, but some states do have registration requirements for planners. The American Planning Association (APA) has standards to accredit planners, who must pass a test and an evaluation of education and experience to become members of the American Institute of Certified Planners (AICP). But AICP standards are very urban oriented and do not necessarily indicate an ability for working on rural and small town planning issues. Membership in the APA does not mean a planner has been accredited by the APA. It only means that a person has paid the membership dues.

You may want to contact other communities in your area, the county planning office, regional council of governments, or state planning office for a list of planning consultants. Otherwise, you can advertise in government journals or contact your state's chapter of the American Planning Association for recommendations on a consultant. You can also contact the community planning department at the nearest university and request the phone numbers of professional planning organizations.

In hiring a planning consultant, your town should be careful to check out the consultant's educational background and experience. Although membership in the AICP or affiliation with a professional society are not crucial, graduation from an accredited master's program in planning is very important. Some universities also offer an undergraduate degree in planning. It is preferable to hire a planner with a successful track record of working with small towns. You should ask the consultant for samples of previous work in small towns and rural areas and contact towns in which the consultant has worked.

Once you have decided to hire a consultant, have the town attorney draw up a contract specifying (1) the work the consultant is expected to perform, (2) the due dates of the work, and (3) the amount and schedule of payments and the procedure of payment. The consultant should bill in installments while the work is being performed, with the final payment (20 percent or more) due when the finished product is submitted. You should also decide whether payment should be made according to hours worked or the complete job. The complete job approach is recommended because it provides a definite figure of total cost.

Costs for planning consultants will vary depending on the size of the town and how much work is required. It is impossible for us to estimate a cost range without knowing the services your community will require and the history of professional services in your region. A zoning ordinance may cost from $2,500 up to $20,000 depending on the size of the town and whether the ordinance needs only to be updated or drafted from scratch. Although the lowest cost may be most appealing, make sure that you understand what you are getting for the price. A good consultant will provide training for your planning commission while the ordinance is being prepared. Training is expensive, but necessary.

If you are satisfied with the work a consultant has done on the town plan or zoning ordinance, you may want to retain the consultant for help in updating the town plan, conducting land use studies, or changing the zoning ordinance.

Finally, the land use section and future land use map of the miniplan should be referred to while drafting the zoning ordinance. The land use plan provides a key link between town planning and land use regulation. The land use section includes a survey of existing land uses, identifies conflicting land uses (industrial and residential uses), and indicates where new development should be located in the future. The zoning regulations then follow to give the community choices on how land use patterns might change over time, how compromises might be made over land use conflicts, and how the community might take best advantage of future growth opportunities.

The Language of Zoning

Zoning jargon must be understood before writing a zoning ordinance. Many of these terms are included in the glossary at the back of this book. A source often used by small town planners is *The Language of Zoning* by Michael Meshenberg, available from the Planning Advisory Service of the American Planning Association.

Zoning involves the creation of zones and districts. A zone is a broad land use category, such as a commercial zone or a residential zone. A *zone* denotes that a certain land area mainly contains or is planned to contain similar land uses. A *district* fits inside the broader zone and specifies the density level which will be permitted. For instance, a residential zone in a small town will generally contain three districts: a single-family district, a two- and three-family dwelling district, and a multifamily dwelling district.

Zones and districts are commonly designated by a system of letters and numbers. Keep the system simple and logical. For ex-

ample, R stands for residential; C for commercial; M or I for manufacturing or industrial; A for agricultural; and P for public use. The district designation is usually a number that follows the zone letter: R-1, A-1, C-1, and so on. The numbers tell the density of development permitted within the district with the higher the number the greater the density of buildings allowed. For instance, R-1 indicates a residential zone and a single-family district; R-3 refers to a multifamily residential zone. M-1 would be a light manufacturing district, M-2 a heavy manufacturing district (see Figure 16–3).

The concept of *use* is very important in zoning. A zoning district allows only certain uses of the land and buildings. The R-1 district, for example, might permit only single-family dwellings and perhaps a few other neighborhood uses such as parks or small in-home businesses. These are called *permitted uses, uses by right,* or *outright permitted uses* because they are specifically listed in the zoning ordinance and are allowed outright with no conditions attached.

Certain other uses, such as schools, churches, a small grocery store, or laundromat, might be allowed in the R-1 district but only if they meet special conditions listed in the standards for the zoning district. Such uses are called *conditional uses.* The applicant must meet these conditions before the town issues a *conditional use permit* or a building permit. Once the applicant meets the conditions listed for the zoning district, the land use is no longer conditional; it now becomes a permitted use. Conditional use standards should be clear and objective. Because the conditional use standards are spelled out in the zoning ordinance, town officials cannot

Table 16-1   Common zoning designations and districts used in small towns/rural areas

Zone	Designation	District 1	District 2	District 3	District 4
R	Residential	Single family	Two and three family	Four - six family	Multi family
C/B	Commercial/business	Center business	Service	Heavy/intensive	Highway use
M	Manufacturing	Light	General	Heavy	Exclusive
I	Industrial	Light	General	Heavy	Exclusive
I	Institutional	x	x	x	x
P	Public	x	x	x	x
FP	Flood plain overlay	Floodway	500 year		x
PO	Protection overlay	x	x		x
A	Agricultural	AgriFarming	Rural use	Undesignated	Resource extraction
AB	Agri-business	Retail	Resource/storage	Rural center/village	
AM	Agri-manufacturing	Light	Moderate processing	Processing	x
AR	Agri-residential	Large lot	Minimum lot	Heavy processing	x
MH	Manufactured housing Park	x	x	x	x
PUD	Planned unit development	x	x	x	x
PURD	Planned unit rural development	x	x	x	x
O	Overlay	Historic	x	x	x

impose new conditions on an applicant without amending the zoning ordinance.

A *nonconforming land use* refers to a land use, lot, or structure that existed prior to the adoption or amendment of the zoning ordinance and no longer conforms to current land use, lot, or structure requirements. Some communities have dropped the nonconforming terminology and refer to them as *previously legally conforming uses*. A nonconforming land use is allowed to remain under a *grandfather clause* in the zoning ordinance. At the same time, the property owners are generally not allowed to expand the nonconforming land use or structure, change to another nonconforming use, or move that use to another location within the same district. If the nonconforming land use or structure is destroyed, it may or may not be permitted to be rebuilt. The rebuilding of a nonconforming structure might be permitted if the new structure's dimensions do not exceed those of the original structure. Some communities place the additional restriction that if the nonconforming use ceases operation for a period of six to twelve months, the property loses the nonconforming use right.

Exhibit 16–2
A Note on Nonconforming Uses

Nonconforming uses can pose very real problems in a small community. An actual example occurred in a town of 1,800 people with a manufacturing firm located in a building previously used by a car dealer in a residential area. The firm employed 80 workers and manufactured steel trailers. The production process involved welding, painting, storage, and considerable noise. The firm had grown from a small business of two people in an old building. The building was surrounded by single-family houses on two sides, the central business district on one side, and an elderly care center on the other. As the firm became more economically important to the community, it also became more of a nuisance to the nearby neighborhood.

When the town adopted a zoning ordinance, the neighborhood was classified as single-family residential. The manufacturing firm became a nonconforming use. When the firm wanted to expand slightly for a storage and new painting area, neighborhood residents correctly pointed out that the zoning regulations did not allow a nonconforming use to expand. The planning commission and governing body were then faced with either following or ignoring their own regulations. This situation often happens in small towns.

Bending zoning regulations is not the way to handle this type of situation. The community first amended its comprehensive plan to include a discussion of the need to address restrictions on nonconforming uses. The zoning ordinance was then amended to permit expansions conditionally if they would not increase the level of activity on the site. In this particular case, the painting building and new storage area were an improvement for the neighborhood. But then town officials worked with the county's economic development director, and within five years the business relocated to the edge of town in a small industrial area. Industrial revenue bonds were used to aid in the financing, and the town supplied the roads. This solution is much better than the town's initial decision, which was to adopt an amortization policy to allow the manufacturing firm to continue to operate without expanding for 10 to 20 years before it must cease operation and conform to the single-family district zoning regulations.

A public discussion of nonconforming uses often produces a major struggle over whether to adopt zoning regulations. Although provisions to accommodate nonconforming uses may attempt to be fair, these provisions may seem unfair to citizens who believe they have a right to do whatever they want to with their property. The strategy in small town zoning regulation has been to handle nonconforming uses in only a superficial way. While this is not correct from a legal standpoint, it is practical in making zoning politically acceptable. Typically, the town officials allow a nonconforming use to retain its right, even if the nonconforming use is destroyed.

ELEMENTS TO BE INCLUDED IN THE ZONING ORDINANCE

Zoning regulations are a set of rules about how land and buildings are used. The purpose of the zoning ordinance is to describe the different land use zones, to explain the regulations that apply in each district, and to set up procedures for administering and changing the zoning ordinance. Because the zoning ordinance helps to put the town plan into action, the zoning ordinance includes a mixture of legal definitions, standards, policy statements, and procedures to guide both local officials and property owners in the development and growth of the town. Figure 16–2 presents a sample of what should be included in the zoning ordinance. The language of the ordinance should be clear and concise.

Legal Framework

The legal framework explains the purpose of the zoning ordinance, how it is enacted, how it is to be interpreted, the legal limits of the ordinance, and the definition of specific terms in the ordinance. The *enactment clause* cites the authority for adopting the zoning ordinance under state enabling legislation. This includes the time and date of the public hearings and the resolution of the local governing body adopting the zoning regulations. This section should also contain a *severability clause* indicating that if one or more parts of the zoning ordinance are ruled invalid by the courts, the entire ordinance will not be invalid. This clause protects the town from having to draft an entirely new ordinance, a costly and time-consuming process.

The *jurisdiction clause* defines where the ordinance applies. The jurisdiction of the zoning ordinance may vary among communities, depending on whether the community has extraterritorial powers. These powers may be granted by the state government to allow a town to zone land or participate with the county in zoning land beyond its boundaries (usually up to two or three miles). In this way, a town can control sprawl or developments locating just beyond the town boundaries that may cause conflicts or burdens on town services. Many towns have no extraterritorial powers and the zoning ordinance applies only to land within the incorporated town boundaries.

Finally, the zoning definitions are very important elements of the zoning ordinance. All words and phrases in the ordinance which have a special legal meaning must be defined exactly. Consult the references mentioned in the Language of Zoning section.

The Zoning Map

The zoning map provides an important illustration of the location and size of different land use zones and districts. Each zone and district listed in the zoning districts (see Figure 16–2) must be identified on the zoning map. For example, the A-1 designation on the map identifies the agricultural district, M-1 is

Figure 16–2   Typical organization and contents of a small town/rural zoning ordinance

1. Introduction, Goals, and Purpose
2. Title, Authority, and Adoption
    2.1 Title
    2.2 Statutory authority
    2.3 Interpretation
    2.4 Overlapping and conflicting regulations
    2.5 Violations, fines and penalties
    2.6 Schedule of fees
    2.7 Notice of adoption of ordinance
    2.8 Establishing zoning districts
    2.9 Adoption of zoning maps
    2.8 Jurisdiction of ordinance

3. General Provisions
    3.1 Duties of the zoning administrator
    3.2 Building permits
    3.3 Obtaining building permits
    3.4 Unlawful acts
    3.5 Exemptions
    3.6 Accessory uses and buildings
    3.7 Previously legal conforming uses

4. Organization, Appeals and Special Procedures
    4.1 Duties of the Planning Commission
    4.2 Meetings, conduct and disqualifications
    4.3 The conduct of public hearings
    4.4 Application for changes to text and map
    4.5 Required findings
    4.6 Criteria for conditional uses
    4.7 Hearings before the governing body
    4.8 Creation of the Board of Appeals (Adjustment)
    4.9 Duties of the Board of Appeals
        4.91 Appeals
        4.92 Variances
        4.93 Exceptions
        4.94 Special Uses
    4.10 Right of appeals
    4.11 Representatives and agents
    4.12 Responsibilities of applicants

5. Residential Zoning Districts
    5.1 R-1 Single family districts
        1. Permitted uses
        2. Conditional uses
        3. District requirements
    5.2 R-2 Two and three family districts
        1. Permitted uses
        2. Conditional uses
        3. District requirements
    5.3 R-3 Multi-family districts
        1. Permitted uses
        2. Conditional uses
        3. District requirements
    5.4 Planned unit development districts
        1. Permitted Uses
        2. Application procedures
        3. Final plan approval
    5.5 Manufactured Homes Park District
        1. Permitted uses
        2. Conditional uses
        3. District requirements
        4. Licenses

6. Commercial Zoning Districts
    6.1 Light commercial districts
        1. Permitted uses
        2. Conditional uses
        3. District requirements
    6.2 General service commercial districts
        1. Permitted uses
        2. Conditional uses
        3. District requirements
    6.3 Planned commercial districts
        1. Permitted uses
        2. Application procedures
        3. Final plan approval
    6.4 Site plans in commercial districts
        1. Contents of plans
        2. Filing and approval process

7. Industrial Districts
    7.1 Light Industrial Districts
        1. Permitted uses
        2. Conditional uses
        3. District requirements
    7.2 General Industrial Districts
        1. Permitted uses
        2. Conditional uses
        3. District requirements
    7.3 Restricted Industrial Districts
        1. Permitted uses
        2. Conditional uses
        3. District requirements
        4. Required plans and specifications

8. Special Purpose Overlay Districts
    8.1 Institutional district overlay
        1. Permitted uses
        2. Conditional uses
        3. District requirements
    8.2 Historic district overlay
        1. Permitted uses
        2. Conditional uses
        3. District requirements
    8.3 Floodplain district overlay
        1. Specifications
        2. Map amendments
        3. Variances

9. General Sign Regulations
    9.1 Intent and purposes
    9.2 Required permits
    9.3 Permitted and prohibited signs
    9.4 Signable areas; computation of area

10. General Requirements
    10.1 Home occupations
    10.2 Table of substitutions and changes
    10.3 Special permits
    10.4 Temporary uses
    10.5 Publication and Notice

11. Definitions

Figure 16-3 Zoning map of Westmoreland, Kansas

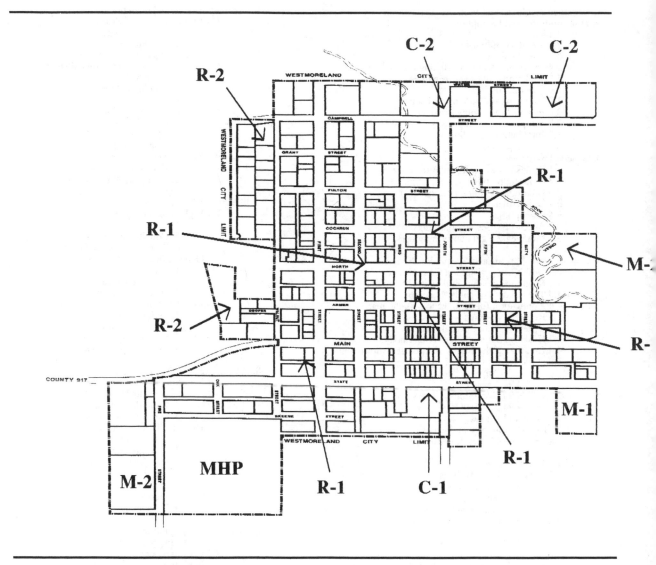

the manufacturing/industrial district, and so on. There may be different densities of development within a land use zone but these will generally require different districts; for instance, the R-1 residential zone is the district for single-family houses and duplexes while the R-2 residential zone is the district for multifamily housing. An example of a small town zoning map is shown in Figure 16–3.

The zoning map must be consistent with the future land use plan map of the miniplan but may contain more detail. The zoning map must clearly show the exact boundaries between zones. Over time, it is likely that changes will be made in the zoning ordinance, and these changes will create new zone boundary lines. The zoning map must be kept up to date to reflect the changes in the zoning ordinance.

The zoning map should have a title indicating the name of the town, the date the map was officially adopted, and the dates of any amendments to the map. The map should be drawn to a scale of between 800 feet to the inch and one-half mile to the inch. A base map like those used in the miniplan should be adequate. The zoning map should also include an arrow indicating the north direction and a legend and legal description of municipal boundaries and zone boundaries.

The amount of land in each zone or district will depend on the character of the town and expected population and economic growth identified in the miniplan. Towns of fewer than 2,500 people will tend to have more land in agricultural zones; larger towns will tend to have more commercial and industrial land. Typically, residential uses will comprise the largest zone, about 30 to 40 percent of the town; streets, sidewalks, and rights-of-way will take up about 20 percent of the total; public and institutional uses, 15 percent; commercial uses, only 5 percent; industrial uses, 5 to 15 percent; and agricultural land and open space, 10 to 30 percent of the town.

Be careful not to zone too much land for a particular use. This often happens when a town wants to attract industry and zones a large amount of land (for example, 400 acres) I-1 for industrial use. The amount of land zoned for industrial use is not as important as other factors, such as the location of the site, the proximity to the town's sewer and water system, accessibility to transportation networks, and the physical capacity of the site to support development.

Zoning should be consistent and maintain the integrity of neighborhoods. The C-1 commercial property noted in Figure 16–4 is a *spot zone* in the middle of an R-1 residential zone. If a commercial use existed on the C-1 parcel before zoning was implemented, the commercial use could be considered a preexisting nonconforming use and allowed to continue as long as there is no expansion of the commercial use. If there is currently no structure on the C-1 lot, the C-1 designation would give an unfair advantage to the C-1 landowner over the neighboring R-1 owners. While a commercial use may be desirable (such as a small grocery store), the proper procedure would be to allow a mixed use (residential/commercial development) or allow the grocery store to be built and carried as a nonconforming use.

In small towns and rural areas, it is not uncommon to allow a grocery store in a residential district, whereas it may be difficult for a landowner to receive permission to build a grocery store in a residential district in a suburban community. The issue often comes down to a matter of space and impact on neighboring property values. A small town tends to have ample space, and a grocery store would generally have little adverse impact on nearby property values.

If the proposed use is not listed under conditional uses or special exceptions allowed in the zone, the remaining alternative is *spot zoning*. This should be permitted only where there is a demonstrated public need for the proposed use that cannot reasonably be met elsewhere. If a spot zoning is allowed, the land use map of the miniplan and the zoning map should be amended. This way, the possibility of favoritism by the planning commission and governing body is likely to be reduced. If one or a few landowners are shown favor through spot zoning and this cannot be justified by the town plan, then the spot zoning may be found to be illegal by the courts. An example of spot zoning is shown in Figure 16–4.

The Zoning Districts

The zoning districts section should list the different districts, briefly describe the purpose of each district, and explain the permitted uses

and conditional uses and development standards in each district. Keep in mind that zoning regulations and standards may vary from zone to zone, but within each district the ordinance must be uniformly applied.

It is important to have an understanding of what land uses should go in the different zones and districts. Many towns have an *A-1 agricultural district* which allows farming, ranching, and agricultural-related uses. In a number of communities, this district may include forestry, mining, and quarrying. Towns normally permit most types of agricultural activity in the A-1 district subject to nuisance

Figure 16-4 Spot zoning example

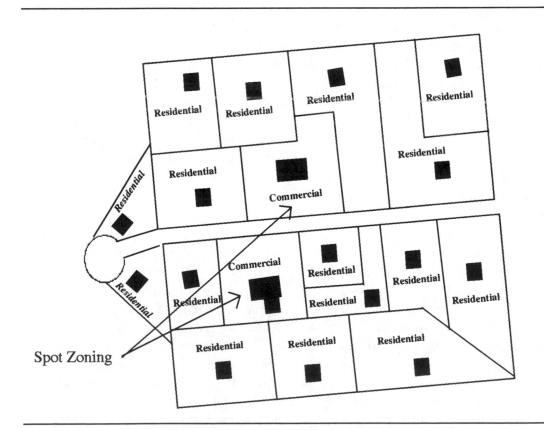

restrictions against keeping livestock near residential areas. Some towns may find it useful to have an A-2 agricultural district for agri-manufacturing and processing and farm-support businesses. These businesses include farm machinery dealerships and repair shops, grain drying, livestock breeding, food processing, and quarrying. Often these businesses are similar to heavy industrial uses and should be located in rural areas away from the community.

While the A-1 district permits and protects agricultural uses, the primary function of this zone is to keep undeveloped land in a large-lot holding pattern with a minimum lot size of 5 to 20 acres. This pattern allows for low-density development and extension of services when farmland is ready to be developed. Agricultural lands not intended for eventual development should not be annexed by the town or zoned for nonfarm uses. The town should also consider de-annexing agricultural land (that is, returning the land to county jurisdiction) if the land is on the edge of town.

The *R-1 single-family residential district* is the most common district in virtually every community that has a zoning ordinance. The R-1 district allows a very limited number of land uses. This district is popular among middle- and upper-class residents as a means of protecting their property investment, their family and lifestyle values, and the neighborhood identity. The purpose of an R-1 single-family residential district might be described as follows: "The purpose of this district is to provide for low-density single-family residences and to provide for certain private and public facilities and services that are compatible with neighborhood surroundings."

The R-1 residential zone might also state that single-family dwellings are permitted outright as long as they meet a minimum lot standard of 8,000 square feet with a lot width of at least 65 feet, side yards of 10 feet, a front yard of 15 feet, a rear yard of 10 feet, and a height of no more than 60 feet. Other permitted uses will have other lot and building dimension standards.

The *R-2 residential district* is usually created for one- and two-family residences and may also include dwellings for three to five families. But, seldom does a small town contain blocks of duplex or triplex housing. Commonly, small towns zone older sections of the community R-2 for rental units or small apartments, and zone newer areas R-1 to prevent most residential rentals.

A town can use the *R-3 residential district* for small apartment complexes or a townhouse style development. Small towns frequently use this district for young couples, public housing, apartments for the elderly, and the increasingly popular retirement complexes where single-family cottages, duplexes, and nursing care facilities are incorporated into one development.

Town planners classify manufactured housing into two types. One type of manufactured home conforms to standard building codes which are based on state or national model codes, such as the *Uniform Building Code*. Common names for these dwelling units are precut, modular homes, sectional, component, or panelized homes. The degree of on-site assembly varies considerably for each type of unit. This type of manufactured home is considered the same as a single-family residence by most states and communities. Many states prohibit towns from excluding this type of manufactured housing from single-family residential zones.

The second type of manufactured home is factory built to a uniform national standard called the HUD (U.S. Department of Housing and Urban Development) code. This unit is almost always called a *mobile home* by local governments, but manufacturers have attempted for years to dispel that image.

An *MH district* for manufactured housing is known as a mobile home park district and is created to accommodate traditional single-family manufactured homes. The mobile home park is essentially a rental neighborhood.

Some towns use the MH district to indicate a mobile home subdivision, which is an addition to the community and consists of privately owned lots. This district allows both types of manufactured housing. It is a popular land planning regulation in resort areas.

Small town planners normally designate from one to three districts for commercial land uses. The most popular is the *C-1 central business district.* The central business district remains a pedestrian oriented trade area. Drive-in food outlets, automobile service businesses, warehouses, and used car lots are not appropriate uses in this zone.

The economic health of the central business district is a major concern in a small town. There are three ways that zoning can help. First, whenever possible, the C-1 district should incorporate government offices, discount chain stores, and other types of businesses that attract large numbers of people. In many towns, chain stores have located on the edge of town or in outlying malls and have drawn a substantial amount of business away from the center of town. In some communities, there may not be enough vacant land

downtown to put a large discount store. Do not ignore the possibility of creating vacant land by demolishing old and abandoned buildings. Second, if the discount store insists on locating outside of the central business district, consider a second C-1 district for the store in an area that brings traffic to the discount store through the central business area rather than around it. Third, if businesses with a large volume of customers are specifically excluded from other commercially zoned areas of town, the central business district can remain or again become vitally active.

A *C-2 district* often includes professional and semiprofessional land uses such as doctors' offices and real estate firms. These businesses require good access to major streets and highways. Such a district can be applied to undeveloped land or to older residential neighborhoods on busy streets where residences can be rehabilitated.

Some towns have a third commercial district, *C-3,* for development on main highways leading into and out of town. These car-related land uses are also called *strip developments* and include fast food restaurants, gas stations, used car lots, and shopping centers. Strip developments tend to compete with the central business district. Towns generally should try to limit the size and type of development along major highways. The C-3 district can require design standards, a landscaping standard of 10 percent of each property, and a limited number of access points (driveways) to the major highway.

Some small towns have two manufacturing districts. The *M-1 district* is for light manufacturing and industrial uses where all or nearly all activity is contained within a single building. Light manufacturing does not require extensive loading and unloading facilities or much outside storage. Normally the effects of the industrial operation cannot be detected beyond the boundaries of the property. Such effects include smoke, noise, glare, dust, and odors. Many light industries are good candidates for industrial parks.

The *general-to-heavy manufacturing and industrial district, M-2,* will contain most of the fabrication, processing, storage, and assembly operations in the community. These uses involve a great deal of activity and storage outside of buildings; large doors are often open; there may be noise, light, heat, smoke, dust, and odors detected beyond the property lines. Also, the hours of operation may fall outside of the normal nine to five routine. An operation may begin very early in the morning and continue late into the evening.

The *planned unit development (PUD)* or *planned development district (PDD)* is a very versatile tool for small towns. It can be used for residential, commercial, industrial, or institutional uses, and it is often used to mix a number of land uses (called mixed-use development) that would not be possible under a conventional zoning ordinance. A planned development district can help to minimize the undesirable impacts that one land use can have on another, and at the same time it can bring a more efficient and desirable land use pattern to a community. Planned development districts have two main characteristics:

1. They are floating or overlay districts which generally do not appear in advance on the town zoning map. Being an overlay district, the planned development concept adds a number of special considerations and rules that are not found in the normal zoning district.

2. The planned development district is a way to promote mixed use development through negotiation between the developer and the planning commission. Under a strict zoning district there is very little, if any, room for negotiation. If a district calls for two dwelling units per acre, then there is very little anyone—planning commission, governing body, or developer—can do to arrive at a result that would yield more units per acre. Planned development overlays, however, can specify low-, moderate-, and high-density development patterns, leaving the choice of two, four, or perhaps eight units per acre to the outcome of negotiation. Essentially, the town gives density bonuses (allows more units per acre) in exchange for developer concessions on the design and siting of the buildings.

A planned development district treats the development site as an integrated whole. For example, a developer proposes to build a nursing care facility, rental apartments for elderly, condominiums for lease or purchase by elderly couples, a pharmacy, medical offices, and perhaps some gift and craft retail facilities. Normally this would require three or four different zoning districts that would probably cause conflict if they were on the same site. Under the planned development approach, the developer can propose this entire plan on a single site, provided that generally accepted rules of site layout, design, and use compatibility are followed.

PREPARING THE DISTRICT REGULATIONS

The district regulations serve to implement and enforce the zoning standards. Each district will have different regulations, but there may be a great deal of similarity among some

Figure 16-5 Planned unit development

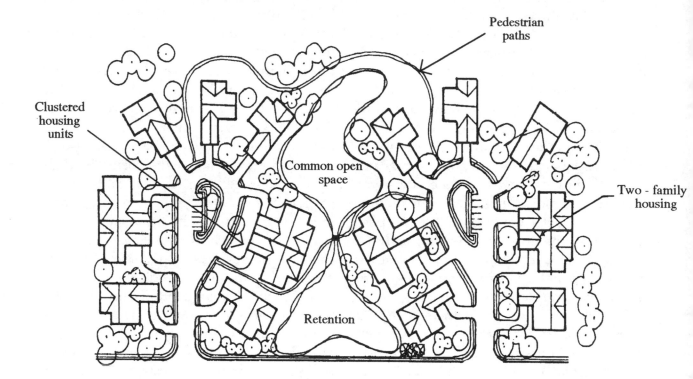

districts. Preparing these regulations requires forethought, discussion, and some objective standards.

The following standards should be addressed in preparing district regulations:

1. Permitted uses.
2. Excluded uses.
3. Accessory uses (rules for secondary uses, such as a storage shed behind a residence, which is a primary use).
4. Special exceptions (if any, rules for exceptions and guidelines for zoning board of adjustment).
5. Conditional uses (rules for conditional uses).
6. Required lot size.
7. Required yard size (front, side, and rear yard setbacks).
8. Maximum lot coverage ratio.
9. Minimum building size.
10. Height limitations.
11. Variances (rules for variances and guidelines for the board of zoning adjustment).

Uses that are to be permitted by right are listed first. Generally, they allow similar uses and prohibit dissimilar land uses. To make sure that the same uses will be understood by town officials and property owners, excluded uses may be mentioned to clarify the permitted uses when necessary, for instance, restaurants but not including drive-ins.

Excluded uses may be spelled out, but it is often difficult to think of all types of development that might be proposed. In some states, excluded uses are not listed in the district regulations; the reason is that if a type of development is not expressly permitted outright, or by a special exception or as a conditional use, it is not allowed in that zoning district.

Uses allowed by special exception are permitted if they meet certain special standards and the uses affect only a neighborhood and not the entire community. Applications for special exceptions are reviewed and ruled upon by the zoning board of adjustment. An example of a special exception might be a telecommunications tower in the agricultural zone. Standards are needed to ensure that the tower is designed and located so that neighbors will not be harmed. If the applicant can meet the standards, then the special exception should be granted.

Conditional uses have the potential to affect the entire community and should be allowed only if they meet certain conditions. Applications for conditional uses are reviewed by the planning commission, but the governing body makes the legally binding decision after holding a public hearing. If successful, the applicant will receive a conditional use permit stating the conditions for the proposed development. But, conditional use applications are often the subject of much debate and even legal challenges.

An example of a conditional use might be a church in a single-family residential district. If built, the church could have an impact on traffic patterns in the community. Also, churches often have weekday meetings and daycare in addition to Sunday services. A church might be allowed in the residential

Home Occupations

A recent land use survey in a small Kansas town found, among others, the following home occupations. Most were unknown to town officials.

- ☐ Family counseling
- ☐ Child care
- ☐ Musical instrument repair
- ☐ Dentist
- ☐ Computer graphics consultant
- ☐ Word processing
- ☐ Photographer
- ☐ Real estate office
- ☐ Wood craft sales
- ☐ Gunsmith
- ☐ Tech repair
- ☐ Cosmetics sales
- ☐ Upholstery
- ☐ Tax preparation
- ☐ Exotic bird sales

district if it met conditions on size (such as no more than two acres) and on-site parking space.

A Note on Home Occupations

Home occupations are common in small towns. A home occupation is simply a business being conducted in a residence. Special rules, however, must be made for home occupations, or they will bring complaints from residential neighbors and downtown business owners who must rent or build commercial buildings to conduct business. For example, the R-1 single-family residential district could list the following rules for home occupations:

1. Home occupations are allowed but are limited to the following activities: clothing alteration, beautician, and professional instruction such as music, art, and dance.

2. The sale of products is prohibited; only services may be offered. Many communities, on the other hand, permit the sale of traditional home products such as crafts, cosmetics, cookware, and stationery. Hobby product sales such as coins, stamps, model trains, and collectibles are often permitted, too.

3. The home occupation area should be limited to no more than 25 percent of the home so that the occupation does not dominate the home.

ZONING ADMINISTRATION

The administration section of the zoning ordinance spells out how a planning commission is created and its powers and duties. This section also introduces two important administrative functions that are special to zoning—the zoning administrator and the zoning board of adjustment. (Some states do not have enabling legislation allowing the creation of a zoning board of adjustment. In those states, the local governing body may perform the board's duties or may pass along those duties to the planning commission.)

The Zoning Administrator

The zoning administrator is appointed by the governing body to help implement the zoning process and to respond to all questions of interpreting and enforcing the zoning ordinance. When a landowner or developer presents a development proposal to the town, it is the job of the zoning administrator to determine whether the proposal meets the town's zoning requirements. First, the zoning administrator checks to see if the proposed land use is permitted in the zone in which the land is located. Then the zoning administrator checks on the special requirements of that zone, such as building size to lot size and building setbacks from the street.

If the zoning administrator finds that the proposed development meets the zoning requirements, the zoning administrator will issue a zoning permit and collect a fee. If a new building or substantial renovation is involved, the zoning administrator will also issue a building permit.

If the zoning administrator denies an application, a response must be given to the applicant in writing, stating how the proposed development failed to meet the zoning requirements. If the zoning administrator finds that the zoning ordinance is being violated, the zoning administrator must notify in writing those responsible and order actions necessary to correct the violation. The zoning administrator may require violators to cease from operating and stop the illegal use of land, buildings, or structures or may require that illegal buildings, alterations, and structures be removed.

The zoning administrator should be available during normal business hours to respond to zoning inquiries and complaints of alleged zoning violations. A number of small towns and counties have a zoning administrator on duty two full days a week and by appointment at other times. For this reason and others, the town clerk is often appointed as zoning administrator. The zoning administrator must have the proper zoning forms to distribute to the public, such as the zoning permit, conditional use permit, building permit, certificate of occupancy, and petition forms for a variance, special exception, and rezoning. As an assistant to the planning commission and zoning board of adjustment, the zoning administrator receives all applications for variances, conditional uses, special exceptions, and rezoning and passes them on to either the planning commission or zoning board of adjustment. Any disputes between an applicant and the zoning administrator on interpreting the zoning ordinance should be resolved by the zoning board of adjustment. The zoning administrator should attend the meetings of both the planning commission and the board of adjustment, when requested, in order to explain the activities of the zoning administrator in the review of a proposed development and to answer questions.

The zoning administrator should also make sure that notices of public hearings are published in the local newspapers and that neighboring landowners, within a specified distance of a property proposed for a zone change or development, are informed of any proposed changes.

The Zoning Board of Adjustment or Appeals

The zoning board of adjustment consists of three to five members appointed by the governing body to handle unusual zoning situations that require individual attention. Without the board, the only solution to individual development problems would be through frequent amendments to the zoning ordinance. Such small amendments would be time-consuming and could weaken the ordinance. The purpose of the board of adjustment is to ensure that zoning is fair and correctly interpreted and does not cause excessive hardship. You should examine your state zoning and planning enabling statutes before creating a board of adjustment because there is not much uniformity from state to state.

The board has three main functions. (In some states, the planning commission can make final zoning decisions if the governing body delegates that power. But many planning commissions must still forward recommendations to the governing body for a final decision.)

1. The board hears appeals by private citizens or public officials of decisions made by the zoning administrator. In this role, the board rules on whether the zoning administrator's interpretation of the zoning ordinance or subdivision regulations is correct.

2. The board reviews applications for special exceptions to the zoning ordinance. A special exception is a use expressly permitted by the ordinance, but the use is allowed only if certain standards are met. A special exception should grant permission to exceptional activities that affect only a neighborhood rather than the entire community. If approved, the board will issue a special exception. The special exception uses must be listed in the zoning ordinance, either in the individual zoning districts or in a separate section. Clear and objective review standards should also be included.

3. The board has the power to grant a *variance* from the strict terms of the zoning ordinance and map. A variance involves a departure from the normal rules which influence the construction or expansion of a building (*area variance*) or the land uses that are allowed in the zone (*use variance*)—though we do not recommend the granting of use variances because of the potential for spot zoning abuses. An area variance refers to minor changes in yard setbacks, minimum lot size requirements, height, and other dimensional standards which, if allowed, would not cause conflicts with neighboring properties. For instance, an area variance might allow a house to be built 10 feet from the side lot line, although the zoning ordinance normally requires at least 15 feet. Only those area variances authorized by the zoning ordinance may be issued. However, standards for variances are rarely spelled out in the ordinance; as a result, a variance is often a judgment call by the board of adjustment. Except in a few states, the variance is used for area regulations (lot sizes, lot lines, setback and yard requirements) and not the actual use of the property. A variance for use, such as to permit a convenience store on the corner lot of a residential neighborhood, is not in fact a variance: it is an amendment to both the zoning ordinance and map.

In order to receive a variance, an applicant must show that three conditions exist:

1. The property cannot be put to a use listed in the zoning district because of limitations in the dimensions of the lot or building. That is, the lot cannot yield a reasonably beneficial use if used only for a purpose allowed in that particular district.

2. The applicant has exceptional circumstances which do not apply to neighboring properties and which are not of his or her own making.

3. The change will not alter the character of the neighborhood.

The board of adjustment should establish a good working relationship with both the zoning administrator and the planning commission. The board, with the advice of the zoning administrator, must decide if a proposed variance or special exception has communitywide impacts and should be referred to the planning commission for consideration as a conditional use. Sometimes it may be wise to hold a joint meeting of the board of adjustment and the planning commission to exchange ideas and promote better understanding of planning and zoning.

The zoning board of adjustment, like the planning commission, must have a definite set of procedures because it is a quasi-judicial board and its decisions may be reviewed in court. These procedures might include rules on board membership, when and how meetings are to be conducted, cases to be decided by the board, the process for hearing individual cases, and record keeping.

Distinction between a Variance and a Special Use

A variance is an authority to a property owner to use property in a manner that is forbidden by the ordinance while a special exception allows the property owner to put his property to a use expressly permitted by the ordinance.

from D. Mandelker, Land Use Law 2d. quoted from *North Shore Steak Houses, Inc.* v. *Board of Appeals,* 282 NE. 2d 606

Exhibit 16–3
A Note on Conflict of Interest
The recommendations of the zoning administrator and planning commission, along with the rulings of the board of adjustment and governing body, should be made fairly and objectively based on the zoning ordinance, the record of the hearing, and the facts at hand. Small town decision makers are often at a disadvantage in their attempt to be fair and avoid conflicts of interest. Often, everyone knows everyone else; family, friendship, and business ties are widespread. Another problem is that there may be too many people from the same profession on a board, commission, or town council.

Rules which specify a conflict of interest or allow disqualification must be drafted with some care and placed in the land development ordinances. Common examples of when planning commissioners or board of adjustment members must declare a conflict of interest and disqualify themselves are:

• When the commissioner is related to an applicant or a person protesting a zoning change at a hearing. Use reason and sensibility to establish this rule. A niece is a close relative; the father-in-law of your second cousin is not.

• When a commissioner is the owner of or holds an interest in the property subject to the request for change.

• When the commissioner is a resident of the area as defined by the enabling statutes (usually 200–1,000 feet) surrounding the property subject to the request for change.

• If the commissioner is a business associate of the property owner or a person protesting a zoning change.

• If the commissioner is an employee or employer of the applicant.

• If, because of a past or current intimate relationship with an applicant, the board member's participation would give the appearance of impropriety.

When commissioners disqualify themselves, they must leave the hearing table and preferably the hearing room. In a small group, quasi-judicial hearing, it is wrong to announce a disqualification and then continue to remain at the table.

A decision maker should disclose in advance any interest that he or she has in the outcome of a decision. If the decision concerns a family member, the decision maker must disqualify him/herself from the case. For example, Doug Jones is a member of the planning commission and his cousin, Amanda Jones, has applied for a rezoning of one acre from R-1 single-family residential to C-1 low-density commercial. If the rezoning is granted, the value of Amanda's land could in-crease by several thousand dollars. In this case, Doug Jones must declare a conflict of interest and remove himself from deciding on the case. If he were to recommend the rezoning, townspeople might claim that his judgment was biased because the land belonged to his cousin. If he were to recommend against the rezoning, his cousin might claim that he was jealous. Either way, Doug Jones tends to appear less than fair and objective. By removing himself from the case, Doug avoids charges of influence pedalling and personal bias.

Enforcement of Zoning, Subdivision, and Other Land Use Ordinances

There is a great difference between passing a law and enforcing it. The enforcement of zoning, subdivision, and other land use ordinances is often weak and ineffective in most towns. Weak enforcement, in turn, leads to disrespect for the ordinances and can even jeopardize the entire town plan.

Enforcement may be difficult for a number of reasons. First, a small town may not have the staff to monitor violations of the land use ordinances. On the other hand, the smaller the town, the easier it is to detect if someone is violating an ordinance. Second, local officials are often reluctant to prosecute violations. The offender may be an elderly person, a relative of someone important, or an important member of the community. No one enjoys being caught breaking the law! Third, convictions for violations may be difficult to obtain. Poorly constructed wording in the ordinance, an improper understanding on the part of the zoning administrator, or a lack of concern from local prosecuting attorneys may pose problems. The courts often tend to view

corous comments or threats have no place in a zoning hearing and only contribute to the perception that such activities will influence the planning commission. Both sides in a zoning hearing have rights and they should be preserved at all times.

8. At this point the first part of the record has been created and the opportunity for the public to speak has passed. The chairperson should ask if the commission members have specific questions for the applicant or any member of the audience. After all questions have been answered, the chairperson should determine if the commission members have enough information for a decision or if the applicant needs to gather more information and appear at another time. If the matter is to be tabled, it should be tabled to a specific date. The applicant should be given instructions, in writing, as to what matters or facts should be gathered by the applicant. When the applicant returns at a subsequent hearing, only these requests will be discussed unless extraordinary matters have come to light in the intervening time.

If it appears that the proposal does not have to be tabled for lack of information or to gather new data, a motion to recommend or not to recommend the proposal should be made. The planning commission discussion of a zoning proposal should always begin with the concept of consistency. In short, is the proposal consistent with the established policies, adopted plans, and previous decisions of the planning commission? If the consensus is yes, the commission should move to an examination of the neighborhood impacts, or if no, to a discussion of the land use change.

Impacts. If the proposed development is consistent with the existing town plan and zoning ordinance, the planning commission should next examine any impacts that might occur when the project is built. The commission should discuss the following questions:

1. How long has the property been in its present use?

2. What is the character of the surrounding neighborhood?

3. Would the change, if granted, be consistent with the types of changes previously recommended by the commission?

4. What were the recommendations of professionals, if any?

5. What relevant points were raised during the public discussion?

If the planning commission feels that some of the development impacts may need to be corrected, the commission may follow two courses of action. One, the planning commission can direct the applicant to study further the specific recommendations set down in a motion to table and to return at a later hearing. The commission may recommend changes to the design, layout, or even the proposed use. Second, the applicant can simply accede to the wishes of the commission and modify the proposal or the commission can impose conditions in zoning. Conditions in zoning should not be confused with conditional uses. The commission may impose certain conditions that the applicant must comply with if they bear directly on the comfort, safety, convenience, and property value within the immediate area. For example, the commission may require the applicant to move a proposed driveway from one lot side to another so as not to complicate an already inefficient traffic situation.

Following a discussion of the possible impacts, the commission should move immediately to the merits of the proposal. The motion to approve (or disapprove) the recommendation should be voted on at this time. If it appears that the commission will disapprove, the applicant should be given a final opportunity to correct any objections that appear on the record and return at a later time. Regardless of a positive or negative outcome, each commissioner should indicate the reasons for his or her vote. After the vote has been taken, the planning commission writes up a recommendation for approval or denial of the zoning change and sends it to the governing body.

Magnitude of the Change. Development proposals that are not consistent with adopted policies and plans will bring about changes in land use patterns. The question for the planning commission is how much change? If the magnitude of change is small, the commission can then consider whether or not it wishes to reexamine adopted policies or simply move on and eventually let the land use change signal a shift in policy. If the magnitude of the change requested is significant (meaning an abrupt shift from one land use pattern to another), the commission will need to focus on the justification or the need for such change. The burden is on the person requesting the change to supply these answers, and it is not the job of the commission to fight the applicant's battles. If the commission reaches a consensus in the need for the change, then the town plan will need to be changed to reflect the new shift. Unfortunately, many planning commissions will simply grant the request for change and let this stand as an amendment to the plan. The correct way to deal with the development proposal is to table it

until the commission has had time to have another public hearing on the question of changing the plan.

Another stage of the hearing process occurs before the governing body. The governing body receives the planning commission's recommendation and schedules a public hearing on the development proposal as part of its regular meeting. The public hearing and discussion should be structured around the record created by the planning commission. If new facts come to light, then the governing body should return the development proposal to the planning commission with specific instructions for review. If the governing body raises serious questions about the proposal, then, likewise, the entire matter should be returned to the planning commission for reconsideration. Under only the most extraordinary circumstances should the governing body reject the recommendation of the planning commission without sending the matter back for reconsideration.

One of the questions that most often occurs during the hearing stage of a proposal is, "What will happen if this matter goes to court?" This question should not influence the decision or actions of any member of the planning commission or the governing body. All the courts and the law have ever required from bodies that deal with zoning is a reasonable review, correct procedure, and a method of resolving land conflicts that does not result in a near total denial of the beneficial use of property. The following are some suggestions that will help to assure that zoning decisions do not end up in court:

1. Always hold a fair hearing. Everyone must have the opportunity to speak and make suggestions. Applicants should always be given the chance to correct flaws in their proposals.

2. Never grant special favors, or appear to grant special favors, to an applicant. The public has a long memory for such actions.

3. Always make and keep a record. Never trust to memory or notes zoning matters.

4. Never tolerate sloppy presentations. Applicants should always be required to bring consistent information to hearings, be prepared to speak, and be prepared to answer questions.

5. Never establish a rule that attorneys may not be present or speak at zoning hearings. Every person has a right to legal assistance.

6. Never hold an executive session. Say everything that must be said on a proposal in front of the public. Never discuss a zoning matter in private with an applicant or discuss the proposal with other members of the commission or governing body until there is a final resolution. The public has a right to hear everything that is said about a public matter.

7. Do not cut corners and do not bend the rules. If a proposal must wait thirteen days, then do not consider it on the twelfth day. It may have worked in the past, but eventually it will cause trouble.

8. Be honest! If there is a personal, business, or financial conflict with a particular rezoning, then a person should disqualify him/herself and leave the room.

9. Always ask yourself, "If this use were located next to my property, would I be voting the same way?"

10. Always consider the rights of the applicant along with the rights of the neighbors and the public in general. There is no excuse for the total destruction of all beneficial use of property; but there is also no excuse for re-ducing neighboring property values and endangering public health and safety.

PERFORMANCE ZONING

Some small towns are reluctant to adopt a traditional zoning ordinance. Often there is a feeling that a landowner should be able to use his or her land in any way he or she wants as long as no one is hurt. A way to incorporate this feeling into a zoning ordinance is through *performance zoning*. Traditional zoning separates land uses that might result in danger to health and safety and welfare. For example, a school should not be located next to a shopping center because of the traffic danger to young pedestrians. Performance zoning regulates the impacts of land uses rather than the uses themselves. For instance, in a typical R-1 single-family residential zone, convenience stores are often not allowed or may only be permitted as a conditional use. Under performance zoning, a convenience store would be allowed as long as the business met certain performance standards relating to noise, air and water pollution, size of building, and parking.

A community can divide the town into zones based on performance standards rather than land uses. That is, no one use can automatically be prohibited from any zone because of the use alone. But different performance standards could exist for different zones. For example, noise and building size standards would be more stringent in a residential zone than in a commercial zone. But it would be possible for a commercial use to locate in the residential zone if it met that zone's performance standards.

Performance zoning involves fewer zoning districts than traditional zoning. The zoning districts separate broadly different land uses (such as residential and industrial) but allow for a mix of land uses within each district (such as residential and commercial). For example, the performance zoning ordinance of Bath Township in Michigan has only five districts: rural, low-density residential, development (along major roads), village core I (commercial), and village core II (the central business district). The ordinance also includes an overlay district for public lands and open space (McElroy, 1985). A buffer yard, similar to a setback requirement, is required to separate incompatible land uses and to reduce noise and visual impact. The greater the conflict in adjacent land uses, the larger the buffer yard should be, including a greater use of trees to screen out noise, dust, exhaust, and visual impacts.

Performance zoning can be especially useful in evaluating development proposals. Traditional zoning has tended to create a cookie cutter pattern of rectangular blocks and lots, whereas performance zoning allows for greater flexibility in the development of a site. Performance zoning features four standards to ensure environmental quality: (1) an open space ratio measuring the amount of open space to the entire site; (2) an impervious surface ratio, measuring the amount of space covered by roads, sidewalks, rocks, parking lots, and buildings relative to the entire site; (3) for residential uses, a density measure of dwellings per acre; and (4) for nonresidential uses, a floor area ratio measuring the square feet of floor area in a building to the area of the entire site.

The determination of specific ratios may involve some trial and error on the part of the planning commission and the governing body. The standards can be helpful in maintaining open space and thus the essential rural character of the community. The density per acre for residential units and the floor area ratio for nonresidential development are similar to traditional zoning standards which look to regulate bulk density and crowding. Also the open space ratio approach allows for the clustering of dwelling units on a site within the town or adjacent to the town while preserving considerable stretches of open space. This approach makes good sense if portions of a site have major physical limitations to development, such as streams, marsh, woods, steep slopes, and shallow soils.

The impervious surface ratio should ensure that water runoff from the site will not be excessive and cause harm to neighboring properties. Many ordinances require that new developments retain 40 percent or more of the rain water on-site by using retention basins.

The advantage of performance zoning is that it is able to handle the problems of variances and conditional uses faster because decisions are made according to definite standards. The difficulty with performance zoning is that definite standards can be difficult to write and administer.

ZONING PRACTICES IN LARGER TOWNS

Zoning ordinances will vary from town to town depending on the physical size of the town, population, and community desires for future development. Towns of 2,500 to 10,000 people may be able to hire a full-time planner to assist with the planning and zoning process. These larger towns often have more complex land use patterns and problems than towns of fewer than 2,500 people.

This section presents some zoning techniques that larger towns may want to explore and of which smaller towns should at least be aware. Towns should know and understand the array of zoning tools available. This way they will be able to respond to a zoning ordinance written by a planning professional and even suggest additions to the zoning ordinance.

One example of a more complex zoning technique is the *overlay zone*, which is particularly useful in areas with natural hazards. An overlay zone is placed on top of a base zone to create a *double zoning ordinance*. For instance, an area is zoned R-1 single-family. This is the base zone. However, part of the area lies within a floodplain. A floodplain overlay zone FP-1 could be placed on top of part of the R-1 zone to create tighter building restrictions, such as all new buildings must be at least 100 feet from the floodway. In other words, a proposed development would have to meet the zoning requirements of both the R-1 zone and the FP-1 zone. The advantage of the overlay zone is that it can be applied on top of any of the town's base zones.

A useful technique in protecting conservation areas and agricultural and forest land is *large-lot zoning*. The restriction on the density of dwellings is designed to protect open space and maintain large parcels of land for farming or forestry. In this way, the rural character of a town is sustained.

Large-lot zoning can be done by stating in the zoning ordinance that land sold in a particular zone must be of a certain minimum size. For example, in a conservation zone, a minimum lot requirement of 25 acres would ensure that individual land holdings would not be broken into parcels below 25 acres, ex-

cept in unusual circumstances. This large lot size would be beneficial to wildlife and plantlife and provide open space in the town.

Care must be used in applying large-lot zoning. Some suburban communities have tried to use large-lot zoning to exclude certain economic classes or racial groups by requiring a 1- to 10-acre lot to build a house. This is called *exclusionary zoning*, and it is illegal where applied to all zones. A large-lot zone must further a particular public goal and must reflect a reasonable use for the land; otherwise it may unreasonably restrict the owner's use of the property.

Incentive or *bonus zoning* can be used by a town to award a developer extra building density or height in exchange for good aesthetic design or other benefits. In larger towns, a developer may want to build several dozen housing units. The town may be better off both in appearance and in providing services to the project if the housing units are clustered together at a density higher than the zoning allows and the developer agrees to maintain a certain amount of land as open space. In such a case, the planning commission and governing body would negotiate with the developer over how many housing units would be built and how much open space retained. The number of units exceeding the density of the zoning ordinance would be considered a bonus for the developer in exchange for the open space.

A *floating zone* is a special zone that exists in the town's zoning ordinance but not on the zoning map. The floating zone can be applied when the town identifies the need for a particular use but is not sure where it should go. Land may be rezoned to the floating zone use based on a case-by-case review if the applicant meets the conditions of the zoning ordinance. Floating zones are typically used for mobile home parks, shopping centers, and multifamily planned unit developments and should not be confused with spot zoning. A floating zone contains definite permitted uses and serves to satisfy an identified public, not private, need. The question with the floating zone is where it should go. Spot zoning usually involves a zone change for a rather small parcel, meeting a private desire.

Spot zoning should be discouraged as it is usually not in keeping with the town miniplan and often may not be legally valid.

SUMMARY

Zoning is one of the most important tools for putting the town plan into action. A zoning ordinance consists of text describing the different land use zones, some general development standards, the administration of the ordinance, and a map showing the location of the different zones. Although a zoning ordinance should be drafted by a professional planner, the zoning administrator and the members of the planning commission, governing body, and zoning board of adjustment should understand what the zoning ordinance contains and how it works.

Zoning is designed to separate conflicting land uses that may pose a threat to personal health, safety, and welfare. Some land uses are not allowed in certain zones, other uses may be permitted on a conditional basis, and some uses are permitted outright.

Zoning also influences the density of buildings and the size of buildings. This is important for reasons of health, safety, and neighborhood appearance.

Zoning is meant to be a flexible tool, and its success depends on the judgment of the officials involved in the zoning process. Under special circumstances, variances may be granted for lot area coverage not normally permitted in the zoning ordinance. Special exceptions and conditional use permits may also be granted after proper review of potential impacts. Amendments to the zoning ordinance and map may be made, based on a petition from private landowners or at the initiative of the planning commission and the approval of the governing body. Amendments are meant to reflect the desires of the community and should occur concurrently with changes to the town miniplan to assure that all zoning decisions have a factual base.

Above all, the zoning process should be open to the public, especially through public hearings. In any zoning decision, the facts should be well documented and there should be good solid reasons for what the town officials recommend or rule. The reasons should be written down and presented along with the decisions. By keeping the zoning process open to the public, more people will tend to become involved in the decisions that affect the future of the community. In this way, townspeople will feel that they have some say in how and where the community should develop.

17

Subdivision
Regulations

Subdivision is the legal process of dividing land into smaller units called *lots* for future sale and development. The creation and sale of several lots and the construction of new buildings can have a major impact on a neighborhood's appearance and on a town's traffic patterns, schools, utilities, natural resources, and tax base. Subdivision regulations help to ensure that new buildings are properly placed on lots, traffic patterns are not hampered, and new areas of development have sufficient access to necessary utilities. The *subdivision ordinance* establishes standards for the division of lots and spells out what services and amenities the subdivider must provide before any lots can be sold or construction can commence.

Why should a community have a subdivision ordinance? There are three major reasons. First, subdivision regulations provide a legal process for registering land ownership. When a large area of land is broken down

into smaller parcels, the number of landowners will increase. Registration of these smaller units of land with the appropriate government official (usually the county register of deeds) assists in providing a secure title to all property. Lot lines, easements, and streets are exactly specified by a mapped survey and not only by the use of words or metes and bounds description. Second, lot purchasers have some official protection because a uniform set of standards is used to review the subdivision prior to its legal registration. Lot purchasers have a high degree of assurance that there will be adequate building space on the lots for their buildings, that the lots will not be flooded, and that they will have proper access to their property. Finally, subdivision regulations are important because they provide a consistent set of standards for all developments within the local government's jurisdiction. Taxpayers can assume that their tax dollars will not be used to reconstruct roads that were not built to established standards. Subdividers can assume that all other subdividers in the jurisdiction must pay similar amounts of money to prepare lots for sale to the public.

RELATION TO PLANNING

As with zoning, subdivision regulation is a land use control that implements comprehensive planning. The relationship between planning and subdivision, however, has historically been viewed as closer than in zoning. Cunningham, Land Use Control, 50 Iowa Law Review, 1965, p. 24.

A town subdivision ordinance works hand in hand with the zoning ordinance and the town plan to ensure that development occurs in an orderly and efficient fashion. The zoning ordinance states the desired density of development in particular zones. The size of the lots in a subdivision must meet the zoning density standards. For instance, if an R-1 zone requires lots of at least 8,000 square feet, all lots in a proposed subdivision must be at least 8,000 square feet. In addition, the zoning ordinance designates different land use zones which the subdivider must follow or else must apply for a rezoning. Finally, the subdivision ordinance should further the goals and objectives of the town plan. For example, the creation of two-acre lots in a conservation area does not support the goal of preserving open space and wildlife habitat. But dividing a two-acre parcel into eight quarter-acre lots in an R-1 single-family residential zone would help achieve the goal of providing more single-family housing in the community.

Major Objectives

The subdivision regulations indicate the steps that must be taken before land can legally be divided into smaller units and sold for building lots. These steps can be grouped under two major objectives: providing adequate facilities and avoiding harm to people and property.

Subdivision regulations are aimed at providing safe, efficient infrastructure—the physical improvements necessary to serve a modern land development. Streets, lights, sidewalks, gutters, water lines, sewers, drainage culverts, and water retention basins are all examples of infrastructure. Rules that relate to infrastructure ensure that all facilities will be properly sized to the development's needs and built to acceptable engineering standards. These rules also guarantee that the subdivider's promise to supply these facilities is met in a timely fashion. These rules place a major share of the financial burden of development on the subdivider and ultimately the purchasers of the new lots. In the past, many towns did not require the subdivider to make these improvements, and the town had to pick up the entire cost of providing public facilities and utilities.

Infrastructure is not limited to pipes and sidewalks. Subdivision regulations can require the subdivider to donate land or money for reasonable off-site facilities such as waste treatment plants, parks, and roads. These requirements are known as *exactions* and the actual donation of facilities or land is called a *dedication*. When pro rata cash payments are required, this is called *money in lieu of dedication* or *impact fees*. (See Chapter 18 for a discussion of impact fees.) Every town has a legitimate interest in making sure that subdividers help pay a major portion of the cost of providing public services to new developments. Otherwise these costs are unfairly borne by existing residents of the community, who must subsidize development from which they receive no direct benefits. Exactions are simply a means of requiring the subdivider to pay a fair share of the cost of servicing the new development.

The second major objective of the land subdivision regulations is to avoid harm to residents of the development, adjacent landowners, and the general environment. Each land development is reviewed by the planning commission prior to the preparation of a final design in order to maximize traffic safety, avoid damaging storm water runoff on neighboring landowners, or perhaps preserve selected open space sites containing valuable trees or other natural features. The subdivision ordinance should not be viewed as a set of precise and unchanging standards, but rather as a set of protection measures that are flexibly applied on a case-by-case basis. For example, one site may be located in an area of heavy traffic and may require special road improvements before it is safe for general use. Another site may contain large amounts of rock with shallow, highly erodible soils and well-defined drainage courses. This site will require a detailed plan to identify those areas most suited for development.

CREATING A SUBDIVISION ORDINANCE

The planning commission is responsible for drafting subdivision regulations and making recommendations to the governing body, which gives final approval to the subdivision ordinance (see Figure 17–1). It is strongly recommended that a professional planner or public works professional write the subdivision ordinance because of the technical and legal specifications involved. However, the planning commission and governing body should have input into the process and understand what elements comprise a subdivision ordinance and how the ordinance works.

If a planning consultant cannot assist with the preparation of your regulations, then it is important that the planning commission and governing body organize a technical study committee composed (at a minimum) of the following professionals:

- A registered land surveyor.
- A civil engineer such as your municipal or county engineer. Some civil engineers are also registered land surveyors.
- A local developer or building contractor who understands the construction process.
- A financial advisor, such as a banker, who understands the process of financing construction, letters of credit, and preparing special obligation bonds (specials).
- A representative of the soil conservation service to advise on soils for building construction, storm water runoff, and suitability for on-site sewage disposal.
- A representative of a local sewer and/or water district who can speak about the installation of public facilities.

Land subdivision regulations are enabled through state legislation. You must know how to prepare and adopt the subdivision ordinance before you start to draft the regulations. Read the state requirements carefully, especially to understand the content and preparation of subdivision plats and the dedication of public facilities. It will be helpful if the planning commission arranges for an attorney to brief them on some elementary points of property law.

Figure 17-1 Creating a typical subdivision ordinance

Governing body

Hires

Planning staff and/or consultant or

Appoints

Technical drafting committee

Holds work sessions with the planning commission and
prepares subdivision recommendations and submits to the

Planning commission

Gives public notice, holds public hearings, makes final changes and
submits recommendations to the

Governing body

Gives public notice, holds public hearings or has several readings
of the ordinance, and officially adopts the
subdivision regulations

Ordinance is signed, published, and becomes official

Subdivision ordinance takes effect*

*Note: Subdivision or allotment procedures vary from state to state and
in Canada. Check state or provincial statutes for exact preparation and
adoption procedures.

A helpful aid for drafting the subdivision regulations is a well-prepared model or adopted ordinance from another community. But keep in mind that your regulations should be tailored to your community's needs. Another important aid is to locate someone who can do simple pencil line drawings, render a line drawing from a photograph, or use a computer software draw tool. Subdivision regulations require examples and illustrations throughout the document as visual guides. A model outline for preparing the subdivision ordinance is shown in Figure 17–2.

The planning consultant, planning staff, or technical committee should hold work sessions with the planning commission to draft the subdivision ordinance. Once the first draft is prepared, the planning commission should review the document and give special attention to clarifying language, items that require visual examples, and problems that are likely to arise because of technical requirements. When the document is ready for a more extensive review, the planning commission gives notice of a public hearing on the proposed subdivision regulations. After holding the public hearing, the commission passes on a revised draft to the governing body. The governing body then reviews the draft, gives notice of its own public hearing, and may (1) return the subdivision ordinance to the planning commission for further study, (2) officially adopt the ordinance, or (3) revise and adopt the subdivision ordinance.

Elements to Be Included in the Subdivision Ordinance

The purpose of the subdivision ordinance is to explain the regulations that apply to dividing land into new parcels, to describe procedures for obtaining exactions from subdividers, and to set out procedures for the administration and amendment of the subdivision ordinance (see Figure 17–2).

The rules of the subdivision ordinance must state that the sale of lots may proceed and a building permit issued only after all requirements of the subdivision ordinance have been met. In addition, no public improvements (roads, sewer and water lines) may be installed until the preliminary plat is approved, but these public improvements cannot be used until the final plat is approved and recorded.

The subdivision ordinance should present a clear definition of the terms used in the ordinance. Perhaps most important is the definition of a *subdivision*. This definition will vary slightly from state to state depending on the definition in the state planning and zoning enabling act. In Iowa, for example, a subdivision is the division of any parcel of land into three or more lots. In Minnesota, a subdivision is the division of a

parcel into two or more lots. In Oregon, a subdivision is the creation of four or more lots from a single parcel. Most states require local jurisdictions to regulate subdivisions. Yet, by not defining a subdivision as any division of land into two or more lots, some state planning enabling acts have opened a serious loophole. A landowner may divide his or her land into two lots and sell off one lot without having to file a subdivision plat. At a later date, the landowner may split the remaining lot into two more lots and sell one of those lots without having to file a subdivision plat. To avoid this problem, the subdivision ordinance should include a beginning date that applies to the creation of three or more lots from an original parcel. For example, the subdivision ordinance could say that "a subdivision must be platted when any parcel of land existing at the date of adoption of the subdivision ordinance is afterwards divided into three or more lots." This provision also takes care of situations where a lot is sold and the buyer wants to split the lot in two. This provision is very important in maintaining orderly growth and ensuring that public services are not overburdened. Many states have enabling legislation which allows local jurisdictions to regulate divisions of land into two or more lots. Although such regulation is generally not required, it is to a community's advantage to review all land divisions. This will allow for better control of development and will enable a community to recoup the costs of extending public services and facilities.

The term *subdivision* is also frequently used to mean "an addition to the community." A new area of town may be referred to as the Meadowlark Subdivision when the area should actually be called the Meadowlark Addition.

Figure 17–2   Elements in the subdivision ordinance

Section 1.0 Title
Section 2.0 Purpose
Section 3.0 Rules or Operation and Definitions
    3.1 Rules - When subdivision is required
    3.2 Definitions
    3.3 Exemptions from platting
Section 4.0 Site Plans
    4.1 Purpose and Requirements
    4.2 Timing and contents
    4.3 Proper form for signature and approval certificates
    4.4 Parking design, landscaping and construction standards
Section 5.0 Utilities and Public Facilities
    5.1 When required
    5.2 Public service districts and developer responsibilities
    5.3 Requirements for on-site water and sewer facilities
Section 6.0 Subdivision Design Standards
    6.1 Street plans and design
    6.2 Utilities and easements
    6.3 Lots
    6.4 Sidewalks
    6.5 Storm water drainage
Section 7.0 Procedure For Processing All Plats
    7.1 The lot split or partition - rules for preparation
    7.2 Predevelopment conference, application and fees
    7.3 Sketch or General development plans
        7.31 When required
        7.32 Required contents
        7.33 General review procedures
    7.4 The Short or Minor subdivision plat
        7.41 Required contents
        7.42 Rules for submission
        7.43 Planning commission review procedures
    7.5 The Preliminary plat
        7.51 Required contents
        7.52 Rules for submission
        7.53 Planning commission review procedures
        7.54 General review procedures and required signatures
        7.55 Notations
    7.6 The Final plat
        7.61 Required contents and signatures
        7.62 Compliance with preliminary plat
        7.63 Planning commission review procedures
        7.64 Governing Body review procedures
        7.65 Certificates and filing procedures
        7.66 Dedications and compliance with conditions
Section 8.0 Post filing procedures
    8.1 Performance bonds and letters of credit
    8.2 Issuing building permits
    8.3 Conflicts with restrictive covenants
Section 9.0 Administration and Enforcement
    9.1 Duties of the Administrator
        9.11 Compliance with regulations
        9.12 Methods of enforcement
    9.2 Variances and waivers
    9.3 Fines and penalties
    9.4 Amendment to plats
    9.5 Amendments to the subdivision ordinance

The land area terms tract and parcel are often misunderstood. A *tract* is land under a single ownership. When you examine the tax assessor's map, you will see large pieces of land that have not been subdivided into lots called, for example, the "Brown Tract" or the "Charles and Edna Williams Tract." A *parcel* is a lot or group of lots under a single ownership or control. A subdivider may divide land into lots, or into lots and tracts at the same time, depending on local terminology. For instance, a subdivider may purchase 60 acres of land from several owners, creating a parcel. The entire 60 acres could be divided into one-acre lots and sold; or 30 acres could be divided into one-acre lots and sold and the remaining land broken into three tracts of 10 acres each and sold to be subdivided at a later time.

A *plat* is the most commonly used term in the subdivision process. A plat is a map, prepared by a professionally licensed surveyor or engineer, which shows the surveyed location of all lots, blocks, roads, easements, and other reservations. The plat is prepared on good mylar, signed by all owners and responsible government officials, and recorded as the official description of the land.

The process of restricting land or use during the subdivision process is an important but confusing process for professionals and laypersons alike. To keep the discussion as clear as possible, only three types of restrictions will be discussed. The first and the most common type of restriction is the *easement*. Although there are several types of easements, the most common definition is "granting a right to another person or persons for the limited use of your land." For example, utility easements are commonly granted to extend power lines, phone lines, or sewer and water lines across a property. The easement is surveyed and indicated on the plat and will allow utility companies or a government to install overhead or underground service lines. The lot owner is restricted from blocking the utility easement or putting a structure within the easement area. An example of a drainage easement is shown in Figure 17–3.

The second type of restriction is known as a *covenant* or a *restrictive covenant*, and sometimes as a *deed restriction*, although this last term is not technically correct. A covenant is an agreement—a contract—between the seller and the buyer of land. The government typically is not a party to the covenant, but special circumstances do exist in a few states and for planned unit developments. Covenants may confer both benefits and burdens on the property. For example, a covenant may require the landowner to refrain from certain actions, such as blocking a scenic view; or a covenant may require that something be done, such as maintaining a common fence. Some covenants are placed on the subdivision plat, such as a certain area can be indicated as "no structure permitted" to reserve land for drainage channels. Covenants are filed with the register of deeds at the same time a final plat is officially recorded. A notation of any covenants should appear on the plat to warn prospective buyers that covenants do exist.

Covenants are useful when a group of people buy lots in a new addition. Covenants may specify several requirements that must be observed when an owner constructs a building or uses the property. For instance, covenants may specify that driveways may only be placed at the corner of the lot—not the center. A covenant may require a homeowner to

Figure 17-3 An easement reserved for drainage
on a subdivision plat

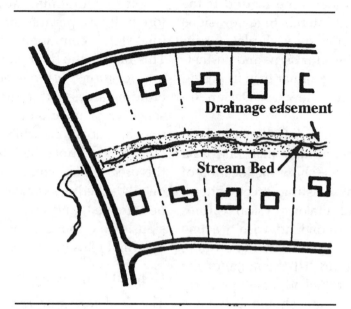

Drainage easement

Stream Bed

build only a pitched roof and perhaps further restrict the roof to wood shingles.

The third type of restriction is known as a *condition* and is often called an *exaction* by community planners. Most building sites are unique: some locations have heavy drainage flows, many are located in areas with difficult traffic patterns, others have physical features which complicate building and site design. Subdivision regulations, no matter how comprehensive, cannot be expected to handle all situations. Conditions (exactions) imposed on the developer during the subdivision review process can help to correct negative impacts that might occur when the property is actually developed. For example, a tract of land proposed for multifamily development is located along a main road which already carries heavy traffic. Residents travelling to and from this multifamily development will have a long wait in the morning and evening during heavy traffic time. Placing a stop sign on the main road is not sufficient. As a condition of platting the subdivision, the subdivider could be required to open a secondary access road to another portion of the tract which would connect with a less heavily travelled road. An area is surveyed for a road and indicated on the plat. The plat contains a space for the property owner or owners to sign in order to dedicate the surveyed road area to the public. When the public officials sign the plat, they accept the dedication of the road area. It is space taken from subdivided lots over which the public can travel.

Conditions can be overused to the point where they cause ill-feelings between subdividers and the planning commission. They should only be imposed to avoid harm to future owners within the subdivision, neighbors, and the community-at-large. They should be imposed only in unique circumstances and not as a routine matter. If the planning commission intends to review signs and building aesthetics on each plat, for instance, then guidelines for signs and aesthetics should be developed rather than imposing conditions with each review (see Design Review in Chapter 21).

Three other important definitions include the sketch plan, preliminary plat, and final plat. A *sketch plan* must show the location of the subdivision, the existing street pattern, and all buildings and major physical features both on the subdivision and within a few hundred feet of the subdivision. In addition, the sketch plan should list the name of the subdivision owner and all adjoining property owners. The sketch plan should present a base map at a scale of at least 200 feet to the inch which shows the proposed pattern and dimensions of lots, street layout, all utilities available, recreation areas, and systems of drainage (storm water runoff), sewerage, and water supply within the subdivision. Finally, the sketch plan should state all the existing restrictions on the use of land in the subdivision, such as easements, covenants, and zoning lines.

The *preliminary plat* is by far the most important element in the entire land development review process. It includes all of the information provided in the sketch plan but in greater detail. All lots, streets, easements, and building lines are shown in precise detail imposed over the topographic features of the land. The *final plat* contains all changes to the preliminary plat, engineering and survey detail, and signature spaces for dedication, approval, and owner certification. The final plat is then ready for official approval by the planning commission and governing body.

Some communities add one final step before building permits are finally issued. This final step is commonly called the *precise plan*. This plan is the final plat with precise building locations (called building footprints), building areas within the lots which exclude sensitive or unsuitable areas from construction, and notations which might limit vehicular access or impose height restrictions. Often, the precise plan contains drainage and road details, schedules indicating which trees may be removed, and areas for the placement of signs. Some communities simply require that two final plats be placed on file.

General Requirements

The *General Requirements section* of the subdivision ordinance (Section 2.0 in Figure 17–2) states that a proposed subdivision must meet the goals and objectives of the town plan and the town zoning ordinance and map. A registered land survey must be completed for any property that is to be subdivided. The costs of the survey are borne by the subdivider and will vary according to the size of the property. The subdivider must preserve all boundary markers and may be required to preserve certain natural features if specified in the subdivision ordinance or design ordinance. For example, the planning commission may approve or deny a request to remove trees above a certain size.

Subdivision Design Standards

Subdivision design standards establish guidelines for the infrastructure of a subdivision, namely, streets, blocks, water and sewerage facilities (including wells and septic systems),

Figure 17-4 Example of different lot configurations

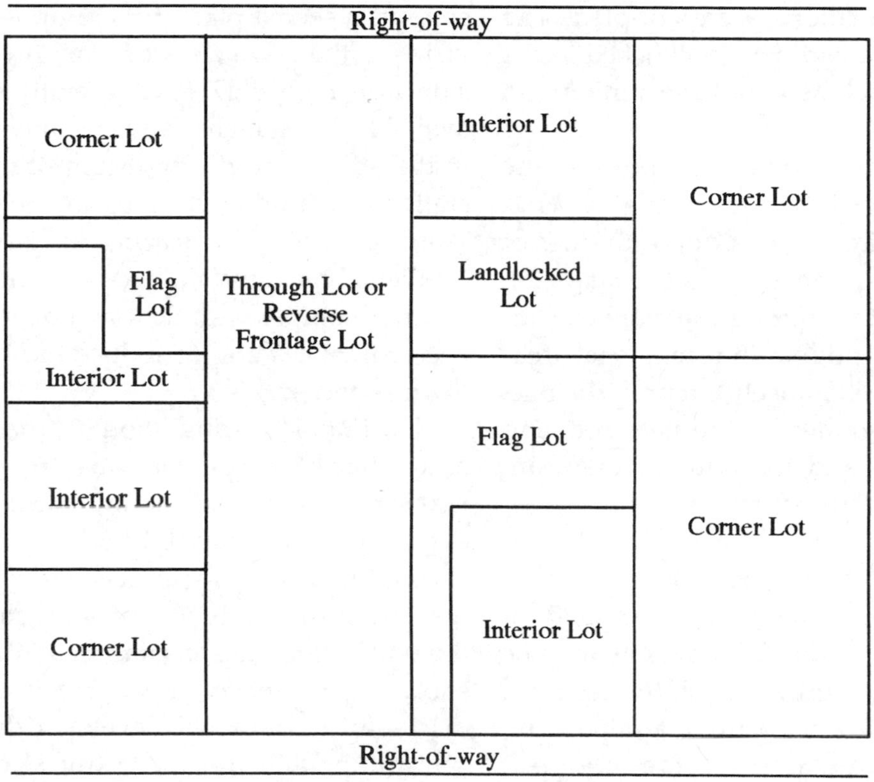

drainage, telephone and electrical utilities, sidewalks, easements, and parks or open space. The design standards also spell out some specific dimensions for new lots. There are two kinds of lots that can pose problems—flag lots and landlocked lots (see Figure 17–4). A *flag lot,* or *panhandle lot,* has a narrow frontage on a street, a long thin strip of land which provides access to a wider area, looking altogether like a flag on a flagpole. Flag lots are generally created to provide access to the street from a lot in the middle of a block. Flag lots often cause conflicts with neighbors, particularly over access, and make

any future subdivision very difficult. The best way to avoid the flag lot problem is to require (1) a minimum road frontage of 60 feet for each lot created by a subdivision; (2) all side boundary lines of a lot to be at right angles to straight street lines and radial to curved street lines; (3) a lot depth-to-width ratio of at least two and one-half to one; or (4) an outright ban on the creation of flag lots.

Landlocked lots have no street frontage and so have no access to the street. The buyer of a landlocked lot must negotiate with neighbors for an easement or right-of-way to construct a driveway. But neighbors are under no legal obligation to grant access to a landlocked lot. Landlocked lots are most commonly found in old subdivisions that were created before subdivision regulations were adopted. The simplest way to avoid new landlocked lots is to require that each new lot have a minimum road frontage.

Some subdivision ordinances prohibit the creation of *through lots* in residential areas. A through lot has frontage on opposite sides of a block and is also called a *double frontage* lot. In residential areas, through lots are considered a waste of land, but in commercial areas through lots are often useful in providing access both for customers at the storefront and for the shipping and receiving of merchandise at the back of the store.

Platting Procedures

Whenever a landowner proposes a subdivision and before any of the new lots may be sold or buildings built, the subdivider must apply for approval from the planning commission (see Figure 17–5). There is a great deal of confusion over the procedure and purpose of subdivision plat review hearings. The subdivision review process should be very clearly defined in the regulations.

The first task for the planning commission or staff is to require the applicant to obtain an opinion from an attorney or abstractor certifying the names of the property owners. This process should be repeated at the time of the filing of the final plat to determine that the applicant is, in fact, entitled to apply for subdivision and legally empowered to offer dedications of the land to the public. All too often joint or common owners, life estates, and corporate parties are not identified in the platting process.

Figure 17–5 shows that the developer is required to make three separate trips before the planning commission. The applicant first submits a sketch plan of the proposed subdivision to the town clerk or planning commission (see Figure 17–6). If a staff planner is available, the sketch plan is usually reviewed in the office with the applicant. If there is no staff, the planning commission reviews the sketch plan and, at a hearing, advises the subdivider about any changes that need to be made to comply with the town plan and land use ordinances and to reduce the impact on town services.

This initial hearing should be advertised as a public hearing (usually as part of the regular meeting of the planning commission) even if it is not required by law. The reason is simple: the developer needs input early in the design stage rather than later when development plans are rapidly solidifying. In short, the sketch plan hearing is a concept discussion session. The developer should present air photos (for large tracts) and well-drawn sketches of roads, lots, special areas, and proposed buildings. The planning commission should discuss:

1. How is the development being financed?
2. What is the proposed density?
3. What types of services will be required?
4. What are some of the physical conditions: soils, slope, drainage?
5. What is the traffic pattern?
6. What are the characteristics of the neighboring land uses?
7. What does the land use plan call for in this area?
8. How is the area zoned?

The public should offer comments after the developer makes the sketch proposal. How-

Figure 17–5 The subdivision application process

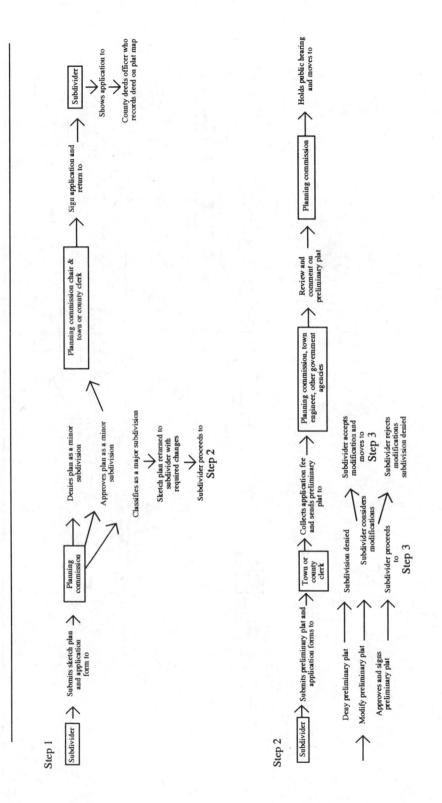

Figure 17-5 – continued

STEP 3

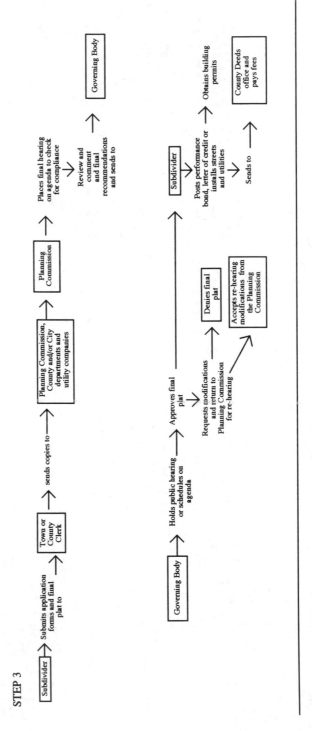

Figure 17-6 Example sketch plan drawn on USGS topographic map

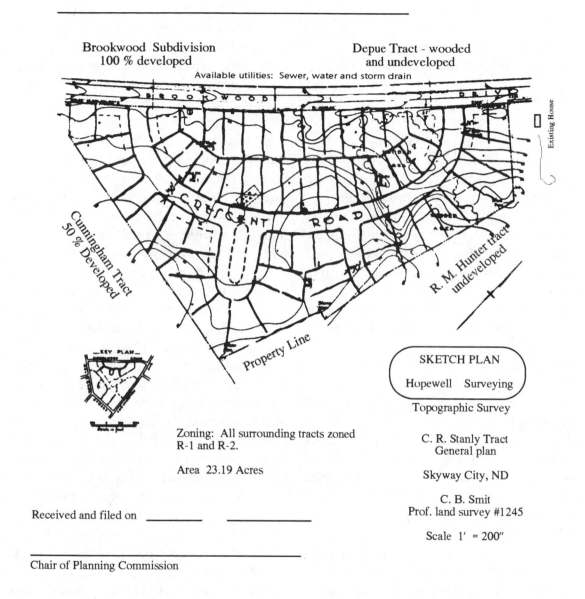

Brookwood Subdivision
100 % developed

Depue Tract - wooded
and undeveloped

Available utilities: Sewer, water and storm drain

Existing House

Cunningham Tract
50 % Developed

R. M. Hunter tract
undeveloped

Property Line

KEY PLAN

SKETCH PLAN

Hopewell Surveying

Topographic Survey

Zoning: All surrounding tracts zoned
R-1 and R-2.

Area 23.19 Acres

C. R. Stanly Tract
General plan

Skyway City, ND

C. B. Smit
Prof. land survey #1245

Scale 1' = 200"

Received and filed on _____ _____

Chair of Planning Commission

ever, unlike rezoning this is not an adversary hearing. The area is already zoned for the proposed use and the debate now centers around the physical character of the proposed development and the relationship of the site to the surrounding environment. The time has passed for meaningful debate over the actual use of the land.

After the public and the planning commission discuss the sketch plan with the developer, the commission should explain in detail which features of the proposed subdivision need to be changed or strengthened by the time the preliminary plat is prepared.

Within a certain time period, usually six months, the subdivider must file a preliminary plat with the town clerk or the sketch plan will be declared invalid and the subdivision denied.

Once the preliminary plat is prepared, the town clerk sends copies to the planning commission, the town engineer, and other government agencies from which the town council would like an opinion. Next, the planning commission holds a public hearing on the preliminary plat (again, as part of its regularly scheduled meeting). At the second hearing, the preliminary plat stage, all surveys have been completed, the property has been divided into cross section (topography), and all roads and easements appear on the plat. The developer is ready to discuss final plans for public utilities, precise road alignments, water courses, and open space requirements (see Figure 17–7).

The job of the planning commission here is twofold—compliance and technical review. *Compliance* is simply a matter of determining if the developer has complied with all requests that were made during the hearing on the sketch plan. A *technical review* determines whether the developer has complied with all requirements in the subdivision regulations, such as whether new streets have the required width and whether all lots are the proper size or if all lots have been tested for percolation prior to the installation of septic systems. A brief sample checklist is presented in Figure 17–8.

If the subdivider proposes to use on-site sewer and water facilities (septic tanks and wells), the county office of the state department of health should at least review the final plat, if not the preliminary plat. On-site sewer

and water facilities generally should not be permitted in towns that have municipal sewer and water systems. On-site facilities may be allowed only if it is not possible to connect the subdivision to the municipal systems and if the subdivider and subsequent landowners sign waivers not to protest future special assessments should public sewer and water be provided. These waivers must accompany the deeds on the lots which are created, thus enabling the community to recoup the costs of servicing the subdivision when sewer and water facilities are extended to it.

The hearing for the preliminary plat is the final opportunity for public input. The public will have an opportunity to see the development as it will eventually appear and make meaningful comments. After approval is given to move to the preparation of the final plan, the time has passed to make changes.

The preliminary plat stage is also the final time that the planning commission will be able to impose restrictions (exactions) on the proposed development. The planning commission should discuss what restrictions, if any, are needed and direct the developer to make these changes. The developer certainly has the right to make counterproposals to the restrictions and should be given the opportunity to do so. When all discussions are finalized, presuming that there is substantial agreement between the planning commission and the developer, the planning commission should indicate that they are ready to review the final plat at a future meeting, but no later than one year.

Once the preliminary plat is approved, the subdivider now prepares the final plat (see Figure 17–9) and returns to the planning commission for approval of the final plat. Gener-

Figure 17-7 Example preliminary plat

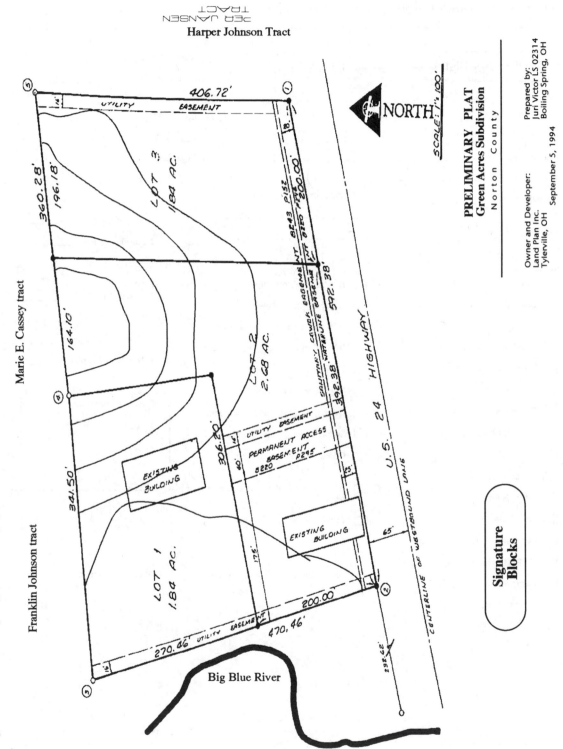

Figure 17–8 Model preliminary plat checklist

(Preliminary Plat) ——————→ Checklist

Public hearing date: _____

First published on: _____

Date submitted _____   Date Checked _____   Checked by: ☐ Clerk

General   ☐ Deeds

Name of development _____   ☐ Engineer

Current zoning _____   ☐ Planner

Amount of fee _____   Name and address of applicant

_____

_____

1. Size of tract _____

2. Number of lots _____

3. Average lot size _____

(Check if OK)

☐ Scale   ☐ Existing features shown   4. Width of utility easements _____

☐ Legend   ☐ Adjacent roads shown   5. Width of r.o.w. _____

☐ North point   ☐ Adjacent tract owners shown   6. Size of plat sheets _____

☐ Legal description   ☐ Internal road r.o.w.   7. Number of copies _____

☐ Name and seal of surveyor   ☐ Utility easements

☐ Title and deed check   ☐ Connection points to utilities

☐ Water retention   ☐ Drainage features and easements

Proposed Variances
1.
2.
3.

☐ Table for lot data   ☐ Setbacks, yards and lot entrances

☐ Lot sizes   ☐ Connecting Roads to other developments

☐ Lot numbers/addresses

☐ Street Names   ☐ All portions of the tract subdivided or phased

☐ Percolation tests   ☐ Copy of proposed covenants

☐ Feasibility study for water

☐ F.I.R.M. (flood plain)

☐ Certificate of elevation

Planning Commission Review Notes: Mandatory Changes

1.   1.

2.   2.

3.   3.

4.   4.

5.   5.

6.   6.

7.   7.

Figure 17–9 Example final plat

Legal Description and Owner's Certificate.

Surveyed representation of all lots and streets

Plat notations

Table of lots

Signature blocks for government officials

FINAL PLAT
MEADOWLARK ESTATES

Norton County

Jural Victor - Registered Land Surveyor

ally, a public hearing is not required at this final stage. The job of the planning commission is to ensure that the final plat complies with all the required changes to the preliminary plat. When the chair and/or secretary of the planning commission sign the mylar, the final plat is sent to the governing body.

The governing body formally accepts any dedications (such as road rights-of-way) offered to the public and approves ordinances that specify development payments, such as money in lieu of dedication or impact fees. When the applicant appears before the governing body, the time has passed for a technical review of the plat design or to discuss density and land use. If the governing body finds flaws in the dedication process or other errors that might have gone unnoticed, the final plat may be returned for correction—but this is a rare event. If state enabling statutes or home rule options create a greater review role for the governing body, the entire process must be redesigned to include these elected officials in the hearing process at the preliminary or sketch plat stages.

When the governing body signs the final plat, the original copy must be filed with the deeds officials and town clerk. Copies are then distributed to the appropriate officials, engineer, the governing body, and utility companies.

Before the final plat is approved, and before any lots are sold, the subdivider must be required to install or pay for the installation of public improvements. Examples of such improvements include paved streets, sewerage, sidewalks, street name signs, and utilities (water, gas, electricity). Alternatively, arrangements can be made to allow the subdivider to post a performance bond, letter of credit, or escrow account to guarantee that all improvements will be installed within two years of the date of approval of the subdivision. The bond or check should be in an amount equal to the estimated cost of the required improvements as determined by the town engineer. If the subdivider does not install the improvements within the specified time limit, usually one year, the bond or credit is called and the facilities are installed under the supervision of the local government. Bonds, letters of credit, and escrows are in the form of a contract, and, therefore, an attorney should always examine the final provisions. Also, it is important that you work closely with the financial institution providing the guarantee for the scheduled improvements.

The posting of *performance guarantees*, often called development assurances, is a difficult task for rural areas and small towns. Rural subdividers seldom have professional development experience and are almost always undercapitalized. Rural subdividers argue that they should be allowed to sell a portion of their lots to gain capital for improvements. Many first time subdividers quickly become disillusioned when lot sales fall below initial expectations and request more time to install facilities. Another argument is that the community or county should pay part of the cost of the mandatory improvements because taxpayers stand to benefit from future property taxes. None of these arguments is consistent with sound public policy, good community planning, or the duty of public officials to protect future lot purchasers. Effective management of the development process means that improvements must be provided and that the cost must be borne by those who will directly benefit.

The best possible way to avoid the problems that inevitably accompany financial assurances is to establish a firm policy that all improvements must be provided under a special obligation bond. Rural officials often reject this route because of the time and effort required to obtain the bonds and administer taxing the special district consisting of the new subdivision. However, in the long run, this system has benefits that far outweigh the administrative costs to government.

What the Final Plat Should Contain

Preparing the final plat is an important process. Failure to observe a few simple rules may cause problems with marketability of title, future recording of deeds, enforcement, and land sales.

Instructions must be given to the person or persons who will actually prepare the final plat. The plat must be drawn on very good quality, acid free paper, or mylar. Plats are permanent records and must last for a century or longer. Nearly all planning commissions require that plats be submitted on mylar, accompanied by a number of paper copies to be specified in the regulations, and drawn with a permanent ink or photocopied on the surface. The user must specify the dimensions of the mylar sheet, such as 24 by 36 inches. With the increasing use of computer imaging, computer-aided design, and geographic-information systems, many plats are now safely stored as graphics on electronic media, ready for instant use.

The final plat must include the following information:

1. The name of the subdivision or development and the name of all new roads.

2. The legal description of the property being subdivided must appear on the plat. The surveyor makes a statement at the end of the survey attesting to all descriptions. The surveyor then signs and dates the survey and applies his or her seal.

3. A statement, usually "The Ownership Certificate," acknowledges ownership of the tract and offers to dedicate easements and land to the public. This is a statement of property ownership conveying to the public all lands that are to be used for roads, utilities, sidewalks, and other facilities. This statement is signed by the owner, or owners, exactly as the signatures appear on the title to the property. That is, if the title to the property appears as John and Jean Smith, it cannot be signed as Mr. and Mrs. John Smith. If the property is titled to multiple owners, then all owners must sign. If other people, businesses, or government agencies have an interest in the property, such as a utility company with an easement, they must also sign or provide a waiver. All signatures on this portion of the plat must be notarized.

4. The final plat must contain signature spaces for a number of public officials indicating their approval. First is the signature of the chair of the planning commission indicating compliance with the land development regulations. The most important signature is that of the chair of the governing body accepting all dedications and approving the plat for filing. A number of other signatures, written as a requirement in the subdivision regulations, are common on small town and rural area plats. The review of the town engineer is very important to assure that roads and utilities will be provided at professional standards. The review of a sanitarian or professional sanitary engineer is vital if municipal sewer and water cannot be provided.

Often the town or county clerk signs the final plat attesting to the fact that all plat fees and taxes have been paid.

5. A table of lots. This table includes the following information for all lots:

- Lot number.
- Size in square feet or acres and fractions.
- Distance of setbacks and yards.
- Dimensions of utility easements.

When all the signatures have been completed, the final plat must be checked just before filing. At a minimum, the following checks should be made.

1. Make sure that the plat is properly signed by all those having an interest in the land.

2. Read the legal description and trace through all the boundaries on the plat. Make sure that the survey distances, courses, and bearings add up to the figures given between each pin. Several inexpensive software programs are available to aid with this calculation.

3. Check that all setback requirements indicated on the plat are equal to or greater than those required by the zoning ordinance. Make sure that a notation of the official zoning designation appears somewhere on the plat. Check that all lot sizes are equal to or greater than those required by the zoning ordinance.

4. Recheck all road widths and lengths of cul-de-sacs for compliance with subdivision requirements.

5. Determine if all signature spaces are properly signed and dated and notarized when required.

6. Check to see if the seal of the preparer (surveyor or engineer) is on the plat and that the survey is properly dated.

7. Be sure to check with the post office a final time to determine if all new road names are acceptable (spelling, length) and not too similar to existing roads within the delivery area.

8. Make sure that any restrictive covenants are filed with the plat.

9. If conditions (exactions) have been placed on the subdivider, then a check must be made to assure that these have been fulfilled or a notation made on the plat that they will be fulfilled. A building permit cannot be issued until the conditions have been met.

At this point the final plat is ready for filing. It should be taken to the register of deeds and the filing fee paid.

Exhibit 17–1
A Few Commonsense Facts
about the Subdivision Review Process

1. A plat should never be released from the preliminary review stage until a majority of the planning commissioners go on record to do so.

2. Objections to the preliminary plat should be clearly stated and presented in writing to the developer. The developer should have a very clear idea of what steps must be undertaken to overcome these objections. The planning commission should ask the developer whether these objections will be met.

3. A hearing for a final plat should be scheduled only after public officials are satisfied that all objections have been addressed. If controversy remains, then the plat should remain at the preliminary stage. If the developer and the planning commission cannot agree prior to the final plat stage, then the entire proposal should be rejected and the reasons for doing so given to the developer in writing.

4. If all obligations have been met, then approval of the final plat should be swift. Planning commissioners should be told that if they plan to vote against the proposal, they should do so only if the record clearly indicates that the developer

has not met the demands imposed by the planning commission.

5. The final plat must be sent to the governing body. Only the governing body, as elected officials, can accept dedications for the public. If the governing body, after a public hearing on the matter, feels that the planning commission has missed essential points or has made a serious error, the final plat should not be rejected: it should be immediately returned to the planning commission, accompanied by the reasons in writing for the return.

The Costs of Subdivision Review and Land Development

Subdividers often consider subdivision ordinances to be unnecessarily detailed and expensive to follow. Indeed, the subdivision review process may take up to several months and involve thousands of dollars in preparing the sketch plan, preliminary plat, and final plat. The subdivider may also be required to bear the cost of installing services before the final plat is approved. This situation puts the subdivider at risk of not recouping major expenses if the final plat is denied.

There are three ways that a town can keep a subdivider's costs down without weakening the subdivision review process. First, the subdivision ordinance can state that a subdivision review shall last for no more than 90 days. This keeps the review process from dragging on and costing the subdivider a fortune. Second, after the preliminary plat is approved, the town can enter into a contract with the subdivider stating that if the subdivider installs the required services and provides the necessary certificates, then the town will approve the final plat. The contract thus removes an element of risk for the subdivider and spells out exactly what is expected.

Third, an effective way to streamline the subdivision review process is to distinguish between major and minor subdivisions. A minor subdivision would involve two or three lots, while a major subdivision would be four or more lots. The review process for the minor subdivision would require less detail in the sketch plan, preliminary plat, and final plat; and the review process could be completed in 45 days. Communities should check their state enabling legislation to make sure that they are allowed to regulate minor subdivisions (also known as partitions).

ADMINISTRATION OF THE SUBDIVISION ORDINANCE

The administration and enforcement of the subdivision ordinance is the responsibility of the zoning administrator (often the town clerk), planning commission, and the town governing body. The zoning administrator collects subdivision application materials and submits them to the planning commission and government officials. The planning commission reviews the subdivider's application and makes recommendations to the town governing body, which either approves or denies the application.

The basic method for enforcing the subdivision ordinance is through the building permit. No permits are issued unless the property is properly split or platted and the required public services are made available.

A building permit should not be issued until the administrator is assured that all improvements will be properly located within the lots. An applicant for a building permit should be required to provide stakes or markers for each corner of a proposed building to allow the administrator or building inspector to measure distances.

Modern subdivision practice includes good records management! A permit tracking process must be established so that parallel programs, such as zoning, floodplain management, variances, and utility connection permits, can be tracked in the future. Adequate software programs exist to allow small communities to record all actions in a database.

Many communities require that a homebuilder obtain sewer, water, and driveway connection permits when a building permit is issued. In addition, percolation tests and inspections must be performed on rural lots prior to construction.

Good administration also includes periodic amendments to the subdivision regulations. The subdivision ordinance may be amended in a similar way to amending the zoning ordinance (see Figure 16–6). Any individual may petition to change the subdivision ordinance or the planning commission may recommend changes to the town governing body. The governing body then holds a public hearing and makes a final decision to approve, modify, or deny the subdivision amendment.

A subdivider may apply for a waiver of certain requirements of the subdivision ordinance when presenting a sketch plan. But unlike a zoning variance, a subdivision waiver means that the applicant must provide an alternative way of meeting the subdivision regulations. Waivers should refer to minor issues and should be treated on a case-by-case basis. A waiver should be granted only if it will not adversely affect the provision of infrastructure or not cause harm to neighbors or future lot owners.

Finally, the subdivision ordinance should list the fees the subdivider must pay in applying for subdivision approval and the penalties for violations of the ordinance.

SUMMARY

The subdivision ordinance is used to regulate the division of undeveloped land into lots for future sale and development. The ordinance spells out standards for improvements and services, such as streets, sidewalks, sewerage, and water lines, among others. A subdivider is usually required to install some, if not all, of the improvements before any lots can be sold or construction can begin. The subdivision ordinance serves to ensure orderly growth which will be physically attractive and not a heavy burden on town finances. There should be consistency between the town plan, the zoning ordinance, capital improvements plan, and the subdivision ordinance. Subdivision regulations also should be administered in keeping with the goals and objectives of the town plan and the zoning ordinance and capital improvements program.

18

The Capital Improvements Program

When, where, and how much a town invests in public services plays a large role in determining when, where, and how much commercial, residential, and industrial development will occur. Public service costs are generally higher per person in small towns than in large communities because of the smaller population and narrower tax base. Therefore, it is important for small towns to plan for the construction and maintenance of public services in order to conserve on limited public funds.

A capital improvements program shows (1) what services a town will build, repair, or replace; (2) where these services are or will be located; and (3) when construction, repair, or replacement will happen. Generally, a capital improvements program will look five to ten years into the future, but this may vary according to a town's estimates of future population growth and service needs. A town experiencing rapid growth may have to draft a new program every couple of years to keep up with rising service demands.

The items commonly included in a capital improvements program are roads and bridges, school buildings, sewer and water lines, treatment plants, municipal buildings, solid waste disposal sites, and police and fire equipment. The program should contain detailed information on the capacity of current facilities, projected future demand for public services, standards for road construction and sewer and water pipes, and estimated future costs and financing arrangements in relation to expected town budgets.

The purpose of the capital improvements program is to anticipate the location and amount of service needs and to provide adequate services at a reasonable cost. In some towns, the program may help conserve scarce resources such as water and energy, especially if the town operates a municipal utility. By not extending services (especially sewer and water lines) to certain areas, the town can discourage development in environmentally sensitive locations. Furthermore, expanding public services can be very expensive, and the capital improvements program can help coordinate projects and avoid mismanagement, such as paving a street one year and tearing it up the next to install a sewer line.

A town should be careful not to expand or upgrade services just because it has decided that growth is desirable. There should be a reasonable assurance that private development will follow the public services. This is particularly true in the case of attracting new industrial plants. These firms like to have industrial sites that already have sewer and water facilities as well as good highway access. Yet, a town may spend up to several hundred thousand dollars installing the services to the site without ever having any industrial plants move in. Some states require that public services—especially sewer and water—be available before a major development can be built. This concept is known as *concurrency* and ensures that new development will not exceed a community's ability to provide services to it.

On the other hand, a capital improvements program may show that some land should not be zoned for a particular use because it is too expensive to service. For example, zoning land for industrial use without nearby sewerage and water lines makes little sense. Many towns have overzoned the amount of land for industrial use; often it is too expensive for the town to install the needed services and no prospective manufacturing firm would be willing to pay for installing the services. Thus, a capital improvements program may help revise both the future land use map and the zoning map. The town would also be wise to adopt a policy for concurrency, which means that private development will be allowed to occur only when adequate public services for

that development are in place. The concurrency policy is especially important for rapidly growing towns that are struggling to restrain skyrocketing property tax burdens.

The best strategy is to coordinate the capital improvements program with the town plan and zoning and subdivision ordinances. The community facilities section and transportation section of the miniplan contain information on the location, capacity, and current and expected demand for town services. The land use section of the miniplan indicates where different kinds of future development are expected to locate. This is important because the type and design of new development (as well as the location) will affect the public costs of providing services. The zoning ordinance and map show the types and densities of development allowed in different parts of the town. The subdivision ordinance states what services the town requires a subdivider to install before new lots can be sold or developed.

The town plan and ordinances will help town officials decide which services to expand, repair, or replace, where, and when. The capital improvements program will often save the town money in the advance acquisition of land for installing services. The capital improvements program should ensure that adequate services will be available in areas of the town targeted for growth. Different zones and districts will need different services and capital improvements. Few developers are willing to develop an area before public services are installed. Here the planning commission should link the capital improvements program with the subdivision regulations to decide (1) what services the town is willing to provide for a subdivision and (2) what services the subdivider must install. These decisions will greatly help in both budgeting town money and setting priorities for capital improvements projects.

Together, the town plan, ordinances, and capital improvements program should aim to create a concentrated pattern of development and avoid sprawl. Scattered development, which may spill beyond the town boundaries, is costly to service, especially when new roads and sewer and water lines must be installed. A capital improvements program may help avoid annexation problems. A capital improvements program should include a map indicating the current location of public services and the boundaries of the area the town is willing and able to service. If the program states that no town services will be extended beyond the town boundaries, this will tend to discourage development on county land adjacent to the town. In the past, service and financial problems have arisen when towns extended services beyond their boundaries into areas of their extraterritorial jurisdiction. Even when towns annexed these areas, the result was greater sprawl and more costly services for all townspeople.

A town may adopt a rule that any new subdivision adjacent to the town will be immediately annexed and provided with services at the residents' expense. In the past, county residents living near a town often resisted annexation because they could use the town services (especially schools) without paying the higher town taxes. Thus, an annexation with services rule may actually discourage sprawl.

CREATING A CAPITAL IMPROVEMENTS PROGRAM

Although few small towns have created capital improvements programs, many towns do have schedules for replacing certain equipment and have targeted money for replacement costs. Currently, there is a growing awareness of the value of budgeting for public facilities. This is especially true since the end of the federal revenue sharing program in early 1987. Most towns are concerned with maintaining roads, streets, and bridges rather than planning for the construction of a new school five years from now. The main value of creating a capital improvements program is that it compels town officials and townspeople to think about the future of the town and to budget town money over time to provide necessary services. Also, it is essential to link a community's land use goals and objectives with the capital improvement program so that growth-inducing public facilities are provided in those areas where the community desires growth and kept out of those places slated for conservation.

A case-by-case, as-the-need-arises approach to capital improvements is a poor way to set priorities to meet current and future service needs. Because public revenue is generally scarce in small towns, there is a need to spend these limited funds as effectively as possible. Some states even require towns to establish an official capital improvements program. More often, a town planning commission draws up an informal program and presents it to the town governing body. Whether or not the governing body formally adopts the program, the point is to use the information in the program as a guide for town budgeting and planning.

Capital improvements programs come to life because of (1) an urgent need, such as contaminated wells requiring an extension of the municipal water system; (2) a foreseeable need, such as the need to provide services for a rapidly increasing population; (3) economic development efforts, such as extending sewerage and water lines to an industrial site; (4) a complaint from residents, such as crowded schools; or (5) a need to spend money more carefully in a town with a stagnant or declining tax base.

Who is responsible for putting together and managing the capital improvements program? Generally the governing body should pass a resolution giving the planning commission the authority to draft a capital improvements program and budget (see sample resolution). Most small towns have limited government personnel to oversee capital improvements. But several individuals could lend their expertise in working with the planning commission (see Figure 18–1). The town engineer, town manager, town clerk, planning staff, the planning commission, and private citizens—all may have good insights on construction, repair, and replacement projects. Public participation is very important and highly recommended. If the public participates in creating the capital improvements program, they will tend to be more willing to support higher taxes, user fees, and bond issues to finance the projects.

Sources of assistance on capital improvements programs include the following:

1. The regional planning agency or council of governments can be especially helpful in putting together grant applications for state and federal funds.

2. The state department of commerce, development, or planning can provide information on construction standards, technology for specific projects, and financing through grants, loans, or bonds.

3. The state association of cities and towns can share the experiences of other small towns in financing and managing capital improvements.

4. Engineering consulting firms can evaluate a town's needs for roads, water, sewerage, and solid waste disposal and can provide designs and cost estimates of potential projects.

The planning commission should draft a list of capital improvements projects and a budget and hold a public hearing as part of its regularly scheduled meeting. Next, the planning commission should submit the capital improvements program and budget to the town governing body. The governing body should use these recommendations in putting together the annual town budget and in planning for future budgets. The planning commission should update the capital improvements plan every two or three years.

Exhibit 18–1
Sample Resolution of the Governing Body for the Creation of a Capital Improvements Program and Budget

The planning commission is hereby given authority to draft a capital improvements program of projects to be undertaken by the town during each of the next five years. The program will describe the estimated costs of the projects and proposed methods of financing. The program will also include a capital budget listing the projects to be undertaken by the town in the upcoming fiscal year, the estimated costs of the projects, and the proposed method of financing. Both the capital improvements program and the capital budget will provide a description of each project, the level of priority, and the overall impact on town operating expenses.

A capital project may involve any of the following projects, either separately or in any combination: (1) a physical improvement including furnishings, equipment, or machinery used in construction, repair, or maintenance; or (2) a study or survey involving a physical improvement; or (3) land or rights in land.

The planning commission may submit recom-

Figure 18-1 Creating a capital improvements program

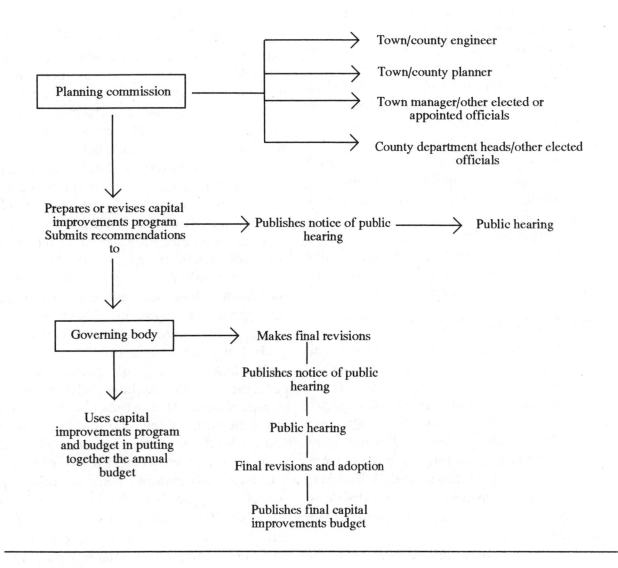

mendations each year to the governing body on the capital improvements program and budget.

The governing body may adopt, amend, or repeal the capital improvements program and budget after one or more public hearings. A copy of the proposed capital improvements program and budget must be filed with the town clerk and planning commission at least 15 days before a public hearing.

Elements to Include in the Capital Improvements Program

The capital improvements program does not have to be a complicated document. The program should be tailored to meet the community's particular service needs, and the program should be presented in a systematic and organized fashion. It may be useful to obtain a current capital improvements program from a similar size town. But remember that each community has its own goals, service needs, and financial capacity.

Elements to include in the capital improvements program are:

1. An inventory of public facilities and capacity and a map indicating the location of these facilities and the area the town is willing to service in the future.

2. A five- to ten-year projection of future service demands and maintenance needs.

3. Policies governing the use of different financing arrangements.

4. A list of priority projects.

5. A capital improvements budget, listing the timing, location, and financing arrangements for different projects.

Inventory of Public Facilities

A helpful starting point is to use the community facilities and transportation sections of the miniplan to compile an inventory of the location, capacity, and current and expected demand for public services. Next, draft a map of existing streets, sewer and water lines, schools, municipal buildings, parks and recreation areas, and the town landfill. The map may also show proposed service extensions, new buildings, and limits to the area the town is willing to service.

Good records on public services make the capital improvements program easier to create and update. A computer can be of considerable help for storing the inventory of town services and equipment, maintenance records, and replacement schedules. It is also extremely useful in showing different budgets and financing arrangements.

An inventory of community facilities should be done by functional departments, such as in Table 18–1.

Projection of Future Demands and Maintenance Needs

The projection of future service demands and maintenance needs should be based on the following information: expected population increase, existing facilities that need repairs or replacement, a change in the goals and objectives of the community, and a change in the structure of the town population.

A population projection should be available from the population section of the miniplan. This will give some idea of how many people are expected to demand services in the future. Also, the economic base section of the miniplan should indicate expected new businesses and industries and changes in the make-up of the economic base, such as more tourism and less agricultural processing. These economic changes will certainly affect service demands.

The town engineer (or public works director in a larger town) should be asked to compile a list of existing facilities that need repairs or replacement. This list should include the age of the facilities, the condition, the capacity and use level (excess capacity), and what and when repairs or replacement will be needed.

Changes in community goals and objectives should first appear in drafting or updating the miniplan. These changes may also surface during public hearings on the capital improvements programs. Changes in goals tend to focus on whether the community should have more growth or less growth. More growth means more capital improvements; less growth means fewer capital improvements. Changes in objectives will affect which projects will be built to achieve certain goals. For example, suppose the town has a goal of improving recreational facilities. The old objective was to acquire more public park space. The new objective is to build a public swim-

Table 18–1 A sample inventory of public facilities

Department	Capital Item	Purchase/ Construction Date	Useful Life	Capacity	Current Level of Use	Replacement Cost	Source of Funds
Fire							
	Fire Station	1968	30 yrs	4 Bays+ Meeting Room	3 Bays	$110,000	Operating
	Ladder Truck	1969	25 yrs	100,000 mi	100,000 mi	$85,000	
	Tanker	1984	15 yrs	100,000 mi	70,000 mi	$50,000	
General Government							
	Municipal Building (to expand)	1964	30 yrs	Five Employees	Six Employees	$90,000	Reserve Account
	Computer	1990	10 yrs	Three Employees	One Employee	$25,500	
	Copier	1986	10 yrs	2,500 Copies per Month	2,500 Copies per Month	$1,500	
Recreation							
	Swimming Pool	1975	30 yrs	300 people per day	200 people per day	$100,000	Gen. Bond
	Baseball Field	1973	not known	1 Ten Team League	2 Ten Team Leagues	$90,000	Grant
	Tennis Courts	1993	25 yrs	50 people per day	20 people per day	$35,000	
Roads							
	Dump Truck	1984	10 yrs	100,000 mi	82,000 mi	$55,000	Operating
	Storage Shed	1976	30 yrs	4 Bays + Sand/Salt Storage	Same	$80,000	
	Loader	1989	20 yrs	100,000 hrs	20,000 hrs	$85,000	
	Grader	1982	20 yrs	100,000 mi	53,000 mi	$100,000	
Schools							
	Elementary School	1971	40 yrs	250 Students	195 Students	$450,000	Gen. Bond
	School Bus #1	1983	10 yrs	100,000 mi	100,000 mi	$38,000	Operating
	School Bus #2	1992	10 yrs	100,000 mi	10,000 mi	$38,000	
Water							
	Well Field	1980	not known	80,000 gal. per day	54,000 gal. per day	$120,000	Special Bond
	Filtration Plant	1980	20 yrs	80,000 gal. per day	54,000 gal. per day	$85,000	
	Pump Station	1975	20 yrs	60,000 gal. per day	54,000 gal. per day	$55,000	
	3.5 Mile Water Main	1975	50 yrs	60,000 gal. per day	54,000 gal. per day	$240,000	

SOURCE: Adapted from E. Humstone and J. Squires, Capital Budget and Program, Vermont Department of Housing and Community Affairs, 1992.

ming pool. This new objective is a construction project with the potential to generate revenues from charging fees for using the pool. The timing, location, and financing of the pool project is likely to be much different from the park land acquisition project.

Changes in the structure of the town population can also have a substantial impact on service demands. Most local budgets are spent on education. If the number of school-age children is increasing, there will be pressure for added school space. On the other hand, many small towns are experiencing a rise in elderly populations. This trend suggests a need for more hospital space, clinics, and nursing homes.

Policies on Financing Arrangements

Before selecting individual projects and drafting a capital improvements budget, the planning commission should establish policies on the use of different arrangements for funding different kinds of projects. For example, many towns are reluctant to go into debt by issuing bonds to pay for major construction projects. These towns will undertake major projects only if state or federal funds are available. Guidelines for financing arrangements will make the budget process proceed more smoothly. One of the goals of the capital improvements program is to avoid abrupt fluctuations in local finances.

Financing policies should address two major questions: (1) How to finance a particular construction project or piece of equipment, and (2) Who should pay the cost. If an improvement or piece of equipment benefits the entire community, then all taxpayers should share the cost. But if the construction project or equipment benefits only a certain neighbor-hood, then user fees, special assessments, or a special district are more appropriate.

Small towns can pay for capital improvements in three main ways: (1) as items in the town annual budget on a pay-as-you-go basis; projects are paid for from annual property taxes, user fees, and licenses; (2) from town reserves; and (3) by obtaining state and federal grants. Town officials should identify what state and federal programs exist to assist with capital improvements. This information may be obtained from appropriate state departments, the local offices of the cooperative extension service, and the state league of cities and towns.

Most towns use their annual revenues and reserves to purchase equipment and to maintain existing facilities, especially roads. Some towns have built up large reserves and use the interest from the reserve account to help pay for capital improvements. Towns commonly apply for state and federal grants to help pay for major projects such as sewer and water lines.

There are a number of other financing arrangements that small towns can use.

Bonds. These include general obligation bonds and revenue bonds. A general obligation bond is paid off out of the town's annual revenues usually over a period of 10 to 20 years. Towns commonly sell general obligation bonds to finance schools, parks, municipal buildings, and recreation facilities. Voter approval may be required before the town can sell these bonds. Some states, such as Illinois, have state programs to pool the sale of bonds to raise funds for several small towns that would have difficulty selling bonds by themselves.

Revenue bonds are sold to develop projects that will produce revenues to the town in the form of user fees. The user fees are then used to pay off the bonds. These bonds often finance projects such as municipal sewer and water lines, where the commercial, residential, and industrial customers pay sewer and water rates to the town. Revenue bonds usually carry higher interest rates than general obligation bonds, but voter approval is rarely necessary.

Impact Fees. If impact fees are allowed by your state, larger towns and towns experiencing rapid growth may want to adopt special fees on new development that can be used to pay for needed park facilities, roads, and other community services. There must a clear link between the fee charged and the demand for additional public services. You should consult your state league of municipalities and other towns that have adopted impact fees for advice.

If you use impact fees, you should include in your annual town budget and your capital improvements program (1) the location of proposed or potential development that could create a need for new capital projects; (2) standards for capital projects to be funded with impact fees, for example, the number of public playgrounds per 1,000 children; (3) cost estimates and funding sources; and (4) the timing of development in the potential locations.

Interlocal Agreements. A town and the county or two towns located near one another can enter into an agreement to share the costs of building a project and share the facilities after construction is completed.

Lease-Purchase. The town can hire a private company to install public improvements and rent the improvements through a lease arrangement. At the end of the lease period, the town becomes the owner of the improve-

ments. The rental payments cover the installment cost to the private company plus interest and profit. Lease-purchase projects often involve the construction of municipal buildings.

Special Assessments. These are charges made to certain property owners to cover the cost to the town of installing capital improvements in the neighborhood. These improvements commonly include streets, sidewalks, water systems, and sewers. Special assessments, unlike property taxes, are paid only by those property owners who directly benefit from the improvements. For example, if several wells in a neighborhood became contaminated and the town extended a water line to the area, the town could charge the property owners in that neighborhood a special assessment to pay for the cost of extending the water line.

The town government will charge a special assessment after development has occurred, unlike exactions, which require the subdivider to install improvements before construction can begin. For instance, if homeowners in a neighborhood want a gravel road paved, the town could do the work and charge the homeowners a special assessment.

Special Districts. A special district is a public agency created to provide a single service such as sewage treatment or water systems or schools. Most special districts exist in the area just outside the town limits where the town has extraterritorial jurisdiction. A special district may be financed through revenue bonds or special assessments, and some districts have the power to impose property taxes.

Tax Increment Financing. Larger towns of 5,000 to 10,000 may want to explore the use of tax increment financing in large-scale redevelopment projects. A town can redevelop a certain area, such as a downtown central business district, with money from the sale of general obligation bonds. The new improvements (streets, sidewalks, etc.) in the central business district raise the property values in the district. These higher values result in higher property taxes for the property owners in the district. The difference between the property taxes before and after redevelopment is called the *tax increment*. This tax increment is set aside from the town's general budget to pay off the bonds the town sold to finance the redevelopment. Once the bonds have been retired, the tax increment becomes part of the town's general fund. The purpose of tax increment financing is to keep the town from spending beyond its means. The higher property taxes generated in the redevelopment district must first pay off the cost of the new improvements; the town cannot use those higher property taxes to pay for other town services until the bonds have been paid off.

Setting Project Priorities

Setting priorities for construction, repair, and replacement projects is often a difficult task. How does the need for a new elementary school compare with the need for a new fire engine or the repaving of Main Street? Capital projects involve different levels of public spending, different timing, and different financing arrangements.

One way that a planning commission and its advisors can attempt to set project priorities is to identify the importance of various proposals. Some towns use four categories: essential, desirable, acceptable, and deferrable.

Essential projects feature matters of public health and safety and meeting state and federal regulations, for example, the installation of a municipal water system to improve town

drinking water. *Desirable projects* are generally not as important as essential projects and certainly are less urgent. Still, the town will want to undertake desirable projects in the not too distant future. Repaving Main Street might be a desirable project. *Acceptable projects* have merit but are not urgent. They can be put off for a few years without threat to public health and safety. Acceptable projects tend to include quality of life improvements such as a community center for senior citizens. *Deferrable projects* are not pressing, nor are they necessary. The town can examine these projects at a later date and decide if money is available to fund them. Such a project might be the installation of benches along Main Street. Although benches might make a nice addition to Main Street, they are not necessary and should have a low priority. The needs assessment survey of the miniplan can provide information on which public projects the community feels are most important.

**Exhibit 18–2
A Note on State and
Federal Grant Programs for
Local Capital Improvements**

"Why should the town pay for a major improvements project when someone else is willing to pick up the tab?" This type of reasoning makes sense for most small towns, but there are some dangers in relying on state and federal grant programs to fund local public improvements.

1. State and federal programs may create a bias in the choice of local projects. In other words, do not apply for a grant unless you are sure it fits the needs and priorities of your community.

2. Programs may be cut or funding reduced in any given year. Applying for grants is a competitive process; the scarcer the funds, the greater the competition is likely to be.

3. It is not uncommon for federal project standards to exceed local desires. For example, the federal government may build a sewer and water system with a capacity for 10,000 people in a town of only 3,000. This could open up much more area for development than called for in the town plan.

You should contact state and regional planning agencies for information on available grant programs—both funding levels and technical project standards—to determine which programs fit the needs of your town.

Figure 18–2 provides a checklist to help evaluate individual projects and set priorities. You should decide which projects are too ambitious, too costly, or not necessary. For example, the town may want to build a swimming pool. An olympic size pool may be too ambitious and costly when a smaller size pool will adequately serve the need. In addition to pointing out the benefits of a project, you should ask, "What will happen if the project isn't built?" This will help identify projects that are not necessary or can be put off to a later date. Small towns will usually consider only a few projects, and a simple way to set priorities should be adequate. Common sense will play a key role.

The Capital Budget

The capital improvements program should present a budget listing the individual projects, their timing, location, and the financial arrangements for each project.

For each project, make a rough estimate of all of the costs involved over the life of the project and in what years these costs will occur. Costs typically include land, construction, maintenance, operation, personnel, and debt if bonds are used. You should make the cost estimates in current dollars and you should account for future inflation. Builders,

architects, engineers, bankers, and bond underwriters will be able to help in making the cost estimates. In addition, you should try to contact a town that has recently undertaken a similar project to obtain cost figures. Other information sources include the state departments of transportation, commerce, and planning and development.

The capital budget should then present an estimated budget for the coming fiscal year.

In describing the financial arrangements for each project, the planning commission should be aware of the town's overall financial picture. The commission would be wise to examine town finance trends over the past few years. The commission should ask, "How close is the town to its mandatory debt limit?" Most states set a limit on the amount of debt a town can incur based on a certain percentage of the town's taxable property value. The amount of debt the town can support will affect whether or not the town can finance new projects with bonds.

Town annual revenues and expenses in recent years will give an idea of cash flow and whether projects can be financed out of current revenues (see Tables 18–2 and 18–3). The property tax is the single largest source of local revenue. The planning commission should determine if property taxes are high, low, or moderate in relation to the income of the townspeople. Some states have limits on the property tax rate that can be charged, and property value reassessments typically occur only once every five years, sometimes even less frequently. Thus, there may be limitations to increasing property taxes to pay for projects.

In the sample town in Tables 18–2 and 18–3, the town does not appear to be bringing in enough surplus revenue to pay for

Figure 18–2   A capital improvements project checklist

	Yes	No	Not applicable
1. Will the project be financed by:			
a. annual town reserves	___	___	___
b. town reserves	___	___	___
c. sale of bonds	___	___	___
d. developer or subdivider	___	___	___
e. other _____	___	___	___
2. Is the project in accord with:			
a. the town plan	___	___	___
b. the zoning ordinance and map	___	___	___
c. the subdivision ordinance	___	___	___
d. other town ordinances and plans	___	___	___
3. The rating of the project is:			
a. essential	___	___	___
b. desirable	___	___	___
c. acceptable	___	___	___
d. deferrable	___	___	___
4. The cost of the project to the town is:			
a. major	___	___	___
b. minor	___	___	___
5. The project involves:			
a. maintenance and repair	___	___	___
b. replacement equipment	___	___	___
c. new construction	___	___	___
6. The project will be a major benefit to:			
a. commercial development	___	___	___
b. industrial development	___	___	___
c. residential development	___	___	___
d. other _____	___	___	___
7. Will the project require additional public investment in the near future?	___	___	___
8. Is the project only of benefit to a certain area or neighborhood?	___	___	___
9. The time involved in completing the project is:			
a. long term (5 years or more)	___	___	___
b. mid-term (2-3 years)	___	___	___
c. short term (1-2 years)	___	___	___
10. The project will generate revenues in the form of:			
a. user fees	___	___	___
b. higher property values/taxes	___	___	___

Each project can then be evaluated as part of a department budget as follows:

Department	Capital Item	Urgency (year needed)	Cost	Source
Fire				
___	___	___	___	___
General government				
___	___	___	___	___
Recreation				
___	___	___	___	___
Roads				
___	___	___	___	___
Schools				
___	___	___	___	___
Sewer and water				
___	___	___	___	___

Table 18–2   Trends in town expenditures

YEAR	1989	1990	1991	1992	1993	1994
Operating						
Fire Protection	$20,000	$20,000	$22,000	$25,000	$25,000	$35,000
General Government	$125,000	$135,000	$148,000	$155,000	$166,000	$185,000
Recreation	$15,000	$18,000	$20,000	$22,000	$22,000	$25,000
Roads	$155,000	$165,000	$175,000	$180,000	$200,000	$220,000
Schools	$750,000	$770,000	$810,000	$835,000	$850,000	$860,000
Sewer/Water	$50,000	$50,000	$55,000	$60,000	$60,000	$65,000
Total	$1,115,000	$1,163,000	$1,230,000	$1,277,000	$1,323,000	$1,385,000
Capital						
Fire Protection	----------	----------	----------	----------	----------	----------
General Government	----------	$3,000	----------	----------	$35,000	----------
Recreation	----------	----------	----------	----------	----------	----------
Roads	$80,000	----------	----------	$30,000	----------	----------
Schools	----------	----------	----------	----------	----------	----------
Sewer/Water	----------	----------	----------	----------	----------	----------
Total	$80,000	$3,000	0	$30,000	$35,000	0
Debt Service						
Town	----------	$50,000	$50,000	$50,000	$50,000	$50,000
School	$75,000	$75,000	$75,000	$75,000	$75,000	$75,000
Total	$75,000	$125,000	$125,000	$125,000	$125,000	$125,000
Grant Total	$1,270,000	$1,291,000	$1,355,000	$1,432,000	$1,483,000	$1,510,000

Source: Adapted from E. Humstone and J. Squires, Capital Budget and Program, Vermont Department of Housing and Community Affairs, 1992.

Table 18-3 Trends in town revenues

YEAR	1989	1990	1991	1992	1993	1994
Assessed Property Value (Assuming 100% of fair market value)	$430,000	$450,000	$460,000	$470,000	$480,000	$490,000
School tax rate	1.40	1.40	1.50	1.50	1.50	1.55
Town tax rate	0.60	0.60	0.60	0.65	0.65	0.70
Property tax revenues	$860,000	$900,000	$966,000	$1,010,500	$1,056,000	$1,102,000
Other local revenues (Fees, licenses, reserves)	$90,000	$85,000	$90,000	$95,000	$98,000	$100,000
State sources	$290,000	$290,000	$290,000	$300,000	$310,000	$315,000
Federal sources	$30,000	$16,000	$11,000	$28,000	$20,000	$15,000
Total	$1,270,000	$1,291,000	$1,357,000	$1,433,500	$1,484,000	$1,532,500

Source: Adapted from E. Humstone and J. Squires, Capital Budget and Program, Vermont Department of Housing and Community Affairs, 1992.

needed capital projects. Surplus funds should be put into a town reserve account for future capital projects. A town of the size profiled in Tables 18–2 and 18–3 should have an annual surplus of about $150,000. Note in Table 18–1 that several capital projects are scheduled for the 1990s to replace old and worn-out equipment.

The planning commission should examine the town reserves. Are they growing or shrinking? Should they be used to finance new projects or as an emergency fund?

The planning commission must be careful to list which projects will be financed with state or federal grant money. Unless the grants have been obtained, these projects may be wishful thinking. Never count on state or federal funding until the money is received. Grant programs are generally competitive and always subject to change.

Finally, the governing body can use the capital improvements budget in putting together a five-year projection of anticipated expenditures and revenues, such as in Table 18–4. This projection will give an idea of what the town's financial situation is expected to be and can alert town officials to particular needs in the near future.

SUMMARY

A capital improvements program offers a way of joining land use planning and management with the town budgeting process. A capital improvements program outlines a schedule of public service expenditures over several years. The program typically includes the construction, repair, and replacement of roads, streets, bridges, sewer and water systems, fire equipment, and solid waste disposal sites. The program presents a capital improvements budget showing both the costs of different projects and the proposed financing arrangements. The program helps town officials make better cost estimates, identify state and federal funding sources, establish priorities among different projects, and determine what improvements developers should contribute in the subdivision process.

For towns in the urban fringe areas that are experiencing rapid growth, or in rural boom towns, a capital improvements program can help establish a growth management system to control and direct growth. The program can also be useful to towns in meeting mandated state and federal standards for water treatment plants and solid waste disposal sites. Stagnant or declining towns can use the program to carefully budget shrinking tax revenues and to try to stimulate economic development.

The capital improvements program is an important way of putting the town miniplan into action. Like the miniplan, the program serves to meet the needs of town residents to maintain and improve the quality of life in their community. The program is closely related to the zoning and subdivision ordinances, which also put the miniplan into action and help determine where development and improvements should go. Public participation in creating and updating the capital improvements program is very important because then the community will be more likely to support the higher taxes, user fees, and debt needed to finance the individual projects.

Table 18–4 Trends in town expenditures and revenues

Year	1989	1990	1991	1992	1993	1994
1. EXPENDITURES						
Operating						
Fire protection	$34,000	$35,000	$36,000	$38,000	$42,000	$44,000
General government	$195,000	$215,000	$225,000	$245,000	$266,000	$285,000
Recreation	$28,000	$34,000	$38,000	$42,000	$48,000	$55,000
Roads	$255,000	$265,000	$275,000	$290,000	$320,000	$340,000
Schools	$900,000	$940,000	$960,000	$1,000,000	$1,050,000	$1,100,000
Sewer/Water	$75,000	$80,000	$85,000	$90,000	$98,000	$100,000
Total	$1,487,000	$1,569,000	$1,619,000	$1,705,000	$1,824,000	$1,924,000
Debt Service						
Town	$100,000	$100,000	$100,000	$100,000	$100,000	$100,000
Schools	$100,000	$95,000	$95,000	$95,000	$95,000	$95,000
Total	$195,000	$195,000	$195,000	$195,000	$195,000	$195,000
Total Expenses	$1,682,000	$1,764,000	$1,814,000	$1,900,000	$2,019,000	$2,119,000
2. REVENUES						
Assessed Property Value (Assuming 100% of fair market value)	$510,000	$540,000	$560,000	$570,000	$580,000	$600,000
School tax rate	1.60	1.65	1.70	1.70	1.75	1.80
Town tax rate	0.85	0.85	0.85	0.85	0.90	0.90
Property tax revenues	$1,249,500	$1,350,000	$1,400,000	$1,453,500	$1,537,000	$1,620,000
Other local revenues (Fees, licenses, reserves)	$110,000	$120,000	$130,000	$140,000	$150,000	$160,000
State sources	$329,000	$335,000	$340,000	$350,000	$350,000	$375,000
Federal sources	$20,000	$20,000	$15,000	$20,000	$20,000	$20,000
Total	$1,708,500	$1,825,000	$1,885,000	$1,9635000	$1,964,000	$2,175,000
3. FUNDS AVAILABLE FOR CAPITAL PROJECTS						
	$26,500	$61,000	$71,000	$63,500	$48,000	$56,000

Source: Adapted from E. Humstone and J. Squires, Capital Budget and Program, Vermont Department of Housing and Community Affairs, 1992.

19

Other Local Land Use Regulations

The miniplan, zoning and subdivision ordinances, and the capital improvements program set out the fundamental policies and procedures for determining where and how a community should grow. The codes and ordinances presented in this chapter are generally optional but are recommended for most small towns. These codes and ordinances address specific problems such as the health and safety of buildings and houses, agricultural uses, tree cover, storm water management, signs, nuisances, and access to the sun for solar energy devices. Often, town governments can use these codes and ordinances to quickly resolve land use problems and avoid lengthy and expensive zoning and subdivision reviews.

THE BUILDING CODE

The *building code* is a set of regulations that describes standards for the construction of new buildings. A building code can spell out what materials can or cannot be used in construction as well as establish minimum standards for plumbing, electrical wiring, fire safety, structural soundness, and overall building design. The purpose of the building code is to ensure the safety of new buildings and alterations to existing buildings.

Nearly every local government has the authority to adopt building codes. Towns do not draft building codes, but rather adopt a standard form of code. Some states have a state building code which town governments must follow or may want to follow. You may want to contact a professional planner or the state or regional planning agency for help in locating a standard building code. Professional building officers' organizations have issued model building codes for different parts of the United States. *The Code of the Building Officials Conference of America* is widely used in the Midwest and Northeast states. In the West, *The Uniform Building Code*, published by the International Conference of Building Officials, is used. The model code most used in the South is *The Southern Standard Building Code,* published by the Southern Building Code Congress. Many communities change, add, or delete sections of the model code to meet local needs and desires.

The building code works together with the housing code and zoning and subdivision regulations to ensure that new development meets community health and safety standards (see Figure 19–1). Normally, a town will not issue a building permit unless the property owner has complied with the building code and the zoning ordinance. Finally, before a new building can be used, the town will issue a certificate of occupancy indicating compliance with the conditions of the building permit.

Administration of the building code varies considerably among small towns. In larger towns and cities, a building inspector will be hired to inspect all new buildings to ensure compliance with the building code. In small towns, the building inspector may be a county building inspector or town employee who also serves as the zoning administrator, town clerk, or town engineer. Some towns hire someone for one day a week from the town utility or local sewer and water district. In some rural areas, the building inspector is a circuit-rider who serves several towns on an on-call basis.

Americans with Disabilities Act

The Americans with Disabilities Act, passed by Congress in 1991, requires businesses and governments to provide people with disabilities equal access to jobs, transportation, and public facilities. This means that all public meetings must be accessible with no physical barriers. The law also requires that all goods and services be available to people with disabilities. Places such as restaurants, hotels, theaters, laundromats, and daycare centers are included, both for new construction and for alterations to existing buildings. Zoning regulations should include a review of access to public structures and private commercial establishments. Design standards must also incorporate accessibility requirements. Local governments can follow either the Uniform Federal Accessibility Standards or the guidelines published by the Architectural and Transportation Barriers Compliance Board. For a copy of the regulations and guidelines, contact The Office on the Americans with Disabilities Act, Civil Rights Division, Department of Justice, P.O. Box 66118, Washington, D.C. 20035–6118.

THE HOUSING CODE

In most small towns, the building inspector is also responsible for administering the town housing code. The housing code defines standards for how a dwelling unit is to be used and maintained after it is built. These standards typically include crowding, indoor plumbing and heating, air quality, and fire safety (see Figure 19–1). For example, a housing code might define substandard housing as lacking all plumbing facilities or having more than one person per room. Other housing standards might be borrowed from the definition of standard, substandard minor, substandard major, and dilapidated dwelling units listed in the housing section of the miniplan. You should probably contact the county health office, the state housing and planning agencies, the regional planning agency, or a

Figure 19–1 Building and housing codes and their relation to zoning and subdivision regulations

Principal Participants in Developing Standards and codes	Building Codes Engineers - Architect -Fire Safety & Housing Specialists	Housing Codes Health and Housing Specialists, Community Development Specialists	Zoning Ordinances Planners	Subdivision Regulations Planners - Civil Engineers
OBJECTIVE:				
1. Natural light (penetration, quality, location)	Windows, yards, courts, light-wells, habitable room size, building separation.	Natural light, internal lighting, habitable room size.	Court yards, building envelope, open space, height and separation.	Open space, density, separation.
2. Access and Egress	Access to streets, corridors, stairs, doors; exits; access to bathrooms and bedrooms	Corridors, stairways, access, doors, exits, obstructions; distances and access to bedrooms and bathrooms.	Access to streets, obstructions, parking	Access to streets, circulation pattern, curb cuts.
3. Occupancy	Room dimensions (area, least dimensions, ceiling height); minimum area per person.	Room dimensions (area, least dimensions, ceiling height); minimum area per person.	Density and minimum areas, prevention of overcrowding; definition of family.	----------
4. Air Supply	Air exchange, ventilation, windows.	Windows, ventilation, temperature.	Windows, walls, building separation, height.	----------
5. Water Supply	Sizes, materials, construction; fixtures	Materials, temperature, fixtures and maintenance.	Infrastructure capacity.	Plats, facility plans, materials, sizes, construction and timing.
6. Air Pollution (discharge into air)	Vents and venting systems, blowers and exhaust systems, incinerators.	Ventilation, operation and maintenance.	Performance standards for industry, traffic generators.	Site plan review.
7. Water Pollution	Plumbing systems, septic tanks, leaching fields, lagoons, mounds and dosing systems, wells.	Maintenance and functioning of facilities and fixtures.	Performance standards, use separation, runoff controls, waste storage.	----------
8. Heating	Flow, distribution, conservation, efficiency, design and construction.	Design, distribution and maintenance.	----------	
9. Fire Safety	Construction and materials, fire detection and suppression, separation, access and egress.	Maintenance of life safety equipment for interiors, exit ways, and heating equipment.	Land use locations, density, separations, obstructions, access.	Density, building footprints, circulation, length of cul-de-sacs...

Source: Adapted from DeChira, Joseph and Lee Koppleman, *Manual of Planning/Housing and Design Criteria,* Englewood Cliffs, NJ: Prentice Hall, 1975, p. 511.

professional planning consultant for help in drafting the housing code.

Enforcement of the housing code may be difficult, given that most small towns have limited personnel. Penalties may include a daily fine for each day the dwelling unit is in violation of the housing code.

SPECIAL PURPOSE ORDINANCES

A town or county can use some *special purpose ordinances* to protect and improve the appearance of the community and to resolve neighborhood conflicts. These ordinances may be added as part of the zoning ordinance or may stand alone to emphasize their importance. The exception is the *nuisance ordinance,* which must always be drawn up separately. The planning commission, with the help of state and regional planning agencies, other towns, or a professional planning consultant, can draft these special purpose ordinances, except for the nuisance ordinances, which should be drafted by the town attorney or other lawyer in conjunction with the planning commission and town police department. When special purpose ordinances are drawn up separately, they must be cross referenced in the appropriate places in the zoning ordinance. All of the special purpose ordinances must be approved by the town governing body before they can take effect. Special purpose ordinances include a health or septic system ordinance, agricultural use ordinance, design review ordinance, historic building ordinance, tree cover ordinance, storm water management ordinance, sign ordinance, solar access ordinance, and nuisance ordinance. The design review ordinance and the historic building ordinance are discussed in Chapter 21 on small town design.

Health Ordinance

Many towns have a health ordinance that regulates the siting and type of septic system. This ordinance is designed to ensure that lot sizes and soils are adequate to absorb on-site sewage disposal and thereby prevent groundwater pollution and other health hazards.

It is common for rules applying to septic systems to be included in the town subdivision ordinance. Before the subdivision of a new lot or lots is approved, a percolation test must be performed by a professional engineer to determine whether an on-site septic system can be used and, if so, what would be the best kind of system for the property.

The state of Pennsylvania has gone so far as to ban the use of on-site septic systems if the groundwater contains more than 10 parts per million of nitrate. High concentrations of nitrates can be especially harmful to newborn babies.

Agricultural Use Notice

Agriculture as practiced today is an industrial process which involves the use of chemical fertilizers, herbicides, pesticides, and heavy machinery. Although farms are attractive to look at, there may be some inconveniences and even hazards in living next to a farm. Each state has a right-to-farm law which gives farmers some protection against nuisance suits from neighbors who complain about normal farming practices. These laws, however, have not been widely tested in the courts.

A better way to reduce conflicts between farmers and nonfarm neighbors is through an agricultural use notice included in the town's zoning ordinance. Prospective buyers and current landowners of any property located in or adjacent to an agricultural zone must be forewarned that farming operations generate noise, dust, odors, and sprays which often spill over onto neighboring lands. The following agricultural use notice is strongly recommended:

All lands within the Agricultural Zone are located in an area where land is used for commercial agricultural production. Owners, residents, and other users of this property or neighboring property may be subjected to inconvenience, discomfort, and the possibility of injury to property and health arising from normal and accepted agricultural practices and operations, including but not limited to, noise, odors, dust, the operation of machinery of any kind, including aircraft, the storage and disposal of manure, the application of fertilizers, soil amendments, herbicides, and pesticides. Owners, occupants, and users of this property should be prepared to accept such inconveniences, discomfort, and possibility of injury from normal agricultural operations, and are hereby put on official notice that the state "Right to Farm Law" may bar them from obtaining a legal judgment against such normal agricultural operations.

(Warwick Township, Lancaster County, Pennsylvania)

Resource Management Easements

Another technique, used in Bonneville and Fremont counties in Idaho, is to require resource management easements for new residential development in or adjacent to an agricultural zone. The easement recognizes that the proposed residence is located in or next to an agricultural area and may be subjected to noise, odors, dust, and other impacts

of normal farming operations. The easement waives the homeowner's legal right to object to lawful farming operations on adjacent lands. The easement is recorded as part of the landowner's deed before a building permit is issued and before any construction begins.

It is important to note that right-to-farm laws, zoning disclaimers, and resource easements protect only normal and legal farming operations. Farming practices that violate state or federal laws, such as water pollution from feedlot runoff, are grounds for lawsuits by nonfarm neighbors. Finally, the town government can pass a resolution not to enact nuisance ordinances which would restrict normal farming practices.

Setbacks

Another good technique for reducing conflicts between farmers and nonfarmers is the use of specific setback requirements both in the agricultural zone and in an adjacent residential, commercial, or industrial zone. For example, the agricultural zone could require that all new farm buildings be located at least 200 feet from the nearest property line. A residential zoning ordinance could state that no dwelling can be built closer than 100 feet from a farm boundary. Manor Township, Pennsylvania, even prohibits a residential landowner from planting trees within 30 feet of a farm boundary because shade from the trees would reduce crop yields.

One design solution worth considering is to require that houses built next to farmland be clustered so that open space on the residential land can serve as a buffer to limit the impacts between the dwellings and the neighboring farm. Cluster developments are recommended only next to already built-up areas of the town, especially where public sewer and water are available. The use of cluster developments in rural areas away from public services only encourages sprawl and the conversion of farmland to nonfarm uses.

Environmental Impact Checklist

The following checklist is useful as a guide in reviewing the impacts of proposed developments on the natural environment. Although this checklist is not a land use ordinance, it may help the planning commission to identify environmental problems that can be resolved in the subdivision review process. For example, changing the design of the development could reduce storm water runoff which could cause soil erosion and stream sedimentation.

1. Does the proposed development involve more than five acres?

2. Will the development have an impact on groundwater supplies or quality?

3. Will the development have an impact on the water quality of a lake, pond, stream, or wetland?

4. Will the development change storm water drainage or produce greater soil erosion and sedimentation?

5. Will the development affect any rare or endangered plant or animal species or hunting and fishing areas?

6. Will the development affect any scenic views or unique land forms?

7. Will the development affect any archaeological or historic sites or historic buildings?

8. Will the development cause major traffic problems?

9. Will the development cause significant air pollution?

10. Will the development generate noise, odors, or other off-site effects that might be considered a nuisance?

TREE COVER

A town can adopt a tree preservation ordinance to maintain existing tree cover, to require the use of trees to act as buffers to protect sensitive lands, and to encourage the planting of trees along streets. The town can require developers to retain a certain percentage or number of trees, to replace trees destroyed during construction, and to plant trees on a site, particularly along roads or among parking lots. Flexibility is important because the preservation or planting of trees on some sites may be virtually impossible. Also, the tree ordinance should ensure that utility rights-of-way are kept free of trees.

STORM WATER MANAGEMENT ORDINANCE

Storm water runoff can cause major damage to a landowner's property and to neighboring properties. A town can adopt a storm water management ordinance to control the impact of development on runoff, groundwater recharge, and overall water quality. The ordinance should include guidelines to assist developers in choosing appropriate storm water management techniques for their development. The ordinance should list storm water management facilities, such as year round ponds or temporary retention basins, which can provide open space, wildlife habitat, and recreational activities, such as fishing and ice skating. Larger towns may want to explore the construction of storm sewers. Other techniques include porous pavements and seepage pits. Meadows or grass strips can also be used to slow runoff and increase the recharge of groundwater.

SIGNS

Signs attract attention and provide advertising or information. A local *sign ordinance* is a special kind of design review ordinance that may restrict the type, size, and location of signs as well as sign materials. For example, many town zoning ordinances already limit the location of billboards to commercial and industrial zones.

The control of signs is a matter of safety and aesthetics. Most sign ordinances restrict advertising signs which could create traffic problems and visually clutter an area. Along strip developments, large, bright signs can dangerously distract motorists, and on commercial main streets, a jumble of signs detracts from the town's appearance (see Figure 19–2). The content of the signs is not at issue. To attempt to control the content of signs is to risk violating the sign owner's constitutional right of free speech under the First Amendment.

In drafting a sign ordinance, the planning commission should consult with local business owners. This cooperation and shared

Figure 19–2 Sign variety, uniformity, and individual expression

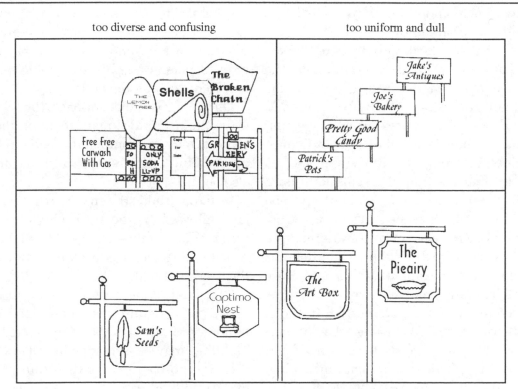

too diverse and confusing   too uniform and dull

When some degree of unified design elements are used,
signs can still express the individual character of each business

knowledge will tend to produce a more workable and acceptable ordinance.

Many towns have prohibited signs above a certain height or signs which extend beyond a certain distance from a building. Some towns have outright prohibited billboards and portable signs. A fair and successful way to eliminate nonconforming signs is to impose a time limit of three to five years for owners to remove or replace the obtrusive signs. This method, called *sign amortization*, causes no immediate hardship and gives owners reasonable time to make their signs conform to the sign ordinance.

SOLAR ACCESS

A *solar access ordinance* helps to ensure that new buildings and alterations to existing buildings do not interfere with the access to the sun of solar heating devices (either active or passive) on neighboring buildings. The ordinance may impose restrictions on the height, bulk, and siting of new buildings and alterations to protect the exposure of existing buildings to the sun. Similarly, the ordinance may allow for certain different siting, such as a zero lot line (no building setbacks from a property line), to enable new buildings to be located to best capture the sun's rays. The ordinance should take into consideration a building's exposure during the winter months when the sun's rays are at a low angle. State enabling legislation may be necessary in some states before towns can enact such ordinances. The state of Oregon, for instance, has permitted local solar access ordinances since 1981. Solar heating devices can help individual building owners conserve their use of nonrenewable energy and save money. On a townwide scale, solar heating devices can reduce a community's energy bill in the long run and keep more money in the community.

NUISANCES

Nuisance ordinances are special laws enacted by the town governing body to protect the health, safety, and welfare of the townspeople. A nuisance is a use of land or behavior that brings harm or annoyance to adjacent property owners or the general public. A nuisance ordinance is a way to resolve land use conflicts that could otherwise lead to harm or aggravation.

State laws commonly provide enabling legislation for towns to regulate a wide array of nuisances, including the following:

Noise. Barking dogs, loud music, construction, and other noise may be regulated. It is helpful to have specific regulations, such as no offensive noise allowed between 10 p.m. and 8 a.m. and requiring that the aggrieved person attempt to resolve the problem before calling the police.

Odor. Obnoxious odors from burning leaves, toxic sprays, manure, and other substances may be regulated. Aside from the odors being offensive, a health hazard may also occur.

Visual. Junk strewn about a yard or a lawn allowed to grow overly high can reduce a neighbor's enjoyment of his or her own property as well as reduce property values in the neighborhood.

Dangerous Structures. A nuisance ordinance could require that abandoned and dilapidated buildings be demolished. Such buildings may be attractive nuisances to children and pose a threat to their safety because of the buildings' rundown condition.

A nuisance complaint is the responsibility of the local police. Violation of a nuisance ordinance may be punished by a fine, a prison sentence, or both.

SUMMARY

A small town should adopt building and housing codes or special purpose ordinances only if the town is willing and able to enforce the regulations. Towns above 5,000 in population should have a building code and a housing code; these codes are also recommended for smaller towns, except those below 1,000 in population where adequate personnel may be a problem.

Special purpose ordinances are often useful in protecting and improving the appearance of a town and resolving neighborhood conflicts. Agricultural areas should be separated from nonfarm residential development. Towns with several buildings of historic or architectural value should consider adopting a design review ordinance to protect these buildings from unsightly alterations and the siting of visually incompatible buildings next door (see Chapter 21). If several old buildings are clustered together in a distinct area, then the town should consider creating a historic district. The district could become a tourist attraction and help diversify the local economy. A tree ordinance can help to provide shade, windbreaks, buffers, and an attractive appearance. A storm water management ordinance can help to protect water quality and property. The sign ordinance aims to ensure that business signs are not a hazard or grossly unattractive. The solar ordinance is intended to protect the exposure to the sun of existing buildings for the use of solar heating devices. These devices can help conserve energy and save money in the long run. Nuisance ordinances offer a simple solution to land use conflicts. These ordinances can regulate a wide range of issues—noise, odor, sight, and dangerous buildings—which may pose a threat to health, safety, or the enjoyment of one's property.

20

Putting the Town Plan into Action

For every problem, there is a solution that is simple, neat, and wrong.

—H.L. Mencken

A town plan is useful only if the town government and townspeople put it into action. We have all heard of plans which have been developed only to be "put on the shelf to gather dust." You should be careful to avoid thinking that the writing of the miniplan means the end of the process. It is, in fact, just the beginning of a continuous planning effort.

How well the plan operates depends on the quality of the plan, the accuracy of its projections, citizen participation, and how town officials administer local land use ordinances and capital spending programs. Local administration is often the weakest feature of town planning efforts. The creation of a town plan, workable ordinances, and capital spending programs is not overly difficult. But the true test comes in putting the plan, ordinances, and programs into action on a day-to-day basis. In short, planning is only as good as the commitment and abilities of the people responsible for carrying out the town plan.

Town officials should have certain quality standards to protect the health and safety of the townspeople. Officials should seek to maintain the appearance of the town and be able to evaluate the impact of any development on public services and finances. On the other hand, economic growth is an important concern and development helps support local jobs and income.

Overall, town officials with citizen input need to decide how best to accommodate growth—whether the town wants to encourage growth or tightly control growth. What kinds of land uses are best located in which areas of the town? Where do the soils, topography, and water table pose limitations to development? What land use regulations are fair? When should a variance be allowed? What improvements should a subdivider install? These are all decisions that rely on the guidance of the town plan and ordinances but ultimately are determined by personal judgment and experience.

In implementing land use regulations, town officials must be sensitive to the rights of landowners and the financial requirements of developers. Officials should try to make the zoning and subdivision review process a timely, open, and helpful experience. Dragging out reviews over several months discourages and angers landowners and developers, adds to the cost of development, and may not improve the quality of the review. Town officials should show applicants what changes are needed to comply with the zoning and subdivision regulations. Townspeople must also have the opportunity to respond to development proposals at a public hearing.

Town officials should not be timid about introducing new, and sometimes controversial, regulations which could benefit the community as a whole by raising the quality of life for town residents and making the town a more attractive place for investors and tourists.

From time to time, the community will want to measure its progress toward achieving the goals and objectives of the town plan. Questions such as "How well is the town managing new development?" and "Were the population projections of the miniplan accurate?" should be debated. These questions are the start for updating the town plan and revising the land use ordinances and capital improvements program in order to meet the

changing needs and circumstances of the community. The town plan and ordinances should be updated at least every five years, the capital improvements program every few years.

Other questions such as "Are development controls discouraging desired growth?" "Is development happening too rapidly?" "Are ordinances being fairly administered and enforced?" and "Have any state or federal programs caused major changes in local development?" are important to ask. A survey of townspeople would be helpful here to give the planning commission and governing body ideas about future directions in town planning and land use regulations. The town may move to avoid unneeded regulations, drop ineffective ones, or add stronger standards to some ordinances. Updating and revising plans, programs, and regulations is crucial to making community planning an ongoing and responsive process.

There are many potential benefits from planning. First, planning is a way of getting people involved in their town and looking to their town's future. Planning shows a caring attitude that can be very attractive to prospective new businesses, industry, and residents. Second, planning helps to coordinate the activities of the town government and to budget town finances. Third, planning is often very useful when a town submits an application for state or federal grant money. Because these funds can have a major impact on local development, government agencies want to know how the money will be spent and the effects on the community. Some state and federal programs may require a town plan before the town can receive any grant money. If a town can show that grant money will be

Planning shows a caring attitude that can be very attractive to prospective new businesses, industry, and residents.

spent in accord with the goals and objectives of the town plan, then the town has a better chance of receiving the grant.

Planning is a long-term, continuous process. A town cannot plan for a year or two and expect to be ready for the future. Times change. Needs and desires change. Plans change. Planning is a learning process that stops only when a community becomes a ghost town! Planning compels town officials and residents to learn more about their town and to educate themselves about the decisions which will shape the future of the community.

21

The Design and Appearance of Small Towns

I had the great good fortune to have been raised in a small town.

—Dwight D. Eisenhower

Small towns conjure up images of tree-lined streets with sidewalks, slow, easy moving traffic, and a town square where people shop and socialize. The houses are well kept among all income groups. Industries are on the edge of town, often on the other side of the railroad tracks. And from almost anywhere in the town, you can see out to the surrounding countryside. There is order, neatness, and safety. The town works as a place to live and to make a living. It works as a community. It has a sense of identity of its place in the world.

But the design of small towns goes beyond the tree-lined streets and the store fronts of Main Street. A town's overall appearance, how it presents itself to the world, is a key component of the quality of life of the people who live and work there. The visual quality of a town is important for both residents and visitors. Visual quality defines the town's character and shows how the townspeople think of themselves. Attractiveness can also be an economic resource, a draw for visitors and new businesses. A messy, rundown community says that the people do not care. A tidy, attractive town shows pride. Good town design reflects an orderly character and style but also encourages diversity and individual expression. No one wants to see a new building that looks out of place or signs that block views of the countryside. But change puts pressure on a community's appearance.

Good communities and good design evolve over time. While community needs and tastes change over time, designers and builders of new buildings must show respect for older buildings. Buildings from different eras with different styles must blend together into coherent districts, neighborhoods, and streetscapes. Individual buildings, spaces, and streets have their own unique features which can work together or against each other. How a building fits in with other buildings depends on how the building faces and its size, style, and color and materials. But before creating ordinances to regulate the design of new buildings and the renovation of old ones, townspeople should understand what makes up the design of a town.

Building Blocks of Small Town Design

The noted planner and designer Kevin Lynch identified five design components that are the building blocks of a town and work together to give it form. How these components interact greatly influences the town's appearance and how the town functions.

Two of the most enduring images in a small town are the tree-lined residential neighborhoods and the commercial Main Street. The quaint neighborhoods and the downtown have distinct identities that are created by their location, type of buildings, and purpose. A person is aware of being in a certain part of the town and speaks of that *district* with a specific area in mind. For example, the central business district is an easily recognized area where the commercial and government buildings, churches, and cultural sites are within walking distance of each other.

A *path* enables movement between districts or within a district or provides an entrance to or exit from the community. For instance, a path may be a street, sidewalk, canal, or railroad line. Paths form the skeleton of the town; they give it organization and shape. People see the town while moving through it on paths, and paths determine the pattern of circulation and activity within the town and between the town and the outside world.

A *node* is a gathering place. It may be where two or more paths intersect, and it may form the core of a district. A town square as the center of the central business district is a good example. A public park or village green could be another node. It is a clearly defined place and often serves as a symbol of a district.

A *landmark* is a prominent building or public site that is easy to find and provides a reference point. It is common to find landmarks located within a node, such as a courthouse in the middle of the town square. Other landmarks may be outside the town but are within view, such as a hill, mountain, or water tower. It is important to keep landmarks in clear view to enable them to stand out.

Edges help to organize the town into distinct areas. The edge of a district defines the boundaries of a district and shows how sharp the break is between that district and another part of town. For example, a river or stream may provide a clearly recognized edge. Perhaps the most important edge in defining the small town is the transition between the built-up town and the surrounding countryside. An attractive feature of many small towns is being able to stand within the town and see out to the countryside. In recent years, this important visual edge has often been clouded by the sprawl of new development.

Small Town Form and Function

These five design elements, together with the mix of land uses and economic forces, give the small town its structure, character, and charm. The five design elements create districts which are organized by nodes, intersected with paths, set apart by edges, and dotted with landmarks. Figure 21–1 shows how these elements work together to form the overall pattern of land use and appearance of the small town. The absence of clearly recognizable places and confusion over how the pieces of a town fit together produce a lack of identity and even a lack of beauty.

Small town design will vary according to each district. In the *industrial district,* we often see large aging buildings at the edge of town. The more modern facilities are low, sleek buildings that are functional but contribute little of visual interest. The renovation and upgrading of older facilities and appropriate landscaping can make this district an important visual as well as economic part of town.

The *residential neighborhoods* present the most diverse visual environment. Along the tree-lined streets are homes that express the individuality of the owner. Yet, the homes of small town America have a fairly consistent character. Programs to assist the homeowner in maintenance and a town forestry program can help. One of the most common changes in residential areas is the altering of large older homes into apartments. New housing should be sensitive to the character of the surrounding community. Even new subdivisions located at the edge of town should complement the character of the older neighborhoods.

The *commercial strip* is found along the highways leading to and from the town. The commercial strip caters almost exclusively to the automobile. Parking lots dominate the side of the road, and signs and oddly sited buildings detract from visual harmony. If businesses along the strip cannot be integrated into the commercial core of the town, they should be developed to reflect the character of the town. For example, see the discussion of highway greenbelts in Chapter 12.

In many small towns, the *downtown commercial area* has over the years experienced a decline in economic strength and physical appearance. The commercial part of town depends on an attractive pedestrian setting, good automobile access, and public activities. In many communities, one can still find locally owned stores with commercial uses on the street level and residences on the upper floors. Although most business owners now choose to live away from their businesses, the upper stories can provide interesting and affordable apartments. These residential places help to keep people in the downtown—people to shop in the stores, eat in the cafes and restaurants, and provide vitality to the area.

In addition to the commercial and government roles played by Main Street, the downtown is the center of social interaction. It serves as the back drop for the 4th of July parade and farmers' markets, as well as the place where friends and neighbors meet. The heart of the traditional small town is the *town square, courthouse square,* or *commons,* a broad open space adjacent to or supporting government buildings. The square acts as an open space for the town residents and visitors and also as a landmark and focal point for community activity.

Figure 21-1 The townscape

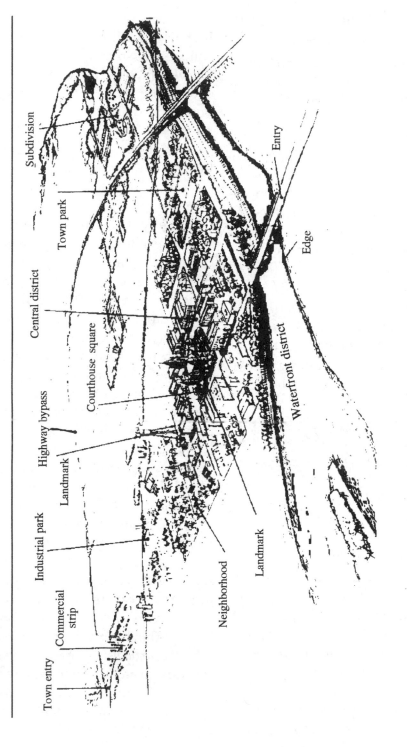

Source: Harry Eggink, AIA, Professor of Architecture, Community - Based Projects Program, Ball State University

The circulation system of streets and sidewalks provides the basic framework of the community by linking together the different districts. It connects where we live to where we work, shop, and play. The street pattern of the small town often consists of a grid of straight streets at right angles to each other. Although this pattern may not bend or curve with the landscape, it does provide a convenient way to organize the town and lets you know where you are: First, Second, Third, or Fourth Street. Often the streets are named after prominent families in the town's history or simply refer to the tree-lined streets: Elm, Oak, or Maple.

Circulation systems should provide clear direction and safe, efficient transportation. Curved roads should generally be avoided because they can be inconvenient for local residents and can easily disorient visitors. Travelers should be able to identify landmarks from the path, and thus it is important to protect views from paths.

Paths have the greatest potential to shape both districts and the overall town. If you look at a map of a town, the most apparent feature is the network of roads and streets. Different paths have different purposes. Recall that the transportation section describes three kinds of streets: arterials, collectors, and local streets. Commercial and industrial uses are best located along arterials. Local streets are essentially residential. And collectors may be framed by a variety of residential and commercial buildings. Small towns, unlike the suburbs, often do not separate residential and commercial areas. In a small town, it is common to walk to the local store, rather than get in a car and drive there. Walking is important to the vitality of the small

town and should be encouraged by providing sidewalks.

Parking is always a challenge to the visual character of the town. Most communities have adequate parking spaces, but they are often scattered, inconvenient, and visually unappealing. The use of a well-crafted parking plan with easy access to businesses and visual screening with trees and other vegetation can help make parking areas fit in with the town's appearance.

The small town also derives much of its character from the street furniture that decorates the paths. This furniture includes signs, lighting, plantings, benches, and so on. These details are often afterthoughts in the town design process, but they can have a noticeable impact on the appearance of a community. Figure 21–2 shows some examples of street furniture that match the pedestrian scale of the small town.

Two other important components of small town design are the *viewshed* and the *entry* into the town (see Figure 21–3). The viewshed begins where the community makes the transition from the surrounding countryside. The entry establishes the first, and often lasting, impression of the community. The entry could be as subtle as a curve in the road or it could be enhanced by well-designed welcoming signs. The entry into the community can often serve as an invitation to explore the town. Care should be taken to clearly identify the entries and key views and protect them from clutter.

Protecting and Enhancing Small Town Character

How do we accommodate and even encourage growth without losing the unique charac-

Figure 21–2   Street furniture

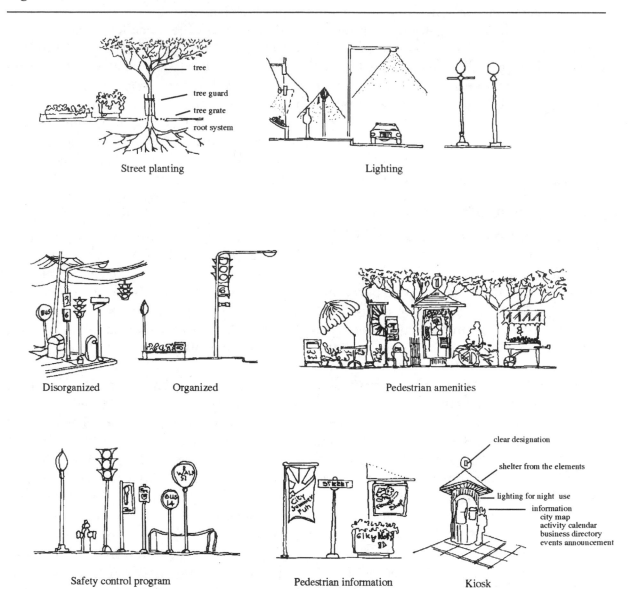

Source: Harry Eggink, AIA, Professor of Architecture, Community - Based Projects Program,
Ball State University

Figure 21-3   The community viewshed

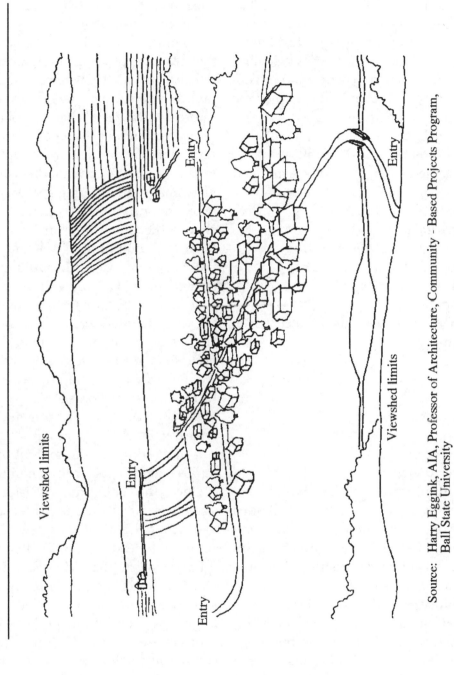

Source: Harry Eggink, AIA, Professor of Architecture, Community - Based Projects Program, Ball State University

ter that is the heart of the small town? The small town design process requires public officials and the public-at-large to develop an understanding of the community's visual resources. The first step is to conduct an inventory and identify and record on a map all the significant physical features of the town and its setting. Much of this information will have been gathered as part of the drafting of the miniplan. Elements that should be examined include:

- Unique natural features.
- Sensitive areas.
- Views, vistas, and viewsheds.
- Entry points to the community.
- Organizational structure.
- Open spaces.
- Buildings of unique or historical character.
- Scenic roads.
- Landmarks.
- Edges.
- Nodes.
- Districts.
- Pathways.
- Blighted areas.
- Obstructed views.

In making this inventory of the town's visual assets, you should especially look for groups of buildings or spaces. These groups are more important than individual features in establishing and maintaining districts and the town's overall character.

The inventory should be done by the town planning staff or consultants who can evaluate the structural integrity of the buildings and the sensitivity of the visual appearance to change. The local citizens, however, play a critical role in this process. They can provide historical background, such as photographs, scrapbooks of newspaper clippings, and anecdotes, that sheds light on the special importance of buildings or places.

Comments from local citizens about what they want the physical environment to become are also crucial. This step in the town design process will set the stage for establishing the future desired visual character of the town.

Two techniques, often used together, have proven to be particularly helpful. A *visual preference survey* invites the community to view images of differing spaces, buildings, or other environmental characteristics and choose the ones they prefer. Often images from the community itself are included to provide comparisons. To avoid fixing the outcomes, this visual preference survey should be facilitated by experienced consultants.

Often included with the visual preference survey is community *visioning*. This usually occurs in a design workshop where teams of planners, architects, landscape architects, and historic preservationists work with the local citizens to develop pictures and designs of what the community might look like. These can show different design and planning scenarios and options for the community.

Once the community vision has been agreed on, it is time for the community to take action. Local citizens, organizations, and community leaders should identify and coordinate projects that will move the town toward its design goals. This townscape plan should include small projects as well as larger, more ambitious projects. The smaller projects are critical, because they keep the community interested and involved by providing success on which to build momentum and ongoing community support.

In getting the projects underway, local leaders and the planning commission can coordinate efforts to seek out funding, professional resources, and volunteers needed to help make the vision a reality.

Small Town Design Do's and Don'ts

No town wants to be thought of as Anywhere, U.S.A. There are a number of mistakes that a town can avoid without stifling development and creativity. Three design rules of thumb are to keep blocks fairly short, to keep the scale of buildings small, and to protect historic architecture. Short blocks add to visual clarity and encourage walking. The standard commercial building in most small towns is two or three stories tall. The main streets of many towns have a row of three-story buildings. A ten-story building would look out of place in a small town. Similarly, a ten-story apartment house would tend to dominate a residential neighborhood. A district should have buildings of more or less the same size. For instance, in a residential area, single-story ranch homes could sit beside two- or three-story houses. A good rule of thumb is to avoid abrupt changes in the size, height, and character of buildings.

In the 1950s and 1960s, many small towns tried to modernize the appearance of their downtowns. Older buildings were made over with aluminum covers, large signs, or big display windows that covered or replaced attractive architectural detail. Most of the modernizing attempts failed. Beginning around the nation's bicentennial in 1976, the renovating of historic buildings became popular. Not only were older buildings recycled and given new life, but the storefronts and facades were cleaned up to reveal the original handsome design. This is not to say that every older building should be refurbished

to mint condition or that no new buildings should be built! But a town should increase awareness of its historic architecture and take pride in this special asset (see Figure 21–4).

Perhaps the best advice in drafting land use and design ordinances is that they should encourage the existing town to be built (see Suzanne Sutro, 1991, p. 5) to reflect the historic pattern of development of the town.

Zoning can be a useful tool in creating districts and in determining the location of buildings; however, zoning should allow for some mixed uses. For example, the central business district should allow for a mix of residential, commercial, and public uses. Ground floor businesses with apartments upstairs make for an efficient use of space that also brings customers to live downtown. Commercial uses should include grocery stores, hardware stores, business and professional offices, and specialized retail. A maximum floor area might be set at 10,000 square feet, though a grocery or discount chain might require more space. The zoning ordinance establishes rules on the height of buildings, floor area ratio, lot coverage, and setbacks from property lines. In a downtown, a zero-lot line, allowing a building on the edge of the property with no setback from the sidewalk or a neighboring property, may be appropriate. The zoning ordinance can influence the scale of buildings and thus how new buildings or renovated structures would fit in with the existing buildings in terms of size and setting (see Figure 21–5).

1. Avoid large lot residential zoning with a minimum lot size of half an acre or more. Large residential lots are a suburban design that wastes land and discourages neighborliness. In most small towns, a 10,000 square

Figure 21–4   Downtown storefront rehabilitation and restoration

Arcade - A row of arches, carried on columns; also a covered shopping street.
Base - The bottom section or pedestal on which a column stands.
Brackets - The small (often triangular shaped) section of material which supports a projecting element.
Building Mass - The visual weight and balance of a building.
Canopy Awning - The canvas roof extension used for sun and weather control.
Capital - The head of the top section of a column, sometimes ornamental.

Cornice - The molded and projecting horizontal member that crowns a facade.
Dimensional scale - The proportion and dimension of intricate detail of a building's horizontal and vertical articulation.
Dormer - A window placed vertically in a sloping roof with its own roof.
Eaves - The section of a sloping roof overhanging the supporting wall.
False Front - A second facade that has been placed over the original facade.
Gable - The triangular upper portion of a wall below a pitched roof.
Human Scale - The sizes of elements which relate to the size of people.
Keystone - The central stone of an arch.

Lintel - A beam bridging an opening.
Parapet - A low wall of railing, often used to protect an area where there is a sudden drop.
Pediment - A low pitched gable.
Pier - A solid masonry support.
Pilaster - A shallow rectangular pier projecting from the wall.
Projecting eaves - The section of an eaves standing out over the edge of the supporting wall.
Oriel - Windows which normally project from an upper story, supported on a bracket or corbeling.
Ornaments - Building details that help establish historic style and character.
Rhythm - Regular recurrence of particular elements, windows, trees, buildings, street, etc.

Scale - The relative size of the elements.
Spandrel - The triangular space between the side of an arch and its vertical and horizontal components.
String Course - A projecting horizontal band on the surface of a wall which is usually molded.
Transom - A horizontal bar across the opening of a window or panel, also a window above an opening such as a door.
Trim - Ornamental material.
Turret - A small, slender tower.
Uniformity - Having a similarity in scale, character, and/or use.
Wall Opening - The window/door openings of a facade.

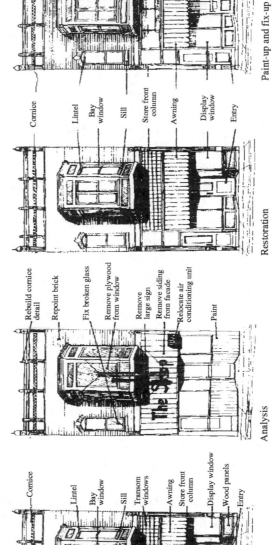

Concept

The concept of the facade is the major pieces that make up the store front and its historic character

Analysis

The analysis of the facade comments on and analyzes the existing store front

Restoration

The restoration of a facade involves reconstructing the facade to its original character, color, scale, material and detail

Paint-up and fix-up

The rehabilitation program attempts to bring the building back to its historic intent, not original character, through minor repair

Source: Harry Eggink, AIA, Professor of Architecture, Community - Based Projects Program, Ball State University

Figure 21-5 The use of vernacular architecture

Require new commercial structures adjacent to existing residential structures to use vernacular architectural styles such as that of older buildings in town, if the neighborhood is older, or similar to newer buildings if in a new development. Place parking in rear on busy streets or utilize street parking in quiet residential sections of town

Source: Grand Traverse Bay Region Development Guidelines, 1991 p. 85.

foot lot (just under a quarter of an acre) is plenty big, and even 8,000 square feet is adequate. Smaller lots are less expensive to purchase and are easier to service with public amenities. Also, allow for a short setback from the street. Long setbacks create large lawns, which are generally more typical of a suburban style and take up space.

2. Avoid strip commercial development along roads leading in and out of town (see Figure 21–6). The entrance to a town makes a powerful impression on visitors and residents alike and says much about the town's character. Too many towns have allowed commercial strips to steal business away from the downtown. These commercial strips are often not well maintained over the years, are often cluttered with signs, and may pose traffic hazards. Also, do not allow public buildings such as the post office or town hall to be relocated out of the downtown to a strip development in the name of convenience. Arguably the nicest design feature about small towns is their compactness which allows for pedestrian travel. Sprawl is the enemy of compactness and draws the vitality out of the downtown. One of the biggest challenges in small town design, especially in rapidly growing communities, is to preserve the town's edge with the countryside. A variety of land use techniques can be helpful, including conservation or agricultural zoning, the purchase of development rights to lands on the edge to keep them as privately owned open space, or even the outright purchase of land on the edge for a greenbelt or recreation area.

3. Allow for flexibility in the use of zoning controls. Traditional zoning is designed to separate land uses, residential from commercial, residential from industrial. But in small towns, stores and homes are often located

Figure 21-6 Avoiding clutter and traffic problems along the highway strip

Shared access drives limit the number of turning cars from the main road.

Parking behind building

Frontage roads, rear service drives, alleys and shared driveways are all better design alternatives. They simplify roadside visual character, minimize conflicts and hazards, and increase road carrying capacity. Placing the parking behind the building increases green space and makes fewer and smaller signs more practical.

Source: Grand Traverse Bay Region Development Guidelines, 1991

close together. This pattern helps to create a neighborhood and makes walking to shops convenient. Pedestrians increase social interaction, unlike suburbs which are heavily dependent on the automobile to link residential and commercial areas.

4. Avoid architectural themes and styles that are not native to your community. For example, a fake Tudor timber design will probably not capture the charm of Merrie Olde England, but rather appear out of place and even silly. Do not try to copy Disneyland!

5. The typical small town downtown is made up of older two- and three-story commercial buildings. These buildings form complementary and consistent blocks. Buildings of greatly different heights make a streetscape appear uneven, like crooked teeth. The three-story commercial building has three parts: the storefront on the first floor, the upper facade on the next two floors, and the cornice which connects the roof to the facade. Design standards should help maintain the balance among these three elements. For example,

storefronts have often been remodeled in loud colors to attract the customer's eye. Sign controls could help minimize this situation by limiting the size of signs. The upper stories of many commercial buildings sit unused or are used only for storage. Upper stories have many potential uses, such as office space or they can be renovated into living space. In Albia, Iowa, upper stories have been turned into housing for senior citizens. This has brought more people back into the downtown and helped local merchants.

6. Owners must have some flexibility when restoring buildings. Do not require that buildings be restored to museum standards. Buildings are supposed to be functional. This usually means an affordable combination of contemporary design (such as modern windows) and historic features.

7. Do not allow new buildings or renovations to existing structures to block the sunlight on public open spaces. The loss of sunshine detracts from the public space as a meeting place (node) and from any landmark within that space.

DESIGN REVIEW

A design review ordinance is aimed at protecting the town from unsightly development which would detract from the appearance of the community and reduce property values. A design review ordinance is especially recommended for towns where tourism is a major economic activity and the town's buildings have historic or architectural importance. An attractive town will also have more appeal to prospective businesses, industry, and residents; and, above all, a good appearance gives the townspeople feelings of pride and caring about their community. A common criticism of American communities, especially suburban ones, is that they have no distinctive features: they all look the same. Design review criteria can help small towns maintain or establish a sense of place.

Guidelines and regulations for the design and appearance of new buildings or renovations to old ones must be based on state enabling legislation. Some design standards can be incorporated into the zoning ordinance. Other design standards can be written into a separate design ordinance. If a separate design ordinance is used, the town governing body should appoint a *design review board*. The board should examine all architectural drawings of proposed development in the town, especially in a historic district or near any historic sites or buildings, to determine the design implications of potential planning decisions. Citizens with knowledge of construction and/or local history would be good choices. The review board would then make recommendations to the governing body but, it is hoped, in coordination with recommendations made by the planning commission on the same projects.

In most small towns, the planning commission can serve as the design review board, with advice from an architect. The commission should draft a town design review ordinance containing design standards and design control districts (for example, the central business district) that address the special local appearance. The commission then holds a public hearing on the design review ordinance and makes recommendations to the governing body.

Often, the planning commission can incorporate the design standards into the zoning ordinance. For example, the zoning ordinance may state that "no excessively dissimilar buildings" are allowed within a certain district. In Freeport, Maine, McDonald's built a white clapboard fast food restaurant, without the telltale golden arches, to blend in with the other white clapboard buildings in town. The zoning ordinance might also require a minimum distance between buildings that look different in style and size.

The design standards should address new construction or building alterations before a building permit is issued. The standards may be general, as in no dissimilar building, or very specific about building height, setbacks, materials, colors, architectural features, siting, and roof type as well as landscaping.

Design guidelines should include standards for:

- The bulk of new buildings (floor area ratio), height and width, lot coverage, and setbacks from adjacent properties and streets (zoning ordinance).
- Landscaping and trees.
- Paving and overall impervious surface (zoning ordinance).
- Parking spaces for commercial uses or multifamily housing.
- Roof style.
- Porches.
- Color, texture, signs, building materials, decorations.

Design regulations should include:

- Sign controls.
- Controls over building demolition.
- Controls over renovations and new construction.
- Controls over landscaping.

If a design review ordinance is part of the zoning ordinance, property owners may apply for a variance to the zoning administrator and may appeal the administrator's ruling to the board of adjustment. If the design review ordinance stands alone, the planning commission receives the variance applications and the governing body and the courts hear appeals.

Some property owners and developers may feel that design is not important for the approval of a project, and they may be reluctant to spend money on improving a project's design. The design review commission or planning commission should be careful to educate landowners and developers about why good design is necessary.

The community should also consider providing incentives to help developers meet the design standards. These incentives might include quicker project approval or financial assistance such as revolving loan funds or tax increment financing.

To a large degree, design is about aesthetics, and what is appealing to one person is not to another. Design standards should be specific in order to be fair to landowners and developers as well as to give the design review commission or planning commission a sound basis for its recommendations on proposed developments.

Design Ordinances

Design ordinances should be based on some kind of visual plan for the town. The visual plan can simply be a set of recommendations or guidelines on the overall appearance of the town, or they can apply to specific districts and neighborhoods. As mentioned earlier, a visual plan should begin with an inventory of the existing built and natural environments and should clearly establish the image of different parts of town in the minds of the townspeople. The design review commission should then conduct a visual survey to identify scenic vistas, scenic roads, pretty groups of buildings, as well as eyesores.

The design review board may want to examine photographs or drawings of what a development would look like and how it would affect the appearance of a street, neighborhood, or the entire town. It may also be possible to use a computer to simulate the proposed development and study the results.

From the inventory and survey could come drawings or brief reports on areas with visual problems (blight, eyesores, and obstructed views) as well as opportunities to improve appearance. The visual plan could include recommendations on the creation of historic districts, the location and protection of landmarks, the location of paths and nodes and appropriate land uses along different paths and within nodes, and the maintenance of edges.

To the extent possible, new buildings and vegetation should not hinder scenic views or disrupt the appearance of a neighborhood. This is not to say that all new buildings should be architecturally the same or that new plant species are forbidden. But visual similarity and continuity and the protection of views are desirable. The design review committee should also identify:

1. The historic buildings that should be preserved.

2. Those buildings that contribute to the character of a historic area.

3. Buildings that could be replaced with new buildings that would have to blend in with the existing structures.

The plan can be a useful reference for a design review board in making recommendations on proposed private development projects and public investments and beautification efforts.

Like the miniplan, a visual plan should be revised every few years to reflect changes in goals and needs. The ultimate goal is to achieve an appearance and a town form that promote a good quality of life for the residents.

HISTORIC BUILDINGS

The *historic buildings ordinance* is a design review ordinance to help maintain the character of historically important buildings (see Figure 21–4). The purpose of designating these buildings as historic is to preserve existing structures and facades, provide alternatives to demolition, and prevent the construction of incompatible adjacent buildings. The historic buildings ordinance gives the planning commission authority to review the design of all proposed demolitions, alterations, and new adjacent buildings before granting a demolition permit, building permit, zoning permit, or subdivision approval.

Officially designated historic buildings or a historic district (where historic buildings are grouped together) may help bring new investors to town and may spur current property owners to spruce up their buildings. This increase in construction activity provides jobs and raises local property values. Furthermore, a historic district could become a tourist attraction and stimulate the creation of new businesses.

Federal State and Local Partnership

Historic protection has become popular since 1966 when Congress passed the National Historic Preservation Act. Since 1980, states may certify local government historic preservation ordinances and transfer 10 percent of their annual federal historic preservation funds to the municipalities. To qualify, a community must show the state historic preservation office that it:

1. Has adopted and enforced a local historic preservation ordinance through a historic preservation review commission.

2. Maintains an inventory of historic properties.

3. Provides for public participation.

4. Fulfills the requirements of the National Historic Preservation Act.

The National Park Service then certifies that a particular building is historic and that planned uses and rehabilitations will not substantially alter historic buildings. For example, the local historic buildings ordinance should require that major exterior alterations to designated historic buildings must not detract significantly from a building's historic value. Demolition of a historic building should be permitted only if there are no reasonable alternatives, such as sale to another party, rehabilitation, or protection by the state or town.

Investment Tax Credits

The Tax Reform Act of 1976 established the use of investment tax credits for the rehabilitation of certified historic buildings for commercial uses. The credits enable property owners to deduct a certain percentage of their investment from the federal taxes they owed for an approved rehabilitation. The Tax Reform Act of 1986 reduced the size of the tax credit from 25 to 20 percent of invested funds. The act also limited the amount of tax credits to $7,500 and required that the credits be used to offset income from the rehabilitated prop-erty. In addition, depreciation rates on commercial real estate were lengthened. These changes in the tax law have sharply reduced the number of restoration projects.

The Historic District

Some towns have several old buildings that are still in use and are grouped together into a clearly defined district. To protect the integrity of the district, a town may decide to create a historic district. Currently over 10,000 historic districts exist throughout America. There are three kinds of districts. The first is a local district which will have its own design review ordinance. The second kind is a local historic district which has been certified by the state historic preservation office. The third kind is a local district which has been listed on the National Register of Historic Places.

The advantage of the National Register designation is that owners of nonresidential buildings and rental properties within the district can qualify for federal income tax credits to offset the costs of renovation. Within a National Register District, which has been certified by the state and National Park Service, there is a 10 percent investment tax credit for the rehabilitation of any income-producing property.

For more information on the requirements for investment tax credits and historic districts contact The National Trust for Historic Preservation, 1785 Massachusetts Avenue, N.W., Washington, D.C. 20036 or your state historic preservation office. The National Trust and the state historic preservation office can also provide technical advice on historic buildings ordinances and historic building design.

Other Tax Incentives

In addition to a historic buildings ordinance or a historic district, a community may encourage the rehabilitation of historic structures through a tax incentive known as a *facade easement*. The owner of a historic building is not assessed additional property value for property tax purposes when the owner improves the facing or facade of the building.

Another technique that a private, nonprofit historic preservation organization can use is the *conservation easement*. The building owner voluntarily agrees to place design restrictions on the building so that the historic character will be maintained. The building owner donates the conservation easement to the nonprofit organization in the form of a deed of easement which runs with the property. The building owner can use the value of the conservation easement, which is the amount that the market value of the building is reduced by the design restrictions (as determined by a qualified appraiser), as a charitable deduction against federally taxable income. The nonprofit organization obtains the right to review and approve changes to the building and to monitor and enforce the terms of the easement and to compel the owner to rectify any violations.

SUMMARY

The design of small towns is often overlooked in planning efforts, especially when economic development through industrial recruiting is a top priority. A quality appearance, however, is both an economic asset and a source of community pride. Tourists enjoy visiting aesthetically pleasing places and prospective businesses are drawn to neat, organized communities. Above all, an attractive town shows that the townspeople care and are willing to invest in their town. For example, the Main Street Program, discussed in Chapter 22, shows how good design can be part of a downtown revitalization effort.

The creation of design ordinances must be based on state enabling legislation. For towns below 2,500, the design ordinances are probably best included in the zoning ordinance. For larger towns, the governing body should appoint a design review committee to examine development proposals, especially if the town contains several historically significant buildings that could be affected by development or renovation.

Good design is also important for wise investment in public services and beautification projects. Design is more than just a quality of life issue; it is ultimately how a town expresses itself to the world. But zoning and design ordinances alone cannot ensure good design. Good town design comes from the commitment of local citizens and landowners to maintain properties and to develop in a functional and visually attractive way.

22

Economic Development in Small Towns: Making It Happen

The inventory of economic assets and the setting of economic goals and objectives are important steps in the comprehensive planning process. Economic assets and how they are used help to influence the growth of the community. While many of the aspects of comprehensive planning are related to land use, economic development is more complicated, especially when it comes to putting economic goals and objectives into action. But it is crucial that economic development programs work together with the comprehensive plan, zoning and subdivisions regulations, and the capital improvements program in order for community change to occur as smoothly as possible.

WHAT IS ECONOMIC DEVELOPMENT AND WHERE DOES IT COME FROM?

Economic development is the major goal of many small town planning efforts. Economic development is a long-term process of change in how people earn a living in the community. The goals of economic development are more and better paying jobs, a growing tax base, the reduction of poverty, a more stable and diversified economic base, and improved public services. Economic development occurs when more goods and services and better quality products are produced per person because of new technologies, new companies, and better trained workers. The keys to this greater productivity are innovation, creativity, and public and private investment. The private sector is the primary source of economic activity, but the public sector plays an important and, ideally, complementary role.

Many people think that economic development programs were born during the economic hard times of the 1980s. Actually, economic development programs have been around since the settlement of the United States. For example, dozens of North American communities were established by town companies or railroads which lured new families and businesses to new communities. In this century, economic development has been called *community betterment, industrial development,* and *retail trade recapture,* among others. But most of the economic development policies and programs in use today were developed shortly after World War II. The shortcoming of many of these local economic development efforts is that they have not been integrated into a community comprehensive planning process, and sometimes even seem to have occurred with little thought of community character or long-term need.

IS ECONOMIC DEVELOPMENT REALLY NECESSARY?

The answer is yes! Economic activity is simply the source of community wealth and well-being. Economic development is necessary for a community to renew itself and grow. Many rural communities and counties are losing people, jobs, and quality of life. There is a great temptation to assume that a community is self-sustaining: somehow it repairs itself; jobs are lost or created because that is just how things happen. By contrast, we are well aware of the consequences that follow from a lack of investment in our housing, automobiles, or businesses. When a community stops investing in itself, decline soon sets in, and the threat of becoming a ghost town suddenly seems very real.

Maintaining economic quality—good jobs, good public services, and a broad tax base—in a small town is no easy task. Some residents will protest vigorously if public money is spent to maintain this quality. Nevertheless, most small towns do not enjoy a growing economy; they do not have the luxury of anticipating that new companies will move to town next year or that new public services will result from population increases. Visit any small community with a static or declining population base. It will not take long to learn why the community is not growing. It is not because the population is getting old or because most young people leave the community. It is because the shoe factory closed; car dealerships no longer operate in communities under 1,500 residents; or, where there were once 57 small businesses on Main Street, there are now only 35. These are the real reasons for decline and they can only be addressed by an active community planning process with a strong economic development program.

The size of a community has little to do with the need for an economic development program. There are many communities with roughly 1,000 residents which recognize that their largest employment base is the school system, the retirement center, or perhaps even a small hospital. The most important activities for an economic development committee are not only to support these small employers, but to work to retain the day-to-day services that create a sense of community: a grocery store, cafe/restaurant, funeral home, pharmacy, and a newspaper. All other services can be purchased in nearby communities. But if you have to leave town to buy a loaf of bread, fill your prescription, be buried, eat an occasional meal, or read the newspaper, then you are probably no longer a true community.

Economic development is also important to support community awareness and a sense of belonging. Public information programs can promote buy local campaigns and undertake price comparison studies of merchants' commodities to help raise awareness. Economic development projects teach important management and marketing lessons about life and business in a small town.

WHAT CAN GO WRONG?

All too often, small towns have mistakenly viewed economic development as a quick fix to replace lost jobs or to bolster local tax revenues. Typically, a town tries to attract a single manufacturing plant that would employ a large number of people. This strategy often fails because a town does not have an adequate industrial site or a sufficiently skilled labor force or the town is remotely located. In addition, the town may be compelled to grant generous tax concessions that result in little or no expansion of the tax base.

Avoiding the quick fix is probably the single most valuable lesson you can learn in an economic development program. There are many measures of success or failure in small town economic development, but the most important factor is time. It is essential that a community take time to get organized and plan how it wants to grow. It has taken a decade or more for most small communities to succeed in attracting new firms and creating new jobs from existing firms. Some communities have used serious industrial recruitment (generally through small industrial parks), new service drives (such as hospitals), and start-up business programs. Other communities were able to attract the fast food chains, discount firms, and bulk sales stores. In short, years worth of economic development work resulted in enough jobs in the form of a new Pizza Hut, McDonald's, K-Mart, or Wal-Mart to replace those lost through factory closings.

Other reasons for economic failure in small towns include (1) a lack of local institutions, such as an economic development organization, and talented local leaders to push for change; (2) poor location; such as places that were by-passed by the railroads or the interstate highways; (3) the depletion of natural resources, such as timber or minerals, which removed the economic base; for example, Veneta, Oregon, was dismantled by the Boise Cascade Company in 1983 because the town was no longer profitable for timber production; and (4) pollution and other factors associated with high levels of environmental impact; for example, high levels of lead poisoning compelled Smeltertown, Texas, to shut down.

Most small towns rely heavily on one or two industries such as agriculture, mining, tourism, or manufacturing and are vulnerable to economic changes. Several towns have recognized this problem and have sought to diversify their economic base. The bottom line is that each community has to tailor an economic development strategy that reflects its labor skills and will meet its own needs and goals.

There are two trends that suggest economic opportunities for small towns. First, the aging population means more retired senior citizens. Of the nation's 2,500 rural counties, about 500 have a significant number of retirees. Most of these people have moved from cities and suburbs to retire in small towns. Retirees do have special health service needs, but they do not have young children to educate, and education is the main portion of local government budgets. Retirees bring in income to a community through social security payments and pensions. A strategy aimed at attracting senior citizens may make good sense for many small towns.

Second, about 270 nonmetropolitan counties have major recreation areas. These counties are among the fastest growing nonmetro counties. But economic growth has transformed the appearance and character of communities and driven up land and housing costs and the demand for public services.

In designing economic development programs, small towns will be wise to create an information network among themselves. This is one instance where outright copying, if done creatively, is no mistake. Although each community experiences its own unique economy, there are often common attributes, especially among smaller communities. Thus, a successful economic development program in one town might work in another similar town.

SIX INGREDIENTS FOR SUCCESSFUL ECONOMIC DEVELOPMENT

Researchers have identified six ingredients as important for successful economic development.

1. The community must take advantage of local resources, such as location, physical setting, financial resources, and people. This includes a willingness on the part of local banks, businesses, and private citizens to donate time and money.

2. There needs to be a strong comprehensive planning effort to guide growth and to improve the community. Local responsibility and problem solving are the foundations of long-term success.

3. Good leadership is essential. Economic development cannot be mandated. Only through a consensus can a town form a coordinated economic development effort. Unless influential leaders and the public-at-large are willing to work for community economic development, not much will happen. Economic development takes time, patience, and commitment. Often a town will set up and fund an economic development committee, but the committee loses momentum after a few months. Leaders must keep economic development efforts alive and on track in both the short term and over the long run. Key individuals for serving on a local economic development committee include local bankers, utility executives, accountants, real estate brokers, attorneys, and small business owners. This will help to create public-private partnerships and joint projects. When the public sector and the private sector are at odds with each other, not much will be accomplished.

4. Good job training and educational institutions are a real plus.

5. The community should be aggressive in its pursuit of state and federal grants. Again, the planning process is key to identifying needs and providing information for grant applications.

6. Finally, there usually is a certain amount of luck involved in economic development! It is common that success breeds success, but some successes may come unexpectedly. Do not be afraid to be creative!

FORMING AN ECONOMIC DEVELOPMENT PLAN

An economic development plan is essentially the economic component of the comprehensive plan or miniplan (see Chapter 8). The economic development plan is a plan of action that spells out in a few pages what the community wants to achieve, how, and when. The economic development plan includes a projection of current economic trends, a desired level of jobs, tax base, and so on, and the gap between where the community is going and where it wants to be. The projection of community activity serves as a best guess of how the town's economy will perform if nothing is done. The strategy required to achieve the desired level of economic activity will depend largely on the size of the gap between the expected trends and the desired level of economic activity. The strategy of a community with only a small gap will be much different from that of a community with a big gap.

The first step in devising an economic development plan is to identify the community's economic performance over the past 20 years. This will aid in projecting economic activity into the future. The historic data will also reveal strengths and weaknesses in the community: why is this a good place to do business, why is it not a good place for business? The economic base section from the town miniplan will be very helpful to show the contributions and limitations of the labor market, lending institutions, tax base, and the export base and the secondary base. The transportation and community facilities sections will show the strengths and weaknesses of the community infrastructure. Also, from the needs assessment survey used in creating the town miniplan, the community can identify businesses that are wanted.

Historic data on unemployment, retail sales, community income, and property taxes may be found through old newspaper records, the town clerk, regional planning commission or council of governments, the state department of commerce, or even the cooperative extension service of your state's land grant university.

Next, it is useful to determine what the community's competitive advantage is. What goods and services can the community produce better than other communities in the region or state? Exports of goods and services enable the community to import goods and services. Export businesses have the potential to grow in regional, national, or international markets. Local-oriented businesses, such as taverns and gas stations, have very limited markets. Competitive advantage is mainly determined by costs. That is, how much does it cost to produce a certain good or service? Major costs include labor costs, transportation costs, local property taxes, and state taxes. Local labor skills and technology will be reflected in labor costs; the location of the community will influence transportation costs; the financial condition of the community will affect local property taxes; and the economic health of the state will largely determine state corporate and personal income taxes. Competitive advantage is constantly changing, especially in today's global economy. What a town may produce efficiently in one decade, may not be true a few years later.

Retail trade is still an important part of the local economy. As part of the economic development effort, the community should determine what its trade area is (from how far away do people travel to purchase goods and services in the town) for different goods and services. Generally, towns with small businesses that offer mainly day-to-day goods and services will have a limited trade area of a few miles. Towns that also provide big ticket items such as washing machines, electronic goods, and automobiles will have larger trade areas, up to 40 miles.

In discussing strategies for retail trade, you should consider consumer confidence, loyalty, and needs. You can use a survey questionnaire similar to the sample below. The goal of the questionnaire is to find out:

1. Why some residents shop in their community while others do not.

2. How local consumers view merchants' prices and service.

3. Which goods and services are not available in your community; why they are not, and can they realistically be offered locally.

4. The consumers' opinions about the friendliness (or lack) of the shopping atmosphere in your community.

Next, your community can estimate a retail trade pull-factor, which is the ratio of the average per capita retail sales in the community to the average per capita retail sales in the state. This will yield a rough measure of whether your community is doing better, less, or about as well as can be expected in retail trade. The pull-factor ratio usually ranges from a low of about 0.4 to a high of 1.5. A ratio of less than 1.0 suggests that retail dollars are leaking out of the community to cities and other towns. A ratio of greater than 1.0 implies that the community is pulling in retail dollars from shoppers from other towns and the countryside. Since sales tax data and retail sales amounts are generally released on a quarterly basis, you should average the pull-factor data over several years. The pull-factor figure from only one quarter does not show the fact that sales may be seasonal (such as around Christmastime) and will lead to an inaccurate picture of the community's retail activity. If you have difficulty in estimating the pull-factor, economists at the state land grant university should be able to help you. The steps for calculating a pull-factor are:

Step One: Divide the total dollars collected from local sales taxes by your community's population. This equals the local per capita sales tax. Local sales tax / local pop = per capita sales tax.

Step Two: Divide the total dollars collected by the state from sales taxes by the total population of the state (this figure can be obtained from numerous sources). This equals the state per capita sales tax. State sales tax / state pop = per capita sales tax.

Step Three: Divide the local per capita sales tax by the state per capita sales tax. This is the local retail sales pull-factor. Per capita local sales tax / per capita state sales tax = local retail trade pull-factor.

Example:

If the local per capita sales taxes   = $345
and the state per capita sales taxes   = $459
then the local retail trade pull-factor = .7516

This result suggests that the community is losing about 25 percent of its potential sales to other places. More information, such as through a questionnaire and analysis are needed before any judgments can be made about sales potential and retention of retail activity within the community.

Finally, it is essential for the community to be realistic in its economic goals. These goals should help promote the community's economic strengths and overcome the economic weaknesses. However, five trends are making long-range planning difficult. First, there is much greater competition among communities for new and expanding businesses and manufacturing plants. Towns that attract plants often have to provide sites with public sewer and water and offer property tax breaks. As a result, the local tax base may not expand as expected.

Second, the consolidation of retail trade among discount chain stores in towns of 5,000 to 25,000 people has meant a sharp decline in retail trade in small towns within commuting distance of these regional centers. Even moderate scale discount chains have the potential to draw buyers from far out in the regional trade area. The main streets of many towns under 2,500 people were much more active 40 years ago, before the advent of discount chains, than they are today, often with no turnaround in sight.

Third, small towns in America are now part of the new global economy in which companies and capital move quite freely across international borders. The economic policies of a foreign country can have a real effect on distant American towns. The result is greater international competition and, therefore, greater uncertainty in planning for economic development. For example, low-wage industries face stiff competition from abroad, and many low-wage firms have moved their operations overseas. On the other hand, *direct foreign investment* is an important source of job-creating capital in the United States.

Fourth, the federal government has been reducing economic development grants for the past decade, including the elimination of the Federal Revenue Sharing Program in 1987. Meanwhile, competition among towns has increased for the remaining funds. Small towns are being asked to supply more of the dollars for economic development efforts.

Fifth, the future of small rural banks and savings and loan institutions is important to communities looking to diversify their economies. Small town banks are a critical source of financing for local inhabitants by channeling savings into local businesses and by purchasing locally issued municipal bonds. The savings and loans play an important role in lending for the construction of new housing. But, the deregulation of these financial institutions in the 1980s, together with the move toward interstate banking, may not benefit small towns and rural areas. Larger urban banks and money market funds can offer more attractive interest on deposits than small rural banks, thus drawing away local capital. Also, when small local banks are taken over by urban-based bank holding companies, local lending may decline. In addition, many small town banks were hard hit by the prolonged Farm crisis of the 1980s, and bankers have since been careful to make only quality loans. These trends in banking may make it difficult for communities to create low-interest loan pools to help existing businesses to expand and to foster the start-up of new businesses.

Once the historical data of economic performance, a projection of economic activity if trends continue, and specific, realistic goals and objectives for economic activity have been formulated, you are ready for action.

This features (1) selecting a specific mission, (2) formulating an economic development strategy and, (3) drafting a schedule of specific projects.

FORMING AN ECONOMIC DEVELOPMENT MISSION AND STRATEGY

A mission is a definite assignment to be accomplished. The mission remains in effect until it is accomplished or changes. The term mission comes from the practice of strategic planning and military planning. The military symbolism is appropriate. No competent military force would attempt to enter a campaign without a well-defined mission; it is essential to the concept of command and control and to the development of strategies used to complete the mission. In contrast, many communities view the mission development stage as an exercise in nebulous thinking. They begin their economic development program believing that they will try something and then learn from their mistakes. Many town leaders also compound this error by visiting a community or two and borrowing ideas too freely.

A mission is not a target or a benchmark, such as "to create 70 new jobs and attract two new firms over the next three years." A mission is simply a statement which summarizes the economic purpose of your community over the next decade and how that purpose can be strengthened. Develop your mission by asking:

1. What is it that we do well in this community?

2. How can we best adapt to change occurring around us?

3. What are some steps necessary to address our problems: such as more resources,

better organization, new ways of thinking, a deeper understanding of our challenges?

4. Is our way of living or the way we do business making the problems worse?

5. In a word or a short phrase, identify concepts that should define your efforts:

Examples:

Doing the right thing	Comprehensiveness
Quality	Quantity within limits
Balance	Opportunity
Fairness	Progressiveness
Entrepreneurial	Public trust
Steady progress	Manage around priorities

Exhibit 22–1
Sample Mission Statement

The town of Skyway exists primarily to provide a quality place to live for its inhabitants. The town will encourage entrepreneurial efforts to provide new jobs. The town aims to achieve steady, balanced economic growth. The town will form an economic development corporation to identify and capitalize on opportunities, including recruiting new businesses, retaining existing companies, and fostering new businesses. In the past, we have been too passive. We must seek funding for street improvements and refurbishing the downtown. If we do not take action now, Skyway's population will continue to decline.

STRATEGIES

All economic development strategies are based on four principles of action:

Plug the Leaks. Plugging the leaks is the most obvious economic development strategy and yet often the most frustrating. Possibly the only major economic leakage that can be addressed at the small town level is the loss of shoppers to other towns. Even this limited task is exceptionally difficult because of the drive and consume pattern of American shoppers, and because rural people are quite accustomed to driving long distances to purchase many of their big ticket items. You must first know where the retail leakages are occurring. There are no really reliable ways of determining the leakages other than to calculate retail trade pull-factors and use well-designed consumer surveys.

When you develop a strategy to plug the leaks, make sure that you do not limit yourself to retail goods. Services are a vital part of the economic structure of a community. In a 1990 survey of rural health care in small Midwestern communities, several towns reported that nearly half of the residents preferred to use health care services in nearby communities rather than in their own town. Even after adjusting for the fact that some types of health care are not available in small towns, and that recent in-migrants often drive large distances to see their long-term health care professional(s), the data still indicated high levels of leakage. Several of the communities, especially those with municipally funded hospitals, were shocked to see hundreds of thousands of dollars in health care revenues flowing out of their town.

Plugging economic leaks from goods and services requires three actions.

1. You must establish an effective public information program to inform the residents of the gravity of the situation, the likely outcome if it continues, and the damage that is being done to local providers and merchants. A quarterly newsletter is best, but publicity in the area media is adequate.

2. You must target information provided by consumers to area merchants and service providers. They are, after all, part of the problem. Working directly with and through the local chamber of commerce, business associations, and professional organizations is usually the best strategy.

3. You must develop a public relations campaign through a network of community interests and organizations. One town of 1,100 people devised a very effective campaign. Each week for one year the chamber of commerce sponsored an ad in the local newspaper which compared prices from a selected business for common goods with the prices from five other similar businesses in the area. Given the reality that there will always be some surly merchants, uncaring, or unscrupulous service professionals, and some consumers for whom price is the only factor in buying, the campaign was quite effective.

Invest in Yourself. The two most popular economic development strategies for investing in yourself are (1) revitalization of the town's central business district and (2) infrastructure investment or renewal.

The revitalization of the town's central business district involves visual design, renewed attraction of customers, public facilities, special events, and merchant participation. A facelift (visual design) for the downtown can create an attractive, well-organized central business district which increases both consumer and merchant satisfaction. And increased retail sales, or at least the potential for increased retail sales, follow increased satisfaction. We know, however, that people are strongly attached to low prices for frequently purchased goods. Wal-Mart, for instance, is not known for architecturally attractive stores, but the prices are low and customer satisfaction is very high.

Renewed attraction of customers involves developing a special environment to entice shoppers back downtown. Large communities try malls; small communities try historic preservation of selected buildings, attempt to lure a small movie theater, a building for arts, numerous antique stores, or even a new retail anchor store. Some actual examples of new attractions are:

• A brand name outlet in a small town of 950 residents. The outlet is located in an old restaurant along the interstate highway.

• A storefront chocolate factory in a town of 350 people.

• A combination continuous auction/flea-market in an old auto sales and repair garage on Main Street in a community of 1,600 people.

• Five antique stores along Main Street in low-rent, older buildings in a community of 500 people.

• A restaurant located in a restored turn of the century home located on the main street in a community of 1,400 people. The city owns the building, the chamber of commerce recruited the chef.

Providing public facilities for revitalization is an important element of success. Consumers will not become repeat customers unless they can find a good parking space, a good sidewalk, and a few awnings to get out of the rain. They also require clean public restrooms in which they are welcome, food and drink, and a place to sit. And, of course, shoppers want to be safe.

Retail establishments in the downtown will be influenced by retail strength in neighboring communities and the proximity of those communities. For example, strategies featuring special events in the downtown may be required in a town of 1,500 when a large discount chain store has opened up in a community of 15,000 only five miles away. Community economic development specialists insist that a community must find its niche, search for marketing strategies, and create an attitude of consumer loyalty. It can be done! We have seen unpromising communities capitalize on assets that were 10 years before given little thought.

Encourage New Local Enterprise. The success of small businesses is critical to any community's economic development. Therefore, growing new businesses can be a very effective economic development strategy in small towns. Four out of five new jobs in America are created by small businesses. At the same time, nine out of ten small businesses fail within five years. New businesses in rural areas and small towns face special challenges. First, there is a lower concentration of resources and markets than in cities or suburbs. Second, the physical area of the market is likely to be much greater, often regional in size, because of the less dense settlement pattern. Third, seed money and management help are harder to find. And fourth, an entrepreneur must have greater savvy because profit margins are often small and the business depends more on cooperation with other businesses.

To help small businesses get off the ground and to nurture them in their early years, small business incubators have been formed in many rural areas. In 1986, only 14 percent of business incubators were located in rural areas. By 1992, one-third of all incubators were in rural places.

New businesses face three main barriers: high overhead, undercapitalization, and poor management. An incubator presents a package approach to lower these barriers. An incubator features flexible, affordable space, usually at a below market rent. A renovated building or empty space over a downtown store is a good choice. Ideally, several new businesses can be housed in one building in order to share clerical services and office equipment, such as computers, copiers, and fax machines. But the space provided for a business is meant to be temporary. It is hoped the business will grow into a full-fledged commercial operation and move to a new site outside the incubator, making way for another start-up company.

An important function of the incubator is to provide new companies with advice on management and financial matters. Some of this advice should come from an advisory board of local business people and some from a network of business people from beyond the town. In Pennsylvania, the Ben Franklin partnership works with Penn State University to provide managerial and financial assistance to incubators through three circuit-riders who visit small towns throughout the state.

Business incubators hold the promise of creating not only new jobs, but also economic diversification of the local economy, increased sales and exports, and more minority- and women-owned enterprises. The more businesses in the community, the greater stake people have there. Business incubators should be included as part of a local comprehensive plan or economic development plan.

Recruit Appropriate New Business.   The competition among towns for manufacturing plants is intense. Moreover, recent studies have found that most new jobs are created in service industries by local small businesses employing fewer than 20 people. In fact, large corporations have recently been *downsizing,* shedding workers rather than expanding their work force. In small towns, the addition of a few jobs here and a few there is more likely than the recruitment of a large employer. Small business development and retention are reasonable goals, and local efforts are aimed at assisting local businesses with expansions and fostering the start-up of new businesses.

Local officials and citizens must be aware of how these trends are affecting the economic performance of their town and how these trends may influence current and future economic development efforts. In short, a community must decide what economic goals and strategies are realistic, what actions it can take to improve the local economy, and what factors are beyond the community's control. All of these decisions will be reflected in the implementation schedule: what is to be done and by when. Finally, there is a need for visible accomplishments or all the economic development participants are likely to become frustrated and give up.

ORGANIZING FOR ECONOMIC DEVELOPMENT

Understanding the Local Economy and Creating a Favorable Business Climate

Step 1—The Organization.   The first step in organizing for economic development is to create a nonprofit local economic development corporation. At least one study has shown that a good organization is often more important than the size of the community in attracting outside industry. The corporation should establish goals and objectives and explore strategies for recruiting new businesses, retaining and expanding existing firms, and fostering new local businesses. It will become apparent that important elements of an economic development effort include public improvements (sewer and water, roads), the availability of low-interest loans, the centralized management of the downtown business district, and the continued involvement of business leaders, government officials, and the public-at-large. In the Minnesota Star Cities program, for example, a community does not attain the Star Cities designation until it has (1) formed an economic development corporation; (2) completed a five-year economic development plan, a one-year action plan, a five-year capital improvements plan, a community profile, an audiovisual presentation, a labor force survey, and a survey of local industries; and (3) successfully attracted a new industry. Once a community becomes a Star City, prospective companies know that this is an organized community that can get economic development projects done.

Step 2—Land Use Plans and Ordinances. A town plan, zoning and subdivision regulations, and a capital improvements program are all important elements in the economic development effort. Business people like to have certainty. A good town plan lets investors and business people know where development is desired and what type. This is not to say that the town should not be open to rezoning land to a commercial or industrial use. However, a good plan together with good zoning and subdivision regulations gives companies a reasonable assurance that conflicts among neighboring land uses will be minimized and that necessary public services will be available.

A town can use the planning process to assist local business development in several ways. A town can help with land acquisition and assembly for businesses and can provide needed infrastructure through the capital improvements program. Also, the town can offer advice on how to meet regulatory standards and obtain necessary permits. The town may even wish to change existing zoning and building regulations that may stifle appropriate development. Care must be taken because some companies actually seek a community with rather strict land use regulations to protect their new office building from a junkyard or other conflicting use next door.

Step Three—Actions, Programs, and Projects. The active programs and projects for economic development depend on the strategies selected from the list of plug the leaks, invest in yourself, encourage local enterprise, and recruit appropriate new businesses. The Main Street revitalization program, for example, is an attempt to include all four of these strategies. Other programs, such as industrial recruitment, reflect a single strategy. The point is that it is useful to know whether or not your actions are in keeping with your strategies!

MAIN STREET REVITALIZATION: RETAIL AND TOURISM

Local government and private business people are starting to learn how to cooperate to organize community resources and generate economic development activity. For towns of 5,000 or more people, the Main Street Program makes good sense as a way to bolster the community's retail trade and to improve the overall appearance of the downtown shopping area. The Main Street approach features four points: organization, promotion, design, and economic restructuring. The organization is headed by a full-time central project manager, as in a mall, who works with business owners, local government, and the public. The project manager should be part of a nonprofit downtown association which can build consensus and cooperation to create a consistent program and long-term planning for the downtown. Funding for the central project manager can come from local and state governments and private contributions.

Promotion consists of advertising the downtown as a special place to shop, live, and work. Promotion includes publicity about the downtown and the staging of special events to bring people into the downtown. Uniform business hours and security personnel can be a boost in making downtown a draw. Design goals focused on improving the visual quality of the downtown. The rehabilitation of older commercial buildings and facades is a major priority. This reinvestment in the downtown can be helped in part through federal investment tax credits for renovating historic buildings. But also important are improving signs and window displays to reinforce the image of quality. Economic restructuring has the goal of maintaining, strengthening, and diversifying the town's economic base. This can be achieved through creating a better mix of stores and businesses and modernizing marketing methods. An important feature is to develop a low-interest loan pool for recruiting new businesses and retaining existing ones.

Communities with fewer than 5,000 inhabitants are rarely recommended for the Main Street Program because they do not have a sufficiently broad market to justify the new investment in retail trade.

To date, the Main Street Program has been adopted by 17 states and over 300 communities. In Oregon, for example, the Main Street Program generated $8.5 million invested in 128 projects. The formation of a network of Main Street towns in a state can be especially helpful for towns to share experiences and information.

The Main Street process has been successful in about three out of every four towns. The Main Street Program is not a quick fix. It takes about three years for the Main Street Program to work. Some towns lost patience and abandoned the Main Street approach within three years. Other towns failed to emphasize all four points, such as trying to promote special events without a central manager or without economic restructuring.

Successful Main Street communities have enjoyed the creation of new businesses, greater investment in the community, refurbished store fronts and rehabilitated buildings, and, perhaps above all, a greater sense of community and pride. This example of a public-private partnership in economic development is a model for towns of over 5,000 inhabitants.

TOURISM

Tourism is viewed by many small towns as a major economic development component. Retail districts may become oriented to tourists as is possible with the Main Street approach. Recreational tourism is important to hundreds of small towns. With either active or passive tourism, the assets and location of the town are determining factors. Towns along the sea coast or other body of water have a special advantage. Places with scenic views, historic sites, museums, and other unique attractions also have an edge in competing for tourists. Another draw is a festival, whether it be based on music, crafts, theater, or an ethnic celebration. For example, Junction City, Oregon, has over 200,000 visitors each year to its Scandinavian Festival.

Although advocates of the Main Street approach do not recommend the use of theme architecture, some small towns have used theme designs to make their community stand out. These themes range from ethnic or western to waterfront and historic. In essence, the Main Street Program advocates a high quality historic theme with renovated and refurbished older buildings.

There are four pitfalls to promoting tourism. The first is that tourism is seasonal and produces wide swings in population, employment, and economic activity. For towns not linked to the ski trade or sunny resorts, the months from late fall to early spring are especially slow. Ski-related towns have had to look for additional activities to try to draw visitors year round. The second danger is that the town experiences growth as it is discovered and the new development overwhelms the town's original appearance. Carefully crafted land use and design ordinances can help to minimize the negative effects of tourism development. For some suggestions, see Chapter 21. A guiding rule of thumb is that the residents should enjoy the town's appearance and attractions as much as the tourists. But the tourists are usually more affluent and hence can afford more upscale types of restaurants and retail stores. Also, if housing becomes tight, the local residents could begin to see themselves priced out of the local housing market. The third problem is that many small towns lack the necessary infrastructure of lodging, restaurants, entertainment, and general retail needed to support tourism development and growth. The fourth threat is the possibility of increases in the price of gasoline or gasoline shortages as happened in the 1970s. The higher the cost of travel, the more likely people are to stay close to home. In sum, to achieve lasting success with tourism, a town must be accessible to fairly affluent tourists who live within 200 miles.

A state role can be very helpful in promoting a town's tourist attractions. Also, cooperation with other communities can be beneficial, such as in the creation of a heritage trail with sites in several towns.

DOES HIGH-TECH HAVE A PLACE IN A SMALL TOWN?

Technology has changed small towns in the past and will continue to do so. In the 19th century, railroads brought life and economic vitality to hundreds of towns. In the 20th century, cars and highways have enabled people to live farther from where they work and shop. The next important technology is telecommunications for sending information cheaply across long distances. Telecommunications should encourage more dispersed settlement and result in the growth of some small towns and remote places. Local officials and businesses should determine how the community can best take advantage of telecommunications. For example, digital switching service for telephones is essential for high volume mail order businesses and franchises of regional and national chain stores. Touchtone phones are necessary for using modems and fax machines and the transmission of national newspapers.

Your community may want to contact the local telephone company, the state public utilities commission, the state department of commerce, and other towns about obtaining digital switches and fiber optic cables if not already available.

Another economic development activity related to high-tech development is investment in human capital. Small towns have often experienced the loss of many young people who leave in search of better training and job opportunities. Job training programs can be helpful in attracting new businesses. Job training can tie in with new high technology manufacturing in electronics, robotics, and computers. But often these high-tech firms congregate on the edge of major urban areas.

CAPITAL AND FINANCING: CREATING A LOCAL LOAN POOL AND BRINGING IN GRANT MONEY

Federal dollars for economic development are available from many sources. The Small Business Administration has programs to assist towns in forming community development corporations under Section 503 of the Small Business Act, providing financial advice to small businesses, and offering small business loans. The Economic Development Administration makes grants for sewer and water lines, especially for developing industrial sites. It also makes money available for economic development planning.

The U.S. Department of Housing and Urban Development (HUD) provides Community Development Block Grants, which are administered by the states and are intended for economic development and public services projects that will benefit low- and moderate-income people. For example, CDBG funds can be used to buy land for an industrial site to attract an industry that would employ primarily low- and moderate-income people. Or funds could pay for the installation of sewer and water lines to service houses where low- and moderate-income people live. Also, the HUD Small Cities Development Program Grants can be used for local projects related to business development: one new job must be created for every $15,000 in grant funds.

The Farmers Home Administration (FmHA) sponsors a variety of economic development programs for small towns and rural areas. The FmHA makes loans and offers rent subsidies for low-income housing. The agency also makes loans to governments for public sewer and water systems and fire equipment. The FmHA, like the Small Business Administration, makes loans to small businesses. Since 1992, most of the economic development programs of the Farmers Home Administration have been taken over by a new agency, the Rural Development Administration, within the U.S. Department of Agriculture.

The U.S. Forest Service, also within the U.S. Department of Agriculture, has economic action programs for communities that are heavily dependent on forest products. These programs feature market development and expansion, economic diversification, and recycling of forest products.

Federal funding sources and requirements are published in the *Catalogue of Federal Domestic Assistance,* featuring a complete list of federal grants and qualifications; *The Federal*

Reporter, which contains information on new grants and qualifications; and *The Federal Assistance Program Retrieval System,* operated by the Department of Agriculture's Soil Conservation Service, which determines the eligibility of small towns for a variety of grants. Copies of these catalogs can be obtained from your congressional representative's office.

Public grants and private donations can be combined to create a revolving fund of low-interest loans to help start-up companies and existing businesses expand. Such a fund is a logical link to both a Main Street Program and a business incubator. Capital is almost always in short supply in small towns. And high risk venture capital for new and expanding companies is very hard to find. In a revolving loan fund, new loans are made as old ones are paid off, recycling economic development money back through the community. A loan fund is an excellent example of a public-private partnership and creative financing.

The Community Reinvestment Act (CRA) of 1987 requires lending institutions to serve the credit needs of their entire community. The initial purpose of the CRA was to ensure that loanable funds did not all leave the community where the deposits were made. The more loans that are made in the community, the more economic activity is stimulated. The lenders are also expected to develop partnerships with other lenders, community groups, and local government. For example, a bank could loan money to a business and take an equity stake in the company as well. A bank could also contribute to a small business loan pool to encourage start-ups in the community.

ENERGY CONSERVATION

Most energy supplies are imported into a community. This means that dollars flow out of the community to pay for energy imports. If the town imports less energy, then more dollars stay in the community to be invested in new jobs and to buy local goods and services. Energy conservation is an economic development strategy that has not been fully explored. In Osage, Iowa, energy conservation efforts in home weatherization and air conditioning management have produced lower natural gas and electric rates and have helped the community to attract new manufacturers. Successful energy conservation requires leadership from the town government and cooperation among the public.

In the wake of the energy crisis of the 1970s, nearly every state created an energy department to help communities to implement energy conservation programs and develop alternative energy sources.

ENTERPRISE ZONES

Enterprise zones have recently been touted as a way to stimulate development in cities and towns with high unemployment rates and large numbers of low-income people. An enterprise zone features the abatement of property taxes and investment credits for jobs created as the relaxation of some development regulations. An enterprise zone makes good sense if the state will pick up the cost of the foregone property taxes. Also, it may be necessary to provide new infrastructure in the form of roads, sewer, and water to establish an enterprise zone that will attract manufacturers. Contact your state department of commerce for more information.

REGIONAL COOPERATION FOR ECONOMIC DEVELOPMENT: CLUSTERS OF TOWNS

In some rural areas, where there are only a few dominant regional centers, economic development seems elusive. In rural Iowa, the idea of cooperation among several towns and between towns and counties has taken hold. Schools and utility companies have been especially supportive. Residents in towns mostly below 2,500 population recognized that political boundaries were not barriers to working on common economic and social problems. To date, some 78 clusters have been formed, mostly since the mid-1980s. Clusters feature nonprofit organizations that work to coordinate town and county government actions on a variety of needs, including industrial recruitment, new business start-ups, retention of existing businesses, tourism, leadership development, grants, special events, and housing. The state of Iowa has begun to use clusters as an efficient way to provide financial and technical assistance to several towns at once, rather than individually. For example, the Iowa Department of Economic Development has included clusters in its database for companies that are considering locating in Iowa.

The *town clusters approach to economic development* is very different from the recent trend of a regional center ringed by many small towns in a hub and spoke pattern. In this pattern, the jobs and shopping are concentrated largely in the regional center and the small towns are essentially bedroom communities. By contrast, the town clusters approach has the potential to spread economic activity more evenly across towns. In many rural areas, it is common for people to work in one town, send children to school in another, and go shopping or to church in a third town. In short, each town is really a part of a regional community.

STATE ROLE IN LOCAL ECONOMIC DEVELOPMENT

So far, state-level economic development programs have not been very well coordinated or especially targeted toward smaller communities. The most important state role in influencing the growth of towns is deciding which towns receive how much money for education, transportation, and economic development. Education costs are usually the biggest single expense in a town budget and local schools are important images and reasons to live in the town.

State governments also have the most detailed information necessary for economic development. For instance, state agencies have computerized data banks on job opportunities and labor availability, local sales tax receipts, employment, and wages.

Town and county governments receive state gasoline tax revenues from the state department of transportation for the maintenance and construction of roads. Roads are the lifelines of small towns, and many towns have survived or prospered because of road systems which make them accessible. But the maintenance of interstate highways is often a costly top priority for state governments.

State industrial recruitment efforts and the creation of enterprise zones (in which property taxes are eliminated or greatly reduced) have had some success. Also, state corporate and personal income tax policies are important for creating a favorable climate for business. Several state agencies accept proposals for grant and loan dollars for local economic development projects. These sources can usually be identified through state departments of commerce, community affairs, or economic development. In Iowa, for example, communities under 2,500 people may receive up to $300,000 in state block grant funds for one year or multiyear projects. These state grants are awarded on a competitive basis, and many small towns do not have the expertise to draft and submit a competitive proposal. In Pennsylvania, the Ben Franklin program provides grants, loans, and training for new businesses.

The state government is also increasingly important as a source of infrastructure funds. For example, Illinois set up a rural bond program to help communities pay for infrastructure. The state purchases the bonds issued by small towns and then sells state securities to investors.

In sum, the huge federal budget deficits and the need to reduce federal spending will put greater pressure on the states to provide grants, loans, and technical advice to small towns that are trying to develop infrastructure and economic development programs.

A SUCCESS STORY: WHAT DOES YOUR TOWN HOPE TO ACHIEVE?

In Maquoketa, Iowa, population 6,300 and county seat of Jackson County, several dozen store owners donated $104,000 to hire a full-time business recruiter. The town produced an eight-minute video which tells about the advantages of living and working in Maquoketa. An added attraction was the availability of industrial revenue bonds to offer low-interest financing for new industry.

Another draw was that Maquoketa had built several hangarlike buildings for potential use by manufacturers. In 1985, a Chicago-based manufacturer of automobile oil pumps opened a 50-employee factory and a Wisconsin-based boat trailer company opened another factory employing 30 people. In 1986, the maker of automobile radiator parts opened a 26-employee plant.

Several factors contributed to Maquoketa's success, some of them common to other towns and some unique. First, Iowa and many other rural areas have an abundance of low-cost, hardworking labor, often from farm families or recently displaced from farming. Second, Maquoketa is a county seat town with a sufficient population base and labor force to attract new business and industry. Third, Maquoketa is located in eastern Iowa where manufacturing is a major economic sector and there is a critical mass of manufacturing and business support services. Fourth, Maquoketa is well situated, only a three-hour drive from Chicago and near the Mississippi River. And finally, Maquoketa used speculative buildings and industrial revenue bonds effectively.

One of the most important functions of local leadership is to be able to assess the community's advantages and convince existing companies to expand and prospective businesses and industries to move in. Maquoketa appears to have brought in businesses without giving away the town. The three firms that came in were relatively small. None of them dominates the town. The leadership that existed prior to the arrival of these firms is not threatened.

There are many examples of successful economic development programs and projects in small town America. Small towns typically have several advantages to offer over metropolitan areas. Small towns have cleaner air, less traffic congestion, lower property taxes, lower crime rates, cheaper labor, affordable housing, outdoor recreation opportunities, stronger community values, and the feeling that an individual can make a difference. On the other hand, small towns often have limitations, mainly featuring a lack of size and distance to markets. Other shortcomings may include limited shopping and social life and inadequate infrastructure to support large employers. The distance problem can be overcome through telecommunications and transportation. It is interesting to note that two of the leaders in mail order retail, L.L. Bean and Lands' End, located successfully in towns of under 10,000 people. In fact, author David Heenan (1991:viii), in his book *The New Corporate Frontier,* believes that "U.S. corporations are demonstrating a clear and growing preference to domicile in smaller, relatively remote townships."

This does not mean that every small town will land a Kellogg's or a Herman Miller (the second leading maker of office furniture) or a Smucker's. But if there is an economic development effort tied to a town plan, then there is at least hope.

SUMMARY

There is much debate about whether economic development is an art or a science. It is much more difficult to teach and transfer the art of economic development than a scientific approach. One of the key ingredients is the people involved in the economic development process. Good leadership is hard to teach or duplicate. Good leadership is necessary to organize the community, plan, and take action.

Small town economic development involves many other factors, some of which can be copied and some not. National trends away from manufacturing employment and toward service industries do not bode well for small communities. Yet, there remains some potential for small-scale specialty manufacturing in small communities. But given the large number of small towns, there are probably not enough manufacturing plants to go around. On the other hand, there are many cases of maverick entrepreneurs who have started very successful businesses in small communities. These entrepreneurs give hope to even the smallest towns but baffle public officials as to how to get more of them started. Techniques such as enterprise zones, business incubators, and low-interest loan pools offer considerable promise.

Still, a town must have assets and resources which make the community an attractive place to live and work. Towns of fewer than 2,500 inhabitants often lack a variety of economic assets and human and financial resources. The town cluster approach being pioneered in Iowa may prove a workable model for cooperative economic development on a regional basis. Otherwise, small towns within commuting distance of a regional center will increasingly become bedroom communities, and those small towns beyond commuting distance will tend to shrink.

The bottom line is that there are no guarantees of economic success. Economic development is best seen as a slow, long-term process of change. Persistence, innovation, and continual work are essential. Economic development should be pursued within a general framework of comprehensive community planning. It makes little sense to sacrifice community character and quality of life for the sake of economic growth.

Small town planning has two main components: the promotion of development and land use regulation. Both tasks need to be balanced to ensure that a community will continue to be a desirable place to live, work, and grow.

23

Strategic Planning
for the Future
of Small Towns

One must plan to plan. This is true whether the plan is the first or the fifty-first. . . . It is as true in the public sector as in the business world.

—GERALD GORDON, *Strategic Planning for Local Government*

Strategic planning is about preparing for change. Large corporations often use strategic planning to look five to ten years into the future and plan for how the company must adapt now in order to compete and grow. A company that fails to anticipate changing needs, markets, and opportunities may not grow or even survive. Although *community strategic planning* has become popular in the 1990s, it is not a new program. Strategic planning is what successful communities have been doing for many years to help themselves.

It is important to note that strategic planning is not a substitute for the comprehensive planning process discussed throughout this handbook. A community must first know itself, assess its resources, and develop workable land use regulations and capital improvements programs before undertaking strategic planning.

Strategic planning involves people viewing their community as a group of stakeholders who are trying to built a consensus on a common vision or mission for the town. Strategic planning often fits well with the local decision making process where important decisions tend to be made by a few movers and shakers. With citizen participation based on consensus, it is easier to agree on a single course of action than to select alternatives—which is the heart of the comprehensive planning process. If decision makers are part of the consensus, then taking action as a community will not be difficult.

Strategic planning for a small town begins when the townspeople form a vision of the community they want, given the economic and social realities that are likely to exist in the next 10 to 20 years. The following six guidelines from Frank So (1988, p. 462) are helpful in the visioning effort:

1. Use existing data and past studies and never use the lack of data as an excuse for inaction.

2. Rely on facts that are known and shared.

3. Promote creative and innovative thinking.

4. Separate those things about which you can do something from those that you cannot do much about.

5. Emphasize solving the most important problems.

6. Discuss your town's mission and purpose and how the management of your local government can be improved.

After the visioning process has been completed, the next step is determining "How do we get from where we are to where we want to be?"

A WORD OF CAUTION AND THE NEED FOR STRATEGIC PLANNING

The economic and demographic future of many small towns is not promising. The 1990 census identified about 19,300 places in the United States. About 85 percent of these places are communities with under 10,000 residents; more than 12,000 communities have less than 5,000 people; and approximately 7,800 communities have fewer than 1,000 inhabitants. In the 1980s, two-thirds of the counties in the Midwest, containing thousands of small towns, lost population.

Rural isolated communities under 1,000 people will be especially hard pressed to survive in the next century. These communities are in need of a planning process which encourages an evaluation of their town's purpose, a sense of mission, and a renewed consensus for action. The strategic planning process is an excellent instrument for this size community; it well may help to change the destiny of some small communities.

BUILDING A STRATEGIC PLANNING PROCESS FOR SMALL TOWNS AND RURAL AREAS

Many strategic planning efforts have succeeded in small towns and rural areas throughout the world. Despite the diversity of small communities, there are five key ingredients that are necessary in all community strategic planning.

Leadership and Organization

Strategic planning requires leaders who are willing to take responsibility for community action. Although elected officials often view themselves as leaders, election to a public office neither guarantees nor necessarily builds leaders. Leadership comes from individual spirit, personal skill, dedication, and willingness to serve. Leadership can be lost from misuse or lack of use, gained quickly in times of stress, or developed slowly through long-term community service. Some people have this quality but do not use it, while others will never have it. Leadership is the most important ingredient in all successful planning programs.

Leaders must build networks to leaders of other groups. Civic leaders build networks to leaders in education, business, cultural affairs, and other important groups in the community. In organizing for strategic planning, leaders must identify what is at stake in the community and then encourage groups (the stakeholders) to actively support their best interests. In short, the first step in strategic planning is to identify those in the community willing to take action.

Finding leadership in a small town may at first seem to be a difficult task. The real secret is to identify the major stakeholders in the following community activities:

Civic Betterment	Health and Hospitals	Service Organizations
Media	Bar Association	Government
Recreation	Youth Activities	Historical Society
Downtown Association	Chamber of Commerce	Sports
Farm Interests	Agriculture Support	Education
Religious Service	Senior Citizens	Vocational-Technical
Culture and Arts	Ethnic Groups	Fairs and Crafts

From leadership springs goals, dreams, visions, and action. Leaders are supposed to identify opportunities and act on them. Strategic planning for the entire community is an important, if sometimes sobering, process. In all stages of planning, the community must look at itself honestly. For some communities, there may not be much optimism or hope. For others, there may be several options. The task of leadership is to be forward looking, to work on and hopefully solve problems before they get out of hand.

Community Assessment

The second key ingredient is the ability of townspeople to assess the assets and liabilities of the community—the strengths, weaknesses, opportunities, and threats. The community leaders and planning groups must assess what the community is doing well, or can do well, based on its resources, talent, and position in the region. This assessment must also involve an inventory (from the miniplan) of basic community strengths, such as an excellent stock of older housing, and potential opportunities, such as attracting retirees. The next step is to evaluate the community's weaknesses and threats. For example, a lack of quality health services, poor retail variety, poor transportation access, or a deteriorating housing base are deficiencies sometimes associated with small towns and rural areas.

The Mission Statement

The next task is the mission statement. The mission statement reflects a recognition of local potential and a commitment to action.

"I really don't know how this town is going to survive in the next century. We have to beg people to run for city council—and then they sit around for hours arguing whether to spend a few thousands dollars on a university consultant to help with downtown improvement. We rejected the Main Street Program just last year. Even our newspaper helped to defeat the small industrial park proposal my group suggested in 1988. I don't think the people in this community have a future."

Some Rules of Strategic Planning

- Professionals Plan with People, Not for Them
- Needs Should Not Be Discovered, People Should Be Asked about Them
- Shared Leadership Results in Effective Organization
- Never Go Outside the Experience of Your People
- A Group Must Be Committed to Its Cause

The community leaders must set a course of action based on strengths and liabilities, vision, and the commitment of the local stakeholders. The mission statement is not a wish list. The mission statement shows what the community stands for and what it intends to do to sustain itself in the future. It must be clear, succinct, and purposeful.

Innovation

Another ingredient in successful strategic planning is innovation. *Innovation* is a process of discovery and learning; change involves risk and, therefore, the possibility of failure, but there is also a risk of failure by not doing things in new ways. Innovative people try to strike a balance between new actions and tradition by retaining the best qualities of both.

Innovation is sometimes threatening to small town dwellers because it means change. Other times, innovation may not produce quick results. Many individuals and groups may criticize community leaders who promote innovative action—especially when the results of the action are uncertain and public dollars are involved. When opponents see an industrial park populated with only a few

firms, they may be quick to point out the folly of the project. But, when the industrial park is full and thriving after 25 years of operation, they may look back and wonder at the vision of community leaders.

Innovation is hard to find in many small towns. Some towns actively oppose change and others are content just to let things happen. Only when a retail chain store opens in the neighboring town and begins to take business away do the townspeople look for solutions. But innovation involves anticipating change and organizing people to prepare for change and to shape change.

Small town dwellers have to be adept at innovating. One such example comes from Flora, Illinois, population 5,700, which wanted to attract a new state prison. The townspeople put together a rap video and sponsored a communitywide parade to gain attention. The effort failed to win the prison, but soon five Fortune 500 companies decided to locate in Flora. The companies liked the community's spirit.

Cooperative Action

The final ingredient in strategic planning is cooperative and coordinated efforts at the local, county, regional, and state levels and, in some cases, with the federal level as well. Communities can rarely go it on their own. For example, successful industrial park development requires county or regional assistance for land acquisition and planning and state assistance to search for new firms or provide advice on expanding local companies. Regional agencies are frequently invaluable in preparing Community Development Action Grants to help provide local infrastructure. Although there are a few instances of total local determination, the large majority of strategic planning efforts in small towns involve intergovernmental, private, or interagency cooperation at some point during the process.

Gerald Gordon (1993, p. 65) suggests that leadership groups follow five rules of involvement and organization in the strategic planning process:

1. Ensure that the group is large enough to incorporate a wide range of perspectives but small enough that it does not become unwieldy.

2. Ensure that the support of top management for both the group and the process is clear to all who are involved.

3. Make available to the group the resources and status necessary to carry out the function of strategic planning, including access data and people.

4. Include the city and county manager, the mayor, or some other key official in the planning process and encourage this person to check with the group on a regular basis.

5. Encourage the development of new ideas and programs and creative approaches to existing programs.

The team effort necessary in local strategic planning also extends to private individuals and businesses. The private sector plays a vital role in the strategic planning of a community through donating money and services. The following is a short but representative list of projects in small towns during 1992 and 1993.

• A lifetime resident of a rural small town bequeaths $1 million for a multipurpose communication/library/meeting facility if community residents match half of the amount in donations.

• A local stone products company donates $50,000 in material and labor for attractive monument signs at the community's entrances and new industrial park.

• A small bank agrees to underwrite all of the photocopying, mailing, commercial printing, and secretarial help for an industrial recruitment effort.

• A local resident grants a 99-year lease to a community of 500 residents on 10 acres of land for an "Oregon Trail Memorial Park." Two regional artists donate their time to prepare the monuments, and the county provides funds for the materials.

• More than 1,000 residents pledge $500,000 to match two private grants to build a primary care hospital in a community of 3,500 people.

All of these private efforts show a commitment to the future of the community. Without that commitment, strategic planning will not succeed.

Further Concepts of Change

Many small communities resist change rather than try to manage change. They may study development proposals for too long and miss a good prospect, or they may shut their doors to new development and possibly sow the seeds of their own decline. Although there are many vibrant small towns in the United States, there are still far too many communities that are their own worst enemies. They are downright resistant to new ideas, unwilling to innovate, and stubbornly incapable of leadership, even when the alternative is quite likely to be a long, slow death. Their watchword is "if it ain't broken, don't try to fix it," and they are resolute in their faith that government has no right to mingle with the private sector. Their elected officials limit themselves to patching streets, watching over the police, detecting corruption, and generally avoiding the larger issues of life.

Strategic planning requires a community to take a medium- to long-term view and ask "What kind of community does this *have* to be in 10 or 20 years in order to survive and provide its residents with a good quality of life?" This question is quite different from the general question behind the miniplan process: "What kind of community do we want?" Although the goals and objectives of the strategic plan should be realistic, they should also contain an awareness that today's plans and actions will influence tomorrow's options.

Strategic planning, like all management and planning programs, has certain weaknesses. Perhaps the most serious weakness, especially in small communities, is the tendency to promote sameness. The gradual loss of unique character can be as damaging to community identity and survival as economic neglect.

Another serious concern about strategic planning is the tendency to follow a top down approach—that is, to involve only the community's leadership and key stakeholders. This lack of public involvement can fatally damage the vision, mission, and action program if these elements are viewed by the general populace as an attempt by the local elite to impose their standards on the community.

A Strategic Plan in the Making

One response to the need for strategic planning has started in northern Iowa where several small towns realized that they could achieve more by cooperating than by competing with each other for economic develop-

ment. Two networks have been formed, the Northern Iowa Rural Area Development and the Area Community Commonwealth. Both groups are working to (1) coordinate economic development efforts, including a loan fund and business directory; (2) provide adequate housing; (3) cooperate on schools; and (4) build leadership in the communities with a regional perspective. In the process, these communities have shared some services and helped keep those costs under control while maintaining quality.

These Iowa communities recognized that they share a common future (Wells et al., 1991:25–27). In today's small towns, it is not unusual for someone to live in one town, work in another, and even send children to school in a third.

Nonetheless, many small towns are reluctant to participate in joint ventures because of long-standing rivalries (especially between high schools and businesses) and overall distrust about losing their own identity. The old adage "united we stand, divided we fall" may be the rallying cry of long-range strategic planning for many small towns.

Strategic Planning and the Sustainable Community

A frequently heard phrase today is *sustainable community*. A community is sustainable if it has the right mix of economic assets, leadership, and luck. A sustainable community not only survives, but provides its citizens with a good place to live and work. Strategic planning is a key ingredient for creating a sustainable community over the long run. Strategic community planning focuses first on identifying overall community strengths, weaknesses, opportunities, and threats. Next, land use, design, and economic development plans are formed to maintain the strengths, improve on the weaknesses, seize opportunities, and address threats to community well-being. Although the goals and objectives of the miniplan and economic development strategy should be realistic, they should also contain the awareness that today's plans and actions will influence tomorrow's options. In sum, planning for population change, land use, economic development, and sustainable communities is essential for today's small towns to shape an uncertain future.

Appendix

Economic Development Contacts and

Resources for Small Towns

The following are a variety of contacts and resources for economic development in small towns. Some of these resources have national programs, while others operate on a regional basis. The Small Business Administration and Farmers Home Administration have offices in every state, usually in the state capital.

Federal Agencies

Appalachian Regional Commission
1666 Connecticut Avenue, N.W.
Washington, DC 20235
(202) 673-7874

Economic Development Administration
U.S. Department of Commerce
Division of Technical Assistance
Room H 7866
Herbert C. Hoover Building
14th and Constitution Avenue, N.W.
Washington, DC 20230
(202) 377-4085

Small Business Administration
1441 L Street, N.W.
Washington, DC 20416
(202) 653-6768

Farmers Home Administration
U.S. Department of Agriculture
Room 5014 South Building
Washington, DC 20250
(202) 447-7967

Tennessee Valley Authority
Old City Hall Complex
Knoxville, TN 37902
(615) 632-6499

Office of Community Planning and Development
Office of Block Grant Assistance
U.S. Department of Housing and Urban Development
451 7th St., S.W., Room 7128
Washington, DC 20410
(202) 755-6587

The Rural Information Center
National Agricultural Library
Beltsville, MD 20705
(800) 633-7701
 Ask for: *Federal Funding for Rural Areas*

Nonprofit Organizations

Midwest Research Institute
425 Volker Blvd.
Kansas City, MO 64110
(816) 753-7600
 Published: *A Rural Economic Source Book: Selected Training and Technical Materials.* $15
 An excellent list of readings for rural and small town economic development. Also published: *Profiles in Rural Economic Development.* Dozens of case studies of successful small town economic development programs and projects. $15

National Association of Towns and Townships
1522 K Street, N.W.
Washington, DC 20005
(202) 737-5200
 An excellent source of ideas and information on solutions to a wide range of small town problems. NATaT publishes a newsletter 10 times a year and has published a number of books on small town economic development.
 Membership fee.

National Rural Electric Cooperative Association
1800 Massachusetts Avenue, N.W.
Washington, DC 20036
(202) 857-9562
 Publishes monthly newsletter on economic development and works with rural communities on development.

Center for Agriculture and Rural Development
The Council of State Governments
P.O. Box 11910
Iron Works Pike
Lexington, KY 40578
(606) 252-2291

Glossary

The following words and phrases are common in the planning process and are used throughout this manual.

Aesthetics: The pleasantness of the total environment. Aesthetics relates to the perceptual aspects of the physical surroundings—their appearance to the eye and the comfort and enjoyment offered to the other senses. Aesthetics are viewed as a legitimate though minor purpose of planning. They are frequently accepted in combination with a major planning element: that is, economy, health and safety, control of densities and hazards, and convenience.

Age composition (population structure): A profile of the persons in a particular planning area shown in terms of age and sex. The total population is divided into males and females and then further separated into four-year age groups. The four-year age groups, called cohorts, are then graphed as a percent of the total population. All cohort graphs taken together form a population pyramid which illustrates whether the community is normal or whether there appears to be a disproportionate number of young, middle-age, or elderly citizens.

Alteration: A change made to a building or structure. Small alterations, such as painting and routine repairs, generally do not involve building and zoning codes. Larger alterations, such as additional rooms or stories, will require review under building codes and may also involve the zoning process.

Appeal: A private individual, group, or public agency may take the decision of the zoning administrator or planning commission to a higher authority for review of that decision. The administrator's decisions may be appealed to the zoning board of adjustment; the commission's decisions may be appealed to the governing body. Similarly, the decisions of the zoning board of adjustment and the governing body may be appealed to a court of law.

Assessment: The process of determining the worth or the market value of land and buildings for taxation purposes. Most communities in the United States assess property at only a fraction of its real value; the percent of real value is called the assessment rate. Thus, multiplying the true value of all community property times the assessment rate yields the total assessed value of all real estate in the community.

Base zone: The zone underlying an overlay zone. Base zones are typically for standard uses, such as residential, commercial, and industrial. The overlay zone adds special restrictions.

Blight: Social and/or physical decay of the community is usually seen as a decay of the central business district and a certain segment of the housing stock. Blight is due to many factors, such as declining population, loss of economic base, changes in roads and highways, lack of public investment, and so on.

Building code: A set of regulations governing the construction of buildings. A building code can spell out what materials can or cannot be used in construction as well as establish minimum standards for plumbing, electrical wiring, fire safety, structural soundness, and overall building design. The purpose of the building code is to ensure the safety of new buildings and alterations to existing buildings.

Building permit: An official document issued by a city, township, or county which grants permission to a contractor or private individual to erect a building or make improvements to an existing structure. A building permit is usually issued only after a public official has certified that a building or structure will be in compliance with all local regulations.

Building starts: The total number of new buildings under construction in a given year. Each building permit issued is counted as a building start.

Build-out scenario: When zoning an area at a certain density, you may want to determine the maximum number of dwelling units or businesses that are actually allowed in that area. A build-out scenario can show on a map or series of maps whether the area would contain too much, too little, or the desired amount of development under the proposed zoning density.

Bulk regulations: Zoning ordinance restrictions on the density, height, location, and lot coverage of buildings. Bulk regulations are aimed at providing buildings with sufficient access, air, fire protection, light, and open space.

Capital improvements program (CIP): A program of when, where, and how much a town plans to invest in public services over the next five to ten years. The program presents a capital budget each year which is useful in drafting the overall town budget. Items commonly included in a capital improvements program are roads and bridges, school buildings, sewer and water lines and treatment plants, municipal buildings, solid waste disposal sites, and police and fire equipment.

Carrying capacity: The ability of an area or unit of land to absorb human development without experiencing a significant decline in environmental quality.

Census data: Information published every 10 years by the U.S. Bureau of the Census for each state, incorporated towns and cities over 2,500 persons, and for all counties. There is a wide range of data available, including populations, ages, sexes, ethnic groups, housing conditions, property ownership, incomes and commuting patterns, to mention but a few.

Central business district (CBD): A central area of the community where citizens carry on commercial trade and purchasing. The central business district is distinguished from satellite business centers, shopping districts, and highway strip commercial districts.

Certificate of occupancy: Official notice that a building is in accord with the zoning ordinance or building and housing codes and may be used or occupied. The certificate is issued for new construction or for changes and additions to existing buildings.

Concurrency: A policy that development can occur only if and when adequate public services are in place.

Conditional use: A land use in a certain zone which is neither permitted outright nor prohibited outright. A conditional land use permit may be granted after review by the planning commission. For example, a convenience store may be a conditional use in a residential zone. Conditional use may also refer to certain conditions placed in the permit that the holder of the permit must meet.

Cumulative impact assessment: The evaluation of the impact of several recent and proposed development projects on community services and land use patterns.

Dedication: The deeding of land by a developer or landowner to the public. Dedications of land commonly occur in the subdivision process; a subdivider may donate land for schools, parks, roads, and other public uses.

Density: The number of buildings, offices, or housing units on a particular area of land. High-density development leaves little open space; low-density development has few buildings or housing units per acre.

Design review: A formal process for reviewing the design and aesthetics of proposed new developments and building alterations; and for determining what improvements or changes might be made to make new developments compatible with the surroundings. A design review board, appointed by the governing body, or the planning commission itself can draft a design review ordinance listing design standards and design control districts (such as a historic district). The design standards may also be incorporated into the zoning ordinance.

Deteriorated or dilapidated housing: A classification for housing conditions indicating major structural damage, unsafe access, fire hazards, insect infestation, and other problems which result in a structure that is not safe or healthy to live in.

Disclosure problem: A problem that often develops during research and information gathering, especially in small communities. The disclosure of private information may occur when information being sought allows the researcher to discover the private circumstances of families and individuals in the planning area.

District: Part of a general land use zone. A district specifies the density level permitted. For example, an R-1 zone is a residential zone and a low-density single-family dwelling district. An R-3 residential zone would be a high-density multifamily dwelling district.

Downzone: A change in a property's zone designation to require a lower density or a less intense use. For example, downzoning would include land changed from eight residential units per acre to only two residential units per acre or land changed from an industrial zone to an agricultural zone.

Dwelling unit: A building designed for and intended for human habitation. A dwelling unit generally, but not always, contains the following facilities: (1) toilet and bath or shower; (2) separate room for sleeping accommodations; (3) kitchen for the preparation and storage of food; (4) space, other than that listed above, for eating and/or living.

Easement: A right to use property owned by someone else, usually for a specific purpose. Most easements are used by utility companies for utility lines and maintenance access. Easements are also used to provide access to otherwise landlocked lots.

Economic base: One of the major studies contained in the comprehensive plan. The study of the economic base investigates the assets and commercial and industrial activities of a community. The economic base is usually expressed as the export-base and secondary-base of local goods and services. Community wealth is defined as property value and the type and worth of public facilities. The labor force consists of the available work force and their educational levels. The economic base of a particular community also indicates the overall ability of a community to invest in itself and the relative desirability of investing in a community from the standpoint of an outsider.

Environmental impact statement:　A specific type of planning study. The impact study represents the combined efforts of many professionals, such as biologists, environmentalists, planners, engineers, etc., and concentrates on the likely impact on the local environment that a certain project might be expected to have.

Exactions:　The donation of land or money, the installation of improvements, or other conditions required of a developer by the town government in return for approval of a proposed development. Exactions are most often used in the case of subdivision applications.

Final plat:　The final application proposal submitted by a subdivider to the planning commission. The final plat should include all recommended changes to the preliminary plat. Signed approval of the final plat, along with certification of title and filing the plat, means the legal creation of a subdivision.

Flood hazard:　An area, properly identified, which is subject to periodic flooding capable of causing property damage and/or injury to people. The degree of flood hazard is usually expressed at the highest flood of record or as the greatest flood of 100 years.

Frontage:　The part of a lot that touches a road, street, or watercourse; it is usually expressed as a specific amount such as 100 feet of road frontage.

Functional planning:　Planning for specific functions of the community, such as water resources, sewer, health, recreation, and so on.

Growth management:　The use of regulations and incentives to influence the rate, timing, location, density, type, and style of development in the community.

Historical data:　Information for a particular characteristic, such as population, that can be gathered for several decades into the past.

HUD:　United States Department of Housing and Urban Development.

Improvements:　Facilities which aid in land development. Improvements include streets, sewer and water lines, curbs, sidewalks, street lights, fire hydrants, and street signs.

Land use:　A broad term used to classify land according to present use and according to the suitability for future uses: that is, for housing, open spaces and parks, commercial, industrial, etc.

Land use and development controls:　Codes, resolutions, and ordinances enacted by communities, townships, and counties under the authority of state enabling legislation. Such controls are designed and intended to be used for the protection of the public health, safety, and welfare. Common land use controls are (1) zoning, which separates the planning area into zones and districts and regulates the use to which land can be put in those districts; (2) subdivision, which guides and controls the division of land for building purposes and the addition of new building areas to the community; and (3) the official map, which designates present and future community areas in which new development may or may not proceed.

Lot:　A piece of land divided from a larger parcel.

Lot coverage:　The amount of a total lot covered by buildings. Many zoning ordinances impose limits on the area of a lot a building can cover. For example, in single-family residential zones a maximum lot coverage of 35 percent is common. This restriction is designed to ensure adequate light, privacy, and open space.

Minimum lot size:　The smallest lot or parcel that can be built on in a particular land use zone. Also, the smallest lot that can be created by dividing a larger parcel. For example, in a single-family residential zone, a minimum lot size of 8,000 square feet (just under one-fifth of an acre) is reasonable.

Model:　In this manual, model refers to a mathematical representation of a particular activity within the planning area. Models used in planning are predictive or descriptive or both. Mathematical models are commonly used in population analysis, economic base studies, land use, transportation and community facilities.

Natural resources inventory:　Natural resources include the soils, water, forests, minerals, geologic formations, and plant and animal species found within the planning area. An inventory of the quantity and quality of natural resources can help the community to identify areas of the town that are suitable for development, other areas that can support only limited development, and, finally, areas that should be protected from development.

Nonconforming use:　A land use that does not comply with the ordinance of the zone it is in or does not comply with other land use regulations. A nonconforming use that existed prior to the zoning regulation will generally be allowed to continue under a grandfather arrangement.

Nuisance: The use of land or behavior that brings harm or substantial annoyance to adjacent property owners or the public in general. Nuisances typically involve noise, odors, visual clutter, and dangerous structures. A nuisance ordinance enacted by the governing body is a way to resolve nuisances.

Parcel: A lot or group of lots under a single ownership or control. A parcel is usually viewed as a single unit for development purposes.

Performance zoning: The use of standards in regulating land use location and density, rather than specific zones and districts. Performance standards regulate the impacts of land uses. Landowners and developers must meet these standards to be in compliance with the zoning ordinance. Performance standards typically refer to noise, traffic, odors, air pollution, and visual impact.

Planned unit development (PUD): A zoning development management approach to physical growth which combines housing, commercial, light manufacturing, and open space uses all in the same zone, while maintaining an overall density comparable to conventional development.

Planning commission: An official body appointed by the governing body of a city, township, or county that is responsible for making the comprehensive plan. In addition, the planning commission makes recommendations to the governing body on the zoning ordinance and zoning decisions, on subdivision regulations and subdivisions, and on development proposals.

Planning data: There are three types of planning data: primary, secondary, and estimated. Primary data are gained from firsthand observation, such as traffic counts or housing and land use surveys. Secondary data are obtained from the estimation of records and text sources. Estimated data are obtained by making assumptions that certain factors are held constant or that certain past trends will continue.

Plans: Major plans include the master plan, comprehensive plan, and the general plan. These plans explore the present condition of an area, project possible futures, and investigate needs in order to develop the general policy goals and objectives through which planning can be implemented. Minor plans include sketch plans, reconnaissance studies, and so on.

Plat: The map of a subdivision, showing the number and dimensions of lots, public rights-of-way, and easements. The plat must be filed with the town clerk in the town plat book.

Police power: The right of government to restrict an owner's use of property to protect the public health, safety, and welfare. Restrictions must be reasonable and be conducted according to due process.

Preliminary plat: The formal application proposal submitted by a subdivider to the planning commission. The preliminary plat should contain the commission's recommended changes to the sketch plan. The preliminary plat shows the property to be subdivided, lots, all roads, and easements. The planning commission may impose restrictions and exactions at this stage (see also final plat).

Professional planner: Planners are of many types and specialties. Many architects, engineers, and landscape architects are, and can be considered, professional planners in certain functional planning areas such as transportation and community design or subdivision layout. However, a professional planner is a person who is qualified to make plans—or to coordinate the making of plans—in all functional areas of the community. A professional planner will be the recipient of an advanced college degree, such as the master of regional and community planning, and often will have obtained a professional registration.

Region: An area including one or more counties which contain certain geographical, economic, and social characteristics in common.

Rezoning: See zone change.

Right-of-way: The right to cross over property. A right-of-way usually refers to public land. For example, public land on which a street is built is a right-of-way. The right-of-way includes not only the street, but land between the street and sidewalk and the sidewalk. Rights-of-way across private property are usually for utility lines or driveways.

Setback: The distance required to locate a building from a road, property line, or other building. This distance is specified in the zoning ordinance and may differ among zones.

Site plan: A map of a proposed development or subdivision. A site plan usually is submitted as part of an application for a zone change, variance, conditional use permit, or subdivision. The site plan should show property lines, buildings, roads, natural features, and the north direction.

Sketch plan: A preapplication proposal submitted by a subdivider to the planning commission to find out what changes and improvements the commission would require for approval of a formal subdivision. The sketch plan should include a map of the proposed subdivision, adjacent properties, and existing improvements.

Special district: A special unit of local government created to provide a specific service, such as schools, water and sewer, and fire protection. Special districts may be supported by special tax levies and/or the sale of bonds.

Special exception: Under unusual circumstances, an applicant may apply for a use not normally allowed in a particular zone or district. A special use may be granted but only if the use is allowable as a special exception listed in the zoning ordinance. Special exceptions may involve decisions of the zoning board of adjustment, the planning commission, and the governing body. Special exceptions should be used very sparingly.

Spot zoning: The zoning of a particular lot for a use that is different from the uses permitted in the surrounding zone. For example, a lot zoned for commercial use in the middle of an R-1 single-family residential zone would be spot zoning. This practice should be avoided because of a potentially negative input on neighborhoods and likely invalidation by the courts.

Subdivision: The separation of a parcel of land into lots for future sale and/or development. A subdivision may be three or more lots or four or more lots depending on the particular state planning and zoning enabling act.

Substandard housing: A broad classification for housing condition, rated in degrees of major and minor, which indicates that a certain dwelling unit is deficient for general use. Common criteria for assessing substandard housing include whether a dwelling unit is wired for electricity (or properly wired), contains plumbing and indoor flush toilet facilities, and has proper sewering and adequate win-

dows for light and air; the condition of exterior surfaces; and many others.

Tract: Land under single ownership or control. A tract usually covers a substantial acreage and has the potential to be subdivided into lots.

Trip: A term used in transportation planning and analysis to denote travel within the planning area. Origin and destination studies, used to describe the trip process, attempt to interpret the point at which an individual trip originates, the path which the trip takes, and the final destination of the trip.

Variance: The decision to alter the provisions of a land use ordinance, usually on a single piece of land. An area variance involves changing the zoning requirements for building height, lot coverage, setbacks, and yard size.

Zone: An area or areas of the town in which certain land uses are permitted and other uses are prohibited by the zoning ordinance.

Zone change: An action taken by the local governing body to change the type of zoning on one or more pieces of land. For example, a zone change or rezoning would be from C-1, low-density commercial, to C-2, medium-density commercial. A zone change for specific properties can happen in two ways. A property owner may ask for a zone change, which is a quasi-judicial action. Otherwise, either the planning commission or the governing body may seek a zone change through a legislative action. If a zone change is approved, the zoning map must also be amended. Some zone changes may require amending the comprehensive plan map.

Zoning ordinance: A set of land use regulations enacted by the local governing body to create districts which permit certain land uses and prohibit others. Land uses in each district are regulated according to type, density, height, and the coverage of buildings.

Bibliography

Alguire, Frank, T. Daniels, J. Keller, and L. Mineur. *Small Town Economic Development.* Planning Advisory Service Memo. Chicago: Planners Press, January 1987. This is a useful summary and description of economic development strategies for small towns.

Allor, David J. *The Planning Commission Guide.* Chicago: Planners Press, 1984. A sensible and down to earth guide for conducting planning commission business, Allor's book is based on a wealth of experience and interviews with planning commissioners. The book focuses on how planning commissions can make more efficient and intelligent community decisions especially in the face of controversy that often occurs in community planning.

American Planning Association. *Land Use Law and Zoning Digest.* Published monthly. This publication is similar to *Zoning and Planning Law Report,* but it has a more comprehensive coverage of zoning and land use law topics. The Digest is more suitable for the professional planner or the practicing attorney than for the planning commission.

American Planning Association. *Zoning News.* Published monthly. This newsletter covers the latest zoning issues and zoning techniques. It is suited to the practicing planner.

Ayres, Janet, et al. *Take Charge: Economic Development in Small Communities.* Ames: North Central Regional Center for Rural Development, Iowa State University, 1990. This publication is a step-by-step approach for strategic planning for community economic development. It is a very useful book and approach.

Babcock, Richard F. *The Zoning Game: Municipal Practices and Policies.* Madison: University of Wisconsin Press, 1966. A classic, but somewhat dated look at the zoning process.

Bair, Frederick H., Jr. *The Zoning Board Manual.* Chicago: Planners Press, 1984. Fred Bair has been writing books for planning commissions and zoning boards for many years. This is one of the best for small towns and rural areas. *The Zoning Board Manual* is especially well indexed and useful as a quick reference for briefing before rezonings. Many rural and small towns have used it to establish guidelines for issuing variances and conditional uses.

Brower, David J., and Daniel S. Carol, eds. *Managing Land Use Conflicts: Case Studies in Special Area Management.* Durham, NC: Duke University Press, 1987. Interesting case studies of special land use management practices are written by different authors. Planning commissions operating in natural resource and high quality farmland areas will find useful comparative information in the chapters on "The San Bruno Mountain Plan," "New York's Adirondack Park Agency," "New Jersey Pinelands Commission," "Impasse on the Upper Delaware," and "Montgomery County Agricultural Preservation Program." Planning commissions located near parks, recreation areas, and national forests will find the cases especially useful.

Brough, Michael B. *A Unified Development Ordinance.* Chicago: Planners Press, 1985. The author seeks to help communities draft a single land use ordinance that combines elements of both zoning and subdivision regulations. It is especially useful for small towns.

Brower, David J., C. Carroway, T. Pollard, and C. L. Propst. *Managing Development in Small Towns.* Chicago: Planners Press, 1984. A well-presented collection of growth control techniques that may be appropriate for large towns.

Browne, Carolyn. *The Mechanics of Sign Control.* Chicago: Planners Press, 1980. This book shows how to prepare and administer an ordinance to control business signs, explains the components of a typical sign ordinance, and describes various procedures for enforcing a new ordinance. It is recommended for planning commissions and practicing planners.

Bryson, Bill. *The Lost Continent: Travels in Small Town America.* New York: Harper Collins, 1989. A funny, off-beat account of one man's journey through small towns.

Clark Boardman Company. *Zoning and Planning Law Report.* New York. Published 11 times a year. This publication provides a very informative summary of recent court decisions on land use regulations and small, topical reports. Many topics relate to small towns and rural areas. The report can be used for periodic briefing of the planning commission and to assist in updating regulations.

Crawford, Clan, Jr. *Strategy and Tactics in Municipal Zoning.* Englewood Cliffs, NJ: Prentice Hall, 1969. This book rates as essential on the list of references that should be purchased by all communities. The book is extremely well written and understandable—perfect for new planning commissioners. Although this book is over 20 years old, its material is classic and will never be dated.

Daniels, Thomas L. "Small Town Economic Development: Growth or Survival." *Journal of Planning Literature,* 4:4 (1989):413–429. A comprehensive review of the literature on small town economic development, it is of interest to practicing planners.

Flora, Cornelia, Jan Flora, Jacqueline Spears, Louis Swanson, with Mark Lapping and Mark Weinberg. *Rural Communities: Legacy and Change.* Boulder: Westview, 1992. This is an up-to-date and very readable assessment of the problems and issues confronting rural areas and small towns.

Glassford, Peggy. *Appearance Codes for Small Communities.* Planners Advisory Service Report No. 379. Chicago: Planners Press, 1983.

Goodman, William I., and Eric C. Freund. *Principles and Practices of Urban Planning,* 2d ed. Chicago: International City Managers Association, 1967. A planning classic, but this book is more appropriate for academics.

Gordon, Gerald L. *Strategic Planning for Local Government.* Washington, DC: International City Managers Association, 1993. This book has a wealth of information on how local governments can plan and act strategically.

Green, Gary, Jan Flora, Cornelia Flora, and Frederick Schmidt. "Local Self-Development Strategies: National Survey Results." *Journal of the Community Development Society,* 21:2 (1990):55–73. This article outlines the results of a national survey which looked at how rural communities have pursued self-initiated programs for economic development. It is both instructive and heartening.

Haas, Gregory. "Minnesota Star Cities: Lighting the Path of Economic Development." *Small Town,* 16:2 (Sept./Oct. 1985):12–15. A good summary of the Star Cities Program and organizing for local economic development.

Heenan, David A. *The New Corporate Frontier: The Big Move to Small Town USA.* New York: McGraw-Hill, 1991. This is an interesting study of successful big companies in small towns. Most of the towns are in the 50,000 people range, but the trend toward locating headquarters in smaller places is compelling.

"Historic Preservation in Small Communities." Ellensburg, WA: Small Towns Institute, 5:9 (March 1975). A set of very basic, yet informative examples of small town restoration and preservation is presented in this special issue of *Small Town.* Many of the now classic ideas of small town preservation are presented in this issue.

Hinds, Dudley S. *Winning at Zoning.* New York: McGraw-Hill, 1979.

Illinois Department of Local Government Affairs. *Downtown Improvement Manual.* Springfield, IL: Office of Research and Planning, 1975. This manual is an important aid to local planning that should be obtained by the planning commission. It contains a comprehensive and well-written description for the layperson of the downtown improvement process. Although some of the material and concepts are now out of date, the bulk of the information is extremely useful. Local officials and planning commissions will find chapters 2, 3, 4, and 5 (surveys, improvements, parking, and circulation) very helpful when evaluating downtown projects.

Jaffe, Martin, and Frank DiNovo. *Local Groundwater Protection.* Chicago: Planners Press, 1987. This is an excellent source of information on identifying groundwater supplies and drafting protection strategies and ordinances.

Frank, James E., and Robert M. Rhodes, eds. *Development Exactions.* Chicago: Planners Press, 1987.

Kelly, Eric Damian, and Gary J. Raso. *Sign Regulation for Small and Midsize Communities.* Planning Advisory Service Report No. 419. Chicago: Planners Press, 1989. This book is a helpful explanation of when and how to use sign controls, with several examples.

Kendig, Lane, et al. *Performance Zoning.* Chicago: Planners Press, 1980. This volume is a comprehensive presentation of the concepts, ordinance language, and techniques of performance zoning. The model ordinance would need to be adapted to a small town setting. Towns and planners looking for an alternative to traditional zoning should read this book and have it on hand as a reference.

Koppleman, Lee, and Joseph De Cheara. *Planning Design Criteria.* New York: Van Nostrand, 1968.

Lapping, Mark. "Changing Rural Housing Policies: Vermont's Mobile Home Zoning Law." *Small Town,* 12:4 (Jan./Feb. 1982):10–11. A study of zoning for mobile homes, this article is of interest particularly to practicing planners.

Lapping, Mark B., Thomas L. Daniels, and John W. Keller. *Rural Planning and Development in the United States.* New York: Guilford Publications, 1989. A wide-ranging discussion of the issues involved in rural and small town planning, it is especially useful for practicing planners and planners new in the field.

Lynch, Kevin. *The Image of the City.* Cambridge, MA: MIT Press, 1961. This book is a classic of urban design and contains useful concepts for small town design.

Mandelker, Daniel R. *Land Use Law,* 2d ed. Charlottesville, VA: Michie Company, 1988. This law book in one volume is suitable for use in small towns and rural areas. There are many reference books available in planning which examine the legal issues involved in regulation and development; most, however, are multivolume sets that are not particularly suitable for the layperson and the small town office. Mandelker's *Land Use Law,* on the other hand, is a comprehensive reference guide to the many questions that will arise in day-to-day operations and at planning commission meetings. The book is indexed nicely and is an essential aid for the planning commission.

McClendon, Bruce W., and Ray Quay. *Mastering Change: Winning Strategies for Effective City Planning.* Chicago: Planners Press, 1988.

McElroy, Joseph J. "You Don't Have to Be Big to Like Performance Zoning." *Planning,* 51:5 (May 1985):16–18.

Mcshenberg, Michael J. *The Language of Zoning.* Planning Advisory Service Report No. 322. Chicago: Planners Press, 1984. A clearly written explanation of zoning concepts and practices, this report also presents helpful illustrations. It is a useful reference tool for the planning commission, zoning board, zoning administrator, and practicing planner.

Minimum Guidelines and Requirements for Accessible Design. Washington, DC: United States Architectural and Transportation Barriers Compliance Board, 1981. A clearly written and illustrated guide for designing local codes to comply with handicapped accessibility standards, this book is an absolutely essential reference for local government. Most of the book contains drawings with dimensions and measurements.

National Association of Home Builders. *Cost Effective Site Planning: Single Family Development.* Washington, DC: NAHB, 1986. This manual tells the local community everything it needs to know about planning for single-family development. This book is probably the best of its kind and is an essential reference for the planning commission.

Porter, Douglas R., et al. *Covenants and Zoning for Research/Business Parks.* Washington, DC: Urban Land Institute, 1986. This book is a concise guide to establishing an industrial or business park. It is very useful because of the numerous examples and model covenants throughout the book. Most of the case examples in the book are for research parks in large cities, but the models can easily be scaled down to small town needs.

Powers, Ron. *Far from Home: Life and Loss in Two American Towns.* New York: Random House, 1991. This book provides an insightful look at two towns, one overcome by newcomers, the other struggling for economic survival.

Roddewig, Richard J. *Preparing a Historic Preservation Ordinance.* Planning Advisory Service Report No. 374. Chicago: Planners Press, 1983. This report provides good advice on the drafting and implementation of a historic preservation ordinance. It includes sample design guidelines and ordinance examples and is useful for planning commissioners and practical planners.

Rohse, Mitch. *Land-Use Planning in Oregon: A No-Nonsense Handbook in Plain English.* Corvallis, Oregon: Oregon State University Press, 1987. Although geared to the Oregon Land Use Program, this book contains a clearly written glossary of planning terms. It is useful to planners in explaining planning to the public.

Rood, Sally A., and Philip Rosenberg. "Capital Budgeting: Small Town Practices in Four States." Unpublished manuscript prepared for the National Council on Public Works Improvement, 1986. This is a study of small town capital improvements needs and the creation of capital improvements plans. It has many valuable insights for practicing planners and should interest academics who work with small towns.

Sargent, Frederick O., Paul Lusk, Jose A. Rivera, and Maria Varela. *Rural Environmental Planning for Sustainable Communities.* Washington, DC: Island Press, 1991. This is a useful text on environmental planning for rural communities looking to balance natural resource protection and economic growth.

Schiffman, Irving. *Alternative Techniques for Managing Growth.* Berkeley, CA: University of California, Institute of Governmental Studies, 1989. Although somewhat geared to California, this book provides a clear explanation of 26 growth management techniques. It is of use especially to larger towns and to towns experiencing rapid growth.

Small Town. Ellensburg, WA: Small Towns Institute. *Small Town* is the journal for small communities and rural areas. It is a well-written, informative journal which uses a format of presenting how projects, programs, and research can be useful to town citizens and organizations. This journal is a must for officials and planning commissioners seriously interested in learning about successful small town projects around the country.

Smith, Herbert H. *The Citizens Guide to Zoning.* Chicago: Planners Press, 1983. As the title indicates, this book was written for the layperson. It contains easy to understand concepts for the planning commission.

So, Frank S., Israel Stollman, Frank Beal, and David Arnold, eds. *The Practice of Local Government Planning.* Washington, DC: International City Managers' Association, 1988. *The Practice of Local Government Planning* and its forerunner, *The Principles and Practices of Local Planning,* has served cities, towns, professional planners, and students for nearly three decades. Besides being a textbook, it is also a handbook for office practice. All aspects of planning and land use regulation are covered in its 21 chapters. Although there is not a specific chapter on small town and rural planning, there is a wealth of information on how to collect data, conduct surveys, and educate people about planning; it also contains several important chapters on zoning and subdivision regulations, economic development, and citizen participation. Because of its distinctive color and its near universal recognition among American planners, it is generally referred to as the "Green Book."

Solnit, Albert. *The Job of the Planning Commissioner.* Chicago: Planners Press, 1987. This popular and very useful explanation of the planning commissioner's role in the planning process is recommended for planning commissioners and practicing planners.

Steiner, Frederick. *The Living Landscape.* New York: McGraw-Hill, 1990. This book presents an ecological approach to planning.

Stephani, Carl J. *A Practical Introduction to Zoning.* Washington, DC: National League of Cities, 1990. This is a straightforward explanation of the purpose and use of zoning.

Stokes, Sam N., A. Elizabeth Watson, Genevieve P. Keller, and J. Timothy Keller. *Saving America's Countryside: A Guide to Rural Conservation.* Baltimore: Johns Hopkins University Press, 1989. A thorough guide to the conservation of rural resources— natural areas, historic buildings, and productive lands—this book has many illustrations and examples, including 28 case studies.

Sutro, Suzanne. *Reinventing the Village: Planning, Zoning, and Design Strategies.* Planning Advisory Service Report No. 430. Chicago: Planners Press, 1991. This report contains good advice on how to develop zoning and design ordinances for village centers.

Tweeten, Luther, and George L. Brinkman. *Micropolitan Development.* Ames, Iowa: Iowa State University Press, 1976. This is an in-depth discussion of the theory of rural development with some practical applications. It is written primarily for an academic audience.

United States Economic Development Administration. *Zoning for Small Towns and Rural Counties.* Washington, DC: U.S. Government Printing Office, 1975.

Vermont Agency of Community and Development Affairs. *Capital Facilities Scheduling and Financing Handbook.* Montpelier, VT: State of Vermont, 1984. A thorough introduction to capital improvements programs, this book is useful for practicing planners and planning commissioners.

Wells, Betty, Laura Sternweis, and Timothy Borich. "Intercommunity Cooperation: How Iowa Towns Band Together for Community Development." *Small Town,* 21:6 (May–June, 1991):25–27. This article explains how Iowa communities have worked together in planning and economic development.

Whitten, Jon. "The Basics of Groundwater Protection." *Planning,* 58:6 (June, 1992):22–26. This article is a good introduction to the problems of and potential solutions for protecting groundwater supplies.

Williams, Norman, Jr., Edmund H. Kellogg, and Peter M. Lavigne. *Vermont Townscape.* New Brunswick, NJ: Rutgers University Center for Urban Policy Research, 1987. This is a study of the historical development and current aesthetic problems in small towns in Vermont. It has some useful information on design controls that are relevant to any town looking to create a historic district.

Ziegler, Arthur P., and Walter C. Kidney. *Historic Preservation in Small Towns.* American Association for State and Local History. Available from Chicago: Planners Press, 1980. An excellent source book which successfully adapts urban historic preservation techniques to the small town and rural area, it has a very basic approach to small town preservation and is valuable to those who want to form a preservation group, survey historic property, or apply for National Register status.

Index